Bulgaria in British Foreign Policy, 1943–1949

Bulgaria in British Foreign Policy, 1943–1949

Marietta Stankova

ANTHEM PRESS
LONDON · NEW YORK · DELHI

Anthem Press
An imprint of Wimbledon Publishing Company
www.anthempress.com

This edition first published in UK and USA 2015
by ANTHEM PRESS
75–76 Blackfriars Road, London SE1 8HA, UK
or PO Box 9779, London SW19 7ZG, UK
and
244 Madison Ave #116, New York, NY 10016, USA

First published in hardback by Anthem Press in 2014

Copyright © 2015 Marietta Stankova

The author asserts the moral right to be identified as the author of this work.

All rights reserved. Without limiting the rights under copyright reserved above, no part of this publication may be reproduced, stored or introduced into a retrieval system, or transmitted, in any form or by any means (electronic, mechanical, photocopying, recording or otherwise), without the prior written permission of both the copyright owner and the above publisher of this book.

British Library Cataloguing-in-Publication Data
A catalogue record for this book is available from the British Library.

Library of Congress Cataloging-in-Publication Data
The Library of Congress has cataloged the hardcover edition as follows:
Stankova, Marietta.
Bulgaria in British foreign policy, 1943–1949 / Marietta Stankova. pages cm
Includes bibliographical references and index.
ISBN 978-1-78308-232-2 (hardcover : alk. paper)
1. Bulgaria–Foreign relations–Great Britain. 2. Great Britain–Foreign relations–Bulgaria. 3. World War, 1939–1945–Bulgaria. 4. World War, 1939–1945–Great Britain. 5. Great Britain–Foreign relations–Balkan Peninsula. 6. Balkan Peninsula–Foreign relations–Great Britain. I. Title.
DR73.G7S74 2014
327.49904109'044–dc23
2014015728

ISBN-13: 978 1 78308 430 2 (Pbk)
ISBN-10: 1 78308 430 8 (Pbk)

Cover image: General Walter Oxley, General John Crane and General Sergey Biryuzov in Sofia, 10 May 1945, reproduced with the permission of www.lostbulgaria.com

This title is also available as an ebook.

CONTENTS

Acknowledgements   vii

List of Abbreviations   ix

Introduction   1

Part One: Allied Cooperation during the World War: 'What Will Be the Place of Bulgaria at the Judgement Seat?'

Chapter One: Bulgaria in British Postwar Planning   15

Chapter Two: Getting Bulgaria Out of the War   37

Part Two: Rising Tensions and Lowering Expectations during the Armistice: 'Britain Has to Be a Little More than a Spectator'

Chapter Three: The Principles of British Postwar Policy towards Bulgaria   73

Chapter Four: Observing the Establishment of Communist Rule in Bulgaria   97

Chapter Five: Recognizing the Bulgarian Communist Regime   125

Part Three: Consolidation of the Cold War Frontline: 'We Are Supporting Certain Principles'

Chapter Six: British Acceptance of Communist Rule in Bulgaria   159

Conclusion   193

Notes   201

Bibliography   233

Index   245

ACKNOWLEDGEMENTS

I was fortunate to draw on the expertise and support of many scholars and friends during the considerable time I worked on this book. Any effort to detail here their actions and assistance would be inadequate. I wish to thank them all, but in particular Prof. Richard Crampton and Prof. Anita Prazmowska, who guided my studies and research in Oxford and London respectively. The late Dr Maria Dowling was the first to encourage my interest in exploring the present subject during a memorable year at the CEU in Budapest, and Dr Edmund Green offered lots of practical help: I remain indebted to both of them not only for the invaluable academic advice but also for their kindness and unique sense of humour.

The late Dr Eduard Mark readily shared his insights into documentary sources and historiography. In the early stages of my work I had the chance to hear and discuss the recollections of several witnesses of the events of the book: Dianko Sotirov, Malcolm Mackintosh, F. L. Simpson and Lord Denis Greenhill are no longer here but are gratefully remembered.

The professional assistance in libraries and archives of Boyka Parvanova in Sofia and Olga Khavanova and Sergei Listikov in Moscow was indispensible. I am also thankful to the staff of the archives and libraries where I carried out research over some years: the National Archives at Kew, the British Library of Political and Economic Science, the Library of the School of Slavonic and East European Studies and the British Library in London, the Bodleian Library in Oxford, the General Department of Archives, the Archive of the Ministry of Foreign Affairs, the St St Cyril and Methodius National Library in Sofia, the Foreign Policy Archive of the Russian Federation and the Russian State Archive of Socio-political History in Moscow.

Above all, it was the love, patience and trust of my husband, children and parents that are in equal measure the strongest incentive and the greatest reward for my work.

LIST OF ABBREVIATIONS

AFHQ	Allied Forces Headquarters
AMVnR	Archive of the Ministry of Foreign Affairs, Sofia
AMVR	Archive of the Ministry of Internal Affairs, Sofia
AVPRF	Foreign Policy Archive of the Russian Federation, Moscow
BAN	Bulgarian Academy of Sciences
BANU	Bulgarian Agrarian National Union
BBC	British Broadcasting Corporation
BCP	Bulgarian Communist Party
BLO	British Liaison Officer
BMM	British Military Mission
BoT	Board of Trade
CC	Central Committee [of the Bulgarian Communist Party]
DII	Department of International Information [of the CC of the Soviet Communist Party]
EAM	National Liberation Front, Greece
ELAS	National Popular Liberation Army, Greece
FF	Fatherland Front
FO	Foreign Office
Force 133	SOE section dealing with the Balkans
FORD	Foreign Office Research Department
HMG	His Majesty's Government
KKE	Communist Party of Greece
MEW	Ministry of Economic Warfare
NC	National Council [of the Fatherland Front]
NKID	People's Commissariat for Foreign Affairs, Moscow
NKVD	People's Commissariat for Internal Affairs, Moscow
OSS	Office of Strategic Services
PID	Political Intelligence Department
PRB	Press Reading Bureau
PWE	Political Warfare Executive

RAN	Russian Academy of Sciences
RTsHIDNI	Centre for Preservation and Study of Modern History Documents, Moscow
SIS	Secret Intelligence Service
SOE	Special Operations Executive
TsDA	Central State Historical Archive, Sofia
TsPA	Central [Communist] Party Archive, Sofia
UNO	United Nations Organization
UNSCOB	United Nations Special Commission on the Balkans
VKP(B)	All-Soviet Communist Party (Bolsheviks)
WCO	War Cabinet Office

INTRODUCTION

Modern Bulgaria's development was continuously affected by the changing balance of power in Europe: Bulgaria's very emergence as a separate nation-state in 1878 was as much the outcome of great-power conflict and arbitration as it was of the struggle for self-determination. Starting with the somewhat misleadingly labelled 'Russophiles' and 'Russophobes' just after it gained independence from the Ottoman Empire, right through to pro- and anti-Western predilections in the post-Communist period, foreign-policy orientation has been a defining force in Bulgarian internal affairs. The involvement of a succession of great powers in the Balkans shaped not only the country's place on the international scene but above all the configuration of the domestic political forces. This reflected largely the fact that in the late nineteenth and the first half of the twentieth century, the Bulgarian political elite looked abroad for models of modernization and sought external support for Bulgaria's territorial ambitions.

It was Bulgaria's key geographic location that attracted the attention of European powers bidding for regional and continental influence. At the centre of the Balkan Peninsula, with a long coast on the Black Sea, the country constituted a natural stepping stone towards the Straits, a hinterland for extending control over the Eastern Mediterranean and a possible base for the penetration of the Middle East. Important as it was, Bulgaria's strategic position was often exaggerated in both popular perceptions and foreign-policy doctrine. For the great powers, dominance over the country was desirable but rarely indispensable, and even Russia – predominantly seen as Bulgaria's protector – at times played the rivalling Balkan neighbours against one another.

The role played by Bulgaria in different historical periods contributed to the struggle among the major European states for leadership in continental and world affairs. In the nineteenth century the interests of Russia and Great Britain consistently clashed in the Balkans as the former used its cultural and historic links with the South Slavs as an instrument for advance towards warm-water ports, while the latter relied on influence in the Mediterranean countries to protect the routes to its overseas imperial possessions. The resulting controversy crystallized in the so-called 'Eastern Question' centring on the legacy of the declining Ottoman Empire. This in turn intensified attention to Bulgaria, which could be used as an outpost for pressure on, or a stronghold for the defence of, the Eastern Mediterranean and the Straits.

Similar reasoning informed the policies of the European powers, when revisionists and supporters of the post–First World War status quo played out their conflict in the Balkans, using the region as their political and economic base. The interwar years were marked by the relative detachment of both Britain – which concentrated on vital states like Greece and Turkey – and Russia – which tried to overcome its isolation after the Bolshevik Revolution through less traditional methods. However, at the end of the Second World War it was these two powers as members of the victorious Grand Alliance that re-emerged as the main contenders for power in the Balkans following their wartime military and political involvement in the region. In the new realities and in reflection of the evolution of their long-term geopolitical priorities, the region retained its value for the preservation and promotion of larger strategic interests.

Examination of British foreign policy in different parts of the globe is a fertile topic in the history of international diplomacy and strategy. The search for British objectives in any particular area draws attention to the essentially practical non-ideological approach of the Foreign Office and the other foreign policy–making institutions. Doubtless, there were overarching principles and beliefs underpinning Britain's specific actions and engagements: emanating from the ideas of national interest, security and balance of power they allowed for flexibility of methods and a variety of approaches to individual partners. As a major determining factor in and outside Europe, Britain's bilateral relations formed the building blocks of regional policies and beyond, and their investigation forms a necessary element in the scrutiny of wider historical processes. For this, the end of the Second World War is an especially opportune moment: the imminent defeat of Germany left a vacuum on the continent and initiated a new phase of political settlement. Against such a background, the study of dealings with Bulgaria in the final stages and immediately after the Second World War illuminates Britain's self-perception as a great power, its ability to sustain various and sometimes clashing international interests, as well as its views and reactions to the aspirations of the other leading players in world politics.

British involvement in Bulgaria during 1943–49 formed a critical aspect of the renewed Anglo-Russian controversy in the Balkans. In turn, the evolution of the British–Soviet relationship had an impact on Britain's approach to Bulgaria. In order to rationalize this two-way process it is necessary to establish not only the rudiments of British planning for Bulgaria but also how these related to the acknowledgement of prevailing Soviet interest in the country. It is challenging also to compare British interpretation of Soviet ambitions to the actual plans and their implementation. This can be meaningfully analysed in the context of the complex strategic factors and mental dispositions bearing on Britain's behaviour. Not only did Britain fear that the Soviet Union coveted traditional British domains of influence but it suspected that the spread of Communism would be used for the achievement of such a goal.

From Britain's perspective, Bulgaria's vulnerability to Soviet pressure exposed to Soviet penetration the southernmost Balkans, where Britain had long-standing interests. An adequate explanation of British actions in Bulgaria hinges on the emphasis that these were undertaken in view of their projection on Britain's Mediterranean and Middle Eastern interests rather than because of their effects on Bulgaria alone. This was the fundament of Britain's approach to Bulgaria and it is necessary to underline that for strategic purposes in the period Bulgaria was predominantly treated as a part of the Balkans, which should be differentiated from the even more elusive category of Eastern Europe. Wartime experience shared with Romania and Hungary, as well as the similarity of the postwar pattern of communization to that of Poland and Czechoslovakia, provided additional dimensions.

A useful line of query is the reflection in British actions towards Bulgaria of the advancing division of Europe into two hostile military and ideological blocs in 1943–49 and how this affected Bulgarian internal affairs. The reverse side of this question is to consider whether the relatively small and weak Bulgaria added to the tensions among the great powers. Bulgaria's position can be investigated as a test case for some of the early inter-Allied clashes which gradually developed into the Cold War. Investigating the points of confrontation over the country would reveal whether these could be placed among the immediate and specific causes for the conflict. This would situate British policy to Bulgaria in a broader analytical framework and address the problem of Britain's aims in areas of secondary importance.

All these issues demand tracing how Britain's objectives were transformed into particular military, diplomatic and political actions regarding Bulgaria. It is essential to explore the process through which Britain's Balkan interests and the renewed British–Russian tension took the shape of, for example, support for the Bulgarian non-Communist politicians or opposition to the South Slav confederation scheme. To that end, the three parts of the book cover three consecutive periods, each reflecting a distinct stage of European developments at the end and immediately after the Second World War. The analysis aims primarily at revealing the attitudes and strategies which eventually contributed to growing international tensions regarding Bulgaria and the whole of the Balkans. For this purpose the most logical starting point is 1943, which marks the intensification of British attention to the country, in both conceptual and practical terms. Thus the analysis underscores the continuity of British policy since wartime while maintaining the focus on Bulgaria's role among the early testing grounds for the Cold War. The closing chapter covers in detail developments until 1949, when British treatment of Bulgaria had gradually become less dynamic and settled into a distinctly recognizable Cold War pattern. While the chapter necessarily mentions events which fall outside this chronological frame, the spotlight is firmly on the transition from world war to Cold War in a specific national context.

Firstly, the focus is on the dual-track efforts during 1943–44 of detaching Bulgaria from Germany and influencing its postwar orientation. The relation between the two throws light on Britain's short- and long-term priorities and establishes lines of comparison and assessment of subsequent British strategies. Here, the historic background is presented as one of the pillars of British planning for Bulgaria, while effort is made to demonstrate its intersection with wartime priorities and the evolving nature of the Grand Alliance. The balance of interest is firmly on the increasing British awareness of limitations imposed by the simultaneously expanding Soviet influence.

The second part covers the years 1944–47 – that is, the armistice period – when Bulgaria was administered by the Allied Control Commission, to which the British military and political representatives were accredited. Following the latter's impressions of local events, their subsequent recommendations and the actions undertaken after consultation with experts in London reveal how the mechanisms of policy making were employed; it also underlines the available choices, and examines the consistency of principles and outcomes. As this is the time of Britain's association with the Bulgarian anti-Communist opposition, it allows investigation into the practical interaction of strategic and ideological objectives in British foreign policy.

The final part tackles the period following the conclusion of the peace treaty with Bulgaria in 1947. This is an attempt to take the analysis of British policy to Bulgaria further than has so far been done in the international historiography of the subject. It maps Britain's diminishing interest in a country where the Communist Party's position was consolidating under undisputed Soviet tutelage and where Britain's opportunities and willingness for active policy were severely restricted.

* * *

The historiography of the latter stages of the Second World War and the early postwar period has discussed events in Eastern Europe as both a cause and a consequence of the deteriorating relations of the Big Three Allies.

The origins of the Cold War have been predominantly explained with the role of domestic political developments and the outside pressures to which the region was subjected. This fundamental historical issue has been approached from a multitude of perspectives and within different scholarly disciplines, making for a variety of narratives. In the still proliferating literature it is not uncommon or unexpected to find little on the part played by Bulgaria alone, or for that matter by most other East European countries which were engulfed in the Soviet bloc, with few exceptions.[1] The rationale is found – at least in volumes posing the 'grand' questions of the Cold War – in historical perspective; it is also explained by historiographical expediency.

Consistently prevailing in the broad field of Cold War studies are volumes on the policy elaboration of the two superpowers, the United States and the Soviet Union, and the pivotal relationship between them. Despite the shifting of research interest towards the middle stages and the ending of the Cold War – stimulated by increased archival availability and opportunity for innovation – the formative first decade of the conflict has proven continuously rewarding for scholars. With regard to it, 'the post-revisionist synthesis' is firmly established as methodology, rejecting earlier theories of sole responsibility of either of the two opposing sides for the emergence of the global clash.[2] Based on the thesis of mutual misunderstanding and misconception of objectives, the early influential works of Vojtech Mastny and John Lewis Gaddis still offer pertinent and informative analysis which has been updated and extended in subsequent works.[3] Mastny's pioneering discussion of Soviet foreign policy during 1941–47 in terms of the complex relationship among Moscow's military strategy, diplomacy and management of international Communism bore particular relevance to the question of Eastern Europe, the more so since he integrated documentary material from the region.[4] Even so, shortly after the collapse of the Soviet bloc, there were voices persisting that Stalin had 'made up his mind' regarding Eastern Europe, where Soviet security would be achieved through ideology and exploitation of the postwar revolutionary situation or a 'blueprint' could be deducted from actions in particular countries.[5] In a more sophisticated and provocative manner, Gaddis still construed Soviet behaviour in postwar Europe as expansionist, driven by Marxism and replicating its domestic model abroad, an amalgamation labelled 'authoritarian romanticism'.[6] Recent scrutiny of the sources of Soviet policy has mostly revisited the well-known dilemma between ideology and *Realpolitik* resulting in comprehensive volumes distinguished by depth and texture of interpretation. Jonathan Haslam highlights the 'deep-seated ideological foundations' of the Cold War, expounding on the intrinsic suspicion and mutual hostility between Russia and the West ever since the Bolshevik takeover of power. This is what ultimately precluded an alternative to the zones-of-influence model which determined the fate of the states in the south-eastern part of Europe.[7] Vladislav Zubok, in turn, advances a conviction that Soviet political and military elites exhibited an 'expansionist mood' which underpinned Stalin's foreign policy, both in and outside Europe. The author terms it 'Socialist imperialism', while acknowledging that it could coexist with interest in continuing cooperation with the Allies.[8] On the whole, post-Communist Russian scholars with access and understanding of Soviet archival materials have stimulated and integrated seamlessly in the ongoing discourse. The various established trails of interpretation can be discerned in their writings, ranging from the assertion that senior Russian diplomats were guided mostly by geostrategic considerations rather than desire for communization of Europe to the view that the ideas of world Communism and Russian imperialism were not only far from sharply contradictory but indeed frequently complementary.[9]

That contradiction between cooperation with the West and Soviet transformations was not inevitable is also affirmed by Geoffrey Roberts, whose work has been permeated by the conviction that Stalin 'neither planned nor desired' the Cold War. Yet Soviet actions and ambitions undeniably contributed to its outbreak: as the penetration of Eastern Europe was deemed by Stalin natural, defensive, limited and possibly justified by a Europe-wide swing to the left, outside observers doubted whether this was not the means to a further goal.[10]

As a consensus is reached on the weight of ideology, outlook and perception in the explanation of the start of the Cold War, Melvyn Leffler puts the light back on personalities, in particular the new superpowers' leaders, showing how their 'fears and hopes' governed policies. He therefore sees the tensions and crises of the early Cold War as lost opportunities for cooperation.[11] On his part, Marc Trachtenberg devotes a chapter of his formidable volume on the 'constructed peace' on negotiations regarding the postwar settlement in Eastern Europe, debating the applicability of the 'spheres of influence' concept by the Allies. He finds that once Western policy was unable to secure a compromise on the central issue of Poland, the prospects of democracy in countries like Bulgaria and Romania sank: the US accepted the reality of the situation and it was not this quarrel which led to the Cold War but the subsequent clash over Iran and Turkey.[12]

Indeed, the division into spheres of influence is among the most recurring paradigms of inter-Allied relations towards the end of the Second World War and beyond. Culminating in the 'percentages agreement' of October 1944 and possibly confirmed at the Yalta Conference in February 1945, it is often seen as standing at the core of Britain's postwar strategy and interlinked with the nature of its postwar objectives.[13] This in turn evokes discussion about the dynamics of the British–US relationship, with some of the literature treating Britain as a junior partner. The view of Britain's secondary role in the onset of the Cold War has been reiterated by the British historian Elisabeth Barker, herself a witness to some of the events which she subsequently investigated. She describes Britain's position 'between the superpowers' as motivated by a growing concern for its own weakness and acknowledgement of its limited ability to influence world events and pursue independent policy.[14] In contrast, Anne Deighton has consistently traced the roots of British postwar diplomacy back to the precedents of wartime thinking and planning. She claims that it is vital for the interpretation of British policy to understand that Britain regarded itself as a great power able to determine the course of events in Europe. Above all Britain justified its right to do so not by its military or economic strength, but by virtue of its expertise in international affairs.[15] Nonetheless, she confirms that Britain's initial Cold War strategy was driven disproportionately by the military and intelligence services whose outlook and objectives differed from those of the diplomats.[16] Haslam too argues for a bigger role of Britain, especially in the latter stages of the world war as the United States under Roosevelt did not commit unequivocally to Europe, while implying at key moments that the Soviets' desiderata could be granted.[17]

The cohort of scholars poring over the process of Britain's involvement in the Cold War have employed a range of prisms among which the personality and leadership of Winston Churchill has been most enduring. The breadth of interpretations is tellingly revealed by two monographs with similar titles and subjects which appeared in close succession. Following the line of 'conceptualism', Folly subscribes to the thesis of cooperation with the Soviet Union, whereas Carlton is a firm proponent of the 'appeasement' version, which he finds to be driven by Churchill's irrevocable if on occasion suitably disguised anti-Bolshevism.[18] Previous publications delineated Britain's policy towards the USSR as a more collective government effort despite the inherent institutional and individual rivalries and the effect of powerful personalities. Both Martin Kitchen, who looked at the British–Soviet relationship during the Second World War, and Victor Rothwell, who discussed at length Britain's foreign policy in the early Cold War, mentioned Bulgaria only in passing – in the context of wider issues such as the political connotations of the opening of a second front in the Balkans or the Balkan confederation scheme. The treatment of Bulgaria is overshadowed by attention to developments in Central Europe such as the Polish question or the political evolution of Czechoslovakia.[19] To an extent this follows the priorities of the British Foreign Office; it also infers that Bulgaria's case deserves little attention due to the country's traditional pro-Russian proclivities and the smooth installation of the Soviet political model.

John Kent's articulate interpretation of British Cold War foreign policy as rooted in the desire to sustain its imperial positions has also proven robust. What mattered for Britain was that its domination in the Middle East and the Eastern Mediterranean should not be disputed by any other great power – which in the circumstances after the Second World War could only mean the Soviet Union. As Britain regarded Greece and Turkey as a crucial link in its imperial policy, it was prepared to divert Soviet pressure on these two countries to the northern part of the Balkans.[20] Such an interpretation, which places Bulgaria as well as Romania and Yugoslavia on the fringes of British interest, picks up themes present in the works of Elisabeth Barker. She also sees Bulgaria predominantly as part of Britain's Balkan rather than Eastern European policy. Although quite concise, Barker's analysis of British attitudes to Bulgaria is attentive, consistent and durable. Her most valuable contribution is the assertion that Bulgaria was not unimportant or marginal for British foreign-policy makers and yet they were not prepared for a clash with the Soviet Union over it.[21]

Indeed, the most productive scholarly approach has been to place policy to Bulgaria in a wider Balkan context and judge developments in the country firstly in relation to its neighbours and then according to their wider repercussions, not the least because this was the practice of the relevant government agencies. As this requires expertise in different languages and archives, it has been used in individual essays forming part of larger collaborative works, but above all in thematic clusters within edited collections where the chapters should be read in discussion with each other.[22] Among these, Varsori and Calandri's *The Failure of Peace in Europe* stands out with its international list of contributors. In it a reflective piece by Arcidiacono impresses with a refreshingly novel hypothesis stating that British involvement in the northern Balkan ex-German satellites was deliberately limited so as not to provoke aggressive Sovietization: it is only to be lamented that little evidence is pinpointed.[23]

Undoubtedly, a comparative and interdisciplinary practice requires support from detailed case studies, which were few and far between of the countries behind the Iron Curtain while it was in place. As Barker's research rarely extended beyond 1945, a gap existed in the study of Western policies to the region after the Potsdam Conference and especially after the Moscow Council of Foreign Ministers in December 1945; the more explored Yugoslav and Greek cases were normally presented without much reference to their northern Balkan neighbours. The statutory opening of Western archives led to some advances in the form of works on the Allied Control Commission for Bulgaria, the most comprehensive of which is Michael Boll's.[24] However, as these were predominantly based on US documentary or memoir material, they focused on the activities of the US political and military missions in Bulgaria.[25]

Only with Vesselin Dimitrov's incisive, multilayered analysis of Soviet policy in Bulgaria for the whole decade of the 1940s has the balance of academic coverage of the country as a subject and player in the early Cold War been readdressed.[26] Skilfully using an array of primary sources, he has built a powerful case, stacking up the various levels at which developments in Bulgaria were representative of wider regional and international trends. The clarity and articulacy of his presentation have not compromised the complexity of his analysis of the interplay between Soviet priorities and local Communists' necessities.

Dimitrov's work fits in a small crop of monographs with a big impact factor redefining the field of East European studies in the crucial period of Communist transition. Although unevenly split between those focusing on foreign relations or on internal developments, they seek to challenge the notion that either the establishment of Communist rule or the isolation of the Soviet bloc were linear processes driven by global strategic visions. Anita Prazmowska has depicted the intricacies of the intense confrontation among the different strands of anti-Nazi resistance in Poland and explained its effect on the politics in the period of Soviet occupation after 1945. From such a perspective, the imposition of the Communist model resulted in large measures from the power competition of political elites.[27] On the other side of the historiography spectrum is Elizabeth Hazard's study of US policy in Romania, with its particular focus in intelligence and special operations, an area of interest now reinvigorated with increased availability of documents. The covert actions of US representatives in Bucharest to encourage opposition and resistance to the Communists before and after the conclusion of the peace treaty in 1947 are deemed as sufficient proof for Soviet suspicions and justification for hardening of Soviet control, a combination that made the country 'a crucible of the Cold War'.[28]

One of the most valuable aspects of the country studies is their integration of national historiographies, so bridging a still-existing academic and cultural gap. Like their colleagues from the region, Bulgarian scholars have been lastingly interested in the local and regional engagements of the great powers and studied them from their particular vantage point. Even in the final years of Communist historiography, ideological accounts had been noticeably toned down in order to give way to more neutral 'positivist' expositions after 1989, to a degree explicable through the double effect of generational and cultural changes. The interpretation of British and US policies in the latter part of the Second World War and the armistice period moved from 'imperialist design' to 'special interest' as revealed from the reading of postwar planning and actions on the ground, especially involvement with the Bulgarian anti-Communists.[29] At the same time, findings from the relatively more accessible Soviet archives and from the almost fully open Bulgarian ones secured momentum for the home academic community. Among the most fraught research questions were those on the triangular relationships between the Soviet and Balkan Communists: Georgi Daskalov's writing on Bulgarian–Greek links provides a wealth of new detail on events at the internationally sensitive border, where there were distinct if short-lived attempts to ease the Communist-led resistance into local administration.[30] The dissections of the confusing turns and twists in Bulgarian–Yugoslav affairs have been copious and lengthy, with the prevailing view confirming that Soviet preferences – actual or perceived – were the touchstone for Bulgarian choices. Evgenia Kalinova, Iskra Baeva and Jordan Baev have authored more rounded longer-term accounts of the effects of the Cold War on Bulgaria's foreign relations and its role as an orthodox Soviet satellite and a front-line state in the Balkans.[31]

* * *

Several documentary collections were the starting point of research for this book, primary among them the official *Documents on British Policy Overseas* published by the Historical Branch of the Foreign Office. The volume dealing with Eastern Europe in the mid-1940s contains seminal documents highlighting the turning points in British foreign policy regarding the Soviet Union and its sphere of influence; two other volumes chart the wartime negotiations among the 'Big Three' Allies.[32] Further sources on the wider question of British–Soviet relations in the early Cold War years are found in *The Foreign Office and the Kremlin: British Documents on Anglo-Soviet Relations*.[33] The secret wartime correspondence between Roosevelt and Churchill comprises parts of the discussion between British and US leaders regarding the conduct of the Second World War and its political consequences for the Balkans and Bulgaria. It offers glimpses of the decision-making process regarding such crucial issues as the bombing of Bulgaria in 1943, the October 1944 'percentages agreement' and Soviet behaviour in occupied Bulgaria.[34] In terms of time span and subject scope, the sections on Bulgaria in *Foreign Relations of the United States*, annually published by the US Department of State, are unparalleled.[35] These documents detail the daily contacts between the US representatives in Bulgaria and their colleagues and superiors in Washington. They reveal the mutual influences of British and US views and how the different attitudes to the country were translated into concrete actions directed to Sofia or Moscow. The documentary volume edited by Michael Boll, *The American Military Mission in the Allied Control Commission for Bulgaria 1944–1947*, is a unique English-language publication dealing specifically with Bulgaria.[36]

Although sanitized, the printed versions of Bulgarian Communist party and government documents can still render interesting information for the patient reader, not the least because they themselves are a kind of testament to the era of their appearance.[37] In the post-Communist period, they have been naturally superseded by academic compilations seeking to illuminate wartime and immediate postwar issues, including the methods used by the Bulgarian Communist Party (BCP)[38] to seize control of the country.[39] The diary of the Bulgarian Communist leader Georgi Dimitrov contains unprecedented insights into the various personalities, events and trends with which this book is concerned.[40] Similarly, an impressive number of Soviet publications from the first decade after the change of regime related to Bulgarian developments and placed them in their Eastern European context, tracing the link between party and government in the Soviet foreign policy–making process, as well as Moscow's guidance of the international Communist parties.[41]

As archives have become more accessible, international collaboration among scholars has increased and digital platforms have changed the manner and outcome of historical research, a multitude of new sources appeared in the public domain in the course of this research. Many of these updates have been taken into account, but the book is primarily rooted in the original documents consulted in several national archives. Bearing in mind the central subject, the bulk of material is of British origin and is preserved in the British National Archive, formerly the Public Record Office at Kew. These are mostly documents generated by two Foreign Office (FO) departments: the Southern, which dealt with Bulgaria and its neighbours, and the Northern, which dealt with Soviet Russia. In addition, there were papers produced by the Foreign Office Research Department (FORD), as well as correspondence with various other British governmental bodies such as the Special Operations Executive (SOE), the Political Warfare Executive (PWE), the Board of Trade (BoT), etc. FO files also contain the flow of communications between London and British political and military representatives in the country. This material gives the most complete picture of the decision-making process. Following in detail discussions within and between FO Departments regarding policy towards Bulgaria in 1943–49, the sources reveal the elaboration of British wartime and postwar objectives and track their practical implementation. They also uncover the various options available to British policy makers – uniquely, their assessment of results and consequences.

In Bulgaria, the majority of historical sources of concern to this book are under the management of the Central State Archive, where accessibility has improved impressively in the last decade. The autonomous depositories of the foreign and interior ministries operate under more bureaucratic routines. However, of greater significance is the need to appreciate that the shape and nature of the materials found there – as in their Soviet counterparts – differ from those in London, where much more was committed to paper. Still, the examination of the archival funds of different Bulgarian institutions – the Ministry of Foreign Affairs, the Ministry of Internal Affairs, the Central Committee (CC) of the Bulgarian Communist Party – as well as the personal papers of such prominent Communist Party and state leaders as Georgi Dimitrov, Vassil Kolarov and Traicho Kostov, enables at least partial reconstruction of the policy making process. These materials disclose how far Bulgarian leaders were able to exercise their own initiative regarding Western activities as opposed to merely acting on Soviet orders.

Soviet archives have preserved documents bearing on policy making regarding Bulgaria, the Balkans and Eastern Europe. It is particularly useful to compare the views and intentions deriving from Soviet sources with their concurrent Western interpretations and reactions. Examination of the released Soviet archives is crucial in establishing the relation between Soviet military strategy and postwar planning for Eastern Europe as reflected in the case of Bulgaria. The interaction between the Soviet design and the strategy of the Bulgarian Communist Party is another pertinent issue. Moreover, some clarification is possible of the Soviet position in negotiations over Bulgaria and the limits to which Stalin was prepared to go in the clash with the Western powers over Eastern Europe in general. All this throws additional light upon the validity of Britain's perceptions of Soviet aims and the adequacy of British tactics to meet Soviet intentions and carry out Western objectives for Bulgaria.

Part One

Allied Cooperation during the World War: 'What Will Be the Place of Bulgaria at the Judgement Seat ?'*

---

* Winston Churchill in the House of Commons, 2 August 1944.

Chapter One

BULGARIA IN BRITISH POSTWAR PLANNING

Since the latter half of the nineteenth century, Bulgaria's place in British foreign policy had been determined by a number of interrelated political, strategic and economic factors fused in the so-called 'Eastern Question'. Even after the dissolution of the Ottoman Empire, the intricacies of this great-power controversy for dominance in the Eastern Mediterranean were to a degree still relevant to Britain's Balkan policy. Before and during the Second World War Britain retained its commitment to securing the naval routes to its imperial territories in the Middle East. This overriding objective shaped Britain's relations with the individual countries in the region.

Bulgaria could influence developments not only in the Balkan Peninsula but also across Eastern Europe. At the heart of the Balkans and bordering the Black Sea, the country attracted Britain's attention as it stood close to the Mediterranean Straits, an area of traditional British interest. In the nineteenth century, the approach towards Bulgaria was complicated by the British perception of the country as closely attached to Russia because of ethnic and cultural similarities. Such an opinion continued to hold sway after the First World War despite a number of open rifts between Russia and Bulgaria in the late nineteenth and the first half of the twentieth century. Britain considered Bulgaria a convenient stepping stone for the fulfilment of Russian aims of predominance in the Eastern Mediterranean. Centuries-long Russian conflict with the Ottoman Empire affected the development of the whole Balkan Peninsula and the adjoining areas. Britain had been jealously watching Russian military successes and the increase of Russian influence in proximity to the Straits.[1] Bulgaria's significance lay in its links with parts of the European continent vital for Britain's security and trade. Such attention as was paid to Bulgaria should be placed in the context of Britain's involvement in the Mediterranean and the Middle East, which had to be safeguarded against the encroachment of adversaries like Russia. On its own account, the country had little value for British policy planning after the Second World War.

The Eastern Mediterranean was an internationally recognized zone of British interest to which the Balkans were the natural hinterland. A great power controlling the peninsula could use it to defend or menace the Straits, and with this, communications to the Middle East. Accordingly, strong influence over Greece and Turkey was central for Britain's security in the Mediterranean. This would undoubtedly be enhanced by amicable relations with Bulgaria. The precariousness of Britain's position in the region had been clearly demonstrated by the Bulgarian occupation of Aegean Thrace and Macedonia in 1941–42. The presence of Bulgarian troops there created serious military difficulties for Britain throughout the Second World War. From the British perspective, Bulgarian withdrawal from these territories would bring a distinct strategic advantage to the Allied military effort against the Axis. In the longer term, Britain's position in the Balkans would benefit if, under British pressure, Bulgaria could be persuaded to cooperate with its neighbours and thus cease to be a cause of regional instability.

The Sources of British Policy towards Bulgaria

By the beginning of 1942, after the anti-Axis alliance was bolstered by both the USSR and the United States, the British government began investigating the onerous issue of European postwar settlement. The initial efforts were mostly intellectual exercises, contained within the FO Reconstruction Department. Headed by Gladwyn Jebb, a respected diplomat, the first 'planners' were mainly engaged in constructing different potential scenarios for postwar international realignment.[2] Naturally, the focus was on the big powers and the smaller ones like Bulgaria were considered primarily in their regional setting and in relation to their existing or possible patrons. Attitudes towards Bulgaria, as towards a number of other small states, were governed by tradition and above all by its role in the ongoing armed conflict. In the case of Bulgaria, these two factors reinforced each other.

Military considerations

During the war Britain turned its attention to Bulgaria only occasionally, discussing it mainly as an ally of Germany. Certainly, British observers noted that the country was unique among the signatories of the Tripartite Pact in that it had managed to abstain from active fighting. It was engaged in Axis operations of secondary importance, such as the occupation of Greek and Yugoslav territories and in providing supplies for German regiments in the Balkans. The Bulgarian king had personally withstood coercion from Hitler to send troops to the Eastern Front. Moreover, Bulgaria preserved diplomatic relations with the Soviet Union even after declaring war on Great Britain and the United States in December 1941. Both the Bulgarian government and opposition greatly emphasized this relatively limited participation in the war, hoping that it would secure benevolent treatment by whichever side emerged victorious.[3]

Indeed, in the earlier stages of hostilities those British diplomatic and military experts who had followed the course of Bulgaria's association with the Axis acknowledged the peculiarities of the Bulgarian position. The FO Southern Department had some understanding of the country's predicament between Nazi Germany and Soviet Russia. Nevertheless, the progress of the war led British officials to display decreasing tolerance of Bulgaria's motives and behaviour. They rejected the Bulgarian government's claims of 'symbolic' participation in the war and refused to play down Bulgaria's contribution to the maintenance of stable Axis control over the Balkans. After all, Bulgarian troops held down local resistance thus freeing German divisions for combat elsewhere.[4] Altogether, Bulgaria's exceptional position was of little influence over British long-term policy. Factors going beyond the immediate wartime concerns prevailed in shaping the general attitude towards Bulgaria and ultimately determined its standing in British eyes at the end of the war.

However, Britain's broad interest in the region would benefit from the elaboration of specific policies towards Bulgaria. Historically, Britain had played a role at various points in Bulgaria's modern history, largely through supporting the most beneficial balance of power to Britain and without being too directly involved in internal Bulgarian developments.[5] Britain had predominantly been concerned with Bulgaria's territorial claims which could disturb the fragile post-Ottoman equilibrium in the Balkans. More recently, Britain sought to address first German penetration of the country and then Soviet approaches, both of which raised British sensitivity regarding the Eastern Mediterranean. Yet, in 1943–44, no British diplomat or politician claimed that Britain should aim for unilateral control over Bulgaria.

What continued to matter to Britain was that no great power hostile to its interests should dominate Bulgaria. One way of attaining this in the changing military circumstances was to establish a British physical presence in the country. In early 1943, the Southern Department took the view that 'the obvious and easiest solution would be that we and the Americans by an invasion of the Balkans should be on the spot and in a position to police that part of the world'.[6]

Such considerations had practical value only if supported by corresponding military preparations. In 1943, while Southern Department officials were suggesting the deployment of British military and possibly civilian authorities to Bulgaria, the British Chiefs of Staff were rationalizing Churchill's idea for an attack on 'the soft under-belly of the Axis'.[7] Churchill's initial argument at the end of 1942, much like the subsequent British military planners' recommendation for a fighting front in the Balkans, was based on the necessity for maximum diversion of forces and damage to Axis communications.[8] But neither the British prime minister nor his military commanders were able to overcome their US counterparts' opposition. High-ranking US politicians and officers had a stiff 'doctrinal objection to anything to do with the Balkans'.[9] They considered anything but massive concentration of force for the cross-Channel invasion of Europe to be a wasteful diversion and engagement in 'pinprick warfare'.[10] They also harboured suspicions that the real British motives were rooted in imperial aspirations to secure a sphere of influence in the Balkans.[11] In October 1943, mainly upon US insistence, the three Allies decided against opening a front in the Balkans. This happened despite the fact that Allied forces were engaged in Italy from where it was possible to push towards the north-western Balkans.[12] It also made futile Britain's long-standing attempts to secure Turkey's unequivocal commitment on the Allied side.[13]

In fact, the British commanders in the Middle East and the Mediterranean, notably General Sir Henry Maitland Wilson and General Sir Harold Alexander, who were responsible for the elaboration of military strategy in the Balkans, were comparatively little concerned with the long-term implications of their choices. It was the Foreign Office and the War Cabinet that had to project military decisions into British postwar interests.[14] In late 1943 and even in the first half of 1944, they conceded the priority of immediate wartime objectives over peacetime planning. Even Churchill, the person most aware of – and vocal on – the political consequences of an Allied offensive in the Balkans, or the lack of it, had to bow to the military rationale and accept the prevalence of short- over long-term policy.

Britain's support of Bulgaria's neighbours

Before the Second World War, Britain's attitude to Bulgaria had been linked to longer-standing relationships with Bulgaria's neighbours, especially those to the south. Bulgaria's increasing proximity to Germany confirmed the basic British negative assumptions towards it. Bulgaria's signing of the Tripartite Pact on 1 March 1941 restored the clarity of the interwar strategic situation in the Balkans. This had been temporarily blurred during the period of Bulgarian neutrality proclaimed after the outbreak of hostilities in Europe in September 1939. Searching for foundations of the postwar settlement, the British government could not avoid looking back at the recent pattern of relations. In the First World War Bulgaria had fought and lost on the side of the Central Powers, subsequently displaying vigorous revisionist criticism of the Versailles system. Both previous and subsequent historical examples of amicable political relations between Bulgaria and Great Britain were few and far between.

Between the wars a relatively small number of Bulgarian politicians advocated pro-British orientation. The scarcity of fruitful economic contacts was glaring. Indeed, Bulgaria produced few commodities in demand on the British market, and most of them could be easily obtained from some of its neighbours. In the 1920s and 1930s, Britain was not prepared to make purchases for political advantage rather than economic profit, thus leaving Germany copious space for manoeuvring in the field of investment and trade with Bulgaria. By 1939, Germany was not only Bulgaria's largest trade partner, but also received most of the exportable surplus of the country in exchange for credits and supplies of much-needed armaments. Germany utilized this situation and positioned itself as Bulgaria's reliable ally in peace and war.[15]

In the late 1930s, the FO conducted an extensive internal debate on the need to counterbalance the Third Reich's economic domination of Eastern Europe, including Bulgaria. Few practical solutions were found, as it was obvious that British companies could not beat the prices Germany offered for Bulgarian goods.[16] Any proposed actions had to be relatively mild for fear of being viewed as an economic challenge by Berlin. During 1937–38 the FO was determined to show that Britain's purpose was not to deny Germany access to Eastern Europe but to re-establish economic equilibrium there. Even though the Bulgarian government itself desired to contain the German economic advance, Britain's attempts to activate economic relations with Bulgaria failed. This was predominantly the result of Britain's inability to change its trade patterns in order to achieve diplomatic and political goals.[17]

In diplomatic terms, Britain had also made half-hearted efforts to prevent Bulgaria's attachment to the Tripartite Pact. It had insisted that Bulgaria remain neutral but offered no positive encouragement, which could have been used either by the Bulgarian king or by pro-Western politicians to oppose aligning with Germany. Most importantly, Britain upheld the Versailles Treaty, universally perceived in Bulgaria as the source of all evil, both at home and abroad. Bulgarian statesmen generally overlooked a nuance in Britain's position, namely that it was prepared to contemplate negotiated territorial alterations to the peace settlement.[18]

Britain therefore had little ground for rapprochement with Bulgaria, whose domestic and foreign policy were driven by unfulfilled territorial aspirations. In the years leading up to the Second World War, the only proposition that could have tempted Bulgaria to stay away from the Axis was territorial acquisition, which Bulgarian ruling circles could present as a step in the direction of 'Bulgarian national unification'. This was the very thing Britain could not promise, constrained as it was by commitment to Greece and Yugoslavia. However, belated British approval was declared for Romania's return of Southern Dobrudja to Bulgaria in August 1940. This concession passed largely unnoticed in Bulgaria as it was disproportionate to the support shown by Germany, which had practically forced Romania's hand.[19]

The British government also officially endorsed Balkan unity, even if it insisted that any initiative should originate from the Balkan states themselves. However, the FO understood that the proponents of the status quo who had joined in the so-called Balkan Entente in 1934 stood to benefit from maintaining Bulgaria's image as unwaveringly pro-German; without making any compromises they could rely on British support. While this was accounted for, the value of the Balkan Entente for British strategy remained paramount.[20] Indeed, any attempt to draw Bulgaria closer to Britain risked appearing to favour it at the expense of its neighbours. The strategic advantage of neutralizing Bulgaria would then be outweighed by the danger of antagonizing its adversaries.

In the initial stages of the war Bulgaria was relatively inconspicuous among the enemy states, but as the war progressed the British government became increasingly aware of the military difficulties Bulgaria posed for the Allies. Most British experts grew intensely hostile to any attempt on the part of the Bulgarian government to present itself as merely caught in the vortex of great-power politics. As a result, the significance of the tense interwar Bulgarian–British relations was magnified. To an extent, the state of affairs preceding the war was replicated during its latter stages. Since the autumn of 1943 British military and political planners had agreed on the desirability of knocking Bulgaria out of the conflict. As very small numbers of Allied troops would be available for the Balkans, Britain had to devise effective measures for the application of diplomatic pressure. Any contacts with Bulgaria brought up before British officials the familiar question of arousing 'at once [...] the deepest suspicion on the part of the Greek, Yugoslav and Turkish Governments'.[21]

In late 1943 and 1944, the FO declared that it was impossible 'to give the Bulgarians the slightest sympathetic consideration'.[22] Even when the Bulgarian government showed willingness to establish unofficial contacts with the Allies, the FO believed that it was simply trying to get itself 'out of scrapes' which it had got into through its own fault.[23] British attitude was augmented by what the British Balkan experts recognized as 'the violent anti-Bulgarian feeling in both Greece and Yugoslavia'.[24] The latter governments-in-exile constantly pressed Britain to make a commitment to harsh punishment of Bulgaria for its role in the war. They did not fail to protest at a single instance when, through propaganda or otherwise, Britain tried to display mildness in order to facilitate

Bulgaria's detachment from the Axis. So vociferous were these protests that the head of the Southern Department, Sir Orme Sargent, feared they might have exactly the opposite effect. Some 'latent Bulgarophilia in the British public' could find 'a favourable breeding place in the irritation and disillusionment which our Greek and Yugoslav allies are bound to cause us as time goes on'.[25]

Planning for Bulgaria was further complicated by the territorial demands of its neighbours against it. Britain had repeatedly stated that territorial changes would have to await the peace settlement. Romanos, the Greek representative in London, was eager to secure British commitment to an enlarged postwar Greece. In September 1943, he complained that in a speech the British prime minister had not mentioned the Greek hope for rectification of the frontier with Bulgaria.[26] Even Turkey, still nominally neutral and on relatively good terms with Bulgaria, criticized BBC broadcasts advising Bulgaria to side with the Allies. The Turkish government shared its disbelief that Bulgarian treachery might be 'condoned and forgotten'. This confirmed the FO's impression that Turkey would manoeuvre for the acquisition of the Sakar massif from which Bulgaria presently dominated Adrianopolis.[27]

Accumulating evidence made the FO sceptical as to its ability to induce Bulgaria to abandon the Axis. The British government was precluded from making even the vaguest of reassurances to Bulgaria. Existing British support for Greece and Yugoslavia and attempts at drawing Turkey closer convinced the Bulgarian government that its only chance of keeping the country's territorial integrity and sovereignty was to remain on Germany's side. The FO fully realized that the lack of positive encouragement was tying the hands even of those small Bulgarian circles which could promote the anti-German case. A feeling of impasse made the FO reluctant to explore the possibilities of rapprochement with Bulgaria. It had some historic sense of failure and was anxious not to lay up incalculable difficulties in its plans for the future of South Eastern Europe.[28]

British Perceptions of the Soviet Role in the Balkans

British foreign-policy makers acknowledged that, as long as Britain was seen as the champion of the interests of Bulgaria's neighbours, Sofia would look to another great power for protection. In early 1943, it was judged that incipient uncertainty about Germany's ultimate ability to win the war increased the likelihood of Bulgaria's rulers trying to reinvigorate relations with the Soviet Union. The FO had to estimate the consequences of such a development on British interests.

In early 1943, Sir George Rendel, British minister in Sofia in 1938–41 and accredited to the Yugoslav government-in-exile during the war, reminded the FO that Bulgaria was the first among the lesser powers to realize that 'in modern conditions small states cannot stand alone'.[29] Most British Eastern European specialists believed that at the current stage of the war the majority of the Bulgarian people were 'as always fervently pro-Russian'. But there were also those who predicted that only on the eve of the Red Army's arrival on the banks of the Danube would the anti-Communists in Bulgaria see the imminent dangers of Soviet occupation.[30]

The FO feared that it was not only pro-Russian feelings which might bring renewed Russian influence over Bulgaria. Balkan analysts recalled that when in November 1940 the Soviet Union had proposed a pact of mutual assistance to Bulgaria, the draft included the Soviet right to establish naval and military bases in the country – within range of the Dardanelles. In later negotiations for an Anglo-Soviet treaty in 1941–42, Soviet security guarantees for the Balkan countries had featured prominently on the Soviet agenda. Stalin had additionally confided in Eden his design for domination of Romania – and the FO surmised that he would also aim to secure Bulgaria.[31] It would only be necessary for the Soviet Union to champion some of Bulgaria's prewar territorial claims to become the 'virtual mistress of the country'. Then Britain would encounter difficulties in distinguishing between 'purely Bulgarian and ultimately Russian interests'. Rendel too was certain that Russia would push south until it obtained military, naval and air bases in the Adriatic and the Aegean. He warned that if the British government did not wish to see Russian bases 'at Split and Dubrovnik, and probably at Dedeagatch, Kavalla or even Salonika', it should in the first place prevent the appearance of these at Varna and Burgas.[32]

Rendel argued that the Soviet Union would not resist the temptation to establish its influence in South Eastern Europe. He even foresaw the possibility of 'a spontaneous movement [...] which would result in the creation of a number of small states or republics which would then spontaneously ask for admission into the Soviet Union'. In such a case it would be 'impossible for the Soviet Union to refuse to have anything to do with it, whatever its undertakings before the Western powers about non-intervention in South Eastern Europe'. Such a development could start from Bulgaria but then affect profoundly the internal situation of Greece and even more Yugoslavia, where the extreme-Left anti-monarchists were very strong.[33]

The fact that Communists were becoming increasingly prominent in the small Bulgarian resistance complicated further the issue of the Soviet role in Bulgaria in particular and in the Balkans as a whole. The Communist ideology could become the instrument for spreading Soviet influence to the south and even west of Europe. What the Southern Department began considering in the spring of 1943 was whether Britain could, and moreover should, aim to 'save' Bulgaria from possible Bolshevization.[34]

Uncertainty about Soviet plans

In the latter stages of the war, the biggest hindrance to the elaboration of a clear British policy towards Bulgaria was the lack of solid knowledge of Soviet plans and attitudes. By 1943, the only definite conclusion the FO had reached was that Soviet influence in the Balkans was going to expand. The more intricate question was, however, whether this increased influence was likely to be coupled with the imposition of the Soviet form of government. Stalin had repeatedly proclaimed that the Soviet Union did not aim at 'the seizure of foreign territory', nor did it intend to impose its 'will and regime upon the Slavonic or any other enslaved nations'.[35] The FO perceived these statements primarily as propaganda, especially since no Soviet declaration mentioned the aspirations of indigenous Communists across Europe. Nevertheless, throughout 1943, British foreign-policy makers were prepared to give the Soviet vision of Eastern Europe the benefit of the doubt.

From different pieces of contemporary evidence the FO ascertained that Stalin's ideas about Bulgaria, and indeed other Eastern European countries, fluctuated. In December 1941, when the Soviet Union had desperately needed military support, Stalin had suggested to Eden that Turkey might be given a portion of south-eastern Bulgaria.[36] Such an opportunistic approach indicated to the FO that Stalin was not led by sentiment but was mostly concerned about concrete wartime achievements. That is why later, in 1943, the Southern Department discussed the possibility of asking the Soviet Union to threaten Bulgaria with war and to confirm that unless Bulgaria surrendered, the Soviet Union could not guarantee its independence. Such a proposition, however, bore heavily on the future of the whole of South Eastern Europe. The Soviet government had hitherto shown reluctance to commit itself 'in any way' on this subject.[37] It was doubtful that the British government itself was ready to make such decisions, either.

As the problem remained confined to internal discussions, in early 1944, the FO continued to speculate about Soviet intentions towards Bulgaria. Even in the spring and summer of that year, when Moscow exerted open pressure on the Bulgarian government to desert the Germans, Soviet short-term plans were unclear to British officials. No precise information could be obtained from the Soviet government, leaving British observers to surmise in a vague general fashion that the USSR strove to establish a 'dominating moral position'. This naturally led to further questions as to whether Soviet Russia would demand something tangible, for example air bases, or seek to ingratiate itself with the Bulgarians by offering them an outlet to the Aegean.[38]

Evidence from Soviet and Bulgarian archives suggests that not even the Bulgarian Communist leader Georgi Dimitrov residing in Moscow and working close to Stalin had many clues about the precise Soviet plans for Bulgaria. Indeed, the existence of such plans can be reasonably questioned.[39] The best available indications of Soviet foreign-policy thinking are the papers of three Soviet Foreign Ministry commissions which functioned from the end of 1943 to mid-1945 and dealt with different aspects of postwar reconstruction. These were headed by Maxim Litvinov, Kliment Voroshilov and Ivan Maisky, all experienced Soviet diplomats with a deep understanding of the mechanisms of Kremlin policy formulation. It is therefore acceptable to assume that their analyses could not have differed much from the opinions of their superiors.[40]

Reporting to Molotov between January and November 1944, the commissions considered it vital that the USSR should assert itself as a power so strong as to deter any future aggression. Among the first steps in this direction would be obtaining strategically favourable boundaries and treaties of mutual aid with the neighbouring countries which also provided for 'the necessary number of land, air and naval bases'.[41] Neither Britain nor the United States were predicted to do much more than voice some ideological objections. Moreover, Britain was judged likely to seek an understanding with Soviet Russia on the basis of spheres of security. This was not seen as incompatible with a second, equally important, Soviet aim, namely that the European continent should become Socialist, as only this would preclude the possibility of new wars and thus guarantee Soviet security. As the commissions recommended in unison good relations with the Western Allies,[42] they clearly understood that this endeavour would be greatly challenged by the advances of Communism. Soviet promotion of a proletarian revolution across Europe was considered especially damaging to relations with Great Britain. Yet the Soviet Union was undoubtedly going to support any indigenous movement towards what was termed 'real democracy'.

Interpretations of the references to revolution in the commissions' documents as merely conforming to the overarching ideological framework in which they operated are justified.[43] In this case, the mention of 'Popular Front Governments' can also be seen as acceptance of the dominant political formula of the time, which also explains the relative absence of excessive Marxist ideology. Naturally, during the war the defence of Soviet territory held priority over lending support to foreign revolutionaries. On the other hand, the spread of revolution should not put the security of the Soviet Union at risk. As the stability of the European situation depended on preserving the alliance with the Western powers, Communism should only be established in countries which were not of crucial importance to the Western Allies.[44]

Looking into the enemy countries' future, Soviet officials initially asserted 'the principles of broad democracy in the spirit of the national front': these were preferably exercised jointly by the three Allies.[45] But in Soviet eyes 'the retrograde record of the West' cast a doubt over such a possibility. Therefore, Europe should be divided into zones of interest and each Big Power should abstain from developing close, especially military relations with the countries not falling within its own sphere. The proposed line of division was apparently drawn on the basis of maximum Soviet interest, placing Bulgaria, Yugoslavia and Romania in the Soviet zone of influence. The aim of undermining Turkey's position as the sole guardian of the Straits was also underlined by the Soviet diplomats. They were confident that as long as Bulgaria received no outlet to the Aegean, Britain would not object to Soviet influence over that country or Romania. Soviet foreign-policy specialists emphasized the importance of reassuring Britain that it would not lose control over the Eastern Mediterranean.[46]

On the whole, outlining their maximum aims in Eastern Europe, the Soviet planners demonstrated adequate understanding of the Allies' (and especially Britain's) preoccupations.

British estimate of Soviet objectives

Having little insight into and lacking reliable information about Soviet aims in South Eastern Europe, British foreign-policy makers were confined to making assumptions on the basis of observable developments. Consequently, comparing British hypotheses of Soviet intentions to the actual Soviet plans and actions would reveal the extent to which British planning and strategy rested on reality. Most British analysts correctly underlined the predominance of the geopolitical motive in Soviet foreign policy but were also right not to overlook the role of Communist ideology.

In late 1943 and the first half of 1944, British policy makers held no unanimous opinion regarding the USSR's ultimate foreign-policy objectives in Eastern Europe. The majority agreed that Stalin would strive to preserve and expand the concessions he had extracted from Hitler in 1939–40. The FO generally accepted that, in addition to Poland and the Baltic republics, the Soviet Union would aim to establish a strong influence over the Balkans. How far such plans were going to damage British interests depended on whether the Soviets would seek to dominate only the foreign policy of the region or change their internal regime too.

Within the FO, different perspectives produced varying attitudes to the Soviet Union. The Northern Department, which covered the USSR, expressed serious doubts that the latter had cut-and-dried, long-term plans, let alone that the FO had adequate knowledge of them. The experts on the Soviet Union maintained that Soviet and British interests were not necessarily antagonistic. One opportunity for reconciliation would arise from cautious

British actions in the Balkans. Christopher Warner, head of the Northern Department, repeatedly warned that if the Soviet leadership detected any British preparation for confrontation, they would respond in kind and would ultimately 'hold the higher cards'.[47]

Alternatively, the Southern Department had been long convinced that the Soviet Union would invade the Balkans. This view began to be taken into greater consideration by the British government in the spring of 1944 as Soviet troops were pushing the German armies across the western Soviet border. The beginning of fighting beyond Soviet territory precipitated yet another attempt on the part of the FO to evaluate possible dominant tendencies in postwar Soviet foreign policy. Simultaneously, Eden and Churchill voiced anxiety regarding the consequences of Soviet westward advances and imminent proximity to the Eastern Mediterranean. Neither of the two leaders was categorical that the Soviet conduct would be troublesome; both were increasingly worried and nervous.[48] Eden was also disturbed lest British suspicions were leaked outside the narrow policy-making circles, thus increasing the possibility of confrontation. Eden deemed it extremely important that the FO should not treat the emergence of a direct clash of interest regarding the Balkans as a foregone conclusion.[49]

FO discussion papers from the first half of 1944 reveal British thinking about the potential Soviet threat and the required reaction to it. Acting on Eden's instructions, various FO Departments 'assemble[d] the evidence in their possession of [the] Soviet intention and the manner in which the Soviet government appeared to be carrying it out'.[50] The result was a broad policy paper which was circulated in the FO and became the basis for a memorandum for exclusive distribution to the War Cabinet.

The FO pointed out that the fact that most of Balkan resistance leaders were Communist did not necessarily mean a 'systematic attempt by some organization to communize the whole Peninsula'. The spread of Russian influence and potential communization of the Balkans were acknowledged as two separate trends, not to be confused. Indeed, British officials showed concern not so much for the latter as for the former. They confirmed earlier views that 'Russia was out' for a predominant position in South Eastern Europe. This could be achieved through the establishment of friendly governments in most Balkan countries, for example by the Partisans in both Yugoslavia and Greece. In many cases the Communists were bound to emerge as the governing force after the war and the Soviet government was using them as a means to an end, but not necessarily an end in itself. British experts conceded that the Soviet Union could justify its building-up of Communist-led movements on purely military grounds, especially since Britain itself was supporting – or had supported – Communist guerrillas in most countries. The FO recognized that, ironically, the Russians had 'merely sat back and watched us doing their work for them'. The most important conclusion contained in the FO policy paper was that the Soviet threat to British interests should not be exaggerated, as this could itself precipitate a direct conflict.[51]

The scrutiny of Soviet demands and the means to fulfil them was supplemented by an attempt at defining potential measures to prevent the spread of Soviet influence in the Balkans. Four theoretical alternatives were put forward. Dropping the support for the Communist-led movements and boosting the more moderate elements was one possibility, as was the opposite, namely full support to the Communists so as 'to take the wind out of the Russians' sails'. Either of these options would cause extreme embarrassment to Britain as it would involve reneging existing agreements and military commitments, especially in Greece and Yugoslavia. The same held true of a suggestion for a British–Soviet undertaking not to interfere in the Balkans. The only feasible option seemed that Britain should focus on Greece and Turkey while availing itself of 'every opportunity to spread British influence'. Deliberate efforts should be made to avoid direct challenges to Soviet Russia.[52]

In this and later papers, the FO approached the subject of Soviet influence in the Balkans from a clearly strategic perspective. Its main conclusions were incorporated in subsequent position documents such as the Post-Hostilities Planning Committee study of 'The Effect of Soviet Policy on British Strategic Interests' from June 1944. This repeated that the Soviet Union would most certainly occupy Romania, strengthen its favourable position in Bulgaria and Yugoslavia and demand military bases in the first two countries. The Committee accepted that Britain could only counter such developments by diplomatic methods, which would hardly be effective. Consequently, later in June 1944, the War Cabinet confirmed the original recommendation of the FO, namely that Britain should consolidate its position in Greece and Turkey and try to spread influence in the rest of the region, avoiding a conflict with the Soviet Union.[53]

Thus, the line of British postwar involvement in the Balkans was more or less clearly drawn. As the extension of British influence was restricted by what were perceived to be growing Soviet ambitions, the limited British resources had to be concentrated in crucial areas: Bulgaria fell outside these. The FO did not dispute what it called the 'dominating moral role' of Russia in Bulgaria and realized that to challenge this would only serve to exacerbate Anglo-Soviet tensions. The result would then be precisely the opposite to what Britain needed in order to defend the Eastern Mediterranean successfully.[54]

The need for cooperation with the Soviet Union

In June 1944, the Northern Department of the FO drew attention to the possibility of the Soviet Union and Great Britain mutually recognizing each other's interests in the Eastern Mediterranean and the Straits. The FO Soviet desk thought that any British effort to build influence in Bulgaria and Romania against the Soviet Union was doomed. They recommended that instead of conflict zones these two countries should become the testing ground for cooperation with the Soviet Union.

Eden endorsed the necessity of continuing collaboration with Moscow and repeated the importance of declaring this publicly. He insisted that the British government should appear to be informing, consulting and respecting the views of the Soviet Union:

> We should not hesitate to make our special interests in the Eastern Mediterranean and therefore in Greece and Turkey, and indeed our interest elsewhere in the Balkans, clear to the Russians: but in any steps we take to build up our influence we must be most careful to avoid giving the impression of a direct challenge.[55]

Such views coincided with trends in earlier FO thinking. In late 1943, in messages to Churchill, Stalin had revealed a desire, before discussing military strategy, to resolve 'all the fundamental questions concerning [...] mutual security and [...] legitimate interests'.[56] At the same time British government officials too were becoming aware of the necessity to raise with the Soviet leaders the issue of postwar settlement.[57]

Lack of unity among the Allies had been variously displayed throughout the war. The increasingly rapid military developments after mid-1943 revealed the necessity for making decisions quickly, which in turn increased the possibility of divergence of policy between Soviet Russia and Britain. FO observers were particularly aware of the lack of mutual consultation and information about Eastern Europe. They envisaged a number of political questions that would arise in the event of military operations there. In July 1943, E. M. Wilson at the Northern Department underlined the negative effects of the lack of discussions with the Soviet Union about policy in Europe in general: 'Unless there is some measure of agreement [...] on general political strategy in Europe there will be increasing heart-burning about tactics, and minor disagreements about tactics will become magnified into major disagreements about strategy and principles.'[58]

He recalled that it was British troops who were and would be fighting on other peoples' territory, a fact placing on Britain the primary responsibility for starting negotiations 'to get our practical strategy in respect of these territories agreed'. Unless approached in time, when the Russians began fighting on other peoples' territory they would see very little need to consult Britain, and by that time the situation would have deteriorated 'almost beyond repair'.[59]

Wilson pointed to examples of Soviet compromises such as Stalin's abstention from concluding a treaty with the Czechoslovak government-in-exile. He warned that Stalin was not going to 'behave' so well indefinitely unless Britain made some specific approach.[60]

Such fears were reiterated by higher-ranking government officials. Robert Bruce Lockhart, Head of the Political Warfare Executive, held that an arrangement with the Soviet Union should be a main *desideratum* of British policy. He believed 'that Britain and the United States cannot guarantee frontiers or even comparative peace in Central and Eastern Europe without a full understanding with Russia'.[61] Sir Stafford Cripps, former Ambassador to Moscow and member of the War Cabinet, expressed similar views. He was convinced that 'easy as it is to prompt the Soviets into mischief, it should be easier still to harness them to responsible policy'. He warned that if, for example, the Soviet Union was excluded from the current discussions over Italy, there would be 'hell to pay'. Stalin would interpret this as an invitation to exclude the Western Allies from decisions relating to Central and Eastern Europe: 'This he may in any case. But why provide him with a moral right and legal justification.'[62] Reviewing advice for rapprochement with the Soviet Union, Sargent complained that it constituted 'a minor form of appeasement'. But even so, he admitted that 'a store of goodwill and confidence should be built up, so it could be drawn upon when relations become really difficult'.[63]

Already in mid-1943, Rendel had pointed to the extreme complexity of an agreement with the Soviet Union in relation to the Balkans. He claimed that the importance of urgent political discussions between the Allies could not be overestimated. These should clarify not only 'the fate of the whole of South-Eastern Europe South of the Danube, and possibly South of the Carpathians, but also the major issue of the future relations between the Soviet Union and Western Europe, at a point where the interests of the two are likely to impinge on each other most acutely and dangerously'. Rendel called for the formulating of 'a clear and consistent policy designed to ensure the real independence and prosperity of this important area'. He insisted that the matter required urgent treatment by a special committee which should be guided by political rather than academic aims and should put forward constructive and well-defined suggestions for policy towards South Eastern Europe: 'The various intricate aspects of this vitally important and urgent problem could be collated, classified and simplified, and [...] the issue could be presented in a complete yet compact and manageable form which would enable HMG to take a clear decision.'[64]

Rendel's proposal was welcomed by the Southern Department, which agreed that 'waiting on events was likely to be fatal' as they 'would not wait for [the British government] to make up [its] mind'. Officials dealing with the Balkans saw clear advantages in determining exactly what they wanted in the region so that they 'could seize any opportunity'. They accepted that suggestions were bound to be amended in the light of future developments, but this was preferable to simply waiting on Soviet moves. Nothing came of these ideas. In August 1943, Sargent made some preliminary moves to choose a chairman for the proposed committee. His actions were, however, suspended without explanation shortly after the sudden death of the Bulgarian king Boris III in August 1943.[65]

'Negative' Planning for Bulgaria

On Eden's orders Rendel's letter to the FO from February 1943 was printed for circulation in the War Cabinet. The letter drew particular attention to the importance of Bulgaria for the formulation of long-term British policy towards the whole Balkan region:

> When the last act of the drama begins [...] the centre of the stage will be held [...] by Bulgaria. Bulgaria – insignificant as she may seem when judged by standards of major world politics – holds a key position in South-East Europe out of all proportion to her own intrinsic importance. We have twice been led into misfortune by ignoring or belittling the Bulgarian issue. But its bearing on the problem of the future of South-East Europe as a whole is so vital.[66]

The Southern Department perceived the text to be an elaboration of a 'favourite thesis' of Rendel's. The diplomat's pro-Bulgarian feelings were well known and it was felt this led him to exaggeration and bias. Yet the logic of his repetitive statements was difficult to refute. Partly, the irritation of the FO derived from the fact that simply acknowledging Bulgaria's significance was not sufficient at the current stage of the war. The Bulgarian desk in particular realized that a more active attitude was needed but was hampered by Britain's possessing few contacts with Bulgaria and little information about the state of affairs within the country. Indeed, the brief on Bulgaria compiled for the secretary of state for the Moscow Conference of Foreign Ministers in October 1943 was barely adequate. The FO was reduced to appealing to the Soviet Foreign Ministry for up-to-date information; the reply was in such general terms as to be of little practical use.[67]

No guarantees for Bulgarian sovereignty

The lack of firm knowledge certainly added to the FO's inclination to elaborate policy towards Bulgaria in essentially negative terms. Although some Southern

Department officials had privately expressed understanding for Bulgaria's difficult position, British public pronouncements emphasized that the country could not expect soft treatment at the hands of the victorious Allies. The proclaimed British attitude was in full compliance with the principles of unconditional surrender of Germany and its satellites. Even when in late 1943 and 1944 unconditional surrender was no longer considered an effective approach and was silently dropped from Allied propaganda, no concessions to Bulgaria were ever seriously contemplated.[68]

The British government's primary demand was the cessation of Bulgarian occupation of Greek and Yugoslav territory. This was repeatedly stressed as the first requirement to be imposed by the Allies on a defeated Bulgaria.[69] Even more importantly, the British government displayed ambiguity towards Bulgaria's independence after the war. Some internal FO documents reveal beliefs that Bulgaria should retain its sovereignty, yet it was considered vital that no official statement or propaganda should raise any 'false hopes on this score'.[70] On the contrary, in order to force Bulgaria's detachment from the Axis, it should be constantly repeated that unless Bulgaria changed sides in the conflict, Britain would not pledge itself to the survival of an independent Bulgarian state. These views were communicated to the US State Department and formed the basis of Eden's brief for the Moscow Conference in October 1943.[71] The official British position was in fact milder than some alternatives spelled out within the FO. For example, Douglas Howard, head of the Southern Department, predicted that the resolution of the Bulgarian question lay either in 'carving up Bulgaria between Yugoslavia and Greece with perhaps a separate Macedonian state or annexation of some sort by Soviet Russia'.[72] Such extreme opinions were, however, an exception among British diplomats and civil servants.

British lack of interest in Bulgaria's existence as a separate state was greatly influenced by a negative attitude towards the ruling Bulgarian dynasty. King Boris III was held personally responsible for Bulgaria's siding with Germany and the Bulgarian government's decision to that effect was regarded as 'deliberate and having been taken in full knowledge of the consequences'. The fate of the king was a matter of indifference to the British government, all the more so since his actions fitted with a perceived pattern of Saxe-Coburg treachery towards Britain.[73] Even Rendel, who during his mandate in Sofia had been quite respectful of Boris, agreed that the king's 'continued presence in the country was only likely to compromise the Bulgarian case still further'.[74] Boris's death in August 1943 did not bring a change in the FO's opinions of the Bulgarian monarchy. However, criticism of the Bulgarian royal family was silently dropped from British propaganda. The FO and the PWE agreed that they should not antagonize Bulgarian public opinion, which was generally sympathetic to Boris's young successor and the widowed Queen Mother.[75]

The FO maintained these views in the face of a somewhat more lenient US attitude towards Bulgaria. In early 1944, aiming like the British government to knock Bulgaria out of the war, the State Department elaborated a 'long-range' plan for that country. In US diplomatic thinking it was vital to give some encouragement to Bulgaria. Under the influence of officials, who like Rendel had served in Sofia before the war and continued to monitor Bulgarian developments, several proposals were forwarded for discussion with the FO. Among these was a declaration that there existed no intention to change the Bulgarian borders of March 1941 or to breach the country's independence as long as the occupied territories were evacuated. The State Department went so far as to recommend an enquiry into a possible autonomy of Macedonia within Yugoslavia, and some minor territorial alterations which would benefit the western Bulgarian border.[76] All this was unceremoniously ruled out by the FO, which judged its US counterpart to be too sympathetic to the Bulgarians as a whole and to King Boris in particular. Some Whitehall officials even spoke of an 'American appeasement plan' in direct contradiction to British policy. Therefore, they quickly and firmly 'disabused' their US colleagues 'of any idea that support can be usefully given' to Bulgaria.[77] This was in line with the earlier British rejection of anything but a negative policy and negative propaganda to Bulgaria. In July 1943, Howard had warned that the Bulgarian government could not be expected 'to risk their necks and take matters in their own hands if they are given no encouragement to think that by doing so they will receive better treatment'. That is why he recommended 'a bare announcement on the lines of [the] famous Albanian declaration to the effect that there will be an independent Bulgaria after the war'.[78] But Sargent was opposed to 'the smallest carrot' for Bulgaria, ruling out even a statement about the retention of Dobrudja. Eden weighed in on the side of toughness.[79]

The firm refusal to issue any assurance of Bulgarian independence spelled difficulties for British policy towards Bulgaria. There was little ground on which the FO could initiate contacts with Bulgarian politicians and use them for the promotion of British wartime and postwar interests in the country. An additional problem arose from the uncertainty as to whether Britain should just aim to detach Bulgaria from the Axis or seek a longer-term influence over the country.

The idea of a Balkan federation

With almost no effective tools with which to influence Bulgaria, the FO could only 'wait and see how events turn out'.[80] The only proactive element in its strategy was the concept of a Balkan federation of which Bulgaria would form a part. The idea met with approval from most British diplomats and civil servants concerned with the region.

In May 1942, the Greek and Yugoslav governments-in-exile signed a treaty of friendship and mutual assistance. This had been encouraged by Britain, which recognized the royal Greek and Yugoslav governments as Allies. The treaty itself pivoted on wartime cooperation against German and Bulgarian occupation in the Balkans. The two signatories and their British mentors also viewed it as the foundation stone for a peacetime federal scheme. In mid-1942, Britain supported preliminary discussions on the subject between the Yugoslav and Greek exiled leaders and Bulgarian émigré politicians in the Middle East, represented by Dr Georgi M. Dimitrov,[81] leader of the left wing of the Bulgarian Agrarian National Union (BANU). Even though the latter was not officially recognized by the Allies as the head of a Bulgarian government-in-exile, cooperation with him featured highly in any intentions to extend British influence in Bulgaria after the war. Among the other advantages it could provide for Britain, his organization was known for its open anti-monarchist feelings and its long-held commitment to the idea of a Balkan federation.[82]

Churchill favoured the idea, having spoken in October 1942 of federations making up a future 'Council of Europe'.[83] In early 1943, the FO Research Department was instructed to look into the feasibility of grouping together various Balkan states. This resulted in a comprehensive theoretical analysis of the foreseeable effects of such a development on the economy, internal and foreign policy of the region, as well as its wider international repercussions. As different combinations of states were considered, it became clear that a union of the Balkan countries could form a part of a whole series of new supranational groupings. The Baltic republics could be brought together, as well as the Central European states. The Balkan federation would constitute an important element in a new European postwar order, intended to bring security and stability to volatile regions.

For the FO analysts, a large Balkan state only made sense if it included Bulgaria. In Britain's view, Bulgaria's nationalist pretensions had caused a number of conflicts in the region over the previous eighty years. As on historical and ethnic grounds Bulgaria continued to have territorial claims towards all its neighbours, it would remain a source of Balkan instability. This would be further aggravated by economic difficulties. A federation might be a way of overcoming Bulgaria's grievances, as the country would share economic benefits with its neighbours and have a stake in their prosperity and stability. Most significantly, engagement with the defence of the whole region was likely to constrain Bulgaria's revisionism.[84]

Neutralization of the Balkan 'powder keg' was distinctly advantageous to the whole of Europe and would have positive implications for British security.

Imperial economic and political interest clearly dictated that Britain should seek a long-term settlement for the endemic problems of the region. Of additional but not smaller importance was the fact that a Balkan federation established under the British aegis would have broader consequences for Britain's international position. It could become a vital barrier to the extension of Soviet influence in proximity to the Mediterranean Straits. This in fact was the critical motive for Britain's support and encouragement of a Balkan federation. The FO was predominantly thinking in terms of the need to consolidate British influence in the Aegean region and use it as the basis for penetration further inside the Balkan Peninsula.

Throughout 1943, the British plan for a Balkan federation was elaborated with traditional power-political patterns in mind. It was placed in the context of long-lasting British strategic objectives and gave only marginal consideration to political development inside the countries which were intended to form the constituent federal parts. The establishment of enduring democracy in the Balkan countries was perceived as desirable, and ultimately it would contribute to the stability of the proposed federation. But this was not a prominent concern for British policy makers.

For all the FO papers and discussions devoted to it, the plan for a Balkan federation was in fact only sketchily developed. Questions such as the countries it would encompass, their political outlook, and the fate of their existing dynasties were left unanswered, or sometimes unexplored. However, the most significant error of judgement made by the FO on this subject was to mention it to Turkey in early 1943 in an attempt to ascertain the latter's possible reaction. At that time, the Turkish government was preoccupied with the Communist danger it considered to be emanating from Soviet Russia. This was aggravated by the possibility of the establishment of a large predominantly Slav state along Turkey's European border. The Turkish foreign minister Numan Menemencioglu discussed the tentative British proposal with diplomats from various Balkan countries, including Bulgaria. He also attempted to involve Arab states in what became his own initiative for a Mediterranean bloc. The FO was appalled at the Turkish indiscretion; the proposal was bound to become known to Stalin and be interpreted as a bulwark against Soviet penetration.[85]

Whether this happened is unclear, but the Soviet Union did have the last say regarding the federation scheme. The idea had surfaced during the Anglo-Soviet treaty negotiations in 1942. Then Molotov had demonstrated a studiedly negative attitude, which became all the more pronounced at the time of the Yugoslav–Greek agreement.[86] Nevertheless, Eden reverted to the Balkan federation proposal in Moscow in October 1943, formulating it in terms of a positive step towards the banishment of spheres of influence from international politics. Although this principle was of central importance for the US government, Secretary of State Cordell Hull demonstrated little interest, leaving the issue to be resolved between the Soviet Union and Britain.[87]

Although both Eden and Molotov declared officially that their governments did not favour separate spheres of influence in Europe, they did not reach an agreement on the Balkan federation scheme. There was almost no discussion of the British proposition. Instead, Moscow produced a statement that the plan was not appropriate as the nations concerned had not been consulted. Such an important step as the creation of a federation should be the result of 'free, peaceful and well-considered expression of the will of the people'. The Soviet Union did not view the existing émigré governments or even the future first postwar governments to represent adequately 'the aspirations of their people'. It also believed that in the proposed form the federation resembled too closely a *cordon sanitaire* directed against the Soviet Union.[88]

The federation scheme was among the factors that contributed to the 'balance of mistrust' among the Allies.[89] The unfavourable Soviet reaction forced the British government to drop the whole subject until a more suitable moment. To all intents and purposes, however, the Balkan federation scheme was permanently deleted from British plans for a postwar settlement. There was considerable uncertainty as to what could take its place. An acceptable substitute was not found and Britain did not prepare adequately to exploit the vacuum which would result from German withdrawal from the Balkans.

At the same time, the British government became extremely watchful of any Soviet attempts to take up the idea of a Balkan federation and give it a form suitable for the Soviet Union. In May 1944, an FO paper traced some indications of Soviet intentions to foster the unification of Bulgaria and Yugoslavia. For Britain such a move would have several negative effects. It would isolate Greece and weaken its position vis-à-vis its northern neighbours. It was certain to revive Bulgaria's claim for an Aegean outlet, again to Greek disadvantage. Most importantly, a South Slav federation would certainly be under direct Soviet patronage, and would threaten both Greek and Turkish positions in the Mediterranean. In practice all this constituted a direct challenge to the British interest and influence in the region.[90]

* * *

British planning for postwar Bulgaria was rooted in historic British precedents where relations with Bulgaria's neighbours and the legacy of centuries of rivalry with Russia featured high. The latter factor was complicated by the fact that Russia was now a Communist state, whose power mechanisms and political logic were not yet fully comprehended by British foreign-policy makers.

At this stage, concerns for democracy in Bulgaria, if present at all, played a supplementary part to security considerations.

Suspicions about the ultimate Soviet aims in the Balkans and Bulgaria were common at the FO. Nevertheless, a consensus emerged among officials that there should be no active measures for counteracting Soviet influence that were unfavourable to Britain. This was left for the future, when Soviet aims and claims would be clearer. Not knowing what privileges the Soviet Union might demand in Bulgaria, it was deemed impossible for the British government to determine its reaction in advance.

Britain failed to devise the slightest inducement for Bulgarian withdrawal from the Axis. Neither could it commit itself to any specific plan about Bulgaria's postwar development before it made sure that the Soviet Union would also associate itself. All this clearly amounted to the concession of Soviet predominance in Bulgaria. The only condition imposed was that Soviet interests in Bulgaria did not threaten British influence in the Eastern Mediterranean. Most strikingly, however, the FO could not even consistently follow a policy of disinterest and detachment. While it consciously chose not to take any actions regarding Bulgaria, it continued to regard the country as a possible zone of future interest.

Chapter Two
GETTING BULGARIA OUT OF THE WAR

From the moment Bulgaria joined the Tripartite Pact on 1 March 1941, British strategists sought to disengage it from the Axis. As Bulgaria declared war on Great Britain and the United States in December 1941, following the Japanese attack on Pearl Harbor, Britain aimed to force the country's return to neutrality, if not its turnaround against Germany. British initiatives to that end were continuously influenced by other regional relationships, such as the involvement with the governments-in-exile of Greece and Yugoslavia, which was central to Britain's long-term position in the Eastern Mediterranean. They also had to factor in the possible reaction of the Soviet Union, in view of the latter's known and suspected geopolitical aspirations.

The Frustrations of the SOE

Britain directed a great deal of its wartime efforts in Bulgaria towards establishing a network of special agents and obtaining relevant military and political information. Its activity was hindered by the fact that Bulgaria was not occupied but allied to Germany – which was not conducive to the development of a significant resistance movement.

The Special Operations Executive (SOE), a branch of the Secret Intelligence Service (SIS) was entrusted with 'all operations of sabotage, secret subversive propaganda, the encouragement of civil resistance in occupied areas, the stirring up of insurrection, strikes, etc.'.[1] Since its emergence in June 1940 it had clashed with a number of agencies with which it had to coordinate its actions: the intelligence services bemoaned it endangering informers; the Political Warfare Executive protested the sparse and often contradictory information it received from the SOE; the Chiefs of Staff believed that effort and personnel should not be wasted on operations of limited military scale and impact, no matter how impressive psychologically.

The Foreign Office too resented the SOE's interfering in the domain of external relations. In a prime example, the British minister in Sofia, George

Rendel, strongly objected to the commencement of secret operations in Bulgaria before a declaration of war. The suspicions and reservations towards the SOE, common throughout diplomatic circles, were even more pronounced in the case of Bulgaria, where the FO had minimal contacts and restricted influence, all of which could easily be monopolized by the SOE. The complicated relationship between the FO and the SOE in Bulgaria shaped to a great extent Britain's approach towards the country in the latter stages of the war.

SOE vs FO contacts with Bulgaria

The preparation for work inside Bulgaria combined various political and military elements. As few available sources outline specific objectives, the broad picture can only be extracted from the existing operational material, bearing in mind that plans were constantly altered to accommodate the changing perception of the situation on the ground. Throughout 1942–44 there were several recurring ideas, among which emphasis was given to the need to contact the biggest possible number of anti-Axis organizations and bring them into a coalition, sometimes referred to as a national front. This was to unite all forms of resistance under the broad slogan of Bulgarian independence. Its political aims would be the distribution of propaganda, the mobilization of anti-Hitler public opinion and pressure on the Bulgarian government to exit from the war. Simultaneously, the national front would hinder Bulgaria's war effort in every conceivable way, including by sabotage and subversion. Initially the SOE considered that its ultimate task in Bulgaria in conjunction with the united opposition forces would be the staging of a revolt, if and when the British military authorities judged it appropriate.[2]

In its preliminary work in Bulgaria the SOE did not exclude collaboration with any group which shared anti-government and anti-German feelings. Soundings and contacts in 1940–41 confirmed that in practice there were few political formations which were worth cultivating. Of primary importance was the maintenance of links with the Military League, the organization of serving officers and reservists with undisputed influence over the Bulgarian army and police force. Realism prompted British officials to recognize that though these officers-turned-politicians opposed Bulgarian involvement with Germany, they were not necessarily pro-British. Contacts with the Bulgarian military were also hindered by the conspiratorial nature of their organization and their strong desire for independence, which prevented them from accepting funding from foreigners. In contrast, the federalist wing of the Internal Macedonian Revolutionary Organization (IMRO), the so-called Protoguerovists, were eager to receive as many weapons and ammunitions as possible. Their terrorist methods were ideal for sabotage and, if necessary, for assassination, although in common with the officers they agreed to work 'with', rather than 'for', Britain.³

Shortly before Britain broke off relations with Bulgaria in March 1941, the SOE in London received a report from one of its agents that 'complete understanding' had been reached between the Military League, the Protoguerovists and the left Agrarians, who showed the most categorical commitment. Negotiations with G. M. had not been easy, but once he accepted cooperation with the British secret services, the latter had many occasions to confirm he was 'a man of exceptional judgement and mental honesty'.⁴ Among the first successful operations of the SOE in Bulgaria was organizing G. M.'s escape in a truck transporting the archives of the British Legation to Turkey in February 1941. G. M. was then helped to make his way to the Middle East, where under British supervision he set up the Free and Independent Bulgaria Committee, which was in charge of two radio stations broadcasting into Bulgaria. He also served as the resident authority on all matters Bulgarian. G. M. tried hard to establish contact with his followers and fellow politicians inside Bulgaria. He duly prepared messages to be smuggled over the Turkish border or by sea. Very few of these reached the addressees and even fewer were answered.⁵

When Bulgaria first entered the war the SOE maintained that G. M. was the representative not only of his Agrarian faction but also the authorized envoy of the other two organizations inclined to collaborate with the British services. There is indirect evidence that initially the British government was prepared to treat him and his associates as friendly exiled political leaders. On 21 September 1941, Lord Glenconner, head of SOE in Cairo, wrote to G. M. and his aide Kosta Todorov that they were recognized as the heads of a Bulgarian pro-British organization and as such would be helped on the principles of Lend-Lease.⁶ This was contrary to the intentions of the FO, which vigorously opposed and effectively precluded any official recognition of G. M.'s political status. Consequently, Todorov, who appeared in London in 1942, created some unpleasant incidents for the FO. He remonstrated at being denied what he regarded as promised backing for his attempts to act as the representative of an émigré government.⁷

In the summer of 1943, the relatively smooth relations between the British special services and G. M. suffered further. Upon intervention from the FO, G. M.'s movements and responsibilities for propaganda to Bulgaria were restricted without clear justification. Apart from the recurring FO resentment of the SOE, an important factor could have been the apprehension that G. M. would indeed form a government-in-exile, which would then seek official British support. A British refusal would be embarrassing in view of the erstwhile involvement and recognition would be impossible without scandalizing the vociferous Greeks and Yugoslavs. This precipitated doubts in the SOE whether he would continue the association with it at all; the more so since at the very same time he had been approached by the US secret services.[8]

Meanwhile, the FO tried to establish its own channels for communication with Bulgaria. Among the few means at its disposal were the services of the former Bulgarian minister in London Nikola Momchilov, who had resigned his post following Bulgaria's adherence to the Axis. The Southern Department had a very favourable opinion of him and he was prepared to cooperate, even though he knew the FO had ruled out his idea of setting up a Bulgarian government-in-exile in London. In the summer of 1942, Momchilov had suggested that he write personal letters to three senior Bulgarian officers who were serving with the Bulgarian occupation corps in Yugoslavia. The letters were cleared with the Chiefs of Staff and then dispatched through secret channels.[9]

In his letters Momchilov warned that Bulgaria's future position would be determined in the course of the coming Balkan campaign, which was going to be a joint operation of all three Allies. Above all, he urged responsible Bulgarian circles to stop helping the Germans and not 'to sit back and wait for the Soviet troops'.[10] In early 1943, following the same procedure, Momchilov wrote twice to General Mihov, Bulgarian War Minister, and also to the Bulgarian Ministers in Switzerland, Spain and Sweden. The Bulgarian archives hold evidence only of the letter to the Bulgarian diplomatic representative in Madrid Purvan Draganov which was duly presented to King Boris III and the Bulgarian government in the summer of 1943. However, the Soviets found out about these approaches and immediately requested more information. Even as Eden was alarmed lest the USSR might suspect Britain of dealing behind the Soviet back,[11] the FO had no illusions about the minor value of these communications. At the time, however, their chances appeared no less likely than those of the missives G. M. was preparing. British officials found the effort worthwhile as it could open an alternative channel with Bulgaria, involving political circles different from the ones with whom the SOE hoped to work.

Momchilov, as well as Dimiter Matsankiev, another Bulgarian exile in London, persistently tried to persuade the FO of the enormous importance of securing contacts with the Bulgarian army. According to them not only did this force consist of half a million well-equipped, trained and disciplined men but they also believed that for historical reasons the rank-and-file were anti-German. Elisabeth Barker at the PWE judged these arguments to be imaginative and over optimistic but was inclined to accept the plausibility of the existence of some anti-government centre within the

Bulgarian army; indeed 'it would be contrary to Balkan tradition if there were not'.[12]

The Southern Department was well aware of the advantages that would be derived from stable links with Bulgarian officers. In this it was at one with the SOE, which had made some contacts with representatives of the Military League and was hopeful of renewing them. The SOE estimated that the military were among the few groups in Bulgaria which were capable of bringing about a revolution. The FO agreed with this and was prepared to authorize contacts with the army, although it firmly forbade any political dealings with either Communists or Agrarians. The FO accepted that one British objective should be to cause the fall of the Bulgarian government by revolution. But what it had in mind was, should the opportunity arise, 'to engineer a military revolution which would at the worst neutralize the Bulgarian army as an effective fighting force, and at the best turn it into a pro-Allied force'.[13]

The increased attention towards the Bulgarian army reflected the growing necessity in the course of the war to achieve practical results in Bulgaria. After the successful Allied landings in Sicily it was obvious that a Bulgarian *volte-face* could be decisive for the whole Balkan Peninsula. This overshadowed any political considerations. Action in the field became imperative, all the more so since propaganda broadcasts from London and Jerusalem were the only success Britain could claim. G. M.'s contacts barely gave signs of existence; the previous January the SOE had dropped 'blind' and lost J. S. Morgan, their best-trained officer for work in Bulgaria.[14]

It was at this point that the FO's tolerance of the SOE Bulgarian section wore thin. In August 1943, the death of King Boris III marked an important political crossroad for Bulgaria, of which little became immediately known in London. Sargent recorded the desperate need for information by wondering 'have we any idea what is happening in Bulgaria? Can nobody tell us anything ... C? SOE? Middle East Intelligence?' His subordinates dryly commented that the SOE's Bulgarian contacts were 'rotten'.[15] Ironically, the FO was to a great degree dependent on situation briefings provided by the special services. These were often ambiguous and sometimes downright contradictory, provoking the criticism of the same diplomats who had themselves stood in the way of establishing a secure underground network in Bulgaria in the first instance.

British military missions in Bulgaria

A fresh attempt to collect information and influence events in the country was required. For this the FO authorized the dispatch of a British military mission, led first by Mostyn Davies. Their actions were accompanied by controversy and bad luck, which caused tendentious interpretations of British policy towards Bulgaria.[16] With hindsight, it is now possible to say that in the winter of 1943-44, British policy makers evaluated Bulgaria on purely military grounds and emphasized the necessity to knock it out of the war despite the possible political cost. Most strikingly, both the FO and the SOE regarded work with the Bulgarian Communists as not only advantageous but also highly desirable.

When Bulgaria joined the Axis, the Bulgarian Communist Party was still suffering from the embarrassment and confusion of the Molotov-Ribbentrop Non-Aggression Pact. Only after the Nazi invasion of the Soviet Union were they able to launch their resistance, and in early 1943 reports of their increased activity accumulated in London. The British observers considered them one of the staunchest anti-government forces, which could also boast past terrorist actions and a history of underground survival. British special agents had not sought direct connection with the Communists as the SOE expected that, if necessary, G. M. would be able to attract them for common action. In February 1943 the FO questioned the SOE London headquarters in Baker Street as to why they had made no direct links with the Bulgarian Communists. The SOE's reaction was acid:

> Having been accused by the Foreign Office of working only with the Communists in Greece, we are now politely ticked off for not working with them in Bulgaria. [...] In Yugoslavia they are quite incapable of making up their minds whether to support their accredited Ally the Yugoslavs, or the so-called Communists supported by Russia. [...] It is too much to expect the Foreign Office to be consistent.[17]

The confusion was more apparent than real and lasted only until British policy makers clarified in their minds the relation between the military contribution of the various resistance movements in the Balkans and the future strategic position of the territories in which they operated. Indeed, the news of successful Communist fighting was more often than not accompanied by warnings from people coming out of Bulgaria that the leftist elements were becoming too strong and, in expectation of support from the approaching victorious Soviet army, were clearing the ground for radical social changes.[18] At the same time, officers with leftist and sometimes openly stated Communist inclinations worked in the SOE itself. In the case of Bulgaria it is not obvious whether they played as significant a role as the one attributed to them in relation to the resistance movements in Yugoslavia.[19] In a way, the lack of reliable contacts and sufficient information about the internal developments in Bulgaria freed British policy makers to undertake what they considered the most practicable course. They were not restrained by any alliances with political elements inside the country whose position they might endanger by uninformed action.

Two British missions were dropped in zones controlled by the Yugoslav Partisans on the border with Bulgaria at the end of 1943. They managed to find Bulgarian guerrillas and established contact with representatives of the Central Committee of the Bulgarian Communist Party, which effectively controlled Bulgarian armed resistance. The missions' brief was to estimate the potential strength of the underground Bulgarian movement and gather evidence for a considered opinion as to whether Britain should support it.[20]

The little that was known about Bulgarian resistance made some British officers suspicious of becoming involved with simple 'never-do-wells' who could also turn out to be anti-British. But the belief that even such people could be useful prevailed:

Whether these are good Bulgarians or bad Bulgarians [...] are questions, which do not interest SOE. What interests SOE is that these are Bulgarians who are prepared to fight and commit sabotage against the Bulgarian Government and the Germans although this means risk of torture or death for them. Such men can be useful to us.[21]

The reports of the British Liaison Officers (BLOs) – as the missions' heads were known – were favourable to the Bulgarian Partisans. The latter claimed to have divided the country into twelve operational zones, which were under the command of a central military authority. Data about the numbers and actions of detachments in each zone was forwarded to Cairo, together with information about the political organization behind the resistance – the Fatherland Front coalition of anti-government parties. This body also directed armed town units, which were responsible for a wave of political murders, especially in Sofia. In order to forestall suspicions that the Fatherland Front was simply a facade for the Communists, the latter claimed that not all guerrillas were Communists and that the Communist Party was but one of the founders of the Fatherland Front.[22]

In fact, Bulgarian Communist leaders misrepresented both the strength of the resistance and the role of the Communist Party in it. The British officers were told that there were about twelve thousand Partisans in Bulgaria,[23] whereas in March 1944, the CC reported to Moscow that 'there were twenty-six Partisan detachments altogether with the overall number of Partisans at 2,320'.[24] Not being able to verify it, the SOE in the Middle East had no reason to distrust the received information and supplies were apportioned accordingly. The strong figures seemed to be indirectly confirmed by the constant stream of news about the upsurge of leftist opposition to the Bulgarian regime. The BLOs did not express the slightest doubt about the sincerity of their Communist contacts and could not even guess at the discrepancy between reality and the data they were given. They themselves were attached to what we now know were the biggest Partisan units operating in relatively favourable circumstances on the Bulgarian–Yugoslav border. The BLOs also assessed favourably the opportunities for the Partisan forces in Bulgaria to grow: the population was assumed to be of generally leftist inclinations, attracted by the Partisan slogans and occasional personal examples of courage. Another positive factor was the perceived mounting popular discontent with the Bulgarian government's internal and foreign policy.

Such analysis of the situation in Bulgaria led the SOE to resolve to assist the Partisans. The Bulgarian section highlighted the crucial element of time: at this moment comparatively small supplies of arms would go a long way and eventually make a big difference. An even more significant result would be the knowledge that aid had been sent by Britain and the United States. This would give the British clandestine organizations a good chance of gaining the Partisans' trust and establishing mutual cooperation on a firmer basis. It could convince the Bulgarian guerrillas to provide the SOE with the necessary military information and accept BLOs for other parts of the country.

From the start the SOE realized that the usefulness of the Bulgarian movement depended significantly on the extent of British involvement. For the Bulgarian Partisans to play their potentially important part, it was vital that they receive regular drops of supplies. Sorties were planned to start in February. There should be 20 in that month, increasing to 50 in May. These should provide the Bulgarian Partisans with at least 7,500 rifles, 18 tons of explosive materials and demolition accessories and 2,000 pairs of boots.[25]

After the FO had approved support for the Bulgarian Partisans, the SOE Bulgarian section had been apportioned stores for the equipment of 15,000 men. However, transportation aircraft was not available due to other more urgent tasks, so the original planning was modified to 15 possible sorties in February, with the hope for compensation in the following months. In practice, the combination of lack of aircraft and bad weather conditions reduced the number of successful sorties in February and March 1944 to a total of 3.[26]

These logistical difficulties were further aggravated by the restructuring of the SOE brought about by the general course of the war. Following the move of the Allied headquarters, the SOE operational centre was transferred from Africa to Bari in Italy at the beginning of 1944. For technical reasons, however, the Bulgarian and Romanian sections remained in Cairo. The lines of command and decision making complicated even further when the Balkan Allied Force was made responsible for the operation of special duty aircraft in the region but not for the special operations themselves. At roughly the same time a dedicated Balkan Affairs Committee had been established to coordinate all Allied actions in the region by reconciling conflicting views. This, however, encountered US resistance from the very beginning.[27]

The position of the BLOs in Bulgaria was not made easier by the suspicions of the Partisan leaders. In March 1944, the CC received a letter from its exiled head Georgi Dimitrov ordering that any British approaches were to be treated with caution and that no political undertakings were to be made. Dimitrov warned that 'imperialist' Britain might try to trade immediate material help for future political influence in Bulgaria. After the war, prominent guerrilla leaders asserted that as time went on and supplies did not come, the Partisans began wondering whether Britain had not set out to disrupt the Partisan organization. They suspected that Britain aimed at destroying the Partisans' potential for taking power in Bulgaria at the end of the war.[28] These allegations were made in the early Cold War period and reflect the contemporaneous attitude of the Bulgarian Communists to Britain. The assertions disregard the logistical and other difficulties and fail to take into account Britain's priorities of the moment. They are indicative, however, of the inherent lack of trust of the Bulgarian Communist guerrillas for Britain and therefore of the shaky original basis of the relations of the SOE with the Partisans.

The plan for SOE activities listed purely military objectives. The overall aim was to secure German withdrawal from Bulgaria and to cause the fall of the Bulgarian government. If 'revolution' was mentioned, it was in the sense of a military coup which would neutralize Bulgaria as an active enemy. The FO liaison at the Middle East headquarters Kit Steel admitted that he looked upon the Partisans as an instrument of pressure on the present government: 'What happens after Bulgaria turns on Germany [...] is no concern of ours so long as the damage to the Germans has been done'.[29] Strict instructions were dispatched to the BLOs in Bulgaria not to get mixed up in internal Bulgarian affairs at all. In propaganda, too, the FO insisted on strict neutrality as far as Bulgarian politics was concerned. As late as the summer of 1944, they did not wish to appear to be promoting the image even of their known collaborator the Agrarian G. M.[30]

The same tactical considerations were put forward by high-ranking SOE officers in Cairo and London while assessing the SOE actions in Bulgaria after the Bulgarian army captured and executed Frank Thompson in June 1944. He had assumed the command of the BMM after Mostyn Davies's earlier death in action. The review concluded that the Bulgarian Partisans' actions had a negligible influence on the military configuration in the Balkans. Their inability to engage in serious warfare with the German or Bulgarian army was the primary cause for Britain's decision to cease the contacts. By August

1944 Lord Moyne, the minister resident in the Middle East, had professed that the Bulgarians 'had shown themselves immune' to British attempts to build up a serious resistance movement in Bulgaria proper, one that would have 'appreciable influence on events there'. He concluded that 'the Bulgarian Partisans were incomparable with the Yugoslavs in terms of conquering free zones'. For Lord Moyne, a high proportion of the Bulgarian guerrillas were 'simply traditional brigands'. He questioned whether 'risking the life of spirited young officers not to speak of arms deliveries to most undesirable elements' was 'worth the candle'.[31]

Secret operations in Bulgaria

The Soviet and US secret services also operated in Bulgaria during the Second World War. In terms of intensity and success, the wartime activities of the British secret services in Bulgaria do not stand up to comparison with those of their Soviet counterparts. It was characteristic of the British–Soviet wartime relationship that whereas Moscow was informed about British special operations, Soviet subversive efforts in Bulgaria were not revealed to the Allies. This was partly due to the working habits and ideological outlook of the Soviet services;[32] more pertinent was the fact that the Soviet government kept its cards regarding Bulgaria close to its chest, not wishing to share much about its objectives in the country.

Relations between the British and US special services were on the whole open and, in most cases, mutually beneficial. At first, the US displayed little interest in Bulgaria. The US High Command had made it abundantly clear that in general it preferred not to interfere too prominently in the Balkans. In September 1942, an agreement was reached between the newly formed US Office of Strategic Services (OSS) and the SOE stipulating that the former would subordinate to the latter in the Middle East. The arrangement was adhered to until in the autumn of 1943 Colonel William Donovan, the head of the OSS, proposed to the US Joint Chiefs of Staff a scheme regarding Bulgaria. This was a 'long-range plan' for Bulgaria, but its immediate objective was to contact the Bulgarian government and influence it to withdraw from the war. The plan looked into possibilities to enhance US subversive efforts, mostly understood as attempts to divert Bulgaria from participating in further military operations against the Allies. One part of the scheme envisaged 'organisation and direction of guerrilla warfare and any other form of action against the Germans'. Few US servicemen stationed in the Balkans were available to undertake such operations, and so, even though it was developed at a department responsible for secret warfare and 'black' propaganda, the plan foresaw the predominant use of diplomatic methods.[33]

The British special services were anything but pleased at the sudden outburst of US interest in Bulgaria, which they viewed as threatening to their whole position in the region. Churchill was vehemently against any notion of US actions in the Balkans being carried outside British command and control. His advisers at the FO and the SOE were sure of their superior knowledge and had nothing but scepticism for the US initiative.[34]

These rivalries were purely tactical and temporary, with hardly any implications for the political future of Bulgaria. The British and US special services, which had both been set up to function in the extraordinary circumstances of the war, aimed at specific wartime results. Frictions with the Soviet services were at a different level and reflected the strained relationship with that Ally.

In Moscow, the SOE and the OSS had their own representatives, separate from the military missions of the two Western Allies. Their functions turned out to be little more than representative, even though they passed low-level military intelligence to the NKVD, the Soviet Ministry of Internal Affairs. They arranged for Soviet missions to be transported to Yugoslavia and Italy in the hope that these efforts would be appreciated and reciprocated. But 'sharing secrets with Stalin' remained a difficult and thankless business.[35]

Recognizing the limited nature of its contacts with Bulgaria, the SOE approached the Soviet special services with requests for details on developments in the country. British officials expected that the Soviet services possessed more up-to-date information, as the Soviet Union maintained relations with Bulgaria and had retained its legation in Sofia. All the Allies received from the Soviet side, however, were general political outlines, which gave little insight and hardly went beyond what was known from British and US sources.[36] This clearly illustrates Soviet reluctance to participate in joint actions and Soviet unwillingness to communicate specific knowledge to the Western partners.

In mid-1944, despite erstwhile frustrations, the FO agreed that the SOE should renew contacts with the NKVD, mainly for the purpose of consultation. This followed the separate but similar proposals by the Bulgarian section in the Middle East and the SOE at Moscow that Soviet assistance should be requested again. A joint impromptu plan was made to ask the NKVD to 'lend' the Bulgarian Communist émigré Georgi Andreichin to the SOE, but it was soon dropped as too risky and unrealistic. Nevertheless, the SOE continued its efforts to obtain operational information, mainly enquiring about possible Bulgarian contacts and dropping points for Allied planes carrying supplies.[37]

The SOE was right to suspect that Moscow possessed information on Bulgaria which it simply refused to disclose to its war allies. Indeed, apart from diplomatic relations, throughout the war the Soviet government maintained contacts with the Bulgarian Communists. This was done initially through the Comintern and, after its dissolution in May 1943, by the Department for International Information (DII) of the CC of the Bolshevik Party.[38] Dimitrov, the head of the Comintern, also presided over the External Bureau of the Bulgarian CC and was recognized as the leader of the BCP by the Communists inside Bulgaria. Dimitrov had wireless links and courier channels to Bulgaria, including through Tito, who passed telegrams across the Bulgarian border. Two radio stations broadcast over Bulgaria from Soviet territory.[39] The documentary evidence is abundantly clear that all directives to the Bulgarian Communists were approved and, in certain cases, inspired by Stalin and his close associates.[40]

For instance, in August 1941 Stalin ruled against the BCP's resolution to prepare for an armed uprising, which would be doomed because it was impossible to support it from outside.[41] Instead, the Soviet government encouraged the setting up of armed town units and of guerrilla bands to operate in the countryside. The Soviet government, however, made it clear that it had no arms to spare for the Bulgarian resistance. The first time the Soviet government did send in weapons and ammunitions was on 8 September 1944, practically hours before the Communist seizure of power.[42] In addition, the Bulgarian Communists were directed to gather military intelligence, as was done for instance by the spy ring of General Vladimir Zaimov, who was caught by the Bulgarian police and executed in June 1942.[43] The Soviet secret services also aimed to reinforce the Bulgarian resistance: Bulgarian émigrés[44] were dropped by parachute and transported by submarine to the Bulgarian Black Sea coast in 1941–42.[45] As neither NKVD nor Red Army archives have been opened, the precise information sent to Moscow by its agents in Bulgaria is not known. Undeniably, this information was crucial for the Soviet government's assessment of the political and military situation in Bulgaria.

Neither the Bulgarian Partisans nor the NKVD related any of their operational knowledge to their British contacts; the latter were not even informed that at the time the BLOs were with the Bulgarian resistance, at least two Soviet-trained Bulgarian-born radio operators were sent in through Yugoslavia.[46] The British special services were not aware either that the BCP – with Soviet knowledge – had contacts with Bulgarian opposition politicians. Of these, probably most forthcoming was the future prime minister Ivan Bagryanov, who even promised to soften police and army measures against the Partisans in return for a political compromise.[47]

The Soviet government's unwillingness to work with the British services in Bulgaria stretched to such an extent that it was detrimental to the interests of the Bulgarian Communists. In March 1944, when the weather finally permitted the dispatch of supplies to the Bulgarian resistance, the SOE could not find the necessary aircraft. The Soviet air force was asked whether it could organize drops of British materiel in eastern Bulgaria, including captured German weapons. The Partisans themselves had specifically asked for these and the Soviet army was known to have them. Months passed before the British appeal received a reply: the Soviet military forces would neither send the weapons nor provide safe dropping points.[48]

The Logic of Military Necessities

The subversive efforts of the British special services in Axis territory were intended to complement the overall military strategy of the Allies. Although there were no regular armed forces fighting in the Balkans, SOE activity on the ground took place against the backdrop of military and political discussions of a possible major Allied offensive on the peninsula.

The idea of a second front in the Balkans

The idea of large-scale operations in the region had been first endorsed in 1941, when it seemed that these could be an extension to a successful campaign in North Africa.[49] At that time British military planners put the stress on undermining the Italian position in the Central Mediterranean. Still, they were very much aware that this would have decisive consequences eastward, where Turkey's entry into the war was only one of a series of important strategic objectives.

Churchill, supported by the Southern Department, was the greatest proponent of the idea of a second front in the Balkans,[50] which he put forward whenever he found a suitable opportunity. Although undoubtedly related to various long-term considerations, his initial motives were above all military. Only in mid-1944 did Churchill stress that his cherished Eastern Mediterranean initiative was also designed to resolve 'the brute political issues' between Britain and the Soviet Union. In this he was motivated by imperial concerns at least as much as by anti-Communism, which had been a formidable characteristic of his political outlook before the Nazi invasion of the Soviet Union.[51] Allied military operations in the Balkans would undoubtedly enhance British influence but not necessarily decrease the role of the Balkan Communist parties. Neither did the idea signify a British preference for political over military objectives in the course of the war.[52]

An invasion of South Eastern Europe was continuously deliberated at British–US 'top-brass' conferences, and while none of them endorsed it completely, it was not categorically discarded until mid-1944. In the summer of 1943 the invasion of Sicily not only brought fighting closer to the Balkans but also made military action there physically possible. This had a profound impact on Hitler's satellites: Bulgaria was believed to be particularly impressed and the Allies agreed to attempt to exploit the opportunity. At the Casablanca Conference in January 1943 and the Washington Conference in May 1943, the US Chiefs of Staff had given consent to explore the option favoured by their British counterparts. Yet US military planners persisted in considering a Balkan campaign as militarily undesirable and so the possibility for it became distinctly remote by the time of the Quebec Conference in August 1943.[53]

Eventually, at Teheran at the end of 1943 the US military commanders firmly refused to deploy troops in the Balkans. This did not prevent Churchill from bringing up the question in the summer of 1944, when General Alexander promoted the advantages of the so-called 'Ljubljana Gap'. The last attempts to convert the US chiefs were made in August and September 1944, when Churchill tried to substitute the landings in the south of France for operations in the Adriatic. He could not prevail over the joint front of Roosevelt and Stalin, who – each for his own reasons – remained firm in their preference for a cross-Channel invasion (code-named Overlord). This decision had far-reaching consequences, as the subsequent absence of Western troops in the Balkans proved a major hindrance for British and US postwar strategy. But the course and above all the outcome of these discussions leave no doubt as to the priority of military over political objectives.[54] The possibility of landings in the Balkans was evaluated chiefly in terms of how it would influence the preparation for Overlord by pinning down as many enemy divisions as possible.

Military objectives were also paramount in Soviet planning. Until the end of 1942 Stalin repeatedly urged the Western Allies not only to advance in Europe, but suggested that the second front might be opened in the Balkans. Even if he was merely probing British intentions with the aim of diverting them, as Elisabeth Barker suggests, he was also envisaging short-term military achievements.[55]

Trying to analyse the conditions and consequences of a possible direct attack on Hitler's Eastern European satellites by Britain and the United States, some British observers saw it as distinctly beneficial for the Allied war conduct. A skilful and well-timed action could bring about the surrender of the whole of South Eastern Europe in weeks. The collapse of one Axis satellite would potentially have an immediate effect on the others, and the collapse of more than one would be fatal for Germany. In late 1943 and in 1944, Germany was becoming increasingly dependent on the resources of its satellites. The denial of the Romanian oil fields, which were Germany's only substantial source of natural oil, could have had far-reaching repercussions. The Balkan mountain range which ran across Bulgaria thus assumed the strategic importance of the forward bastion guarding the Danube, itself the essential transport route for Romanian oil. The defence of the mountains, in turn, depended on the possession of Sofia and the railways north of it.[56]

The Balkan countries were aware of their strategic significance to Germany and became ever more apprehensive of Allied strategy after the Allied successes in North Africa and Sicily and the reversal at the Eastern Front. For Bulgaria, one of the high points of alarm was at the beginning of 1943, when the Adana Anglo-Turkish conversations were alleged to have prescribed military action against it.[57] Reports reaching Sofia from most Bulgarian diplomatic missions abroad mentioned the possibility of a Balkan invasion. The ones that refuted it were no less disturbing as they professed some kind of Western understanding with Soviet Russia from which communization of the region would ensue. In short, the Bulgarian ruling circles might soon once again face the difficulty they had experienced at the start of the war, namely how to balance between Germany and the USSR.[58]

This anxiety was exploited by British military planners, who knew about it from intercepted enemy diplomatic messages. Even if a Balkan campaign was not forthcoming, fear of it could divert attention first from Sicily and then from Western Europe, where the real landings would take place. In late 1942, leaflets dispersed over Bulgaria by British planes and broadcasts from the Middle East asserted that the next Allied actions would focus on the Balkans; Anglo-American troops would enter Bulgaria and force its capitulation.[59] This line of propaganda was later extended to augment the strategic deception necessary to guard the plans for Overlord. The British secret services even suggested simulating Allied military activities along the Bulgarian Black Sea coast to imply imminent land invasion of the Balkans. The idea fell through for lack of Soviet support.[60] All the false leads, however, impressed Bulgarian politicians. They also most probably alarmed Soviet intelligence despite the fact that it knew of British deception campaigns in advance. One misconception the Soviet Ally might have shared with the Bulgarian enemy was that since Britain had long-standing imperial interests in South Eastern Europe, it meant to intervene to re-establish a dominant position there. Such thinking was rooted in late nineteenth-century rivalries but was also fed by the prewar perception of Britain as the protagonist of anti-Bolshevism.

The FO Southern Department was of course aware that no substantial troops would be dispatched to Bulgaria, but some officials still hoped that at least a token force would be available to signify British interest there. This was very different from Romania, where the only realistic and desirable option was that of Soviet occupation.[61]

Even when they understood that no major fighting would take place in the Balkans, the Bulgarian political elite continued to believe that if and when they decided to surrender to the victors, an Allied force would be present to protect them from the Germans.⁶² All these political conjectures seemed to be reinforced by the Allied air attacks over Bulgaria.

Bombing Bulgaria

The origin of the idea of bombing Bulgaria can be traced no further than the logistical opportunity offered by the establishment of air bases in southern Italy. These were within reach of important communications and transport points in the Balkans and especially the Ploesti oil fields. Bulgaria itself had few strategic centres of great importance and in fact the first raids over its territory took place when weather or other obstacles prevented attacks on Romanian targets of higher priority. In the autumn of 1943, attention to bombing Bulgaria gradually increased. One reason for this was that attacking German troops on Yugoslav or Greek territory – a legitimate option – carried the danger of inflicting casualties on the civil population of Allied governments.⁶³

Bombing Bulgaria was a justifiable albeit secondary military aim in its own right. The first recorded suggestion was made by the British Chiefs of Staff in early October 1943. This was taken up by the Defence Committee presided over by the prime minister on 19 October 1943. It was revealed that Bulgaria had eight divisions helping the Germans to garrison Yugoslavia and Greece and employed forces against 'guerrillas who are our friends and whose resistance is growing daily'. Churchill spoke in very harsh words insisting that the activities of the 'Bulgarian jackals' could not be tolerated any longer, 'however much they might be under the heel of the Germans'. A sharp lesson had to be administered to Bulgaria with the primary objective of making its troops withdraw from occupied territories and of stretching German forces even further.⁶⁴

The Defence Committee 'carefully considered the best method of bringing the Bulgars [sic] to heel. All agreed that surprise air attacks on Sofia, accompanied by leaflets citing the fate of Hamburg and Hanover, would have best and most immediate effect.' It was thought that a 'relatively small diversion of air resources' would be 'well worthwhile'. All the more so as it could also bring significant political results, especially since the death of King Boris III in August 1943 had destabilized the internal situation in Bulgaria.⁶⁵

The first substantial raid on Sofia was carried out on 14 November 1943, hitting the marshalling yards, the airfield and a number of civilian buildings. The raid's general effect was judged to have been 'out of all proportion to the military significance of the target'. The Bulgarian government had become seriously concerned with both further bombing and the sharp decline in public morale. It was even suspected that continued raids might result in internal upheaval, 'such as would constitute a grave embarrassment and threat to Germany's whole military structure in the Balkans'.⁶⁶

More attacks followed in December 1943 and January 1944, all of which were estimated to have satisfactory results for the Allies. Administrative life in Sofia was brought to a virtual standstill; the inefficiency of the air defence was exposed. The population of the capital fled to the countryside where its tales spread panic and anger against the government and Germany.[67] As a result of the raids, at the beginning of 1944 Bulgaria appeared to have become the most vulnerable of the three Axis countries in Eastern Europe: civil discontent was growing and the morale of the army was falling. In early February 1944, an appreciation by the SOE Balkan team forecast that a concentrated attack 'may be able to break Bulgaria within a few months – possibly in the summer'.[68] Therefore, the Middle Eastern Command which was in charge of the air attacks over Bulgaria decided that the geographical scope of attacks should be extended before Sofia was allowed to recover. For instance, there was a good strategic argument that Plovdiv and Kazanluk should be bombed as both were important railway centres within twenty miles of which Partisans were operating. The latter 'would no doubt secure valuable recruits and encouragement from a breakdown there similar to that at Sofia'. The commanders of the Navy suggested attacks on the Black Sea ports and traffic.[69]

Historiography has practically neglected the fact that bombing was coordinated with the Bulgarian Partisans. As the possibility of a direct military attack on Bulgaria was becoming remote in the spring of 1944, Britain was eager to strengthen its contacts with the Bulgarian guerrillas and give them some evidence of good will. When informed through the BLOs, the Partisan leaders approved of bombing in general. They asked for certain points in Sofia and elsewhere in the country to be struck so as to be particularly damaging for the government in both material and political terms. Simultaneously, they warned the Allies to avoid the working-class quarters of Sofia so as not to inflict casualties on that part of the population best disposed to the resistance movement.[70]

By April 1944, the importance of Bulgarian targets, which was subject to frequent reviews, had fallen. A few minor air raids over Bulgaria took place in the early summer of 1944. Without eliminating Bulgaria as a possible target, priority was given to targets in Romania and Hungary. Attacks on these countries were thought likely to force them to withdraw troops fighting on the Eastern Front.[71]

Bombing was another aspect of Allied policy on Bulgaria on which Britain sought Soviet concurrence. While the question was being discussed in London, in October 1943 in Moscow Eden suggested that Stalin should be informed of the planned air raids over Bulgaria. Stalin turned out to be 'surprisingly forthcoming'. This pleased Churchill despite his insistence that

Stalin's permission had not been necessary as the USSR was not at war with Bulgaria. The FO appreciated Stalin's 'being in the business' and wanted to capitalize on this unexpected success by making it known to the Bulgarian government and population. Indeed, the Bulgarian government had already been given the cold shoulder when it had approached the Soviet diplomatic missions in Sofia and Ankara to ask for mediation to stop the air raids. But this was different from making the Soviet government openly associate with the Allied bombing as such a step could promptly diminish Soviet prestige in Bulgaria.[72]

Even though US bombers had taken part in the attacks, the US government kept an open mind on the subject. In February 1944, while an OSS mission dealing with Bulgaria was still in Istanbul, the United States suggested that bombing should be temporarily ceased in order to allow Bulgaria to send a peace mission to Turkey in relative safety. Churchill refused.[73]

As a rule, plans for bombing were made with no other political objectives in mind than the detachment of Bulgaria from the Axis. There was some notion of the most desirable postwar developments from a British point of view, but this was of distinctly inferior importance in day-to-day thinking before the end of the war. This was a logical result of the limited contacts and knowledge about the political situation in Bulgaria resulting from Britain's failure to establish stable communication with those political elements that it could have felt able to support after the war.

The Futile Peace Negotiations

British Balkan experts were well aware of the political difficulties created by the fact that no Anglo-American troops would enter Bulgaria. There was no enemy army approaching the frontier to which the Bulgarians could surrender, unlike in 1918 when they had asked for armistice from the commanders of the Entente forces at Salonika. On their part, Bulgaria and the other satellites could not fail to notice that the Allies were stretched to the extreme in the Eastern Mediterranean. The small Axis powers used this to procrastinate in their approaches for peace, hoping to extract better terms later.[74]

Renewed political contacts

The Bulgarian government used a number of approaches to its representatives abroad to sound out the intentions of the Western Allies. Most of the contacts took place in neutral countries and produced no particular commitment on either side. They were more often than not initiated by the US special services trying to sidestep British supremacy in the Balkans. In Switzerland, where

Nikola Momchilov had sent letters under SOE tutelage to the Bulgarian ambassador in Bern, Allen Dulles of the OSS was in touch with the Bulgarian consul in Geneva. There were also US attempts to influence Bulgarian political circles through the Bulgarian mission in Stockholm.[75] The most intensive and fruitful contacts were those made with the Bulgarian mission in Turkey. Nikola Balabanov, the Bulgarian ambassador, was a skilled diplomat with a sober understanding of Bulgaria's position in the war. He made good use of the post in Ankara, constantly evaluating the perception of Bulgaria on both sides in the conflict. He also received valuable information from Istanbul, one of the busiest centres of intelligence throughout the war. Balabanov was among the first to recommend to the Bulgarian government the establishment of early links with the Western Allies in parallel to those with the Soviet government. Additionally, he thought contacts with the Greek and Yugoslav governments-in-exile and resistance movements would be useful, as their association with the Allies was likely to have a great impact on Bulgaria's future.[76]

All these contacts yielded little beyond the illusion on both sides that alternative routes of communication were being kept open. Their value faded rapidly in late 1943 and early 1944 in the wake of the air attacks, even though these were intended to speed up Bulgaria's defection from the Axis. Initially, it was even hoped that the three Eastern European satellites would desert Germany at approximately the same time, granting the Allies a considerable strategic advantage before Overlord. Some observers believed that the satellites were following 'limited adherence to the German cause [...] determined largely by the same reasons which determined our Turkish ally, in his slightly more favourable position, to a policy of neutrality'.[77] Therefore, it was essential for the Allies to devise a policy which would lure the satellites with little detriment to their existence as nation-states.[78] Such an opinion of the motives behind the satellites' behaviour was occasionally voiced by some British analysts in late 1943 and early 1944. It was in effect contrary to the Casablanca formula of 'unconditional surrender', to which the US Chiefs of Staff attached the greatest importance.[79] Ostensibly, British military planners went along with their US counterparts but never found this rigid approach either very convincing or effective. Therefore, the FO tried to introduce whatever degree of flexibility the situation afforded.

Apart from the brief discussions of the Balkans at the Teheran Conference, the Allies had not considered joint policy towards Bulgaria. This was partly due to the fact that British actions were dependent largely on the success of bombing. But while the Western Allies were attacking Bulgarian cities from the air, the Soviet armies were moving steadily towards the Bulgarian borders. Even so, by the spring of 1944 military plans had not been synchronized. Attempts to obtain some indication of Soviet views on the future of Bulgaria and the South Slavs had produced little beyond a professed general desire for amenable governments. It seemed to the Southern Department that Stalin was showing a pronounced reluctance to commit himself to any future political or military course in Bulgaria. Such an attitude could be, and usually was, interpreted as a Soviet intention to strike a separate deal. Alternatively, the FO observers were reassuring themselves that, maybe just like the British, the Soviet government had not managed to achieve any definite political results and was loath to admit it openly.[80] Besides, the British diplomats were getting tired of the slow and noncommittal Bulgarian requests for talks in the first half of 1944. They began suggesting that, instead of listening to Bulgarian complaints and explanations, the Allies should present firm conditions not for negotiations but for armistice.[81]

In the autumn of 1943, bombing itself had been planned as only one component of a broader Allied strategy. It was to be part of 'a determined threefold attack' consisting also of support to subversive elements and effective propaganda. The goal would be Bulgaria's detachment from the Axis, irrespective of whether it was done under the present or a new government.[82]

Britain preferred that Bulgaria should emerge from the war as a democratic country. Britain's efforts to influence the policies of the wartime Bulgarian governments revolved around the moderate Bulgarian political elements. The latter, while being opposed to the alignment with Germany, were not aiming at radical internal transformation. Additionally, Britain had to consider the necessity of maintaining a common front with Soviet Russia, not only in combat but in propaganda too. The steady Soviet military advance resulted in extremely good propaganda for the Soviet Union, precipitating complaints in some British conservative circles that the West was deliberately enhancing the Soviet image. On the whole, British policy makers fully realized that without solid Soviet support any Western initiative in the Balkans would have a limited success.[83]

The OSS too sought Stalin's approval before putting its own plan for Bulgaria into action. The plan had been elaborated at the end of 1943 under Colonel Donovan's supervision. It envisaged the initiation of preliminary talks with the Bulgarian government. The central figure in these was the Bulgarian-born financier Angel Kuyumdjiiski, who had recently been granted US citizenship and made colonel of the US Army. Kuyumdjiiski was attached to a special mission headed by Colonel Jadwin and was able in about two months in Istanbul to renew his contacts among Bulgarian politicians and businessmen. At the end of February 1944, he believed that his efforts were about to bring forward a mission authorized by the Bulgarian government to receive official Allied terms for Bulgarian surrender. The OSS and the State Department thought this the best possible outcome as it would not only put an end to

Bulgarian participation in the war but also leave the Bulgarian opposition untainted by surrender and therefore eligible for future office. US diplomats with longer experience in Bulgarian affairs than Jadwin, Kuyumdjiiski or even Donovan were not so optimistic, considering that the Bulgarian government still had room for manoeuvre.[84]

British services dealing with Bulgaria had not been told of the exact nature of the US project before it was outlined in Moscow. On this occasion, the OSS had specifically tried to avoid its British counterpart, as Churchill himself had refused Roosevelt's request to authorize Donovan's initiative.[85] The FO openly disapproved of the Jadwin–Kuyumdjiiski affair: it felt sidelined and above all expressed scepticism about the United States' ability to handle the situation properly. It also insisted that any Bulgarian envoys should talk to representatives of all Big Three powers at the same time. In comparison, the Soviet government seemed content to leave things in US hands. It expressed the desire to be kept informed of the progress of the contacts but abstained from practical involvement in the US initiative. The Soviet ambassador in Cairo – where the Bulgarian emissaries were expected – was instructed to follow possible negotiations but not to present any views.[86]

Bulgarian attempts at double-dealing

The sudden and mysterious death of King Boris III in August 1943 had caused a shock in Bulgarian governing circles that had trusted him to steer the country safely out of the conflict. Gradually realizing that they might end on the losing side, they became more willing to establish links with the Allies but also apprehensive of Allied deliberations on the fate of the Balkans.

Bulgarian handling of the talks with the Jadwin mission revealed both inflated expectations about the outcome of the war and faulty perceptions of the interests of the Allies. Contacts had been authorized in the belief that generally the United States had a more lenient attitude to Bulgaria in comparison to Britain. The government of Dobri Bozhilov (September 1943–June 1944) tried to extract preliminary concessions from Kuyumdjiiski, mainly with respect to the occupied territories, the retention of which dominated national politics.

At the end of 1943 after the Moscow and Teheran Conferences, the Bulgarian legations across Europe were very active in reporting rumours about the intentions of the Big Three. Some claimed that Stalin had taken the upper hand, others that the traditional British diplomatic skill had prevailed, but most concurred that there could be no agreement among the Allies. Entirely dismissive of official communiqués, one diplomat wished that Bulgaria's lot could be made easier by finding out 'who had deceived whom or whether they had all deceived each other'. Naturally, Germany sought to increase Bulgaria's fear that a deal had been reached to apportion the Balkans to the Soviet Union. Bulgarian military intelligence too supported this view.[87] The leading figures in the Bulgarian government also thought that Britain and the Soviet Union were 'playing hide-and-seek'.[88]

A lonely sober voice was that of the Bulgarian minister in Turkey: from the beginning of 1944 his reports stressed that there would be no imminent serious rupture among the three Allies. He advised that Bulgarian foreign policy should not be constructed on the false premise that it would be able to benefit from the existing inter-Allied differences. He was able to point to numerous examples which showed that the principal role in the Balkans had been delegated to Stalin.[89]

But the conviction – or rather hope – of inter-Allied conflicts was difficult to shake off. The Bulgarian prime minister Ivan Bagryanov (June–August 1944) even suspected that both Britain and the Soviet Union were ready to conclude a separate peace with Germany in order to forestall the other's advances.[90] He further believed that both Germany and the USSR preferred Bulgaria maintaining relations with both of them so as not to extend the fighting to the Balkans. The Bulgarian government repeatedly concluded that it was best to avoid committing to any of the Allies until the outcome was clearer and then quickly manoeuvre so as to obtain a satisfactory peace settlement. The Soviet Union could be wooed with the idea that Bulgaria would join it while the very same possibility should be used to threaten Britain. In other words, Bulgaria was to try to keep all sides happy: not to provoke a German occupation and simultaneously to improve relations with the Soviets. The ultimate objective was while keeping a low profile to reach an agreement with Britain and the United States for exiting the war. This was dictated by alarm that, unless Bulgaria joined the West, it would not be able to avoid a Soviet-backed Communist takeover. Concurrently, there was a vague fear that if British troops entered the Balkans, so would the Red Army.[91]

Notably, foreign minister Purvan Draganov had in mind to start conversations, not negotiations. Georgi Kisselov, who was sent on a peace seeking mission to Istanbul in June 1944, was 'provided with a [deliberately] vague formula': he should not promise Bulgaria's pulling out of the war but should maintain that Bulgaria still hoped for a peaceful solution of the national question.[92]

On the other hand, the overriding ambition of securing the Bulgarian territorial acquisitions made even succumbing to Soviet pressure acceptable to some political circles represented in Bagryanov's cabinet. At the beginning of 1944 a number of prominent politicians sought direct links with the Soviet Union, usually through its legation in Sofia. Most of them tried to determine what terms would be offered for exiting the war. The standard reply was that the Soviet government would insist on withdrawal from Serbia,[93] thus confirming the demands of the Western Allies, if not necessarily driven by the same motives.

While Bagryanov felt it necessary to continue his balancing act, events in the Balkans were moving fast. On 2 August 1944 Turkey broke off relations with Germany. The same day in a speech in the House of Commons, Churchill used very strong words in reference to Bulgaria, accusing it of a 'petty and cowardly part' in the war and warning there was little time to repent.[94]

While in late July 1944, the Bulgarian government had curtailed German activities in the country and prepared to repeal anti-Jewish laws and withdraw from Serbia shortly, it still refrained from breaking with Germany before 'leaning' elsewhere.[95] It had taken a month to clear the way for a new official high-profile Bulgarian peace feeler, led by the former president of the Bulgarian National Assembly, Stoicho Moshanov.[96] Three more weeks passed before he actually held his first conversation with the British ambassador to Turkey Sir Hughe Knatchbull-Hugessen on 16 August.[97] Misconstruing British interests, Bagryanov rationalized that ongoing Soviet pressure on Bulgaria would disturb Britain and the United States and consequently make them less demanding towards the country. Unsurprisingly, Knatchbull-Hugessen on his part advised that the Bulgarian government should speed up its extraction from the Axis, although he was not thinking in terms of pre-empting potential Soviet action towards Bulgaria.

While Moshanov was in Ankara, the Bulgarian government tried to support his mission by admitting publicly that declaring war on Britain and the United States had been an error. This, however, failed to impress Britain as the Bulgarian prime minister was contradicted by his foreign minister: for Germany's reassurance, Draganov proclaimed that Bulgaria was continuing with its erstwhile policy, simply using different methods. Neither were the Allies convinced by Moshanov's appeals that nothing drastic could be done before Bulgarian troops were taken out of Serbia. They were hardly helped by the fact that while they were trying to ascertain the earnestness of the new emissary, the latter had to return to Sofia for consultations after the Romanian coup of 23 August 1944.[98]

Despite the setbacks, the FO decided to proceed with the talks and also consult with its Allies. On 27 August the British Embassy in Turkey directed Moshanov to go to Cairo, where he would obtain the terms of armistice with Bulgaria. In his memoirs written about twenty-five years later, Moshanov claimed to have immediately felt that he should procrastinate. Among the various explanations he put forward was a conversation on 30 August with Dr Floyd Black, the former director of the American College in Sofia, who advised delay so as not to create difficulties among the Allies.[99] There is no archival trace of such a recommendation.[100] There is, however, evidence that Moshanov also encountered the opposite view in his conversations; for instance, the Turkish foreign minister stated that the Bulgarian government should surrender immediately in order to prevent the large Soviet army gathering on the Danube from entering Bulgaria.[101]

Moshanov's circumstances were aggravated by the absence of all three Allies' ambassadors from Cairo. The designated head of the British delegation Lord Moyne was in Italy. The US ambassador MacVeagh had not come back from Washington, whereas his deputy was not yet fully authorized to participate in the talks.[102] Such a situation contradicts the thesis of some Bulgarian scholars that both Britain and the United States desired to get Bulgaria out of the war as a matter of urgency.[103] In fact, Britain was not at all in a hurry to conclude an agreement with Bulgaria which corresponds to the difficulties of wartime planning for the country. So, the British failure to act urgently in the Cairo talks fits in the broader pattern of lack of defined strong interest towards Bulgaria.

As the Red Army appeared on the northern Bulgarian border, the nearest British troops were at least fifteen hundred miles away. Moshanov was also acutely aware that the Communists were going to play an increasingly important role in Bulgarian politics after the war; when he had last left Sofia, negotiations to include them in the cabinet had been under way. Yet, waiting for talks with the Western representatives, he learned that there were no Communists in the newly formed government of Konstantin Muraviev. Moshanov found himself in the position of representing a government which he believed could not last long. Also, he was required to sign an armistice which would not be lenient to Bulgaria: he was soon made to understand that instead of negotiations he was merely going to be presented with Allied terms which simply had to be accepted. He therefore feared lest he would be held morally responsible for armistice terms which he would be given no chance to soften.[104] All of this would endanger his hopes for active participation in postwar Bulgarian politics; it explains why Moshanov raised doubts about his own credentials in a telegram to the new Bulgarian premier. Finally meeting Lord Moyne, Moshanov made a long and roundabout statement which prompted the Allies to check his authorization. In communications to Sofia, Moshanov then repeated that he would accept a new mandate 'if entry of Soviet troops does not change the situation'.[105]

In a personal letter sent to the Communist leader Dimitrov three years after the armistice negotiations, Moshanov admitted that he had 'diverted' the handing of the text of the armistice on 1 September 1944 and assumed personal responsibility for the failure of his mission. Apparently, he had decided not to 'betray the future of his country' when its 'independence had been seriously threatened by the West'. He even claimed that he had related the events to the Soviet representative, who had complimented him on having performed 'a great service not only for his country but also for the whole of Slavdom'.[106]

Soviet opportunism

Britain and the United States were keen on three-power joint action in Bulgaria. They were very much aware of the political leverage the USSR had and were eager to use it for what they considered the common purpose of getting Bulgaria out of the war.[107] In February 1944, the FO was looking into ways of intensifying pressure upon Bulgaria. Sargent wrote to Eden that 'the Russians should be asked to enter the picture as well'. So far, whenever approached by the FO, Moscow had showed unwillingness to commit itself. Sargent thought that 'the Russians sit pretty, maintain diplomatic relations and wait for the day when they can step in not as conquerors but as deliverers'.[108]

In the spring of 1944, the Soviet Union began demonstrating greater interest not only in Bulgaria, but in the Balkans as a whole. The pressure applied by Moscow on the Bulgarian government to distance itself from Germany was greeted by the FO as long overdue. However, simultaneous Soviet criticism of British behaviour in relation to Greece was disquieting, prompting Eden to note 'unhappily increasing signs of Russia's intentions to play her own hand in the Balkans regardless of our desires and interests'. In early July 1944, his concerns were recorded in a document circulated to the cabinet, reporting that the Soviet government was using the Communist-dominated movements to gain a predominant position in South Eastern Europe.[109]

This assessment was made at a time when both London and Washington were receiving a stream of intelligence about increased Soviet activity in Bulgaria. Even without firm evidence, the West was practically certain that the Bulgarian Communists operated under Soviet direction. On the other hand, there was reliable information about the renewal of old and the establishment of new contacts between Bulgarian opposition figures and Soviet representatives in Sofia. An illuminating example was that of Petko Stainov, a leading member of the political circle Zveno and hitherto considered a staunch Anglophile. After the devastating air raids over Sofia in January 1944 in which his family had been directly hit, he had made a strong speech in Parliament in support of friendly relations with the Soviet Union and began visiting the Soviet Legation regularly. So did another pro-Westerner, the Democratic Party leader Nikola Mushanov. Other centre-right Bulgarian politicians, for example Atanas Burov and Alexander Girginov, were also in touch with the Soviet minister Alexander Lavrishchev.[110] Records of these encounters are not available, but the context suggests that Bulgarian politicians of all colours were making an effort to keep open links with Moscow as they foresaw an increasing role for the Soviet Union in Bulgarian affairs.

The Soviet government put increased diplomatic pressure upon Bulgaria to break off relations with Germany.[111] In January 1944, Lavrishchev told the Bulgarian premier Bozhilov that the Soviet Union would intercede with Britain and the United States to stop the bombing if Bulgaria withdrew from Serbia. The same offer was repeated in February, when Lavrishchev also stated that it was not incidental that Soviet propaganda omitted the demand that Bulgaria should withdraw from Aegean Thrace.[112] Soviet representatives were signalling a preparedness to make some concessions to Bulgaria, which at the time compared favourably to the air strikes by the West.

In March 1944, Fyodor Gussev, the Soviet member of the European Advisory Commission (EAC) in London, declared that this body should not discuss the terms for Bulgaria. Molotov commented that it was simply too early. Both British and US experts seemed to interpret such Soviet reserve as just reflecting the fact that the Soviet Union was not at war with Bulgaria. Both Western Allies told the USSR that they would welcome any future Soviet observations on developments related to Bulgaria. They accepted that the Soviet government reserved the right to reopen the question when it was in a stronger military position in the Balkans; neither the representatives in the EAC nor their superiors perceived anything worrying in this.[113]

In the spring of 1944 Soviet diplomatic efforts to precipitate Bulgaria's exit from the war intensified. This coincided with the heavy Soviet offensive on the Eastern Front, which marked the advance of the Red Army into Eastern Europe and the Balkans. Records of plans for military and political action regarding Bulgaria are lacking; it is plausible that Stalin simply waited to see the outcome of fighting on Polish and Romanian territory, as well as the development of the internal Bulgarian situation, before deciding on a specific course of action. This does not mean however that he was going to be a passive observer of events either in Bulgaria or the Balkans as a whole.

Gradually, the Soviet attitude towards the Bulgarian government stiffened, and in mid-April 1944 the latter was faced with Soviet complaints that it was aiding the German war effort by providing transportation, ports and airfields to Axis troops retreating from the Eastern Front. To Bulgarian protestations of innocence the Soviet government replied with demands for the reopening of Soviet consulates and the establishment of new ones so as to be able to verify Bulgarian claims for noncollaboration with Germany. The Bulgarian government was told it should appreciate how much Soviet Russia was doing to save Bulgaria from sinister Western designs.[114] Unwilling to comply with the Soviet demands, the Bozhilov government resigned at the end of May 1944.[115]

The new government of Ivan Bagryanov soon realized that Soviet demands could not be postponed for much longer. Foreign Minister Draganov saw his task as satisfying them only partially and so maintaining the balance between Soviet pressure and German influence as long as possible. Prophetically, Draganov wrote to a friend that Bulgaria was left with no more than three months of independence. Therefore, he began preparing for opening talks with Britain and the United States while also sending a special personal letter of good will to Molotov. By return, the Soviet Foreign Ministry demanded whether Bulgaria was ready to break with Germany.[116]

Throughout this intense exchange of communications the Soviet government did not consult with its Allies about developments in Bulgaria or its own part therein. In late August 1944, Sir Archibald Clark Kerr, the British ambassador in Moscow, related to Molotov rumours that Bulgaria was going to ask the USSR for an armistice as soon as the Red Army appeared on the Danube, and in response the Soviet government was going to intercede with the Allies so that Bulgaria could keep the occupied territories. The Soviet foreign minister refuted these stories as complete lies. It was only then that he admitted that the state of Soviet–Bulgarian relations deserved attention, and promised to let the British government have the relevant papers.[117] In the meantime, the Soviet Union had professed no opinion or interest in the most recent Bulgarian peace initiative in Turkey.[118]

In late August and early September 1944, Soviet diplomats in London, the Middle East and Sofia undertook a series of steps regarding Bulgaria which at first sight appear unrelated and confusing. In their entirety, however, they reveal logic aimed at neutralizing as far as possible the Bulgarian armistice talks with the Western Allies, and the transfer of initiative to Moscow. All this was done with the knowledge that the Red Army was crossing Romania and would soon appear on Bulgaria's northern border.

On 24 August, after the Romanian coup which had forced Moshanov to return to Sofia, the Soviet delegate to the EAC finally agreed to participate in the discussions of the Bulgarian armistice. He concurred with most of the clauses dealing with the withdrawal of Bulgarian troops from any occupied territories, demobilization of the Bulgarian armed forces, dissolution of paramilitary organizations, release of Allied prisoners of war, etc. But on 29 August, when Moshanov had again gone to Turkey to resume armistice talks, the Soviet representative withdrew from the deliberations in London. On the same day, the Soviet chargé d'affaires left Sofia leaving only a junior diplomatic officer at the legation. Similarly, Moshanov was astonished to discover that the Soviet ambassador had left Cairo just as his final meetings were scheduled.[119]

Further, on 30 August the Soviet government officially informed its Allies that it refused to recognize the complete neutrality proclaimed by Bulgaria on 17 August.[120] This had been conceived by Bagryanov as a provisional step on the way to breaking off relations with Germany: because Radio Moscow had relayed it, it was assumed to be accepted by the Soviet government. As soon as the real Soviet attitude became known, Bagryanov announced his resignation, hoping once again that a cabinet crisis would delay compliance with the Soviet demand that Bulgaria declare war on Germany.

Coercion from Moscow was well timed, as it followed the Bulgarian decision of 29 August finally to order the Bulgarian occupation forces to leave Macedonia. Simultaneously, German troops began retreating from Greece. Joint Anglo-American intelligence explained the Soviet behaviour by discontent with the plans for negotiations with Bulgaria; the pressure on Bagryanov had specifically aimed at stopping the Cairo negotiations, in which the USSR did not participate.[121] These were indications that the Soviet government was beginning to have second thoughts about Bulgaria. However, Soviet unwillingness to participate in the current talks was not fully appreciated by the West. Britain and the United States were misled by their own preparedness to let Soviet Russia influence or even join the Cairo negotiations at any time. The West also believed that the Soviet Union might be prepared to make concessions in order to alleviate fears of the imposition of Bolshevism. Simultaneously, in conversations with Bulgarian representatives several Soviet ambassadors in neutral countries voiced displeasure that Bulgaria had not approached Moscow for mediation, hinting that Soviet terms would be more lenient than those offered by Britain and the United States.[122]

It seems plausible that only at the end of August 1944 did Stalin make plans for military advance in Bulgaria.[123] It was evident that Bulgaria was not going to offer resistance to the Red Army so that Soviet occupation and the ensuing political influence over the country would be achieved without any material or human losses. But this does not confirm that Stalin had always planned the occupation of Bulgaria. On the contrary, just like the Western Allies, he had been led by military factors above all. As the military situation in the region became clearer, Stalin could concentrate on political developments.

The new Bulgarian government of Konstantin Muraviev, who hailed from the right wing of the Agrarian party, was formed to solve a single issue, that of getting Bulgaria out of the war. It needed to sign an armistice with Britain and the United States and asked for Soviet mediation, hoping to benefit from the fact that Bulgaria still had diplomatic relations with the Soviet Union. The Soviet Ambassador in Turkey Sergei Vinogradov, through whom the request was made, initially agreed readily but then quickly retreated, yet another sign that Soviet plans were not fixed. Similarly, despite Muraviev's extensive efforts to co-opt Communists, their position also fluctuated and eventually they backed out of the deal, most likely in response to changing Soviet plans.[124]

The Soviet government declared war on Bulgaria on 5 September 1944 at 6:00 p.m. Moscow time. It seems that the Bulgarian government learnt of the Soviet declaration of war from the radio and had to determine its authenticity via Ankara. Only half an hour's notice was given to Clark Kerr and the US ambassador Averell Harriman. The Red Army was already poised at the Danube, but when asked whether it would enter Bulgaria, Molotov gave a noncommittal answer. No immediate Soviet intentions were disclosed to either Harriman or Clerk Kerr.[125]

Strikingly, the Soviet declaration of war on Bulgaria was made just when the latter had finally resolved on declaring war on Germany. The public announcement was scheduled for two days later upon the war minister's request for time to evacuate Bulgarian troops from Yugoslavia. The war minister was later revealed to be working with the Communists and the arrangement was almost certainly prompted by the Soviets.

It is debatable how necessary Bulgarian territory was for the westward advance of the Soviet armies. The Soviet commanders considered Bulgaria 'off to one side from the main highway of the war' and accordingly reduced the numbers of troops entering the country.[126] The Red Army waited for three days after the declaration of war before crossing the Bulgarian frontier, just as the Soviet government officially granted the Bulgarian request for armistice.[127] For Moscow the declaration of war on Bulgaria justified occupying the country, which in turn was dictated by power-political considerations.

The delayed Soviet entry could not have been caused by fear of the last retreating German formations, which could have been dealt with by the Bulgarian army alone. It was no secret that Bulgarian fears of German occupation had been exaggerated in order to justify procrastination. The Soviet command was fully aware of the political situation and was supplied with last-minute military information by Communists from northern Bulgaria.[128] Nor did the Soviet troops stand aside so that the Communist-dominated Fatherland Front could take power with local forces only: they were already on Bulgarian soil at the moment of the coup d'état. The Soviet army had stopped to wait for an internal uprising as instigated by Communist Party circulars and a manifesto. However, the country was relatively calm, and once inside Bulgaria the Soviet troops took their time, entering Sofia only on 15 September 1944.[129]

An alternative explanation of the slow march is the necessity to observe and consider the Western reaction to the Soviet declaration of war on Bulgaria. It was not very dramatic. At 5:00 p.m. on 7 September 1944, Lord Moyne informed Moshanov that it would be put on record that Bulgaria had requested armistice, that it had not received the terms and that the talks had ended because of the Soviet war declaration.[130] Only after this final conversation between the representatives of the Western Allies and Moshanov in Cairo did the Soviet armies enter Bulgaria. Stalin's manoeuvres in Bulgaria – planned or improvised – had yielded good results.

British attitude to Soviet occupation of Bulgaria

The FO itself was somewhat taken aback by the Soviet declaration of war on Bulgaria, especially as this came while Bulgaria was finally seeming to make a serious effort to get out of the war. Once the Western ambassadors in Moscow had reported the news to their governments, they were instructed not to express disapproval but return to Molotov to find out the Soviet motives and intentions. Clerk Kerr was directed to enquire whether the Soviet government would join the current Cairo conversations or insist on ending them, as under the new circumstances they constituted separate peace negotiations. Molotov refrained from giving a direct answer and went into a long tirade about the whole course of Soviet relations with the last three Bulgarian governments. He insisted that the Soviet break with Bulgaria was useful for all three Allies. Beyond this statement, which neither of the two ambassadors challenged, he did not give any indication of the next Soviet move in Bulgaria.[131]

Admittedly, Molotov could not have made commitments to any firm course. At the time, the Soviet actions regarding Bulgaria did not follow a firmly set plan. To a great extent they were formulated in response to the attitudes demonstrated by the other Big Powers. Stalin had always shown great interest in Bulgaria but was not prepared to risk a major confrontation over it while fighting with the Germans was still going on. Cautious by character, he waited to see whether the West would protest his unilateral actions. Upon entering Bulgaria, the Soviet troops were given strict orders not to interfere with internal developments as they were not carrying out a Communist revolution but a military operation. Soviet representatives told Bulgarian diplomats that they were not going to quarrel with their Allies over Bulgaria.[132]

Despite displeasure at not being informed earlier, Britain and the United States quickly recognized the new situation. With no hesitation they acknowledged the changed position of the Soviet Union vis-à-vis the Bulgarian armistice talks and suspended the Bulgarian armistice mission in Cairo. This readiness to accommodate, if not welcome, the Soviet actions must have been registered in Moscow. Stalin understood that the West was not going to object to his having dealt firmly on his own terms with Bulgaria. Moreover, this was also a precedent for future relations over the country.

In fact, the Soviet declaration of war on Bulgaria could partially be explained by British insistence that something should be done about Bulgaria by the three Allies in concert. Throughout 1944, the FO had been in favour of increased Soviet pressure on Bulgaria and initially even regarded the Soviet move in this context.

Since the Red Army had began fighting on non-Soviet soil, there had been warnings in Britain against the possibility that the Soviet Union would soon be in a position to determine the future of Eastern Europe alone.[133] However, in the spring and summer of 1944, the FO had been worrying about the opposite, namely how to get the Soviet Union involved in policy towards the region. Britain recognized the Soviet interest, reinforced by geography and tradition, and was eager to use it for the purpose of eliminating Bulgaria from the European conflict. All the more so since it had been long obvious that any effective military measures could be undertaken by Soviet troops only. At this point, Britain considered war operations somewhat separately from positive postwar policy. The FO recognized the need for political planning but at the same time did not forget Soviet susceptibilities.[134] Most Western analysts concluded that the Soviet Union would determine the course of future developments in Bulgaria to a great extent; therefore the less it perceived the Allies to threaten its natural claims, the less severe its eventual dominance would be.[135]

The lack of co-ordination with the USSR had been judged to be detrimental to British political and propaganda efforts in Bulgaria. FO approaches to induce the Soviet government to influence Bulgaria had in most cases ended without success.[136] There was a distinct feeling at the Southern Department that Soviet Russia wanted to preserve its special position in Bulgaria and therefore British intervention could harm British–Soviet cooperation.

In any case, British concerns mainly focused on Greece. In the spring of 1944, the FO began considering how to make sure that the Soviet government understood the great importance of Greece for Britain.[137] At the end of May 1944, speaking to Soviet ambassador Gussev Eden had made it clear that he did not object to the intensification of Soviet pressure on Bulgaria. The latter's withdrawal from Greece would be of great military and political value for Britain.[138]

Simultaneously, the FO was considering how to make Moscow announce solidarity with Britain's actions regarding Bulgaria. British Balkan experts believed that any initiative with which the Soviet Union was publicly associated had bigger chances of success in Bulgaria. Therefore, at the end of August the FO noticed with satisfaction that clandestine stations broadcasting over Bulgaria from the USSR were attacking the Bagryanov government with increasing violence. British observers were not in the least perturbed by Moscow's urging the Bulgarian Partisans to remove the government and bring the Fatherland Front to power even though the newly proclaimed Bulgarian neutrality was seemingly accepted.[139] Western diplomats in Turkey raised some concerns about the contradiction in Soviet statements but were overtaken by events.[140] In any case, as late as 29 August Knatchbull-Hugessen told Moshanov that since the Soviets recognized Bulgarian neutrality, all that had to be done was the conclusion of an armistice with the Western Allies.[141]

At the same time, Britain hoped that the Soviet Union would not be satisfied by the announced Bulgarian neutrality and would continue pressing Bulgaria to turn against Germany. Between 29 August and 4 September 1944 Clark Kerr wrote to Molotov at least twice approving of the Soviet policy of dispelling Bulgarian notions that refuge could be taken in neutrality. On 31 August 1944 Eden thanked Gussev for the views expressed on Soviet radio and said that Soviet propaganda would be of great help while negotiations with Bulgaria were going on in Cairo.[142] As late as 4 September Lord Moyne wrote to London that Soviet propaganda and Soviet withdrawal from the EAC and the Cairo talks meant that 'the Russians would settle on our own terms'.[143]

Indeed, in the spring and summer of 1944, with the Bulgarian question evidently coming to a crisis point, Britain had even considered proposing to the Soviet government that it declare war on Bulgaria. When this happened without its prior agreement, the British government was astonished but not worried.[144] It was eager to find an explanation for the lack of consultation, although its optimism decreased upon the realization that it had not been informed of at least three communications between Bulgaria and the Soviet Union.[145] British experts and diplomats disagreed as to whether the Soviets had always planned to go alone in Bulgaria or undertaken last-minute steps in order to join the armistice negotiations.[146] Turkey, preoccupied with fear of the Red Army on its northern border, blamed Britain for delaying the Cairo talks and thus providing the opportunity for Soviet occupation of Bulgaria.[147] The Bulgarian premier Muraviev later wrote that in the crucial days after 5 September 1944, both Britain and the United States demonstrated a total lack of involvement with Bulgaria.[148]

* * *

The stubborn aversion of the British ambassador to subversive methods coupled with the unfavourable political situation in Bulgaria had hindered the preparation of British special services for operating during the war. As a result the SOE suffered a series of setbacks in Bulgaria and was able to complete only a fraction of its objectives in the rest of the Balkans. The two British military missions sent in with huge difficulties towards the end of the war ended in disaster. As Sargent concluded in June 1944, the work of the SOE had hardly been satisfactory and 'ever since the beginning of the war, their one and only showpiece [had] been [the Agrarian] Dimitrov'.[149] This sober assessment of the futility of wartime links made British foreign-policy makers realize how weak the basis for the promotion of Britain's postwar interests in Bulgaria was.

Whitehall officials generally agreed that it was leftist organizations which were going to force Bulgaria's break with Germany. It was not illogical for British planners to envisage that the detachment of Bulgaria from the Axis could be accompanied by serious political or social turmoil. Such likelihood was usually associated with the growth of the role of the Communists as the most vociferous opponents of Germany. The prospect of increased Communist influence anywhere in the Balkans was viewed by most British policy makers as undesirable. It became even less palatable when considered as a stepping stone for strengthening the positions of Soviet Russia in the region. Simultaneously British officials realized that one of the few methods to diminish the chances of a Communist seizure of power was British preparedness to support anti-Communist elements in Bulgaria. However, in the last months before the Bulgarian surrender, the options and advantages of British involvement in Bulgarian internal politics remained largely unexplored. In fact, there had been steady deterioration of the importance of political planning regarding Bulgaria and attention was increasingly concentrated on military goals. The closer real fighting moved to Bulgaria's boundaries, the more British planners were prepared to drop their political schemes.

Despite Britain's limited ability to affect Bulgaria's participation in the war, most British officials believed it possible and planned for a significant role at the time the country decided to back out of the conflict. The fact that the United States had made it clear that it would not consider occupying Bulgaria and that the Soviet Union was not at war with Bulgaria left the British government with the impression that it would have the leading part in the peace negotiations. British politicians and diplomats had always recognized the special position of Russia vis-à-vis the Balkans. But the radical change of situation, which occurred when the Soviets reached the Danube and declared war on Bulgaria, caught virtually all British planners unprepared. The tortuous peace talks in Cairo lost momentum and it soon became obvious that Britain's plans had to be adjusted to reflect the new balance of internal and external forces in Bulgaria.

Part Two

Rising Tensions and Lowering Expectations during the Armistice: 'Britain Has to Be a Little More than a Spectator'*

---

* Churchill in conversation with Stalin, Moscow, 9 October 1944.

Chapter Three

THE PRINCIPLES OF BRITISH POSTWAR POLICY TOWARDS BULGARIA

Throughout 1943 and 1944, British policy towards Bulgaria had been driven by the necessity to force the country out of the war and so break the main Axis link in the Balkans. British efforts were only partly successful, as Soviet pressure proved to be the primary factor behind Bulgaria's exit from the conflict. British diplomats had foreseen the increased role of the Soviet Union in South Eastern Europe in the final stages of the war and expected it to grow and extend into the postwar period. The sober acknowledgement of Soviet strength implied adaptation of British long-term interests.

Whitehall plans for the preservation of Britain's international role consistently recognized the Balkan Peninsula's strategic importance. Both before and during the war, Britain had paid a great deal of attention to its traditional ally Greece; considerable diplomatic and military resources had also been invested in the effort to enlist neutral Turkey in the Allies' camp. The British government had a vested interest in the security, stability and prosperity of these two countries which guarded the approaches to the Straits. British analysis of the consequences of Soviet strategic gains near the Straits should also cover the possibility of 'export' of the Soviet sociopolitical system to the area. Most importantly, the British government faced the question of whether Soviet Russia would use the countries it had occupied at the end of the war in order to penetrate the continent even further to the south and west.

In view of the significance of these matters, the Foreign and War Offices renewed their attention to Bulgaria, whose position under Soviet occupation was acquiring special dimensions as a potential base for ideological or military expansion. Bulgaria's defeat in the war had not destroyed its claims to adjoining territories: with Soviet support it could emerge as an instrument of Soviet foreign policy. To preclude such a possibility, Britain would have to attempt to build up Bulgaria's abilities and will to resist Soviet pressure. This goal required steering its development into an independent, economically viable and democratic nation-state.

The Consequences of the 'Percentages Agreement' for Bulgaria

Undoubtedly preferring to maintain amicable relations with the Soviet government into the postwar period, quite early in the war, British foreign-policy makers had identified areas where interests overlapped and could become the subject of a renewed Anglo-Soviet controversy. The potential of the Balkans to stir trouble in European relations was readily recognized, especially since they had become a prime factor for the Nazi–Soviet breach in late 1940. British foreign policy required a course of action which would accommodate both Britain's desire for sustained influence in the region and its hope of not alienating the USSR because of this. For a short period between the autumn of 1944 and the spring of 1945, such a delicate balance seemed to have been found in the so-called 'percentages agreement' between Churchill and Stalin.

In the non-Communist world the deal was known before the opening of the British archives from the memoirs of many of the direct and indirect participants.[1] The release of the relevant Soviet documents after the collapse of Communism marked official Russian acknowledgement which had previously been denied. The Russian records seem more detailed than the British but on the whole confirm the veracity of the long-released British papers.[2]

By his own admission of the famous episode on the evening of 9 October 1944, Churchill put on a note a series of percentages, which would show the division of responsibility in the Balkans between Great Britain and the Soviet Union. Stalin then ticked it off in blue pencil, more as a mark of acknowledging Churchill's proposal than as a sign of approval.[3] This rough copy became the document which served as the basis for the following negotiations by the British and Soviet foreign ministers. The system which emerged from the Moscow negotiations over the next two days was intended to represent generally the respective share of the two big powers in Greece, Romania, Bulgaria, Yugoslavia and Hungary.

While Churchill was explaining his idea to Stalin he did not draw attention to Bulgaria at all, fixing Britain's influence there at 25 per cent in the initial note. It was Eden who subsequently accepted adjustments by which Britain's portion in Bulgaria was reduced to 20 per cent.[4]

Messages from the British delegation in Moscow to the British cabinet and the Foreign Office explained that the percentages did not determine the number of British or Soviet representatives on the prospective Allied Control Commissions for Germany's ex-satellites. Nor did the figures signify the presence of pro-Soviet or pro-Western members in the countries' first postwar governments.[5]

Churchill deliberately tried to alleviate the fears of the US administration that an old-fashioned secret bargain had taken place behind the small nations' backs. In telegrams to President Roosevelt and his advisor Harry Hopkins, the British prime minister denied in advance any potential accusations that a spheres-of-influence deal had been executed.[6] This was in accord with an earlier message to Roosevelt in May 1944, in which Churchill had stated that Britain did 'not of course wish to carve up the Balkans into spheres of influence'.[7] Churchill himself had asked Stalin to agree that in official releases the phrase 'dividing into spheres' would be glossed over by suitable diplomatic language.[8] According to the Soviet stenographer, Churchill said:

> The Americans will be shocked at seeing this document. But Marshal Stalin is a realist and he, Churchill, is not distinguished by sentimentality, while Eden is an absolutely wicked man. He, Churchill, did not show this document to the British Cabinet, but the British Cabinet usually consent to what he, Churchill, and Eden suggest. As for Parliament, the Cabinet has a majority in Parliament, and even if this document is shown to the Parliament, they will understand nothing of it.[9]

During and after their Moscow visit, code-named Tolstoy, Churchill and Eden repeatedly stressed what the percentages were *not*. Both vigorously refuted the few attempts on the part of the FO to translate the percentages into practical measures to be taken up by British representatives in Eastern Europe. As early as 12 October 1944, Eden wrote to Sargent that 'too much attention should not be paid to percentages which are of symbolic character only'.[10] Churchill later insisted: 'The system of percentages [is intended] to express the interest and sentiment with which the British and Soviet Governments approach the problem of these countries, so that they might reveal their minds to each other in some way that could be comprehended. It is not intended to be more than a guide.'[11]

Despite the rhetoric, a close inspection of Churchill's offer to Stalin reveals that he had done exactly what he was refusing to acknowledge. The notorious half sheet of paper makes most sense in the context of the spheres-of-influence concept, whereby the rival great powers struck an agreement to apportion disputed territories. In October 1944, the Soviet Union and Great Britain reached a compromise to recognize each other's interests in certain areas of the Balkans and Eastern Europe and drew a line between their respective zones. The later practical complications arose only because the agreement did not envisage closed spheres in which each power would have exclusive influence. Instead of a division on purely geographical terms, Churchill suggested a scheme in which a majority share in one country was offset by a minority share in another, whereby an overall equilibrium seemed to be maintained.

The official record suggests that real bargaining started only after Stalin had 'ticked off' Churchill's original set of figures. It was the failure to reach a complete understanding on Bulgaria that proved the greatest obstacle to sealing the scheme immediately. Until the question of Bulgaria came up, a perfect deal had been struck: the percentages for Greece were reciprocated by those for Romania; in both Hungary and Yugoslavia a fifty-fifty division was contemplated. In these cases, not much discussion had been necessary. From the beginning Churchill conceded a much greater Soviet interest in Bulgaria, declaring that it 'owed more to Russia than to any other country'. In contrast, Stalin challenged the degree of interest in Bulgaria which Britain professed.[12] Several times the discussion deviated from and then returned to Bulgaria, treating it as a part of a broader framework which involved also Greece, Turkey, Yugoslavia and even Italy. Stalin and Churchill were unable to agree on what exactly was included in their respective shares in Bulgaria and eventually referred the Bulgarian issue for clarification to their foreign ministers.[13]

Two subsequent conversations between the leading British and Soviet diplomats dealt predominantly with Bulgaria. In the course of the war this was possibly the moment when the greatest deal of attention was paid to Bulgaria at the highest level. What can be extracted from the Moscow negotiations is the best example of British policy thinking on the country. Two premises ruled Britain's attitude, both related to Bulgaria's geographic position. Firstly, Bulgaria was a country on the Black Sea, where the Soviet Union should have complete freedom. Secondly, Bulgaria should withdraw its troops from Greece, which was in Britain's sphere of influence.[14] Churchill also told Stalin that unlike Romania, where it was a spectator, Britain wanted to be 'a little more than a spectator in Bulgaria'.[15]

The Moscow talks were unique in that the issues were discussed and solved in the undisguised language of power politics.[16] The larger implications of the 'percentages agreement' can be comprehended in relation to the shifting balance of power in Europe in the second half of 1944, which Churchill had been observing with increasing apprehension.[17] Even before the Soviet armies appeared in the Balkans the FO had discussed the traditional Soviet involvement there. Churchill's sensitivities had been triggered not by any definite Soviet actions but rather by what he understood to be Soviet threats to take action.

At the end of April 1944, after the suppression of the Greek forces' mutiny in the Middle East and the dispatch of an SOE Mission to Romania in December 1943, Molotov accused the British government of disregarding the legitimate interests of the people concerned. Before Soviet troops started their march across the Balkans, further small and not necessarily related incidents were constructed by British diplomats into a logical chain of events, which seemed to indicate rising Soviet ambitions in the Balkans. One crucial occasion for display of this suspiciousness was the secret dispatch on 25 July 1944 of a Soviet military mission to the Greek Communists.[18] Eden had already drawn attention to 'Russia's intentions to play her own hand in the Balkans regardless of our desires and interests'.[19] The foreign secretary reported to the cabinet that 'the Russians were using the Communist-dominated movements to gain a predominant position in South East Europe'.[20]

The manner of the Soviet government, not consulting or even informing its Allies of particular actions, was itself another reason for British irritation. In the autumn of 1944, Britain's willingness to clarify its existing and future standing vis-à-vis the Soviet Union in the Balkans grew in proportion to the concentration of apparent Soviet attempts to gain a serious political foothold in the region. In fact, acutely conscious of the strategic issues at stake, British diplomats had tried unsuccessfully to establish a common Allied policy in the Balkans for almost a year since the Moscow Conference of October 1943. At that time, preoccupied with its military agenda, the Soviet government had refrained from entering into political discussions so as not to prejudice its standing at the end of hostilities.[21]

After October 1943, the British Chiefs of Staff had reviewed measures for British defence in the postwar era. In mid-1944, the Post-Hostilities Planning Committee defined the only foreseeable danger as a breach with the Soviet Union. Eden's opinion was that unless it incorporated an Anglo-Soviet alliance, any security scheme would precipitate the very danger it was intended to decrease.[22] The erstwhile conduct of the war had prompted the FO to emphasize the need for an early understanding with Soviet Russia on a number of postwar issues. This was especially true of the Balkans, where British influence was under challenge. In the first half of 1944, it was becoming less certain that the military disposition at the end of hostilities would bear favourably on vital British strategic and economic interests in the region. Realizing that their forces might not be sufficient to safeguard a large and unstable zone, British policy makers had to introduce a degree of flexibility in their tactics. They had to work out a clear idea of what the minimum British interests were and how to secure them.[23] British diplomats could only achieve this clarification in response to a sound understanding of the Soviet objectives.

The value of Greece for British strategy in the Balkans had never been questioned in Whitehall. British influence there had to be retained at any cost and the possibility of any Soviet intervention there would be fatal. Although earlier in the war British analysts had given Soviet intentions towards Greece the benefit of the doubt, they were never inclined to watch developments passively. By mid-1944, the steady approach of the Soviet armies to Greece coupled with Soviet pressure on the Straits seemed to form an ominous combination. What was more, Britain itself had seen to the strengthening of the Greek – and Yugoslav – Communist movements as a part of the general anti-Axis military effort. In the early summer of 1944, the clash between British short- and long-term interests had come to a head.[24]

For two months in the summer of 1944, the prime minister put enormous effort into persuading not only the British War Cabinet but above all the US president and State Department that there was a way to keep the Soviet Union out of Greece. His proposed method was to agree with the Soviet Union that for the duration of the war in Europe Britain should take the lead in Greece, and the Soviet Union in Romania. Overcoming the difficulties posed by an evasive Roosevelt and a State Department adamantly hostile to any idea of 'division of responsibility', in mid-July 1944 Churchill wrote to Stalin that the scheme could go ahead. The initial understanding was that this was a temporary agreement which would be tested in the course of the following three months.[25]

Because of US reluctance and slowness to accept the British proposal, there was some confusion in the FO as to whether the three-month trial period was ever enforced. Also, as the Soviet Union maintained its links with the Greek Communists, it appeared to be acting beyond the temporarily agreed boundaries of its zone.[26]

The provisional wartime division of the Balkans clearly gave Stalin a clue about Britain's ultimate goals. At the same time, Soviet analysis 'of the prospects and possible basis of Soviet–British co-operation' also argued that this could be brought about through 'amicable delimitation of spheres of security'.[27]

British attitude to the other Balkan countries is still subject to differing historical interpretations. Bulgaria is a particularly confusing case. British policy makers were on the whole realistic about their minimal influence over wartime developments in that country, but they were also reluctant to trade it off as easily as Romania for freedom of action in Greece. Indeed, at one moment in June 1944, when Churchill was particularly anxious to bring the US president round to his point of view, he mentioned that the trial agreement would also cover actions in Bulgaria.[28] Yet he did not repeat this, possibly because it seemed to raise rather than alleviate US suspicions.

FO officials preferred to keep Bulgaria in Britain's sphere, or at least not to forsake it at the very beginning of negotiations. They realized that in the worst possible scenario, Bulgaria would have to be assigned to the Soviet zone: the view was for instance expressed in an FO memorandum from August 1944.[29] Eden's own opinion fluctuated. In the spring of 1944, he seemed more inclined to abandon Bulgaria as Soviet danger to Greece was perceived to be too great; in the following summer, as the three-month agreement obliged the Soviets to keep away from Greece, he spoke of retaining British influence, although not at the cost of antagonizing the USSR. It seems that to an extent Eden was waiting for some clarification of the Soviet attitude towards Bulgaria which would then serve as a starting point for the formulation of Britain's own objectives.[30]

During an intensive exchange of opinions about the Balkans between July and September 1944, neither Eden nor any Balkan specialist denied the Soviet Union a greater interest in Bulgaria. What the FO insisted on was that the British government should not reveal its preparedness to abandon Bulgaria in unfavourable circumstances but rather keep it as a reserve bargaining card, possibly to be played in the final negotiations. This is what happened in Moscow and this is why suddenly Bulgaria constituted such a difficulty in October 1944. In the end, Eden was bound to accept less British influence in Bulgaria than Churchill had contemplated. The crucial reason for this – apart from Soviet intransigence – was that from the summer of 1944 the ambiguous British attitude to Bulgaria had made it impossible for the government to decide on any firm demands for privileges in that country. At the October 1944 negotiations Eden repeatedly stated that all he wanted was to make sure Britain had more voice in Bulgaria than in Romania but made it clear that ultimately he cared for Greece and Turkey. As resolve had been lacking in relation to Bulgaria its abandonment 'in the real battle' was almost a foregone conclusion.[31]

Given the FO's down-to-earth approach to Bulgaria, the prime minister's and the foreign secretary's actions in Moscow caused little worry in London.[32] British officials continued to work on the assumption that the Soviet Union would have a greater say in the countries which did not have a special status in British foreign policy; the advantage was that the Soviet government would have no hostile intentions towards those that did.[33]

Sir Alexander Cadogan, the permanent undersecretary of the Foreign Office, characterized the news of the 'percentages agreement' as 'nothing much' but was relieved that some understanding in regard to the Balkans generally seemed to have been reached.[34] Sargent was glad that 'Eden had done well'.[35] Oliver Harvey, Eden's private secretary, who was often markedly critical of Churchill's foreign-policy methods, voiced no objections to the Moscow agreement, at which he was present. He was especially content with the result of 'Eden's plain speaking'. What is more, three months after Moscow, Harvey still thought that there was 'much to be said for Russian claims to play a leading part in the East [...] as we claim in the West'. He even admitted that it was time for Britain to accept that it could not 'have [its] cake and eat it as HMG always expect[ed]'.[36] On the whole, those British officials who were familiar with the 'percentages deal' approved of it or accepted it as the least bad solution. They had probably resigned themselves to granting the Soviet Union a free hand in the Balkans apart from Greece, and had seen in the Moscow negotiations one last British attempt to gain more than the absolute minimum. Churchill himself came back from Moscow sure that he had reached not only a realistic agreement but also the best possible one for British interests in Greece.[37]

Among the positive results of the 'percentages deal' Britain could count the assertion that it would remain the leading Mediterranean power. In exchange, Churchill conceded that the Black Sea was a Soviet lake, probably not forgetting that the Black Sea was significant for the Soviet Union exactly because it opened to the Eastern Mediterranean.[38] At the same time, Stalin increased pressure on the Straits by reiterating a demand for a new international regime of passage through them. Churchill readily recognized the need to substitute the obsolete Montreux convention. Stalin assured Churchill that the Soviet government had no plans to make any country Communist, adding that he was in fact exercising restraining influence on the local Communist parties in the occupied countries. However, by saying that some Communists would not listen even to him, Stalin seemed to be warning of the difficulties he could create in Eastern Europe.[39] Without giving any firm commitment Stalin touched upon British sensitivities.

Because of its ambiguity the 'percentages deal' scheme has been interpreted in radically opposing terms: that the three-month trial predetermined the final disposition of the forces[40] has been disputed by the assertion that the Moscow figures simply confirmed a division that already existed on the ground.[41] A third version claims that instead of trying to perpetuate the situation at the time, Churchill rather made an opportunistic bid for larger British influence in the Balkans than could be secured with the few thousand British troops in Greece.[42] He could only rely on Stalin's good will and this was exactly what he did not trust, and therefore pressed for a division of responsibilities. The most he could hope for was to have Stalin's word so that, if necessary, he would be able to show later that Stalin had violated it. But this could hardly be the case with an unwritten secret understanding which Britain could not admit even to its US ally. The fact was, as Churchill told the House of Commons on 18 January 1945, that he had tried to avoid disagreement with Soviet Russia. The result of his attempt was uncertain because there was no mutually acceptable interpretation of the percentages.[43] Notably, recent historiography – which is not any more enthralled by the 'percentages agreement' – focuses more on Stalin's approach, including that the deal was above all psychologically reassuring for him[44] or that it sanctioned conquests he had not yet made.[45] While Britain succeeded in the safeguarding of Greece,

Bulgaria was allocated the role of a buffer between the predominantly British zone and the Soviet one.

The problems of the Bulgarian armistice

Armistice negotiations with Bulgaria began in the Soviet capital on 15 October 1944 – shortly after the Anglo-Soviet talks were wrapped up.[46] Unaware of the 'percentages deal', the Bulgarian representatives were among the first to experience its practical effects. The elaboration of the terms presented to Bulgaria was a test for the feasibility of the Moscow deal, especially in view of earlier differences among the Allies on the matter.

Britain and the USA had already decided to make Bulgarian withdrawal from the occupied territories a preliminary condition for armistice negotiations. This and some other demands caused some 'pretty vigorous exchanges' between Eden and Molotov which were linked to the final version of the 'percentages scheme'.[47]

The last three wartime Bulgarian governments had felt unable to draw Bulgaria out of the war without extracting territorial concessions from the Allies. The Muraviev government broke off relations with Germany but did not cancel Bulgarian administration of the 'new lands'. Even while the Red Army was overrunning Bulgaria, Bulgarian troops remained in occupation of Yugoslav Macedonia and Greek Aegean Thrace. British observers interpreted this as an indication that Bulgaria was going to try to get from the USSR what Britain had denied it. Indeed, only four years earlier, in its proposal for a nonaggression pact, the Soviet Union had offered Bulgaria an outlet on the Aegean in return for Soviet bases on the Bulgarian Black Sea coast.[48] Another disquieting factor for British policy makers was the absence of US public opposition to Bulgarian territorial claims, reminiscent of US leniency to Bulgaria at the end of the First World War.[49]

To Britain these were unsatisfactory prospects after a considerable part of its war effort in the Balkans had aimed at ending Bulgarian occupation of Greek and Yugoslav parts. While Bulgaria had been knocked out of the war, Britain had been given no categorical assurances that the Soviet armies were going to stop on the southern Bulgarian border.

British wartime planning had deemed it essential that Bulgaria should be forced out of the war in such a way as not to affect the interests of the small Balkan Allies and the security of the Straits. Instead, in September 1944 with Soviet involvement, if not encouragement, Bulgaria might acquire a position from which it could threaten the fragile Balkan equilibrium. There was no regular Greek force to stop any invasion, nor had British detachments yet been dispatched to Greek territory: even if they had, they would not risk clashing with the Soviets. British military and political leaders followed closely the slightest movement of Soviet and Bulgarian troops on the Bulgarian–Greek border. On 16 September 1944, in an attempt to ascertain the intentions of the new Bulgarian government regarding Greece, a British military mission arrived in Sofia from Drama in northern Greece. The British officers informed representatives of the Bulgarian government that imminent British landings were going to take place at Dedeagatch, Kavalla and to the east of Salonika.[50] The message implied that any remaining Bulgarian troops in Greece would soon face British military detachments. It was meant to dissuade the Bulgarian government from harbouring any hopes of continuing the occupation of Greek Thrace. On 21 September 1944, after consultation with the Joint Planning Staff Churchill wrote to Stalin that British troops would soon land in Greece so there was no need for a Soviet advance in that direction.[51] This communication to Stalin was designed to pre-empt any dreaded Soviet move towards Greece. On 27 September, with the British divisions still a week from their arrival in southern Greece, Churchill sent a second message to Stalin containing his wish to go to Moscow.[52]

The timing of these telegrams is not coincidental. They highlight the need Churchill and Eden felt to talk to Stalin in person while the situation in the Balkans was still unsettled. The appearance of the Red Army in the Balkans could be explained by military expediency, yet the British leaders feared mostly about its impact on long-term developments. Most British analysts were convinced that British influence and prestige would sustain a great blow if the Soviet army crossed into Greek territory or Bulgarian detachments were allowed to remain there indefinitely. That is why Churchill wanted to make an effort to compensate with political negotiations for what Great Britain lacked in military presence in the region.

British anxieties were complicated by the fact that Communist guerrillas were especially active in the northern Greek provinces, still controlled by Bulgarian troops. If EAM, the leftist resistance movement headed by the Greek Communist Party, was to have material and military support from Soviet Russia, a Greek civil war could easily flare up. These considerations were on Churchill's mind when in Moscow he told Stalin that they should not 'get at cross purposes' but should work to prevent the eruption of 'mini-wars' in the Balkans.

Even though clearly not intended to provoke Britain, Bulgarian actions in Aegean Greece were also a cause for British concern. Already on 11 September 1944, the Fatherland Front government sent to the Kavalla region two government ministers, the Communists Dobri Terpeshev and the Social Democrat Dimiter Neikov, accompanied by one of the leaders of the Bulgarian Communist resistance in southern Bulgaria. They met representatives of the

Greek Partisans and promised them the Bulgarian government's help. They urged local EAM-ELAS detachments to come down from the mountains and take over power in the countryside. Simultaneously, the retreating Bulgarian civil authorities were instructed to hand over control of local affairs to the population. All this aroused the suspicions of British observers, as it was evidently meant to aid Greek left-wing resistance against nationalist guerrillas loyal to the London-supported Greek government-in-exile. For this reason, Terpeshev's speeches on his tour of Aegean Thrace, which drew parallels between the struggle of Bulgarian and Greek Partisans and extolled the decisive intervention of the Soviet army in Bulgaria, sounded all the more menacing.[53]

The situation in the Aegean, aggravated by the Soviet presence in the Balkans, worried Whitehall officials. Their fears were exacerbated by the panic which had overwhelmed the Greek government-in-exile when Bulgaria had turned on Germany and declared that Bulgarian troops were going to help drive the Germans out of the Balkans. The Greek royal government flooded the FO with protests against any Bulgarians remaining in Greece under any pretext.[54] The possibility of Bulgaria claiming any part in the liberation of Greece or campaigning for a co-belligerent status was in Greek eyes a single step away from renewal of territorial aspirations. Even at such a precarious moment Greek exiled leaders confirmed their own counterdemands for the rectification of the border at Bulgaria's expense.[55] British diplomats found themselves under the double burden of their own apprehensions and the Greeks' genuine alarm, which seemed all the more justified since it was shared by the Royal Hellenic government and the left-wing EAM activists.[56]

In October 1944, British observers detected a threatening stance in the USSR's attitude towards Greece. However, scrutiny of Soviet behaviour reveals that by October 1944 Soviet Russia was prepared to relinquish any position in Greece. Major Micklethwaite-Miller of the SOE, who had spoken with the Bulgarian deputy war minister in Sofia on 16 September 1944, had been explicitly told that 'the [Bulgarian] troops will go out and will not intervene in Greek affairs'. Informing Dimitrov in Moscow about the incident, Traicho Kostov, the most senior Communist in the country, added that 'whether there were new or old authorities in the regions left by Bulgarian troops, this was a Greek affair'.[57] This was echoed in a statement the Bulgarian government issued immediately after the visit of the British officers in Sofia, confirming that it did not want to be dragged into the internal quarrels of the rival Greek groups and asking for instructions by the Big Three Allies on this matter. Evidently, by mid-September 1944 the new Fatherland Front government had resigned itself to the idea that Bulgarian administration of the Aegean territories would be cancelled and recalled the Bulgarian civil authorities from the region.

However, these signals were not taken at face value by the British government; neither were the reports of the SOE officers found reassuring. Instead, British officials observed carefully the activities of the Bulgarian government's delegation and the ambiguous behaviour of the Bulgarian commanders in Greece. British apprehension seemed further justified by the Soviet declaration that the left flank of the Third Ukrainian Front needed to be guarded from possible attack by the Germans retreating from Greece. It was noted in London that in early September 1944 the Soviet 17th Army had already undertaken intelligence operations in Greece.[58] Also, on 17 September 1944 when Soviet troops had entered Sofia, all Bulgarian armed forces including regiments outside the country had been placed under Marshal Tolbukhin, the commander-in-chief of the Third Ukrainian Front. Britain's fear was that if the Soviet army were given orders to take over all territories administered by Bulgaria, it could reach the Mediterranean in hours.[59]

The clash of interest between Britain and the Soviet Union on the question of the Bulgarian withdrawal from Greece surfaced on 10 October 1944 when Eden spoke emphatically to Molotov about developments in northern Greece. He pointed out that 'the Bulgarians were behaving with increasing insolence' towards Britain and 'had even dared' to place British officers under house arrest.[60] So agitated was Eden about Bulgarian behaviour, that he repeated three times in a row how important it was that all Bulgarian troops should evacuate Thrace without delay.[61] He pointed out that he considered the intolerable Bulgarian actions to be condoned by the Soviet government and demanded that the Soviet High Command order the immediate Bulgarian withdrawal from Greek territory. Molotov seemed embarrassed and even though he did not deny responsibility for Bulgarian actions, he made a faint attempt to persuade Eden that no Soviet armies were engaged in any operations in Greece. Only after Molotov promised that Bulgarian troops would be taken out of the northern Greek provinces did Eden agree to a 20 per cent share for Britain in Bulgaria as opposed to the 25 initially claimed by Churchill. A similar change was agreed for Britain's percentages in Hungary.[62]

Recalling the Moscow meeting in his memoirs, Eden expressed general satisfaction. The one particular result he thought worth mentioning was that the Soviet government 'would summon the Bulgars out of Greece and Yugoslavia' the same evening.[63] On 11 October 1944 the Bulgarian government was informed that its troops had a fortnight to clear Thrace as a preliminary condition for the conclusion of an armistice with the Allies.[64]

The question of Bulgarian troops in Thrace resurfaced once again shortly after the Moscow summit – in the European Advisory Commission (EAC), where the Bulgarian armistice underwent final adjustments. In the discussion of Western participation in the Allied Control Commission (ACC) for Bulgaria, the US delegate stubbornly denied the Soviet chairman more powers than those accorded to the British and US representatives. The Soviet delegate then mentioned that Bulgarian military detachments should be allowed to stay in Greece as they now formed a part of the fighting Soviet army.[65] Gussev certainly acted on instructions from Moscow, but it is doubtful that these were intended as anything more than bargaining tactics to obtain concessions on other matters of importance to the Soviet Union. The Soviet diplomat, therefore, demonstrated how easy it would be for the USSR to complicate affairs in the Mediterranean if it did not obtain satisfaction elsewhere.

It is extremely difficult to establish whether in the autumn of 1944 Stalin was prepared to support Bulgarian claims to the Aegean, as was the general impression among British observers at the time.[66] This could be inferred from later Soviet hostility to Greece and pressure on the Straits.[67] However, the Bulgarian troops had in fact been ordered to leave Thrace already on 6 October. On that day Stalin personally spoke with Dimitrov, explaining that it was the British demands that were delaying the Bulgarian armistice. Stalin pointed out that his own priority was to retain the Bulgarian army intact in contrast to Britain's desire for disarming it. Stalin voiced confidence that the Bulgarian armistice negotiations would be concluded soon, especially since he intended to speed them up by pledging an early Soviet withdrawal from Bulgaria, 'at the worst after the defeat of Germany'.[68]

Altogether, Stalin had correctly assessed Churchill's agenda behind initiating the October 1944 conversations. Aware of British priorities, Stalin was able to exploit Britain's weaknesses in the Balkans and use the Soviet bargaining points to the full. For almost a week the secret of the imminent Bulgarian evacuation from the Aegean provinces was not divulged to British leaders, making them nervous and willing to sanction Soviet gains in the Balkans and beyond, as long as the Soviet Union stayed away from Greece.

Abstaining from going beyond Bulgaria's prewar borders, Stalin had not lost long-term interest in the Mediterranean. In accordance with the advice of his foreign policy experts, he preferred to make the control of the Straits part of a lasting larger Soviet–British deal, based on 'amicable demarcation of the security spheres in Europe according to the principle of geographical proximity'.[69] If his recollections are to be believed, Molotov favoured even more restraint than Stalin as far as pressure on Turkey was concerned. Molotov also remembered that the Bulgarian Communists used to urge that Bulgaria be allowed to annex a part of Greece:

> It was impossible [...] you had to stay within limits. Raising this issue would have caused trouble right at the beginning of the peace. The English and French would have been opposed. I consulted with the

Central Committee and was told not to bring it up, that the time was not right. We had to remain silent on this issue. But Kolarov was urging it. It was desirable but not timely.[70]

None of the leading Bulgarian Communists – in Moscow or Sofia – have left straightforward evidence of designs on the Aegean. The government of 9 September 1944 had renounced its predecessors' occupation of Yugoslav Macedonia and northern Greece, calling for peaceful resolution of the territorial disputes with Bulgaria's neighbours.[71] In Craiova on 6 October 1944 it signed an agreement with Tito – who had just visited Moscow – allowing Bulgarian troops to remain in Macedonia and fight against the retreating Germans under Soviet command.[72] The FO did not fail to notice these developments.[73]

The establishment of the Allied Control Commission for Bulgaria

The negotiations on the composition and functions of the ACC for Bulgaria revealed the priorities of both Britain and the USSR, as well as the concessions they were ready to make to secure these. As the armistice administration for Bulgaria, the ACC would be a vital and legitimate channel for British influence in Bulgaria in the immediate postwar period. Of equal significance was that it could serve as a ground-level forum for cooperation – or indeed contest – among the Allies.

Already in the second half of 1943, the British and US governments had begun preparations for the peace settlement. They had mapped out the political, economic and other problems that would arise on the cessation of hostilities and started looking into possible solutions. One of the most urgent issues was that of preparing the armistice terms for Germany and its principal satellites, including Bulgaria. British diplomats believed that the peace settlement should be founded on solid inter-Allied agreement. Accordingly, Eden proposed at the Moscow Conference in October 1943 that 'a clearing house for any European problems connected with the war [...] arising either before or after the cessation of hostilities' should be set up.[74] This became the London-based EAC.[75] To British disappointment, both the US and the Soviet governments considered the commission to be little more than an extension of normal diplomatic activity and consequently their representatives had limited competence.

The British delegate in the EAC, Sir William Strang, wrote later that despite long periods of inactivity and drawn out negotiations caused by the Soviet belief that time was on their side, 'never once [...] was there ever any serious misunderstanding [...] or any breach of given word'. Strang insisted that the work of the EAC 'stood the test of events and [...] plans went smoothly into operation when the time came to apply them'.[76] Such a statement is hardly supported by the example of the Bulgarian armistice. Work on it was initiated in May 1944, but despite the British efforts to knock Bulgaria out of the war throughout the summer, the draft was not ready until late August.[77] This was an additional albeit relatively minor factor for Britain's procrastination during the unfortunate Moshanov mission.

When on 29 August 1944 the Soviet delegate in the EAC pulled out of the deliberations of the Bulgarian armistice, British observers interpreted this as a show of Soviet disinterest. Only with hindsight did they realize that rather than agreement to the Western Allies having the last say on Bulgaria, Gussev's withdrawal meant that the Soviet government had decided to impose its own conditions on Bulgaria under completely changed circumstances.[78] The Soviet government's objective was not simply to participate in the discussions for Bulgaria, as Strang claimed: even while the Soviet Union was not at war with Bulgaria, the Western governments had been willing to accept tripartite participation in the envisaged ACC for Bulgaria.[79] When the Red Army occupied Bulgaria, the Soviet objective changed so as to secure the decisive role in Bulgaria's postwar development.

The EAC dealt with the Bulgarian armistice in earnest only after the end of the Moscow talks in October 1944. However, the EAC only worked out the formalities of the text: all significant decisions had been taken by the Soviet and British foreign secretaries in their talks on 10 and 11 October, and in the letters they exchanged shortly afterwards. Strang himself admitted that British Eastern European experts did not expect to have much say in the Bulgarian armistice regime as Soviet predominance in 'the immediate wartime future' had been expressed 'in the figures given by the PM to Stalin in Moscow'. He also voiced the resignation of most senior British diplomats and civil servants in that 'the effect of the armistice, no matter what the text might say, was to open the way for exclusive Soviet influence'.[80] As the British sought to preserve some input in the armistice settlement for Bulgaria, friction centred on the prerogatives of the representatives of the Big Three powers in the ACC.

By the end of August 1944, the various British and US administrative bodies in charge of armistice preparations had reviewed and reached a broad understanding on the main points of the armistice instrument. Apart from recalling Bulgarian troops within the Bulgarian boundaries as of 1 January 1941, these included demobilization of the Bulgarian army, giving the Allies free passage across the country and securing any required material and financial facilities. In addition, an enabling clause was devised so that the Bulgarian government was obliged to fulfil any demands made by the Allies. Although the preliminary drafts foresaw Anglo-American occupation of Bulgaria in extraordinary circumstances, such a development was not realistically expected by either British or US planners. Most importantly, no provision was made for any foreign control body to be introduced in Bulgaria. It was shortly before the entry of the Soviet army into Bulgaria that the British Chiefs of Staff raised the question of a control commission. This was accepted by the US Joint Chiefs only after the occupation of Bulgaria. When Gussev rejoined the EAC sessions on Bulgaria, he confirmed his government's wish for such a controlling mechanism.[81]

Gussev insisted that the proposed ACC should be run entirely by the commanders of the Soviet forces stationed in Bulgaria. While the British agreed that the Soviet member would be the chairman, they insisted that he should simply be *primus inter pares* in a truly tripartite body. This view was upheld firmly by the US administration throughout the negotiations on the Bulgarian armistice, which in October 1944 moved from London to Moscow and back.[82] The US government had so far displayed little concern for Bulgaria but intended to take a livelier interest in the future, precisely through the ACC.[83] The US ambassadors to Moscow and London were given instructions to endorse the principle of equal participation in the Bulgarian ACC to the end, stopping short of refusal to sign the armistice. Even after the Anglo-Soviet deal in Moscow made the US position untenable, the State Department proceeded to place on record its objections to exclusive Soviet rights in the ACC and reserved the right to bring up the question at a later date.[84] Consistent assertion of the necessity for full tripartite membership in the ACC was motivated above all by general US ideas about the peace settlement and not by particular interest in Bulgaria itself. The impression of the future US representative in Bulgaria Maynard Barnes was that the Bulgarian negotiations were not followed by the US War, Navy or State Departments 'with any particular interest or intelligence'.[85]

As the rather more pragmatic British attitude to the problems of the Bulgarian armistice carried the day in Moscow in October 1944, Barnes did not consider the British leaders 'pulling a fast one' on the USA, but understood that they were trying to get a deal.[86] In the protracted talks with Molotov on 10 and 11 October Eden opened the bargaining on the Bulgarian ACC with the proposal for equal representation. Molotov maintained firmly that this was not feasible. He protested his inability to understand how three people could have the same responsibility and argued that it could only create confusion. Moreover, the 80 per cent share just allocated to the Soviet government would become meaningless if the representatives of the other two had equal shares. Finally, a compromise was found in the decision to allow for two distinctive periods in the existence of the ACC. Until the end of hostilities with Germany, the Soviet High Command would be in full charge; after that until the conclusion of the peace treaty, there would be increased participation of the British and US elements of the commission.[87] In letters to Molotov after the talks, Eden practically gave away the right to any Western participation during the first period.[88]

Historians have claimed that the establishment of the Bulgarian ACC followed broadly the precedent of Italy, where the Western Allies had occupying armies and commanded an exclusive say in the armistice regime.[89] While the situations in Italy on the one hand and Bulgaria and Romania on the other can be superficially compared, it is apparent from the available records that in the Moscow conversations the Soviet leaders did not touch upon this question. Yet it certainly was on the minds of British officials, who were very conscious of Britain's position in Italy and wanted to prevent the Soviet diplomats from raising it officially.[90]

The only concession Molotov made in Moscow was that a representative of the Anglo-American Combined Chiefs of Staff should also sign the Bulgarian armistice along with the Soviet commander of the Third Ukrainian Front.[91] This was a purely symbolic gesture and gave Britain little satisfaction for three years of war with Bulgaria. In the eyes of the FO, it became even less meaningful as worrying developments were shaping on the ground. The Soviet military authorities had already expelled SOE and OSS teams from Bulgaria on the pretext of improper accreditation. In addition, the Soviet High Command in the country insisted that the designated British political representative had arrived without the necessary Soviet permission and so was refusing to receive him and facilitate his work.[92] All this contained little promise for Soviet–British cooperation in and regarding Bulgaria.

The picture was complicated by the fact that the political agreements undertaken by the British prime minister and foreign secretary in Moscow were made known to none of the British diplomatic or military officers sent to Bulgaria. They had been dispatched to the country with little knowledge about the preceding developments and with only the most basic terms of reference for their mission. Unsurprisingly, initially they honestly believed that their task was to take a full and equal part in governing their former enemy Bulgaria.

The Armistice between the Allies and Bulgaria was officially signed on 28 October 1944 in Moscow. The Bulgarian delegation included government ministers from the different parties in the FF. It was given no chance for bargaining: it had been summoned to formalize an act of unconditional surrender. By then an official joint Allied military mission had verified the complete withdrawal of Bulgarian troops from Thrace.[93]

The attitude displayed towards Bulgaria during the Moscow negotiations in October 1944 showed that the Second World War had changed little in Britain's relationship with that country. It was evident that British diplomats gave priority to stabilizing their relations with the other great powers. During the talks between the British and Soviet leaders it became obvious that the general principles determining the approach to Bulgaria were deeply rooted in the traditional power politics of the region. Once again, more than anything else Bulgaria attracted British attention by virtue of its geographic location and complicated relationship with its neighbours. The Moscow meeting also provided a miniature of future British behaviour towards the country.

The Meaning of Yalta and Potsdam for Bulgaria

The Moscow negotiations further demonstrated that the Soviet Union would quickly fill any vacuum resulting from British inability, unwillingness or hesitation to uphold British interests. Throughout the war Stalin had been interested in extending and stabilizing Soviet influence over Bulgaria, Hungary and Romania, especially after establishing that Churchill did not regard these countries as of primary importance. This is precisely what Stalin managed to confirm at the time of the 'percentages agreement'. His political achievement was certainly underpinned by the military advantages the Soviet Union enjoyed in the Balkans. In the months after the Tolstoy meeting, the westward military advances of the Red Army continued and caused British leaders to worry whether it would stop at the agreed line in Central Europe. But this renewed anxiety about Soviet intentions did not mean that top British policy makers expressed any remorse about the rights or wrongs of the 'percentages agreement'.

At the same time, noticeable nuances in Britain's attitude towards the Soviet Union emerged. British observers did not deny Soviet predominance in the ex-satellites, but they resented the methods with which it was being asserted. They were concerned with accumulating indications of Soviet interference in the internal affairs of the occupied countries. Above all, they were perturbed by hostile Soviet behaviour towards the Western representatives there.[94] This gradual change of heart was especially characteristic of Churchill, who did not have much trust in Soviet intentions anyway. Outwardly he maintained his understanding with Stalin and could not but admit that when civil war erupted in Greece in December 1944, Stalin had kept his word of not interfering. Not denying that he had recognized the Soviet lead in Bulgaria and Romania, Churchill was however disturbed by the fact that in these countries Communist-controlled governments were ruling by force, with complete Soviet support. One way for the British prime minister to keep his promise and yet let Stalin know that Soviet actions in Eastern Europe were not considered legitimate was to persuade the United States to exercise some moderating influence on Soviet behaviour.[95]

THE PRINCIPLES OF BRITISH POSTWAR POLICY 91

During the first half of 1945 no British official was given authorization to challenge the 'percentages agreement'. Accounts of the limitations and humiliations under which they were placed became a constant feature of reports from the Western representatives in the ex-satellites. These representatives were equally confused by the failure of their superiors to initiate any adequate action on a suitable international level. A number of men in the field independently came to the conclusion that some quid pro quo must have been achieved. Their bigger concern, however, was the realization that their leaders might be entertaining false ideas about the real Soviet attitude to big power cooperation.[96]

In relation to Bulgaria the 'percentages deal' overshadowed the subsequent three-power summits at Yalta and Potsdam. Despite its increasing unease concerning developments in the ex-satellite states, the British government was not prepared to announce publicly that there had been an agreement, let alone that Stalin was not respecting it. Therefore, one possible course was to try at least to rectify, if not supersede, the effects of the Moscow agreement. British adherence to the US-sponsored Declaration on Liberated Europe at Yalta in February 1945 could be seen as such an attempt through the pledge of assisting jointly 'the establishment of internal peace' and of facilitating through 'free elections' the establishment of 'governments responsible to the will of the people'. This stood halfway between belated reassertion of the principles of democratic government and restraint from confrontation precipitated by the Soviet methods of application of the 'percentages deal'. This was, however, too subtle an expression of disapproval of Stalin's actions in Eastern Europe. He signed the declaration with quite a different meaning of democracy in mind to that of the Western powers, and after Yalta several times reminded British representatives of the October 1944 bargain.[97] This served to make it clear to the British leaders that Stalin was not satisfied with receiving assurances of the strategic security of the Soviet zone. British diplomats realized that for the Soviet Union security was equated with territory, and what was more, complete domination of the acquired territory. Only then would the USSR refrain from meddling in the others' zones.[98]

It is commonly agreed that the fate of Eastern Europe was finally determined at the Yalta summit. In fact, apart from Poland, which of course had been one of the greatest concerns for the British government throughout the war, no other Eastern European country was discussed meaningfully by the Allied leaders. Harvey feared that the conference would be the 'usual scramble leading to the usual half-digested decisions' and was soon able to confirm this prediction.[99]

The internal situation in Bulgaria, which together with Romania was at the time of the Yalta Conference keenly watched by the FO, was not placed on the agenda. The subject of Bulgaria was briefly touched upon when British grievances regarding Soviet domination of the ACC, the Bulgarian–Yugoslav treaty and Bulgarian reparations to Greece were recorded.[100] The closest the Big Three came to paying attention to the Balkans at all on this occasion was in a general and indecisive review of the international regulation of the Straits. Both Stalin and Churchill reiterated their agreement for the revision of the Montreux convention, by which they confirmed their positions from the previous October. Regarding Yugoslavia, it was decided to endorse a compromise between the Partisans and the London-based government-in-exile, which could again be interpreted as practical implementation of the fifty-fifty deal.[101] So, as far as the Yalta talks touched on questions raised at Tolstoy, the general framework tended to be confirmed. The lawyers at the FO argued that neither Stalin nor the British government 'were committed very much' by the Yalta Declaration. The major advantage they saw was that the document provided 'an excellent bargaining counter'.[102] Stalin was given almost no reason to suspect that Soviet actions in the ex-satellites were resented or that they could become the cause for a major inter-Allied controversy.[103]

By late February 1945, the FO had decided to 'let sleeping dogs lie' and not invoke the declaration except for the specific purposes of inducing the United States to accept responsibility for some other areas of British interest, such as Greece. FO officials discussed the idea whether Britain could agree to a degree of Soviet influence in Western Europe in exchange for the same for the British government in Eastern Europe without reaching unanimity. Sargent explored the possibility of Britain joining the United States in invoking the declaration in an attempt to stop the Soviet Union from 'cooking' the elections in Bulgaria and Romania. Eventually, he advised against this and repeated that the only value of the declaration was in committing the United States to European affairs. But Britain had to be very careful with US involvement in Eastern Europe as 'the Americans are only too prone to espouse a cause enthusiastically and later let us down with a bump'. Also, Britain had to consider whether, for example, claims in Romania would not make Stalin take an 'inconvenient' line on Italy.[104]

After the Yalta Conference, however, the relative British complacency with regard to the northern Balkans steadily decreased. Diplomatic signals from the Soviet-occupied countries drew attention to the growing arrogance of the local Communist parties, derived above all from their firm belief in Soviet backing. British doubts that the Soviet military and political representatives exercised a strong influence on the ruling coalitions found constant confirmation. The ultimate proof came in late February 1945 with the Soviet-supported imposition of a Communist government on the helpless Romanian king. At the same time, the FO was markedly loath to take up with the Soviet government the issue of political conditions in Romania and Bulgaria. There was no official British criticism of the Soviet-directed change of government in Bucharest.[105] Nor did senior FO officials wish in any way to get involved in a dispute over the forthcoming elections in Bulgaria.[106] One reason for this was that the problems of the Polish settlement were forcefully coming to the fore of political discussions between the Soviet Union and its Western partners. The FO preferred to concentrate on the solution of this most serious of questions, and not irritate or distract the USSR with disputes of lesser priority. Another inducement for Britain to refrain from making public comments on the situation in Bulgaria and Romania was the ever-present fear that Russia could retaliate in Greece, Italy or another country of primary interest for Britain.[107]

After Yalta, British foreign-policy makers set out to re-examine policy towards South Eastern Europe, which was inextricably entangled with the conduct of Anglo-Soviet relations. They faced the crucial question whether Soviet actions in the ex-satellite states revealed future Soviet intentions for the area. In addition, they wondered whether the Soviet Union was going to maintain friendly relations with its Western Allies or use its powerful position to dominate the postwar continent. As usual, there was not a straightforward answer to these complicated dilemmas and the real task of the FO was to look into possible scenarios and work out relevant solutions. The result was a memorandum signed by Sargent on 13 March 1945 and soon afterwards circulated to the War Cabinet. It reiterated the fear that the Soviet Union had deliberately set out to violate the Yalta agreements. But there was also an allowance for the fact that Soviet behaviour remained consistent with what it had been before Yalta and that the countries concerned had themselves not been renowned for democratic traditions. The overall inclination of the authors of the paper was that the British government would be much wiser in accepting the historic realities in the northern Balkans and resigning itself both to undemocratic regimes and Soviet predominance there. The alternative would only risk deterioration of relations with the Soviet Union without any realistic hope that political conditions could be improved, and would therefore spell the definite failure of all British objectives in the region.[108] At the same time, Sargent was worried that Britain might be seen as abandoning certain countries, like Bulgaria and Romania, in the belief that it would be able to save others. This would amount to admission that it was willingly operating within certain geographical limits and therefore abdicating its right as a great power to be interested in the whole of Europe.[109]

The end of hostilities in Europe brought a new reappraisal of British foreign policy in another memorandum, written by Sargent in July 1945 and entitled 'Stocktaking after VE Day'. Endeavouring to assess Britain's international position in the immediate postwar years, this document recognized the decrease in material resources for which Britain would have to compensate with skilled diplomacy and the support of the United States. Three-power cooperation was still considered central to British foreign policy but depended on accurate assessment of Stalin's long-term objectives. Sargent was emphatically of the opinion that the Soviet Union was not likely to pursue further territorial expansion but would instead opt for the consolidation of its power in Eastern and Central Europe. This meant the establishment of Communism in the countries controlled by the USSR, which in its turn would become the greatest long-term danger for British security and influence on the continent. This time Sargent seemed to reverse his advice of the previous month, writing that Britain should not be afraid to take the lead in an independent, anti-totalitarian policy in relation to Eastern Europe. But once again, he stated that British efforts should differentiate between the countries in the region: on this occasion he mentioned that Communism might have to be accepted in Romania and Hungary but not elsewhere, including Bulgaria.[110]

While the FO was re-evaluating British relations with the Soviet Union, the State Department was reconfirming the basic belief of US foreign policy that spheres of influence should be discouraged. This was directed equally against Great Britain, who was suspected of uninterrupted imperial aspirations. What remained unclear was how US politicians hoped to reconcile the idea of no special zones of interest, with continued insistence on good relations with the Soviet Union, which was evidently going against its undertakings at Yalta. Among US diplomats, Kennan was the only one who saw the postwar international dilemmas in terms close to those of his British colleagues: where it was not able or willing to confront the USSR, the United States needed not challenge Soviet supremacy.[111]

As a rule, however, until the Potsdam summit, the Truman administration continued Roosevelt's search for general cooperation with Soviet Russia.[112] This was in a sense one step behind the British government, which was becoming more conscious that an altercation with the Soviet government was approaching. Nevertheless, British political analysts were realists enough to recognize that the Balkans were not going to be the subject of such a showdown. In fact, confrontation almost flared up in an area close to the Balkans. In May 1945, Tito's troops occupied Trieste in an attempt to annex it to Yugoslavia. This was seized upon by Churchill, who saw in it a suitable occasion to demonstrate to the United States how Soviet foreign policy operated. Churchill was convinced that the Soviet Union had plans for Trieste to become a Soviet-controlled outlet to the Mediterranean and that Tito was acting upon orders from Moscow. In any case Tito withdrew his forces from Trieste only on the insistence of Stalin, who balked in the face of firm and unanimous British and US action.[113] The whole episode was reminiscent of the Bulgarian withdrawal from northern Greece: the British government took an inflexible position, as its Mediterranean interests were perceived to be under a strong threat. Apparently abiding by the 'percentages deal', the Soviet Union, or rather its assumed proxy, pulled out of an area it had recognized as of greater British concern. So, a month before Potsdam, it was confirmed in practice that the Moscow understanding was still in force. It was not superseded by the decisions at the last three-power conference in July 1945, either.

Potsdam changed little as far as British attitudes to the ex-satellite countries were concerned. Of course, President Truman made a strong impression by insisting on the implementation of the Yalta Declaration. In his view the three Allies should agree on the necessity of immediate reorganization of the present governments in Bulgaria and Romania.[114] But these questions were overshadowed by more imminent ones – above all the administration of defeated Germany – and effectively slid into the background. The results of the Potsdam Conference regarding Bulgaria can be best exemplified by the contrasting statements made by the US president and the Soviet foreign minister. On his return to the United States, Truman repeated the assertion that the Balkans were not going to be in any one power's sphere of influence.[115] At precisely the same moment, Molotov privately reassured Dimitrov that 'in general the [Potsdam] decisions are favourable to us. In practice our sphere of influence has been recognised'.[116]

* * *

The period between the summer of 1944 and the Potsdam Conference was vital for the clarification of Bulgaria's place in British policy. This was the time when British foreign-policy planners elaborated and tested the rationale of Britain's position, taking into account Bulgaria's strategic and political significance in Eastern Europe and the Balkans. Concern for Bulgaria's internal development, even the imposition of Communism, was little more than a function of the military danger the country could pose to the Eastern Mediterranean.

British conduct in October 1944 confirmed again that Britain was willing to go to almost any lengths to secure its prevalence in Greece. This tendency was not only unequivocally recognized by the predominant majority of British politicians and diplomats but was also made perfectly clear to the Soviet leaders. As there was no British military presence in the region comparable to the Soviet armies stationed in the northern Balkans, Churchill and Eden tried to extract all the political concessions they could from Stalin. They understood too well that the Moscow deal was going to bear heavily on postwar developments, but justified it mainly as having prevented much more threatening alternatives.

The 'percentages agreement' touched on the most sensitive issue of future Anglo-Soviet relations. It was an attempt to define the limits of British and Soviet policy in an area where both had interests, and so diminish the possibilities for a conflict. It postponed the flaring of full-blown hostility between Russia and the West, and particularly between Russia and Great Britain after the end of the Second World War. However, the negotiations also exposed the fact that a full agreement was hardly possible and therefore served to alert the British government to the need to fortify its Mediterranean positions.

Britain's recognition of its inability to commit enough resources to secure predominance in Bulgaria was combined with the long-standing acknowledgement of Soviet interests. This explained the British government's adherence to the spheres-of-influence idea. It was Churchill who put this approach into practice, but it was in fact intellectually supported by the majority of the diplomatic and political establishment. It was the almost unanimous acceptance of the agreement of those British senior statesmen and officials who knew about it that secured its application throughout the armistice period.

Chapter Four

OBSERVING THE ESTABLISHMENT OF COMMUNIST RULE IN BULGARIA

The conclusion of the armistice invariably changed the substance of Britain's relations with Bulgaria. Securing the withdrawal of Bulgarian troops from Aegean Greece was seen as a significant diplomatic and tactical success for the British government. As Bulgaria's proximity to the Mediterranean continued to govern Britain's interest in the country, participation in the Bulgarian armistice regime was a valuable new channel for influence on Bulgaria's postwar development. Observations made by British political and military staff in Bulgaria would throw light on the actions and aspirations of local political actors, but also – and even more importantly – on the methods and aims of Soviet foreign policy in Bulgaria, the Balkans and Europe in general. Further, the ACC would be a forum for lower-level great-power cooperation: its functioning would test the desire of the Soviet Union to maintain friendly relations with the Western Allies.

Ironically, the importance of Bulgaria for Britain grew as a result of the Soviet occupation, whereby Bulgaria's military facilities were placed under Soviet control and its government looked to Moscow for internal and international support. Bulgaria's dealings with its neighbours and its attitude to the Western powers would be determined by, and therefore would be symptomatic of, Soviet postwar plans. In the second half of 1944, British leaders were increasingly worried that the Soviet Union might use such a newly acquired position of power in the Balkans to encroach on territories beyond those conceded to it and so endanger long-term British interests further afield. An aggravating possibility was that Bulgaria could adopt Communism as a state ideology. British concern over this was deepened not so much by aversion to the ideology as by the understanding that it would cement the Soviet foothold in the Balkans, which could be easily used for offensive purposes.

Altogether, the establishment of Soviet authority in Bulgaria, greatly enhanced by the presence of the Soviet army, had a direct bearing on overall Soviet–British relations. Great Britain, which had few positive ideas on how to influence Bulgarian postwar development, considered its interest to lie in preventing a complete Communist domination in Bulgaria.

Involvement in the First Postwar Elections in Bulgaria

There is little direct documentary evidence on British objectives in postwar Bulgaria. Yet a large quantity of archival material on the first Bulgarian postwar elections suggests that the Foreign Office considered this an event of consequence. Evidently, the manner of carrying out of the elections would illuminate the direction in which the Bulgarian regime would evolve and so indicate whether the USSR would insist on complete domination of both foreign policy and internal developments. Linking this to Soviet actions in other occupied territories, the FO would be able to explore the hypothesis of a Soviet design for the establishment of Communism in Eastern Europe.

British doubts about Bulgarian democracy

Even though the British mission had little initial knowledge of Bulgaria, its members grasped quickly the essentials of the small but complicated Bulgarian political scene. Right after the Bulgarian surrender, they were subjected to the suspicion and outright hostility of the Soviet occupying authorities. In early September 1944, an SOE team sent from northern Greece to Bulgaria was unceremoniously thrown out of the country by the Soviet High Command.[1] In October Soviet heavy-handedness culminated in the refusal of General Sergei Biryuzov, commander of the Soviet forces in Bulgaria, to receive the designated British representative before the formal conclusion of the Bulgarian armistice. That event, however, seemed to bring little change to the Soviet attitude to British officials. On 29 November 1944, an order issued by Biryuzov, in his capacity of acting head of the ACC, forbade the Bulgarian government any direct contacts with the Western missions.[2] Meanwhile, the Soviet High Command in Bulgaria went to extraordinary lengths to obstruct the activities and even physical movements of the Western members of the ACC. This issue was indicative of Soviet attitudes towards the Western Allies and gradually became a legitimate reason for the worsening of inter-Allied relations. It was exacerbated by the Bulgarian Communists, who believed that the inclusion of US and British representatives in the ACC had somehow impaired the internal situation in Bulgaria.[3] By the Potsdam Conference, which marked the beginning of the second period of the functioning of the ACC, 'it had already become a habit for Russia to push us in the face, and they continued to do so', in the words of one American direct witness.[4]

The initial efforts of the British military and political representatives were focused on sending home accurate and balanced reports on people and events in Bulgaria. Analysing the nature of the ruling coalition of 9 September 1944, which had seized power by a *coup d'état* and proceeded to rule by decree, they underlined that it needed to confirm its legitimacy through proper elections and foreign recognition.

British observers also noticed immediately that the Communists who were in charge of internal affairs and justice dominated the government even though it consisted of four members from each of the BCP and Zveno, two each from the Agrarian and Social Democratic parties, as well as some independent politicians. British apprehension that such disproportionate strength would be used to the Communists' ulterior purposes found proof in the setting up of the people's courts and the assignment of special powers to the interior minister.[5] It was obvious to the British representatives that the Bulgarian Communists turned the people's courts into instruments of political vengeance, even though their proclaimed task was to prosecute German collaborators and wartime criminals. Nearly one hundred and fifty of the highest-ranking Bulgarian politicians, civil servants and court officials were shot in the early hours of 2 February 1945, while many others were imprisoned. By April 1945, 11,122 people had been tried, 2,618 sentenced to death and 1,046 executed.[6] Furthermore, already in the first weeks immediately after 9 September 1944 Communists zealots had abused, arrested and murdered their real and imagined enemies, mainly from the wealthy classes and supporters of right-of-centre parties: the government mostly turned a blind eye to the violence. After the people's courts folded up, the intimidation and maltreatment of the Communists' political and intellectual opponents continued through two of the earliest laws of the Fatherland Front government, the Decree for the Protection of the People's Power and the Law for Labour Educational Institutions. These dealt with cases of political opposition.[7] However, the content of the laws if not the spirit of their implementation could be formally interpreted as following the provisions of the armistice to punish fascists and warmongers. Accordingly, without much debate the FO chose not to raise the problem of political persecutions and executions with the Bulgarian government.[8]

The Communists' aspirations to political monopoly could be discerned in their parallel drive for predominance in the FF Committees, which sprang as a countrywide network of support for the government. These were then used by the Communists – at both central and local level – as the means of intervening in the other parties' affairs.[9] The picture was further complicated by the fact that the non-Communist government parties contained numerous factions, some of which were not averse to increased cooperation with the Communists in exchange for more political power. At the same time, tension mounted in the governing coalition, mainly because of Communist brutality and dictatorial aspirations. British representatives did not regard these developments as conducive to democratic practices and foresaw that it would 'be very easy for a one-party government to establish itself': this 'would inevitably take the form of some kind of Communism'.[10]

In the wake of the Yalta Declaration on Liberated Europe, which confirmed Allied commitment to free elections and the establishment of a multiparty system, the British political representative in Sofia, William Houstoun-Boswall, alerted his superiors to the possibility of elections for the National Assembly as early as May. Several Bulgarian government officials – most notably the Communist secretary of the National Council (NC) of the FF, Tsola Dragoicheva – had made pronouncements to that effect, insisting that there would be a single list of FF candidates with an agreed ratio of deputies from each party. The British representative did not think the moment ripe for elections as even some Communist leaders admitted that 'passions were running too high [...] after the [...] trials and executions'. Houstoun-Boswall suggested that Britain, together with the United States, should declare keen interest in the proposal while highlighting their democratic expectations and publicizing their reservations as to the ability of the present regime of ensuring a free and fair vote. Houstoun-Boswall believed that by formulating clear criteria the two Western powers could put off the elections for some time. He sought to stimulate the attention of his own government by reminding them that the Bulgarian postwar elections would be the first in a former German satellite and as such could set a precedent for the rest of Eastern Europe.[11]

In the meantime, the US government had already acted upon developments elsewhere in the region, namely protesting to the Soviet government about the imposition of a new, Communist-dominated government in Romania in March 1945, which had been formed as a result of Soviet deputy foreign minister Andrei Vyshinski's direct intervention. Molotov flatly rejected the US protest, claiming that the implementation of the Yalta Declaration was the sole responsibility of the Soviet Allied Control Commission.[12] In turn, the State Department refuted this interpretation, affirming that it considered itself bound by the Yalta promises. On 5 April 1945, the US ambassador in Moscow remonstrated again to the Soviet government and proposed the establishment of some machinery for tripartite consultation to look into the timing and preparation of Bulgarian elections.[13] The Soviet reply put an end to the exchange by pointing out elections in Bulgaria were not imminent, yet any further US action in relation to the issue would be interpreted as interference in Bulgarian internal affairs.[14]

Available documents make it possible to suggest that in the spring of 1945 the Bulgarian Communists had not yet begun planning for elections. The Western representatives' anxiety about the premature timing of the elections was somewhat exaggerated, if still relevant in terms of the manner in which elections would be carried out.[15] Indeed, the US action in Moscow had been coordinated with the FO, which had reluctantly pledged support: a British representation was handed to the Soviet government a whole week after the US one. Houstoun-Boswall for one was more than sceptical about the US proposal. He predicted that participation in any tripartite body would simply make British and US representatives 'look ridiculous and shoulder the responsibility' for the results. He had in mind much subtler means of influencing the Bulgarian authorities and public, for example British propaganda for democracy, journalistic coverage of events in Bulgaria and above all encouragement of the moderate FF elements by official pronouncements of British interest.[16] On its part, the Southern Department agreed with the general premises behind the State Department's move but considered it unwise to raise the questions of the Romanian government and of the Bulgarian elections simultaneously. They preferred a gradual approach by which matters would be resolved one at a time, while also expressing content that at least it was the United States that had taken the lead.[17]

The FO Balkan specialists were neither too concerned about the timing of Bulgarian elections nor unduly worried about potentially improper behaviour by the Bulgarian government. At the time they were preoccupied with internal deliberations as to whether acceptance of the Yalta principles overruled the Tolstoy agreement and whether they should continue to abide by the elusive ratio fixed in October 1944.[18] The alternative was not only to voice their views regarding Bulgaria and Romania, but above all to insist on these being taken into account by the Soviet government. The main British dilemma was whether to take a firm attitude regarding a country so clearly within Soviet control. This could cause not only 'bitter reproaches from Moscow' but possible retaliatory action in territories in which Britain had 'a much more lively interest than [...] in Bulgaria'.[19]

Although disconcerted by Communist excesses in Bulgaria, Houstoun-Boswall agreed that the question should be approached from the angle of British long-term cooperation with the USSR. Yet he maintained that the elections themselves would show how the Soviet government proposed to apply the Yalta Declaration. He reported that the Soviet compromise on the composition of the Polish government, the Soviet acceptance of Bulgarian withdrawal from Thrace and Tito's abandonment of Trieste were all interpreted across the political spectrum in Bulgaria as signs of Soviet defensiveness.[20] At the Southern Department, Howard found these examples premature and inconclusive with regards to Bulgaria. Indeed, most British observers wondered whether it was worthwhile for Stalin to make some concessions or if Soviet prevalence in the country was too important for him to be put at stake by working together with the West.[21]

British analysts acknowledged that the prospective elections in Bulgaria would validate the existing political structure and lend constitutional authority to the present government.[22] However unpalatable this appeared, knowledge of Balkan history justified doubts as to whether it could be prevented by such measures as a democratic electoral law and mitigation of Communist terror. Sargent repeatedly recorded his scepticism of the outcome of even relatively free elections anywhere in the region. He wrote that the last war had impoverished and reduced most of the population to a state of complete apathy. He did not expect ordinary people 'to fight for parliamentary institutions, which in any case they never learnt to rely on or respect'. Instead, he could understand how they could wish 'to obtain a minimum of security and stable government even [...] at the cost of their political or personal liberties'.[23] Sargent recalled that even in the calmest interwar years parliamentary institutions in the region had been inefficient and corrupt and had, as a rule, been replaced by some form of dictatorship, leading to increased susceptibility to Communist propaganda and opening opportunities for Soviet-style totalitarianism. He believed this to coincide with the intentions of the Soviet government and make British chances of introducing free institutions 'somewhat dim'.[24]

Sargent's reasoning led him to conclude that the establishment of totalitarian regimes across Eastern Europe was almost inevitable. He felt that the British government should resign itself to its inability to change such an outcome. Most importantly, since it was highly unlikely that British protests would alter the overall direction of developments, they should be abandoned as they could only antagonize the Soviet government.[25] Such thinking applied not only to Bulgaria but to most of Eastern Europe and was especially, if not exclusively, directed towards Germany's war collaborators. To some extent, this echoed prewar patterns of Britain's behaviour dominated by reluctance to get involved in a peripheral region to which another great power laid more pressing claims.

Preparing for the elections

Ironically, just when key British policy makers were advising restraint regarding Bulgaria, prominent Bulgarian Communists were forming extremely hostile opinions of Britain. In January 1945, in a report for the DII of the CC of the Bolshevik Party, Kostov accused the British representative of leading the non-Communist Fatherland Front parties to question the Communists' predominance in central and local government, and particularly of encouraging the Agrarians.[26] He was, however, aware that such allegations should be voiced with great caution and used for internal purposes only so as not to affect relations with Britain.[27] Altogether, experienced Communist activists understood the need to maintain outward tripartite Allied cooperation and carry out reforms 'on a more indefinite, more vague, temporary basis of democratic compromises' due to 'the particular international situation and the impossibility for the USSR to interfere openly in [Bulgarian] internal dealings'.[28]

When eventually in June 1945 the regents set the polling day at 26 August, Houstoun-Boswall could report that his grim predictions about the elections looked about to be proven correct: the Fatherland Front parties would stand on a joint electoral list, allocating in advance to the Communists and Agrarians 95 parliamentary seats each out of the prospective 267. Houstoun-Boswall thought that the true support for the Agrarians was three times stronger than that for the Communists.[29] More ominously, in May left-wing splinter groups had overtaken the leadership of both the Agrarian and Social Democratic parties with active Communist support. At the beginning of June, Nikola Petkov, leader of the Agrarians within the FF, was removed from his party position by a pronouncedly pro-Communist faction – which also rendered his cabinet seat questionable.

Judging by such signs, British observers could only guess that the Communists were escalating their interference in the other parties' affairs. What they did not know was that indeed the Politburo had called for increased Communist support for the so-called 'healthy forces' (i.e., leftist pro-Communist elements in the other parties) and was preparing a discrediting campaign against G. M. Dimitrov and Petkov.[30] The Communists continued to keep up the appearance of coalition unity, appealing to the other parties for cooperation and denouncing as yet anonymous enemies of the Fatherland Front.[31] Stalin personally advised dealing carefully with Petkov and his supporters: before throwing them out of the cabinet and the ruling coalition, it would be necessary to 'unmask' them so that they would not 'emerge as martyrs and fighters for freedom'.[32]

One of the first acid tests for Britain's attitude towards the Communist persecution of the Bulgarian opposition was the case of G. M., who was accused of treason for undermining the authority of the FF and demoralizing his supporters in the army. In May 1945 he escaped from home arrest and found shelter with a member of the British military mission. Receiving the news, the FO immediately instructed the British representative to remove the Agrarian leader from the British mission and inform the Bulgarian prime minister that G. M. 'had simply passed through British hands'. The FO resolved to refuse G. M. political asylum without even knowing whether he would ask for it. He was driven to premises belonging to the US mission in Sofia, where he remained for several months until his departure for the United States. Throughout this period, the main British concern was that the British government should avoid confirming even the slightest suspicion of supporting anti-Fatherland Front and anti-Soviet activities in Bulgaria.[33]

Such careful behaviour had no impact on the attitude of the Bulgarian Communists. Their hostility to Britain was motivated by ideological stereotypes rather than concrete British actions. That is why in G. M.'s case the Bulgarian government distinguished little between the British government, which refused to get involved, and the US government, which ultimately granted asylum to the Agrarian leader. The fact that G. M. had worked for the British propaganda services during the war loomed large in the accusations against him. In every subsequent arrest of opposition activists, the charge of being 'an agent of Anglo-American imperialism' was sooner or later brought up.

Nevertheless, with only indirect evidence of Communist interference in the other parties' affairs, the British government could not make Communist behaviour the subject of any official action. Instead, the preferred British course was to raise objections to the electoral law and insist that any government formed as a result of it could not be viewed as representative or democratic. This was done simultaneously by the British delegation at Potsdam and the British representative to Bulgaria.[34] Houstoun-Boswall suggested a joint Anglo-American declaration stipulating that neither power would recognize the Bulgarian government.[35] The US State Department on its part favoured international observation of the Bulgarian elections. This was not acceptable to the FO, sensitive to Stalin's statement that the presence of foreign monitors in the Greek elections – another US suggestion – 'would be an insult to the Greek people and interference in Greek internal affairs'.[36] If Stalin was reluctant to sponsor a precedent, which might then be used to urge similar measures in Eastern Europe, the same may be said of the British government.[37]

Following closely the course of events in Bulgaria, the FO also sought the views of the principal opposition figures, who themselves were eager to consult the British mission. Houstoun-Boswall was able to report that in mid-July the government-sponsored negotiations between the two factions of the Agrarian Union, those of Alexander Obbov and Nikola Petkov, had failed, causing the latter's resignation from the government. This was accompanied by a letter to the Allies' missions, the ACC, the Bulgarian prime minister and regents, protesting against Communist terror against non-Communist candidates and asking for postponement of the elections.[38] As in August the remaining Agrarian and Social Democrat ministers and the finance minister, the independent Petko Stoyanov, left the government, a 'United Opposition' was formed. The centrepiece of its programme was the demand for the restoration of political rights and freedoms, accompanied by removal of the militia out of Communist hands and cessation of Communist interference in public institutions or private life.[39]

Most of the opposition's demands resonated with the views of the British representative that a high standard of electoral conduct should be set in Bulgaria. Meanwhile, the British mission understood that the opposition and wider anti-Communist circles in Bulgaria relied on staunch British support. At the end of July, even the Exarch Stephan, the head of the Bulgarian Orthodox Church, spoke to Houstoun-Boswall about the need to raise interest in the Bulgarian elections in the West. The exarch had just returned from Moscow and was convinced that the Soviet government would listen to British considerations and tame the Communist extremists; he also believed that with Western public endorsement the anti-Communist opposition would be much more willing to precipitate an electoral crisis.[40] In August Houstoun-Boswall received information that the Zveno leaders had not yet withdrawn their confidence from the government solely because they were not sure of consistent British support for the opposition.[41] The same was true of the two non-Communist regents who privately appealed to the British government to take some firm action.[42]

Just as Communists in Bulgaria were certain that the Western diplomats were secretly encouraging the opposition, the latter too seemed to take Western backing for granted. In fact, British policy makers hoped that the impending political crisis in Bulgaria could somehow be avoided.[43] The FO felt that it could be embarrassed by further active involvement with the opposition. Petkov was judged to be in considerable political and personal danger and Houstoun-Boswall was instructed to make it clear that the consequences of the opposition's actions were its own responsibility. The British government did not feel justified in directly encouraging Petkov and his associates as it would not be able to offer them any subsequent protection.[44]

An additional factor accounting for British hesitation was the ever-present concern for Soviet retaliation in Greece, where the political situation almost mirrored that in Bulgaria.[45] Closely supervised by Britain, the Greek government was in the middle of preparations for its first postwar elections. The British government believed that its involvement in Greece would guarantee the democratic conduct of the elections and the veracity of the result. However, the Greek Communists severely criticized Britain for creating unjust political conditions. The British government was particularly sensitive to such accusations as they were believed to reflect the views of the Soviet Union.[46]

The British government's position was also complicated by sudden US activity. Both the US representative in Bulgaria Maynard Barnes and Ambassador Harriman in Moscow had for some time complained to their superiors about the lack of evident US interest in the Bulgarian electoral issue. Their grievances appeared to have been heeded when in a speech on 9 August 1945 President Truman paid renewed attention to Bulgaria, Hungary and Romania. On 15 August, the State Department followed up with a note to the Bulgarian government stating that the United States would only resume diplomatic relations with a representative government, which the one formed after the approaching elections would categorically not be.[47] On 18 August, Secretary of State James Byrnes said the same in a public statement exposing Communist machinations in Bulgaria.[48] The Sofia government did not fail to notice that the British government was slow to associate itself with any of the US declarations.[49]

The FO was greatly offended by the United States' failure to consult it about the final text of the US note of 15 August 1945. Simultaneously, the FO felt under immense pressure to act with regard to Bulgaria.[50] British diplomats in the field saw a chance for 'an outstanding diplomatic victory in Soviet-controlled Europe', where British prestige and influence had reached 'the lowest possible ebb'.[51] In contrast, Whitehall officials preferred to 'keep to generalities' and undertake a course which, while making their views clear, would not expose them to a diplomatic rebuff. The Southern Department had very little hope indeed, that any Western rebuke of the Bulgarian Communists' methods would serve to promote democratic standards in the Bulgarian electoral campaign. British experts predicted a failure for any such initiative and were convinced it would harm Britain's standing in Bulgaria. They recommended instead a very mild approach which would be in step with the United States, without committing Britain to any radical measures in case of falsification or violence at the polls.[52] There was even serious consideration whether it was not better to wait until the Bulgarian elections had taken place: it would be easier to object to a manifest fraud, whereas any superficial change of the electoral law could still conceal Communist intimidation.[53] Finally, on 20 August 1945 the Bulgarian government was handed a note which simply outlined the reasons for British disapproval of electoral conditions in Bulgaria. This was immediately publicized by the British foreign secretary.[54]

The timing, motivation and content of Britain's declaration suggest that British policy makers favoured a distinctly lower-profile campaign in Bulgaria than had been launched by the United States. There had been insufficient high-level coordination between the two Western powers regarding electoral conditions in Bulgaria. The eventual British note resulted much more from unease that Britain should not be perceived as lagging behind the United States than from conviction that a British involvement in Bulgaria would serve a useful purpose.

The unexpected postponement

Dispatching the note of 20 August to the Bulgarian government, the FO felt it had done its best as far as Bulgarian elections were concerned. British policy makers were not optimistic of their ability to influence significantly Bulgarian internal developments and their action had partly been taken as a precaution against future accusations of acquiescent silence in the face of approaching totalitarianism. Three days before the date of the scheduled elections, an unforeseen opportunity for a much greater Western involvement on the ground appeared.

At a press conference on the evening of 22 August 1945, the Bulgarian foreign minister Petko Stainov stated that the British and US notes had produced a great political effect but had no juridical power. He explained that the Bulgarian government was subordinate to the ACC, which was the only institution competent to decide whether the elections could go ahead.[55] Historiography has accepted that Stainov's statement motivated the heads of the US and British missions in Sofia to seek a meeting with the chairman of the ACC and demand discussions regarding the elections. Stainov has been credited with a certain degree of independence, which provided an opportunity for Western action. Additionally, the US political representative is believed to have boldly surpassed his instructions, practically inducing Stainov to make his statement.[56] Available documents reveal that the incident was even more complicated and Stainov's motives less clear.

Events in Sofia were triggered by news from Romania, where the British and US representatives in the ACC had just initiated political conversations with the aim of resolving a government crisis. This provided an impulse for the British and US diplomats in Bulgaria to demand an appointment with Biryuzov about the pending elections. Judging by reports sent to London, Stainov gave his press conference after these demands had been registered.[57] Russian archives, on the other hand, show that on 22 August Stainov twice visited the Soviet mission. During the day he saw Biryuzov and recounted a conversation with Barnes, who had warned that the US and British notes were a step short of pulling out of Bulgaria. In the evening Stainov talked with the Soviet political adviser Stepan Kirsanov.[58]

If Stainov relayed his conversation with Barnes correctly, the latter did indeed exceed his instructions to a much greater extent than already assumed by historians. Barnes's warning might have been the reason for Stainov's press statement. On the other hand, it is equally possible that after being apparently cautioned by the American, Stainov informed the Soviet authorities and it was they who advised him to make his statement in view of their own prevalence in the ACC. As the full content of Stainov's meetings with the Soviet representatives is not known, any suggestion of possible Soviet influence on the foreign minister's statement for the press would be purely speculative. Yet it is significant that the released documents disclose that during the crisis he was in ongoing contact with the Soviet mission.

While the US and Soviet representatives were actively engaged in the events preceding the crisis of 22 August 1945, the British diplomats in Bulgaria seemed to have stood aside. They supported their US counterparts but in line with FO directives did not themselves initiate any action. In the next two days, however, the British representatives in Sofia played their part in the quickly evolving events.

On 23 August, identical notes from the US and British representatives to the Soviet High Command in Bulgaria referred to Stainov's statement of the previous day, asking for postponement of the elections until the ACC devised measures which would assure free and democratic conduct.[59] The FO was less than enthusiastic at the news and Sargent in particular considered a written request a rather unfortunate step. He was anxious lest the Soviet Union would interpret it maliciously as interference and then use it to pose as the defender of Bulgarian independence. He was certain that a mere postponement would not automatically remedy conditions. Most significantly, in his understanding the earlier British note to the Bulgarian government had been intended as 'a warning and nothing else'.[60] In effect, Sargent's comments were critical of Houstoun-Boswall for sending what was practically an unauthorized note to Biryuzov. Even so, the FO did not explicitly order its representative to abstain from further actions.

Upon Biryuzov's invitation, the US and British representatives presented their demands at a full meeting of the ACC at midnight on 23/24 August. They insisted on postponement of the elections until the government secured freedom of speech, press, radio and assembly and guaranteed free and secret balloting. In addition, the main opposition parties should obtain the right to hold their own party conferences and any other parties which could prove sufficient popular support should be legally registered. The fulfilment of these conditions should be entrusted to an interim 'Cabinet of Affairs', in which the powers of the prime minister should be assumed by the Regency Council and all principal parties should hold ministries.[61] The last point had not even been mentioned in correspondence with the FO or the State Department – another indication that the Western representatives in Sofia had acted spontaneously.

The Soviet members of the ACC tried to prevent a meaningful discussion of the Bulgarian situation. Kirsanov made a four-hour exposé going over each article of the electoral law in a legalistic manner and insisting that it was a model of democracy. He was finally interrupted by General Crane of the US mission, who reminded him that Britain and the United States had no intention of recognizing the Bulgarian government under the present circumstances. Crane suggested that the ACC should take responsibility to avoid a major inter-Allied conflict over Bulgaria by simply postponing the elections. Biryuzov simply agreed to refer the question to Moscow and adjourned the meeting at 5:00 a.m. The British representatives were satisfied that finally a frank exchange of views had occurred in a friendly atmosphere.

They did not hold high hopes for postponing the elections literally on the eve of the poll.[62]

At 11:00 p.m. on 24 August Biryuzov convened another tripartite meeting. He read out a letter from Stainov to the ACC effectively asking for postponement of the elections in view of the US and British representations. The ACC briefly discussed the letter and agreed a reply recommending postponement.[63] No one was more surprised at this outcome than the very people who had pressed for it.[64] Indeed, in his first telegram to London General Oxley thanked the Foreign Office for the support he believed it must have provided by coordinating representations in Moscow and Washington.[65] Months after the event Houstoun-Boswall continued to wonder at the Soviet government's climb down in such a short time and could only explain this by the factor of surprise.[66]

In its internal correspondence, the FO frankly admitted that the postponement of the Bulgarian elections well surpassed its greatest expectations. Houstoun-Boswall and General Oxley were congratulated. Senior officials felt, nevertheless, that success could be more realistically attributed to luck or Bulgarian hesitation rather than Western intervention. This attitude might be partly explained by the FO's reluctance to admit that a US initiative it had initially not approved had eventually succeeded. It is also significant of the FO's ability to recast past actions in a favourable light that after the postponement it informed the British press that the matter of the Bulgarian elections 'had been fully discussed' in the ACC and the decision had been reached after 'satisfactory co-operation'. Several months later, even Houstoun-Boswall began to claim that it had always been Britain's objective to postpone the August elections in Bulgaria.[67]

The FO could not but acknowledge that the postponement of the elections was the most important Western achievement in Bulgaria since the signing of the Bulgarian armistice. This could have significant consequences in as far as theoretically it increased the chances of a fairer second electoral campaign. It demonstrated the practical possibility for application of the principles of great-power cooperation and seemed to mark the real beginning of the second period in the work of the ACC for Bulgaria.[68] On the other hand there was renewed British apprehension about the price Soviet Russia would try to extract for its concurrence with Western demands in Bulgaria. Even British foreign secretary Ernest Bevin feared that the Soviet government would raise its stakes on some subject vital for Britain, such as fastening the conclusion of the Italian peace treaty to the international recognition of Bulgaria. The FO expected to witness increased Soviet attention to Greece too.[69]

With these reservations in mind, the FO was bewildered at the subsequent US actions in Bulgaria. On 27 August the US Secretary of State sent a note to the Bulgarian government expressing satisfaction with the decision to postpone elections. In addition, as a token of approval, the United States agreed to the appointment of an unofficial Bulgarian representative in Washington, for which Bulgaria had long asked. The Bulgarian official press quickly seized the opportunity to proclaim that diplomatic relations with the United States were restored. The FO received with incredulity the news that Barnes had even proposed bestowing a suitable US order on General Biryuzov.[70] The FO specialists saw in all this examples of incredibly 'muddled thinking'. Their general conclusion was that success had deprived the State Department of 'all sense of proportion'.[71] They were also worried that the conciliatory US actions would 'stultify the denunciation by Byrnes and Bevin and [...] discourage the moderate elements that there is consistent Anglo-American policy'. British observers were most displeased that the State Department's precipitate action had again been undertaken without consulting London.[72]

Preparation for Elections in November 1945

British policy makers did not overrate the effect of the postponement: the Bulgarian government had only conceded for the moment not to hold elections, which it realized would have been ruled unfair by the Western democracies.[73] However unexpected, this only constituted 'an initial step towards the satisfactory solution of the internal political situation' in Bulgaria.[74] The British political representative in Bulgaria agreed with his US colleague that 'any disposition [...] to rest on our oars can only give final victory in Bulgaria and throughout Eastern Europe to the Communists and the USSR'.[75]

Neither did the postponement of the elections bring any significant change in Britain's assessment of its own capabilities to influence developments in Bulgaria. The incidental success underlined the belief that British interest in the country could be defended only by constant pressure in Sofia and Moscow. To make its views known and taken into account, the British government had to tackle specific cases with determination and a clear notion of its objectives. In practice, in the late summer of 1945 the carrying out of free and unfettered elections in Bulgaria became an objective of British foreign policy in its own right. British representatives saw their role as ensuring the establishment of the conditions they had outlined in the fateful ACC meeting on 23 August.

British involvement with political liberalization

The FO considered that the alteration of the Bulgarian electoral law commanded priority, for instance removing the provisions for the government to disenfranchise opposition supporters or expel opposition members from the future parliament. Houstoun-Boswall encouraged the opposition to publicize its criticism of the law and put forward proposals for amendments. He asked some opposition leaders to prepare for him extensive memoranda on the electoral law with points on which he himself could press the government for improvements. Despite his clear sympathies, the British representative aimed for objectivity, which he considered the best protection against Soviet accusations of prejudice. He had the greatest understanding of the difficulties under which the opposition laboured but also felt frustrated with some of its 'childish demands and complaints'.[76] He and the FO severely criticized several opposition proposals, notably the disenfranchisement of soldiers on the grounds that they would vote according to the orders of their Communist commanders.[77]

By 14 September, when the Decree for the Amendment of the Electoral Law was published, the FO was satisfied that most of its demands had been addressed since the postponement of the elections. The last formal British objection was against the right of the government to remove deputies from the assembly, but the FO decided not to pursue this further.[78] For Houstoun-Boswall, there was not 'very much ground for complaint about the Law itself, at any rate judged by Balkan standards';[79] of more importance was the application of the law 'with a reasonable degree of fairness'.[80]

In the optimistic aftermath of the August electoral postponement, British diplomats had also considered the formation of a neutral cabinet to carry out elections, a possibility welcomed by the leaders of the opposition Agrarians and Social Democrats. Using his influence over the regent Venelin Ganev, an Anglophile member of Zveno, Houstoun-Boswall promoted the idea of a 'Cabinet of Affairs' to the other two regents, including the Communist Todor Pavlov. In early September they had managed to convert Prime Minister Kimon Georgiev himself in favour of 'strengthening and broadening' the basis of the government through including members of the opposition.[81] However, on 7 September, hours after the prime minister had been persuaded to give way to a caretaker cabinet, General Biryuzov had called on the regents to inform them in categorical terms that elections should be carried out under the current government or the USSR would withdraw protection from Bulgaria. Biryuzov's threat had the effect that the prime minister declared that he would remain in office unless the three Allies jointly recommended otherwise. Privately, Georgiev had complained that he was powerless in the presence of about two hundred thousand Soviet troops in Bulgaria, while no more than three British divisions were based in Greece.[82]

In the middle of September the NC of the FF itself initiated negotiations for the inclusion of the opposition in the government. These ended abruptly when the opposition put forward 10 firm conditions, most importantly the appointment of an Agrarian as premier and another non-Communist as interior minister.[83] In all likelihood, the Bulgarian Communists had hoped for some easy show of goodwill which Britain and the United States would accept. Another factor might have been the Soviet government's desire to appear flexible shortly before the upcoming first Council of Foreign Ministers in London. Stalin personally explained to leading Bulgarian Communists who immediately flew to Moscow after the postponement of the elections: 'It would be better if the Opposition was legalized, so you could handle them and force them to act loyally instead of going underground. It is in your interest that there should be Opposition. [...] It is even beneficial for you to have an Opposition of 50–60 people: you will boast to Bevin that you have an Opposition.'[84]

As a result, seeking to regain the political initiative the Communist Party supported political amnesty and politicians who had not entered the Fatherland Front were released from prison. On 7 September, non-FF parties were legalized, allowing for the establishment in opposition of Petkov's Agrarians, Kosta Lulchev's Social Democrats and the Democrats led by Nikola Mushanov and Alexander Girginov. Also, in a desperate attempt to be seen to be broadening its basis, the government included the leader of the re-established Radical Party Stoyan Kosturkov as minister of education, even though until 9 September 1944 he had been staunchly pro-German.[85]

Many Communist activists admitted that the compromises had been made under strong Soviet insistence to comply with the demands of the West.[86] Initially severely shocked by the postponement of the elections on which they had not even been consulted, the Bulgarian Communists accepted Stalin's argument of the necessity of maintaining good relations with Britain and the United States. For the time being the Soviet advice was 'not to shout too much about [...] eternal friendship with the Soviet Union'.[87] Vassil Kolarov, a well-known Communist politician and Comintern functionary, was sent from Moscow to Sofia to boost his party's morale. He led the renewed electoral campaign for the BCP with vigour, stating that the main tasks of the Communists in the new National Assembly would be to adopt a new constitution and proclaim a republic. Kolarov was more than once overheard saying that even though the Soviet government would make some apparent concessions in Bulgaria, he had been sent to make sure that these did not amount to much. He was convinced that the views of neither the British nor the US governments mattered, as both would capitulate once confronted with a fait accompli.[88]

The opposition was far from content with the changes to the electoral law or the relative political relaxation, which it considered to be mere window dressing. It related to the Western representatives the daily threats towards its leaders and supporters by the militia or Communist activists. Such encounters were especially vicious outside the capital where foreign observers rarely appeared and therefore could not report direct evidence to their governments. The British and US diplomats knew, however, that a number of the most prominent prewar leaders had been continually terrorized by being moved from prison to house arrest to hospital and back to prison even before their political activities were legalized.[89]

The British government was reluctant to increase official pressure on the Bulgarian government. As a result, the British mission in Bulgaria had no clear instructions on how to proceed and relied mainly on its own judgement. As the British political representative understood the situation, the postponement of the elections had given the opposition the previously denied chance to present its case and make a bid for power in Bulgaria. The opposition should use this opportunity even in the prevalent atmosphere of incertitude and pressure. The practical goal Houstoun-Boswall and his colleagues set themselves was to keep up the spirit of the Bulgarian opposition and give it moral support. Britain also perceived its role in overseeing the course of pre-electoral developments and scrutinizing the maintenance of general democratic conditions in Bulgaria.[90] Britain's efforts concentrated on the Agrarian Party as it was believed to be supported by at least eighty per cent of the population. Another aim was to convince the various opposition groups to combine their strength and unite against the Communists. This was partly achieved when upon Houstoun-Boswall's advice the right-wing Agrarian Gichev joined Petkov, who had already become the centre of anti-Communist resistance.[91]

One unexpected difficulty encountered by Houstoun-Boswall was that frequently the Bulgarian opposition turned a deaf ear to his doctrine of self-help. He reported an unhealthy tendency among opposition leaders 'to lie back [...] content with the reflection that everything is in the hands of [the Western governments]'.[92] Gradually, the British diplomat himself lost confidence in the aptitude of the Bulgarian politicians. Occasionally, he even doubted the democratic potential of the Bulgarian nation, in whom 'five hundred years of Turkish rule [had] implanted a slave mentality too deeply'.[93]

Daily observation of the Bulgarian political scene convinced British political and military officers in Bulgaria of the truth of the opposition's allegations about the dependence of the Bulgarian Communists on Moscow. As a result both General Oxley and Houstoun-Boswall recommended that the British government, in conjunction with the US government, should apply political pressure in the Soviet capital. Houstoun-Boswall believed that in the face of another joint British and US action, Stalin would not deem it expedient to support the Bulgarian Communists.[94] But Houstoun-Boswall's major concern was that he was left without a clear idea of the political and strategic importance his government attached to the country.[95] He was aware of the inability of the Southern Department to elaborate a consistent general line of policy towards Bulgaria. He accepted the argument that British involvement in Bulgaria would affect relations with Soviet Russia and have a long-term impact on the whole postwar European configuration of forces, but he recommended testing the Soviet will to cooperate in practice. He was not informed of the fact that internal FO debates were leading senior diplomatic staff in London to lean increasingly in the direction of a compromise with the Soviet Union. This would amount to confirming the spheres of interest in the Balkans. Such an attitude was reflected in Britain's decision not to take any action in Bulgaria until the outcome of the discussion of the Eastern European situation at the approaching London Council of Foreign Ministers was clear.[96] There the Western delegations demanded democratization of Bulgaria and Romania, while Molotov insisted that the regimes in both countries were fully representative and should be internationally recognized. In the wake of this deadlock, the FO briefly weighed up and dismissed the chances for a second postponement of the Bulgarian elections.[97]

In September and October 1945, despite great reservations the FO observed with certain satisfaction mixed with mild surprise the progress of the Bulgarian opposition. The latter was praised for taking full advantage of the freedom of the press and showing much courage in its anti-government campaign, all of which seemed to justify Britain's efforts.[98] Therefore, the decision of the opposition to boycott the elections came as a disappointment. The validity of the reasons for abstaining from the vote was fully recognized by British officials and diplomats who had long concluded that the elections would definitely be manipulated. The FO could also foresee one advantage in that, without the presence of the opposition in the future parliament, the latter could not claim to be representative. And yet, the FO instructed Houstoun-Boswall to urge Petkov to go to the polls.[99] Among the motives for such advice was the overriding fear in the FO that anything which could be interpreted as British obstruction in Bulgaria might bring Soviet retaliation elsewhere.

The Consequences of the Etheridge Mission

While British foreign-policy makers gradually realized that their involvement in the Bulgarian elections was not producing the desired results, their US counterparts decided to make another effort to influence political developments in Bulgaria. In October 1945, US Secretary of State Byrnes charged Mark Etheridge, a respected and experienced journalist and publisher, with the inspection of conditions in the country. Etheridge's appointment came on the heels of the conspicuous failure of the London Council of Foreign Ministers a little earlier. Barnes had been present at the London summit and had tirelessly repeated to State Department officials his case for tough pressure on Soviet Russia, in whose hands he believed Bulgaria's fate lay. For this reason, Barnes approved the dispatch of the Etheridge mission.[100] Cyril Black, one of Etheridge's principal assistants, who had profound knowledge and first-hand experience of the Balkans, shared Barnes' impressions. Black believed that the Etheridge mission was called for by the hardening US attitude to the Soviet Union, which had yet to be matched by a shift in US public opinion.[101]

Etheridge spent two weeks in Bulgaria, where he conversed with politicians from all shades of opinion and sounded both the Soviet and the British representatives. The opposition leaders described most forcefully the constant threats and obstruction of their activities by the government. They restated the main political demands they had presented to the government in September. Petkov also explained his decision to boycott the approaching elections partly as a result of the small likelihood that the United States would press for a second postponement. Etheridge considered the opposition's refusal to take part in the elections erroneous and said as much to the Bulgarian prime minister. Etheridge pressed Georgiev to admit that a possible solution was to reconstruct the Fatherland Front in its original form, which had been supported by the overwhelming majority of Bulgarians. But Georgiev repeated the official line that the opposition leaders themselves stood in the way of reforming the government.[102] To the Regency Council, Etheridge spoke of the impossibility of having a representative Bulgarian government without the Agrarian Union. He prompted the regents to extend the deadline for the nomination of candidates for election, an idea suggested to him by a number of anti-Communists.[103]

On 9 November 1945, Etheridge met Georgi Dimitrov, who had just arrived from Moscow to take part in the final stage of the electoral campaign. The leader of the Bulgarian Communists stated firmly that his presence in Bulgaria had been required to make sure a second postponement did not take place. He tried to reassure the US envoy that the Communists had no intention of monopolizing power and proposed to rule in alliance with the rest of the FF parties. He even mentioned the possibility of discussing the inclusion of opposition Agrarians and Social Democrats in the government after the elections. However, the overall impression the US delegation carried away was that all concessions the regime might make before the elections would be purely cosmetic. Etheridge formed a suspicion that the Communists intended to crush any opposition after the regime had won at the polls.[104]

The Bulgarian Communists believed the United States' involvement in Bulgaria to be 'a cunning manoeuvre against the government'.[105] Etheridge's arrival was seen as a pretext to postpone the elections once again, which would severely undermine the authority of the government and increase the ambitions of the centre-right parties. Therefore, even before Etheridge met with the most prominent non-Communist figures in the government, Kostov had achieved a clear understanding with Georgiev and war minister Damian Velchev that the elections would not be postponed, the government would not be reconstructed and any negotiation with the opposition would take place without outside mediation.[106]

In the course of their consultations in Bulgaria, the members of the Etheridge mission were increasingly convinced that the proper conduct of the elections required reorganization of the government and registration of separate party electoral lists, for which a second postponement was needed.[107] It was not certain that the State Department would approve such a solution. Etheridge was under double pressure – to find an alternative means of demonstrating undiminished US interest in Bulgaria and also somehow to prepare the way for a necessary US retreat on the subject of the Bulgarian elections. He proposed that his delegation should proceed to Moscow: after all Dimitrov himself had made it clear that important decisions regarding the Bulgarian elections were taken there. Heading for the Soviet capital, Etheridge was specifically instructed by Byrnes to recommend the postponement of the elections. This would allow enough time for the preparation of opposition electoral lists and for the reorganization of the government to include opposition representatives. Another point to press was the reorganization of the militia, which had to be taken out of Communist hands so that it could not be used as an instrument of repression over non-Communists.[108]

The Soviet government had access to full information about the course of the Etheridge mission as daily reports from Sofia reached Dimitrov while he was still in Moscow. The Bulgarian Communists were even able to relay to the Soviet government details of Etheridge's meeting with the prime minister, who had not hesitated to disclose them to Kostov.[109] The Soviet government had responded to Etheridge's arrival in Sofia by dispatching there the Soviet journalist Ilya Ehrenburg as a special correspondent. His articles for the Soviet press were carefully scrutinized by the DII. They extolled the achievements of the Fatherland Front and insisted that it had wide support from all progressive elements in Bulgarian society just as Etheridge was preparing to present exactly the opposite case to the Soviet government.[110]

In Moscow the special US representative was received by Vyshinski, to whom he made little secret of his negative judgement of conditions in Bulgaria. Vyshinski insisted that his own information was quite the opposite and ruled out postponement of the elections claiming that it would be an unjustifiable intervention. The Soviet government would have considered a request from the Bulgarian government, but Vyshinski was sure that such a request would not be forthcoming. This was the reverse of what Etheridge had found out in Bulgaria: only days earlier the Bulgarian prime minister had indicated that he would have made such a request had he been a free man.[111]

Britain's reaction to the Etheridge mission

Houstoun-Boswall found Etheridge agreeable and 'very level-headed'.[112] The British political representative in Sofia hoped the US mission was going to send a correct picture of the Bulgarian situation to Washington but failed to see how this would influence immediate developments in the country. What is more, in contrast to the Communist Kostov, who expected Etheridge's appearance to cheer the spirit of the opposition, Houstoun-Boswall was afraid that the opposition would lie back and place everything in the hands of the American.[113]

The appointment of the Etheridge mission caused mixed feelings at the FO, where the Balkan experts were slighted that they had not been consulted properly. Throughout the mission, there was an abundance of complaints about the short notice given and US failure to observe the principle of prior coordination.[114] The FO was further overcome by sudden resentment of the increased US role in the region. The Southern Department somewhat hesitantly claimed that Great Britain had a greater interest than the United States, not only in Bulgaria but also in Romania, which Etheridge was to visit too. Only rarely did anyone put forward the idea that as long as they achieved results Britain should not object to the more direct US methods.[115] Therefore, the British government reserved the right to make its own views known to the Soviet government.[116] British distrust of the US approach was to an extent matched by US desire to try to solve the Bulgarian problem alone. The State Department requested that there be no parallel British action as Etheridge's greatest asset was his being regarded as an independent enquirer.[117]

Only when Etheridge arrived in Moscow were British experts able to form a clear and objective opinion of his views. Etheridge talked with the British ambassador Clerk Kerr and the chargé d'affaires Frank Roberts and tried to explain how the specific actions he had recommended fitted in with US long-term policy. Etheridge proclaimed Bulgaria to be of similar strategic importance to Poland, with the added advantage of being accessible to the West from Greece and Turkey. His ideas revolved around the possibility for the West to buy Bulgarian products for political reasons and secure free Bulgarian commercial access to the Aegean through Salonika and Dedeagatch. The West could save the Bulgarian Agrarian Union, just as it had saved the Polish Peasant Party, by showing consistent interest in it. According to Etheridge, the West should also work for the withdrawal of the Red Army from Bulgaria.[118]

Even after this update on the progress of the mission, the FO retained a certain dislike of it. British observers could not overcome the feeling that the whole venture had 'somewhat flimsy grounds' and showed distinct relief at its predicted 'rapid and inglorious conclusion'.[119] British officials were especially sceptical of the practical results of the Etheridge talks but also noted that some Bulgarian Communist leaders were beginning to waver with regard to the elections. That is why Dimitrov had been promptly sent to Bulgaria to force through the elections on 18 November without any compromise with the opposition.[120] Some British analysts even saw the abortive September talks between the Bulgarian government and opposition as a sign that the Soviets had been considering changes in the regime to which the Etheridge mission had put an end.[121] On the whole, the FO concluded that the US action had been too aggressive and had actually stiffened the resolve of the Bulgarian Communists, who did not want to appear vulnerable to Western pressures. This can now be confirmed by evidence from letters from Kostov to Dimitrov discussing the best ways to demonstrate that the Bulgarian government 'would not waver at outside intervention and the Communists would stand firm' in the face of insidious manoeuvres.[122]

The question of another diplomatic note

At the conclusion of his Moscow visit Etheridge recommended that the US government issue a diplomatic note on the question of the Bulgarian elections. This should stipulate that the coming Bulgarian elections were not going to be held in a satisfactory democratic manner and therefore the United States would not recognize the resulting government.[123] Immediately, Houstoun-Boswall took the opportunity once more to persuade his superiors that a strongly worded note would tilt the balance in Bulgaria. It could precipitate the resignation of the Regency Council, which in turn would create enough justification for the postponement of the elections.[124] Neither this nor previous communications on the subject specified the expected advantages of a second postponement. The British representative seemed to be accepting the belief – or rather the hope – of the opposition leaders that another postponement would mean explicit criticism of the Communists, who would therefore alter their behaviour. Indeed, this scenario had been discussed with the regents and some opposition figures, but Houstoun-Boswall overlooked the fact that even the United States was not asking for a new postponement. Apart from that, to the British representative in Sofia, some official pronouncement that the Bulgarian government did not meet the criteria for recognition seemed to be the only 'stick' Britain had left in Bulgaria.[125]

On 14 November 1945, the US government requested Britain's support for a note of protest and the FO's initial reaction was to oblige promptly.[126]

On second thoughts, however, British officials realized that the proposed statement would make it impossible for Britain to recognize the Bulgarian government not just after the elections but for some considerable time afterwards.[127] It became important, therefore, to find a middle course which would keep in step with the United States but also not tie the hands of the British government. The compromise was discovered in a formula which would simply say that Britain did not consider the Bulgarian government as 'democratic and representative'.[128] This subtle distinction was hardly going to be acknowledged outside Western diplomatic circles, and the FO quickly dropped it. The members of the Southern Department began arguing that as the situation in Bulgaria had not changed since August, the note which had been sent to the Bulgarian government then was still in force and rightly expressed the official British views. Foreign Secretary Bevin personally reviewed Britain's position and concluded that it would be a mistake to send a new note. The only remaining problem was how to wriggle out of the US proposal. A pretext was found in the fact that the US Embassy in London had not forwarded its government's request for support to the FO.[129]

At the end of the Etheridge mission, the British government faced the question of whether to repeat its action in Bulgaria from the previous August, namely to state before the ballot that the emergent government would not be regarded as representative. This would amount to admitting that the tactics employed so far had not produced any significant result. Despite the August postponement of elections and the ensuing Western pressure campaign on the Bulgarian government, the conditions for the establishment of democracy in Bulgaria had barely improved. British official circles had to recognize that their best diplomatic efforts regarding Bulgaria were all but wasted. The FO was rapidly moving towards the opinion that since it could not influence Bulgarian developments, it should not object to them and thus merely expose British impotence in the face of dictatorship. What is more, the deadlock in relation to Bulgaria and the other ex-satellites was being used by the Soviet Union to prevaricate on other issues of importance for the West. That is why senior British diplomats began pressing more vigorously than ever for a compromise to be reached at the approaching December Council of Foreign Ministers in Moscow.

On 16 November 1945, the opposition made a last desperate effort to recreate the conditions that had brought the August postponement of elections. It sent identical letters to the prime minister, the ACC and the Allies' missions stating that the political atmosphere in the country had not improved but on the contrary the terror of the authorities had increased.[130] Almost simultaneously, the United States delivered a note to the Bulgarian government expressing conviction that the results of the elections would not reflect the democratic choice of the Bulgarian people and therefore it would refuse to recognize the new government.[131]

This action was not matched by a similar British one, despite Houstoun-Boswall's numerous warnings that the Bulgarian government and, he believed, the Soviet government were 'openly banking [...] on divergence of opinion between HMG and USG'.[132] Indeed, the lack of a British note softened the blow of the US declaration, but Houstoun-Boswall's last-minute appeals did not activate any change of mind at the FO.[133] During the week of the Bulgarian elections, the mission in Sofia was left without any communications from London whatsoever. In vain did the representatives in Bulgaria plead for 'any (even private) indication of the attitude of HMG'.[134] It was almost a week after the elections that an FO letter explained to Houstoun-Boswall that the British government had resolved 'not to tie [their] hands with a public statement'.[135]

As scheduled, the Bulgarian general elections took place on 18 November 1945. There was little overt physical violence on the polling day. The government reported a turnout of 85.2 per cent, of which 88.3 per cent voted for the Fatherland Front. Boycotting the elections, the opposition had campaigned for the casting of blank ballots. The government proclaimed these invalid. The number of blank ballots together with the number of people who had genuinely abstained from the vote constituted just below a quarter of the electorate. The smallest government majority was recorded in the biggest towns, possibly due to more stringent supervision. In addition, the fact that the publication of results in Sofia and some other major towns was delayed suggested falsifications.[136]

On the basis of the official statistics, the FO concluded that at least a quarter of Bulgarians were opposed to the government. This was not considered an implausible result given that a big proportion of the electorate was illiterate, the electoral campaign had taken place in an atmosphere of Communist intimidation and psychological coercion, and the opposition 'had not put up a serious show'.[137] In any case, British observers had not expected more than forty per cent for the opposition in a fair election.[138] At the same time, Houstoun-Boswall wrote that members of the ruling coalition had been allegedly shaken by the real results of which they were aware. There were rumours that local Communist leaders had been 'upbraided' by Georgi Dimitrov, who himself had been reprimanded from Moscow for having misled the Soviets. It was also said that a secret Soviet mission had been sent to Bulgaria to investigate the real state of affairs.[139]

In the anticlimax after the elections, British diplomats tried to analyse the developments of the previous months in view of the necessity to modify policy to Bulgaria. Houstoun-Boswall could claim to have the best insight into the machinations of the Bulgarian Communists, whom he had observed closely for more than a year. He was convinced of their being manipulated according to the objectives of Soviet foreign policy. He expected the radical Left elements in the FF government to work for the implementation of political and economic measures, which would not only consolidate their power but also strengthen the Soviet hold on Bulgaria. Apart from binding the Bulgarian economy to the USSR, the British political representative predicted the proclamation of a republic to be followed by steps for the establishment of a South Slav federation.

Houstoun-Boswall's outlook was inevitably shaped by his proximity to the Bulgarian political scene. Naturally, he felt more involved with events in Bulgaria than his superiors in London but was not misled about the low priority of the country in overall British policy. However, he insisted that the pattern evolving in Bulgaria, where the Soviet hold was the firmest, would illuminate future developments in the rest of Soviet-dominated Europe. Events in neighbouring countries, such as the proclamation of the Yugoslav Republic, could in turn indicate correctly the direction in which Bulgaria would go. For Houstoun-Boswall, only a holistic approach to the region could slow the Soviet determination to fortify Soviet positions in the Balkans. He was categorical that Bulgaria was being permanently drawn into the 'vortex' of Soviet security, with its strategic as well as purely ideological dimensions. The real importance of this was, of course, its bearing on the protection of British communications and interests in the Near and Middle East. This required a thorough reassessment of policy towards Bulgaria and clarification of British long-term objectives.

Houstoun-Boswall's general examination of the unstable British position in Bulgaria was not followed by any concrete proposals for action. He was aware that Great Britain could lend Bulgaria no 'physical aid in any shape or form to stand up to its liberators'.[140] All he could suggest was that British disapproval of the strengthening Soviet control over Bulgaria should be made clear to the Soviet government – from a common Anglo-American front.[141] Houstoun-Boswall's assessment was confirmed by Clerk Kerr, who saw no way to reverse the decisive Soviet influence over Bulgaria. British diplomats in Moscow warned of Soviet malicious capability to interpret British action with regard to Bulgaria as aimed at weakening the Soviet hold. They advised the FO not to bring the question of the Bulgarian regime to the attention of the Soviet government as this would only rock overall Soviet-British relations without any real chance for local advantages. Any momentary British gains in Bulgaria would most certainly be compensated by Soviet troublemaking in areas of far greater importance for Great Britain.[142]

The Southern Department agreed with the gloomy judgement of the picture in Bulgaria and could not see any obvious formula for improvement.

British policy makers became increasingly uncertain that they should try to apply any pressure regarding the Bulgarian issue as they had serious doubts whether Bulgaria could be converted into a genuine democracy at all. Simultaneously, however, some reluctance to give up completely the erstwhile aim of promoting political and economic freedom lingered on at the FO. The two conflicting lines of reasoning informed the search for an adjusted British approach to Bulgaria in the months after the November 1945 elections.[143]

* * *

Britain had followed the United States in the effort to secure the August 1945 postponement of elections in Bulgaria. In the course of this episode, it had become clear for British policy makers that they had managed to slow down the advance of Communist power in Bulgaria only because the Soviet government had apparently been presented with a unified and strong Anglo-American front. At the time, the postponement had assumed an importance of its own, but once achieved it required the elaboration of further means to follow up and build upon the unexpected success. The period between August and November 1945, when elections were finally carried out, was crucial for the clarification of long-term British attitudes to Bulgaria.

In retrospect, the FO realized that the practical effect of the August postponement of the elections was somewhat dubious. It was little more than an exception and did not change the intentions of the Bulgarian Communists, but it certainly alerted them to the need to proceed with their plans more carefully so as not to cause international embarrassment for their 'Big Friend'. But they were also able to consolidate their position by reorganizing the ruling political coalition they dominated and by working for the disintegration of the opposition. Nor had the postponement of the Bulgarian elections brought any change in the pattern of British–Soviet relations regarding Eastern Europe. The momentary Soviet acquiescence in Western demands did not lessen overall Soviet influence in Bulgaria, which was based foremost on the links of the BCP with the Soviet Union. The correct evaluation of this situation drove British foreign-policy experts to the unequivocal conclusion that there was precious little they could do to affect the course of events in Bulgaria, meaning they had to cut their losses and save face while aiming to preserve their influence in the southern part of the Balkans.

British hesitance to become involved in Bulgarian affairs in the second half of 1945 had been overshadowed by unusual US activism at the time of the postponement of the elections. At that time, US recognition of Soviet interests in Eastern Europe was still not judged incompatible with the existence of independent democratic states. The Etheridge mission was launched as an attempt to overcome the deadlock regarding Bulgaria. Its advice for a second electoral postponement served no useful purpose in British eyes. The futility of the US initiative convinced the British government that no precipitate action was desirable in Bulgaria. It also made the FO conscious of the need to persuade the United States that there was no feasible alternative to the increasing British resignation to the situation in Bulgaria.

Chapter Five

RECOGNIZING THE BULGARIAN COMMUNIST REGIME

Continuing to scrutinize the Bulgarian political scene after the elections of 18 November 1945, British representatives in Sofia were especially interested in the balance of forces in the government and the relations between the parties within the ruling Fatherland Front. Details assumed great importance as foreign observers found it increasingly difficult to follow the trends inside the Bulgarian government due to the growing hostility of the Communists to contacts with Western representatives.

The electoral results provided the Fatherland Front government with a certain degree of legitimacy as well as stabilized the position of the Communist Party. While the Soviet Union had restored full diplomatic relations on 14 August 1945, Bulgaria still needed to secure recognition from Great Britain and the United States,[1] which would bestow upon the Bulgarian regime the moral privilege of acceptance in the international community. It would also allow Bulgaria to resume normal international trade which was crucial for the country's postwar reconstruction and internal consolidation.

The Soviet Union too had a stake in both the moral and economic aspects of the recognition of the Bulgarian government. The resumption of normal relations with the Western democracies, therefore, could be interpreted by friends and foes of Communism alike as acquiescence in the exclusive Soviet influence over Bulgaria. Since it was suspected that Soviet activity in Bulgaria formed a part of the larger pattern of establishment of Soviet dominance in Eastern Europe, Britain's attitude to the country had to be consistent with overall British policy to the Soviet zone.

Even though Britain interpreted political developments in Bulgaria in 1945–46 as contrary to the provisions of the Yalta Declaration, concern about the Soviet threat to British positions in the Mediterranean and the Middle East overruled any general anxiety for democracy in Bulgaria in particular and in Eastern Europe as a whole. At the same time, the emerging strategic conflict could be formulated most eloquently in ideological terms with Soviet actions presented as antidemocratic. At the end of 1945, Sargent wrote:

> We are trying to put a limit to Russian expansion in the Middle East and in fact to build up a kind of Monroe system in that area. This makes it of vital importance that Bulgaria should be an independent buffer state. If Bulgaria remains a Russian satellite it will always be in the power of the Soviet Government to use Bulgaria to keep Turkey and Greece perpetually on tenterhooks [...] with disastrous effects to our whole position in the Eastern Mediterranean.[2]

Here was the justification for engagement in Bulgarian affairs in a nutshell. In order to counter Soviet influence in the Balkans, Britain was committed to supporting the opposition, which was not susceptible to control from Moscow but could only thrive if political liberties were observed.

The Moscow Council of Foreign Ministers

The elections of 18 November 1945 produced a National Assembly in which only the parties remaining in the Fatherland Front were represented. In the coalition itself, Petkov's Agrarians and Grigor Cheshmedzhiev's Social Democrats who had broken away were substituted for leftist factions of their own parties prepared to collaborate with the Communists. Pro-Communist interference also forced a split in Zveno, although its most prominent leaders Georgiev and Stainov continued as premier and foreign minister respectively. Having been so far regarded by Western observers as the moderate elements in the Bulgarian cabinet, their behaviour before and during the elections raised suspicions that they might turn into 'not only willing tools [...] but [...] star players on the Communist side'.[3]

In late November and December 1945, the Bulgarian government made several unofficial attempts to find out the terms under which the Western Allies might reconsider their views that it was not representative.[4] The Communists understood that the basic criterion was the provision for normal political activity of the opposition, which should eventually re-enter the government. That is why shortly after the elections the Communists reassessed their attitude to the parties outside the Fatherland Front. At the Ninth Plenum of the Central Committee on 12 December 1945, Kostov stated that 'because of internal as well as international considerations' the Communist Party was interested in cooperation with 'the democratic part of the bourgeoisie and bourgeois intellectuals'.[5] At the same time, leading Communists warned the opposition publicly that unless it returned to the Fatherland Front, it would be regarded as 'a reactionary adversary fascist force', which would be 'ruthlessly revealed and destroyed'.[6]

The Moscow advice

On 7 December 1945, three weeks after the Bulgarian elections, Etheridge submitted his final report to US secretary of state James Byrnes. Etheridge concluded that in Bulgaria, as well as Romania, an authoritarian regime excluded representatives of large segments of democratic opinion. He confirmed that in both countries the local Communists were supported by the Soviet Union, which used them to achieve domination of the Balkans as a stepping stone towards the Mediterranean. While acknowledging the security concerns of the Soviet Union in the region, Etheridge's report did not accept them as legitimate reasons for the denial of free elections.[7]

Etheridge was pessimistic about the prospect for genuinely free elections in Bulgaria. Even so, he proposed a number of improvements that would address the most obvious British and US criticisms. In the first instance, the current government should be reorganized to include leaders of all parties which had originally adhered to the FF programme. An equally important requirement was that the Ministries of Justice and the Interior should be taken out of Communist control. The government should then conduct fresh elections in which all democratic parties should be free to participate on the basis of single or separate lists according to their choice. Further, the current National Assembly should concentrate on calling new elections for a Grand National Assembly which should revise the constitution.[8] Etheridge himself accepted that this was a maximum programme and was prepared to regard the implementation of even half the measures as good progress. He placed his belief in the moderates within the Communist Party, who were allegedly urging for an end to excesses.[9] The report was generally approved by Barnes in Sofia, whose experience with the Soviets prompted him to point out that it was more important to insist on some positive action rather than to expect them to agree with a condemnation of the existing situation.[10]

The members of the Etheridge mission believed that their outspoken reproach of the Communist regimes in Bulgaria and Romania would shock US public opinion.[11] However, the US government itself was not yet ready to reveal publicly its displeasure with events in the Soviet zone. Moreover, open and sharp US criticism of Soviet policy in the Balkans was itself certain to exacerbate tensions among the three Allies.

Etheridge's report was circulated only among a limited circle of US policy makers and was not even forwarded to London. It was used as the main brief of the US delegation at the December 1945 Moscow Council of

Foreign Ministers. The council assembled at the insistence of Byrnes, who was particularly anxious to resume discussion and reach compromises on the issue of the ex-satellites. The US secretary of state thought it essential to overcome the deadlock from the previous meeting in London regarding Bulgaria and Romania.[12] He was guided equally by concern for democracy in Eastern Europe and by compulsion to resolve the controversy on the political situation in the Balkans before the conclusion of peace treaties with the former minor Axis powers.

As the Moscow Conference was a result of US efforts to improve political conditions in Bulgaria and Romania, its outcomes are easily attributed to US action. A closer look at the proceedings reveals that the compromise reached regarding the two Balkan countries was as much a Soviet initiative. Byrnes himself confirmed that initially Stalin had refused to consider any proposal, which undermined the results of the November elections in Bulgaria. Subsequently, Stalin himself suggested an arrangement whereby members of the Bulgarian opposition could be included in the government in exchange for Western recognition. Faced with the prospect of another fruitless conference, the US delegation agreed.[13] On 27 December 1945, the Moscow Council issued a communiqué stating that the Soviet government would give 'friendly advice' to the Bulgarian government to include two opposition politicians. They should be truly representative of their parties and willing to work with the government. On their part, Britain and the United States undertook to recognize the Bulgarian government once these conditions were fulfilled.

It is not easy to explain why the Soviet Union showed willingness to consider favourably some of the Western demands in Bulgaria. It is possible that Stalin desired to regain credit lost in London in September and tried to reciprocate Byrnes' obvious eagerness for an understanding over Eastern Europe. In addition, Molotov was undoubtedly impressed by the US inclination to allow Bulgaria to forego reparations to Greece and even consider the possibility of a Bulgarian outlet on the Aegean.

Archival evidence, however, also reveals that the Soviet government grasped the Moscow decision as an opportunity for mending relations with the West without encroaching on the position of the Bulgarian Communists. Before making his proposal to the conference, Stalin wrote to Dimitrov about the US suggestion that the Bulgarian government should be reorganized. Stalin advised the Bulgarian Communists to consider including one or two ministers from opposition circles in the government. Stalin told Dimitrov that someone 'not too popular' – rather than Petkov – should be given 'some insignificant ministry'. This would achieve the double result of drawing some politicians away from the opposition and giving some satisfaction to the West. Apparently, the Soviet leader considered the Bulgarian Communists sufficiently in control of the situation to be able to grant some minor concessions without tipping the overall political balance.[14]

The Bulgarian Communists faithfully embraced Moscow's line, convinced that Stalin intended to follow the letter of the communiqué without fulfilling the original Western expectations. Dimitrov deliberately misrepresented Britain's and the United States' position as a conspiracy to form a government of the opposition. He stated triumphantly that the Moscow decision indirectly recognized the November elections, the resultant National Assembly and the existing government. He assured the Communist Politburo that the Moscow communiqué merely gave 'Britain and the USA a chance to save their face'.[15] For Kolarov, the decisions of the Moscow Council meant that the two Western powers had acknowledged the predominant interest of the Soviet Union in Bulgaria.[16] Such an interpretation echoed Stalin's boasting to a Bulgarian government delegation that he had been able to limit what he called 'the demands of the Anglo-Americans' and in some cases discard them altogether.[17]

The Moscow decision was welcomed by that part of the US administration which was inclined to compromise with the Soviet Union in the name of good postwar relations. Byrnes spoke publicly of his hope that the application of the Moscow decision would improve the democratic character of the two East European governments and that for the first time after Yalta this would be done in conjunction with the Soviet Union.[18] On the other hand, President Truman, who was believed to be the leading proponent of firmness towards the Soviet Union, stated firmly on 8 January 1946 that the Bulgarian government would not be recognized without guarantees for free and unfettered elections.[19] By then, the first round of talks between the opposition and the government in Bulgaria had already ended in failure.

The British government had little choice but to subscribe to the compromise. Indeed, Bevin had agreed to go to Moscow only after he faced the threat of being left out of any US–Soviet agreement.[20] His reluctance was partly due to the fact that Britain had not been consulted before the US proposal for the meeting was sent to Stalin. More importantly, at the end of 1945 the British government saw little chance for genuine long-term solution of the conflicts with the Soviet Union regarding internal developments in Eastern Europe. By this time, Bevin was convinced that the Soviet Union was aiming to undermine Britain's position in the Mediterranean and the Middle East.[21] British foreign-policy makers were increasingly more concerned with securing British strategic positions in the Balkans rather than with what was perceived as short-lived improvement of political conditions in the Soviet zone. Yet the effort to limit Soviet influence in the Eastern Mediterranean was linked to involvement in internal Bulgarian politics where Britain associated with the ambitions of the Bulgarian anti-Communist opposition.

The first round of negotiations and Vyshinski's mission

The Moscow communiqué spread optimism among leading Bulgarian Communists. They confirmed their intention to avoid unnecessary clashes and take every opportunity to come to terms with Britain and the United States. They also believed that the Western powers themselves had no choice but to 'bow to the existing circumstances' in Bulgaria.[22] Confident in their superiority, the Communists perceived the Moscow decision as a magnanimous concession to the opposition, which should not be allowed to disrupt the balance of the government. In addition, the Communists saw a welcome possibility to split their opponents even further. It was assumed that various opposition groups would want to participate in power, and therefore the Communists would be able to handpick the two opposition representatives to enter the cabinet.[23]

This tactical plan was devised on the background of firm Soviet control over Bulgaria. The Soviet High Command was issuing orders to stop opposition newspapers and even to take plays off the stage of the National Theatre. On 18 December 1945, the Soviet delegation to the ACC had sent the Bulgarian Foreign Ministry a letter categorically insisting that communications from the ACC should be treated as 'official orders which require precise and timely fulfilment'.[24] The government's position was presented to the opposition in a memorandum, which stipulated that the opposition members who accepted office should endorse the present government's domestic and foreign policy. Parliament would sit until the end of the current session in March 1946. The only prospective concession was that future elections should be discussed without restriction of the right to nominate separate electoral lists.[25]

The opposition in Bulgaria judged the Moscow decision on the whole positively. For them, the communiqué had publicly acknowledged the nonrepresentative character of the present Bulgarian government and had stressed the importance of their own existence.[26] That is why, on 4 January 1946, the Agrarians led by Petkov and the Social Democrats led by Pastuhov accepted the government's invitation to talks. They handed the government their own proposals for the fulfilment of the Moscow decision. Insisting on government guarantees for 'liberty of press, thought, assembly and association', the opposition emphasized its requirement for fresh elections to be carried out according to a new electoral law. As a sign of its own good will, the opposition pointed out that it was ready to appoint only two ministers as opposed to the six they had had before walking out of the cabinet in August 1945. Despite this, the Bulgarian government announced that the opposition was disregarding the friendly Soviet advice and ended negotiations.[27]

It is likely that during these brief contacts the Communists were disappointed that the opposition showed no signs of disintegrating as they had predicted.

They might have even feared that the government could have been unwittingly strengthening the opposition by treating it on an equal basis. If the Bulgarian government had acted on its own by closing down the short-lived talks, its actions soon found approval in Moscow.

On 7 January 1946, a Bulgarian delegation consisting of Kimon Georgiev, Petko Stainov and Interior Minister Anton Yugov flew to the Soviet capital for a special meeting with Stalin and Molotov.[28] The visit was shrouded in secrecy and Western observers could only guess that it was part of the process by which Bulgarian leaders were 'being coached to play their part in the formulation of the Russian foreign policy programme'.[29] BCP archives show that Stalin spent two hours with the Bulgarian delegation analysing the whole post-armistice period. He made particular efforts to assure the Bulgarian ministers that Soviet Russia had the interests of Bulgaria at heart, pledging lasting support in return for 'certainty that Bulgaria would never become the terrain for adversary initiative and aggression'.[30] Posing as the protector of Bulgarian interests, Stalin also described how he had succeeded in resisting the Western foreign ministers' demands, which, he implied, were harmful for both Bulgarian and Soviet interests. He had only agreed to a reconstruction of the Bulgarian government as this simply meant the inclusion of two opposition members.[31] Stalin even seriously reprimanded the Bulgarian representatives for entering into negotiations with Petkov and Lulchev: 'You should have just plainly pointed out the decisions of the conference and invited them to appoint two of their representatives loyal to the Fatherland Front. Why was it necessary for these representatives to give you declarations on this or that? You, with your tactic, have made the opposition think that you need them when in fact you don't need them at all.'[32]

Stalin thus castigated what he interpreted as the excessive zeal of the Bulgarian government to fulfil the Moscow advice. On the other hand, he declared the opposition's refusal to follow Soviet guidance to constitute an argument with the Soviet Union itself. For this reason, the Soviet government would assume responsibility for the failure of the Moscow decision if the Bulgarian government strictly followed instructions from Moscow. To show that he meant business, Stalin ordered Vyshinski to depart immediately for Sofia and explain the exact meaning of the Moscow decision to the opposition. To the visiting Bulgarian delegation Stalin confessed that in practice Vyshinski 'had no mission' apart from relaying once again the Moscow communiqué.[33]

Both Lulchev and Petkov refused to bow to what were effectively Vyshinski's threats and commands to enter the government without being granted any concessions in exchange. Vyshinski's unyielding attitude was based on Stalin's personal instructions not to negotiate with the opposition but simply to require it to nominate two politicians for inclusion in the government. After two days in

Sofia, Vyshinski proclaimed that no compromise was feasible and left Bulgaria, thus signalling the end of Soviet endorsement of the Moscow decision.[34] Stalin preferred that the Bulgarian government could have presented itself as representative but he was 'not willing to compromise [...] the realities of Russian influence to obtain this end'.[35]

Britain's Search for Alternatives

By mid-January 1946 the Moscow communiqué had become subject to two irreconcilable interpretations. The Bulgarian government insisted that the opposition should take up ministerial posts thus showing willingness to cooperate. The latter pointed to the provisions that those entering the government should be truly representative of their parties and therefore required preliminary concessions. These differences were reflected in the opinions of Soviet Russia and the Western powers, which backed the interpretations of the government and the opposition respectively. This situation gave confidence to the Bulgarian Communists and Dimitrov proclaimed at the Parliamentary Commission for Foreign Affairs that the lack of unanimous opinion among the three Allies 'untied' the hands of the government to follow the more advantageous Soviet interpretation.[36]

The Bulgarian Communists were anxious to attribute the refusal of the opposition to comply with their demands to British and US influence. In documents for internal Communist use, Petkov's group was portrayed as 'organized and inspired by British and US intelligence', who urged the opposition towards 'more energetic terrorist actions'.[37] In contrast to such allegations, the British and US archives reveal that while feeling unable to advise the Bulgarian opposition to enter the government, the Western governments did little to bolster it. The British and US representatives in Sofia expended substantial energy urging their governments to activate policy towards Bulgaria. Britain and the United States, however, experienced difficulty in deciding how to react to the failure of the Moscow decision. Both subscribed to the view that nothing in the communiqué stopped the opposition from laying down advance conditions. They did not feel compelled to insist on the opposition just entering the government under any circumstances.[38] Despite analysing the situation in similar terms, British and US policy makers proposed different actions, just as their motives for signing the Moscow communiqué had been different.

The US political representative in Sofia urged the State Department to accept that the Moscow formula had not been based on an honest appraisal of the situation. He was in favour of firm action to resolve the deadlock but also warned that if the great powers did not try to enforce some compromise, 'much blood will be spilled in Bulgaria'.[39] Even if sceptical of these extreme pronouncements and radical recommendations, the State Department considered the moment ripe for some new 'constructive proposals', such as new elections after the dissolution of the present assembly, to be advanced to the Soviet government.[40]

Unlike the State Department, the Foreign Office had little faith in Britain and the United States' abilities to exert pressure on political developments in Bulgaria. The discussion of Bulgarian affairs rarely went beyond the FO and there is no evidence that the Moscow decision was discussed by the British cabinet. Occasional references to the difficulties of the Bulgarian opposition were made in the House of Commons, but mostly these were prompted by the FO itself. Whitehall officials had long realized that there was precious little they could do to stop Communist advances and Soviet domination in Bulgaria. Analysing events from the latter half of 1945 and the beginning of 1946, they were deeply sceptical that any course short of confrontation with the Soviet Union would produce the changes Britain desired in Bulgaria. And since a definitely anti-Soviet stance was out of the question, the only rational attitude was that of conciliation and downplaying the differences with the USSR. This line of reasoning was gradually crystallizing among British foreign-policy makers, but its adoption was preceded by some contradictory behaviour.

Signals from Sofia unmistakably pointed out that parallel to the consolidation of power of the Bulgarian Communists, the Soviet government was entrenching itself even more firmly in Bulgaria. The FO concluded that it was useless to pursue any further the implementation of the Moscow advice, or for that matter, to put forward any new initiative. At the end of January 1946, the FO told the State Department that as far as Bulgaria was concerned they should both wait for the next move to come from Moscow.[41] Such a decision was a far cry from the recommendation of Houstoun-Boswall that the British government assume a firm attitude, abandon half measures and refuse to negotiate with the unrepresentative Bulgarian government at the forthcoming Paris Peace Conference in May.[42] In fact, the FO had in mind exactly the opposite – that is, not to cause any hold-up of the peace negotiations.

The confusion in the FO is especially obvious from the contradictory messages it sent to the British representative in Bulgaria. Within the same week at the end of January 1946, Houstoun-Boswall was instructed to uphold the demands of the opposition, then to take special care not to antagonize the Soviets and finally also not to oppose any new action initiated by the United States.[43] Senior British civil servants were reluctant to make a definite public statement about the existence of disagreements with the Soviet Union regarding Bulgaria. This was exasperating to British officials in the field and irritating to the State Department.[44]

Contradicting his own initial recommendation for silent firmness, Houstoun-Boswall proposed a strong-worded British declaration to sober up the Soviet government. His superiors, though, were not worried by the prolongation of the indefinite state of affairs in Bulgaria, and at times even mentioned that there was 'a good scope for bargaining' there. The latter judgement was based on the assumption that eventually the Bulgarian government would seek recognition, and on this score Britain possessed advantages.[45]

Sargent himself wrote inconsistent notes. He was most certain that the prospects of genuine free elections seemed distinctly unlikely. He was extremely pessimistic of British ability to influence Bulgaria and yet, even he occasionally suggested some approach to the USSR for 'diluting' the existing Bulgarian government. Then, he thought, additional concessions for foreign journalists and for a greater degree of individual freedoms could be achieved through 'nagging'.[46] But this contained the inherent danger of actually signalling British lack of deep interest in the future of the country and above all lack of resources to underpin open disagreement with the USSR. Britain's ill-defined course towards Bulgaria was exposed even further against the background of disturbances in the Peloponnese and Soviet–British friction at the United Nations. From this, it would be obvious to Soviet foreign-policy specialists as well as to political observers in Bulgaria that the real concerns of Great Britain in the Balkans were related to the strategic defence of the Mediterranean; any interest in the establishment of democracy in Bulgaria took a distinctly secondary importance. Such conclusions would make it difficult for the Bulgarian opposition leaders to maintain a courageous attitude in the face of renewed political attack from the Communists.[47]

As if sensing this hesitation, at the end of January 1946, the Bulgarian minister of foreign affairs pleaded with the British representative not to place his government in the position of 'having to choose between one Ally who is here in force and the two Allies who are not physically here'. He repeated that any solution of the Bulgarian situation must be imposed from without and only by the Big Three Allies in agreement.[48]

During the later half of January and in February 1946, the US State Department was actively trying to elaborate yet another initiative regarding Bulgaria which would be acceptable to the Soviet Union. The best option which emerged was to persuade the Soviets to send new advice to the Bulgarian government, this time proposing dissolution of the National Assembly after its current session and the calling of fresh elections. The United States would then respond by agreeing to recognize the Bulgarian government if the latter guaranteed full civil liberties.[49] It is not clear how the State Department hoped to induce the Soviets to adopt the proposed course. In any case, some US government advisors understood that the proposition was inherently flawed since it would commit the United States to recognizing the Bulgarian government in exchange for promises, which in the light of past experience were unlikely to be honoured.

In view of this, on 22 February 1946, the United States sent the Bulgarian government a note urging the renewal of negotiations between the Bulgarian government and the opposition. In practice the note restated the provisions of the Moscow decision.[50]

The British representative in Sofia was instructed to support the US note only verbally. The British government's intention was to register disapproval of the Bulgarian government without entering into formal discussion. Unwittingly, this complicated the situation as the Bulgarian foreign minister Stainov was able to tell the press that he had not received any written British communication.[51] In the meantime the Soviet government practically accused the United States of violating the Moscow decision by encouraging the Bulgarian opposition to resist it.[52] In its turn, the Bulgarian government was quick to declare that until the evident differences between the Allies were cleared, it could only follow Vyshinski's authoritative interpretation of the Moscow agreement.[53] Finally, the FO was pushed to issue on 11 March 1946 an official communiqué confirming its subscription to the US interpretation of the Moscow decision.[54] Not long afterwards, on 22 March 1946 a British note was also presented to the Soviet government, detailing arguments against the actions of the Bulgarian government and disagreeing with the Soviet interpretation of the Moscow decision.[55]

To some extent, the two notes represented a bolder British attitude towards events in Bulgaria. For this the FO had long been pressed by Houstoun-Boswall, himself influenced by Petkov's requests that Britain take a firm stand against the Bulgarian government. While Houstoun-Boswall maintained that Britain's manner should be as rigid as the USSR's, he fully realized that there could be little concrete achievement in Sofia where British actions would mostly be of 'nuisance value vis-à-vis the Russians'. He also saw the problem of reconstructing the Bulgarian government in terms of 'which side holds long enough in Bulgaria while the main issues are outlined elsewhere'.[56]

At this moment the British government was closely involved in the first postwar Greek elections and would resent even remote Soviet interest, which might be incited by the diplomatic exchanges regarding Bulgaria. Anxious that British actions should not be seen as provocative at such a sensitive juncture for British policy in the Balkans, the British foreign secretary ruled that the note to the Soviet government regarding Bulgaria should be postponed for a week. Bevin also opposed any British accusation of a Soviet breach of agreement.[57] In these circumstances, FO officials sought to devise a course of action which would enable them to overcome the stalemate in Bulgaria with as little loss of prestige as possible. They hoped for but a few concessions by the Bulgarian government to the opposition. Even these had to be extracted in a careful and timely manner which would not jeopardize positions elsewhere, and above all the relations between the great powers. It was of utmost importance that the attempts to resolve the Bulgarian deadlock should not hinder the continuing preparation of the peace treaty with Bulgaria. Then, if the Bulgarian government could be seen to be reformed, the British could easily extend recognition.[58] The latter consideration motivated British support for another round of negotiations between the Bulgarian government and the opposition.

The final negotiations

In the time between the verbal communication and the British note the Bulgarian prime minister submitted his resignation and began negotiations for a new government.[59] The British political representative judged this to be the result of nervousness in the FF and popular discontent with the present political situation. Houstoun-Boswall believed that even the Communists respected the strong support the opposition commanded throughout the country. He found confirmation of his opinion in the fact that Petkov had again been approached by the Communists to 'work out some *modus vivendi*'. In addition, a special Soviet emissary had urged Petkov to come to terms with the Fatherland Front 'at almost any price except fresh elections'. For Houstoun-Boswall these were signs that a firm attitude impressed the USSR and made it anxious to find an internationally acceptable solution to the Bulgarian question.[60]

The recess of the Bulgarian parliament which started on 28 March 1946 provided an appropriate moment for reconstruction of the government. Prime Minister Georgiev was prepared to agree to Petkov becoming deputy prime minister and to discuss the other demands of the opposition. The latter had not changed since the negotiations of the previous January: the reconstruction of the government had to be accompanied by cessation of political persecution against opposition leaders and supporters.[61]

The US and British representatives in Sofia were kept informed of the talks through contacts with the opposition. While pleased with the very fact of the negotiations, Barnes and Houstoun-Boswall estimated the possibility for a compromise differently. The US diplomat felt that the opposition had held out for so long that it should not stay out of the government much longer or it would never get in. Instead, Oxley and Houstoun-Boswall advised Petkov not to abandon his erstwhile demands but to propose some compromise himself. For example, he could admit that the opposition was not in the assembly due to its own actions and to confirm its commitment to a republic. Britain cautioned that the opposition should exercise 'the greatest possible moderation of speech and in the press, not to create the impression that they were only die-hards who were less able to compromise than the Fatherland Front'.[62] Both the US and British representatives in Sofia were prepared to accept once more that Georgiev's attempts to negotiate were genuine and accordingly pressed for a joint British–US message to facilitate further talks.[63]

At that moment, unknown to the Western diplomats the Soviet Union had already begun a broad offensive against the reorganization of the Bulgarian government. Stalin personally criticized the Bulgarian Communists for their 'modesty and lack of initiative'. In mid-March 1946, in a letter to Dimitrov and Kostov, Stalin and Molotov rejected the legitimacy of the opposition's demands after the November 1945 election.[64] Replying to an appeal for support by Dimitrov, Stalin's new recommendations to the Bulgarian Communists explained: 'First, the opposition should be ignored in every way and no negotiations with them should be held. Second, a number of well-thought and cleverly organized measures should be undertaken to strangle the opposition.'[65] All British observers in Bulgaria learnt was that the Soviet ambassador had explained to Georgiev that the opposition's demands were unacceptable to the Soviet government. As a result, just when the State Department expressed satisfaction with the offers made to the Bulgarian opposition, Georgiev claimed that he had not made any such proposals.[66] For the Western diplomats there was no doubt that Georgiev's reversal was caused by the stiff and obstructive Soviet attitude.[67]

On 28 March the negotiations between the Bulgarian government and the opposition broke down. The opposition had not even had a chance to reply to the government proposals before these were withdrawn.[68] A new government took office on 31 March 1946: far from making the executive more representative, the Communists actually obtained additional ministerial posts. Five ministries, including that of finance, on which the Soviet government had specifically insisted, were now in Communist hands. Of the two deputy prime ministers who were added to the cabinet, one was Communist. This happened at the expense of the other FF parties, whose positions were weakened; the Social Democrats retained only two ministerial posts. The new government issued a declaration that it would adhere to the policies of the previous one.[69]

These developments rendered the possibility of fulfilment of the Moscow agreement in Bulgaria extremely remote. Both the British and US governments had to face their failure to bring about the inclusion of the Bulgarian opposition in the government. British and US policy makers were aware of their lack of adequate diplomatic and political means to outweigh Soviet influence on Bulgarian political life. The Foreign Office concluded that there was nothing it could do at the moment since its communications to the Bulgarian government had elucidated the British position and should have deprived the FF of any illusion of British lack of interest.[70] However, the hope that the Bulgarian rulers would appreciate British firm actions was increasingly overshadowed by the growing realization that the Moscow communiqué had never really been appropriate for Bulgaria but Britain had been drawn into it by the United States. In April 1946, M. S. Williams at the Southern Department called the Moscow decision 'a millstone around [Britain's] neck', especially since it could not be easily renounced.[71] It would be impossible to nullify it in Bulgaria without impairing its credibility in Romania and therefore risking expulsion of the Romanian opposition from the government. Of even greater significance was the fact that British officials could propose no alternative to the Moscow agreement and therefore preferred to uphold it publicly since at least it committed the Soviet Union to the reorganization of the Bulgarian government.[72]

British behaviour was also dictated by an unwillingness to enter into an open confrontation with the Soviet Union regarding Bulgaria. Stalin had persistently refused to recognize the legitimacy of British and US views, and had even begun accusing his former Allies of deliberately breaking the Moscow agreement. Soviet military presence in Bulgaria was coupled with unrestrained meddling of Soviet officers and political representatives in all aspects of Bulgarian politics and economy. This was facilitated by the close political links between the BCP and Moscow. British observers admitted that attempts to check the pace of communization could have no more than nuisance value and would be perceived by the Soviet Union as illegitimate interference in its sphere of influence.

Towards Recognition of the Communist Regime in Bulgaria

The failure of the Moscow agreement on Bulgaria took place against the background of general worsening of inter-Allied relations. The end of the war exposed the lack of long-term cohesion between the Soviet Union on the one hand and Britain and the United States on the other. Increasingly, disagreements which signalled different strategic aims were coming to the fore of international politics. In a pre-election speech of 9 February 1946, Stalin prophesied that the rivalry between the Soviet Union and the West would inevitably lead to future wars. As he underlined the incompatibility of Communism and capitalism, he was judged by contemporary analysts in London and Washington to be announcing the beginning of new militancy in Soviet foreign policy.[73] Stalin's pronouncement provided the occasion for George Kennan's 'long telegram' of 22 February 1946, which explained Soviet aspirations to dominate territories beyond the Soviet borders in the context of both centuries-long Russian policy and Communist ideology. Kennan's analysis confirmed the US policy makers' worst fears that the consolidation of Soviet power in Eastern Europe was going to become the basis for a more aggressive attitude towards the former Allies. As this was generally seen to call for a correspondingly tougher policy, it was welcomed by diplomats stationed in Eastern Europe, where those in Bulgaria were among the most vocal and active.[74]

British policy makers drew similar conclusions from the recent Soviet acts. In concurrence with reports of the Joint Intelligence Committee of the Chiefs of Staff, most British diplomatic experts had little doubt that the USSR aimed at the consolidation of a belt of Communist satellite states around its borders. The chargé in Moscow Frank Roberts fully agreed with Kennan's assessment as to the motives and aims of Soviet foreign policy.[75] His views influenced thinking in the FO, where undersecretary Christopher Warner suggested firmer British measures to attack and expose Communism wherever it demonstrated itself.[76] Although not an authorized government statement, Churchill's Fulton speech of March 1946 represented truthfully the swing of opinion taking place among senior British civil servants.[77]

The familiar difficulty of policy formulation

The noticeably firmer British stand towards the Soviet Union was motivated by developments in Iran and Turkey where Soviet pressure openly threatened the security of the British Empire.[78] This hardening attitude was not reflected immediately in dealings concerning Bulgaria. The first months of 1946 were devoted to relatively quiet observation of the consecutive failures of the political forces in Bulgaria to reach any agreement, mainly as a result of Soviet support for the radicalism of the Bulgarian Communists. The final breakdown of the Moscow decision was followed by a period of bewilderment as to how Britain could overcome the ensuing deadlock.

While not a primary cause for the conflict with the Soviet Union, Bulgarian developments added to Soviet–British tensions. In April 1946, the FO once again grappled with the question of granting recognition to the Bulgarian government as it would be broached at the forthcoming Paris meeting of the foreign ministers, where peace treaties with the ex-satellites were on the agenda. The problem reappeared as the British government had made it clear that it would sign no peace treaty with a government which did not match its criteria for legitimacy and democracy. At the same time, Houstoun-Boswall, who was aware of the FO's prejudice against new initiatives in Bulgaria, strove to precipitate the reactions of his superiors. His communications challenged the indecisiveness of the Southern Department by insisting that 'by studiously avoiding any action which Russia might think provocative and aggressive as she jolly well pleases', the British government was bound to repeat its 'great prewar mistake with Germany'.[79] Passionately, he declaimed:

> It is surely better to think and do something consistently and then be slightly wrong, than to wobble and reflect and inevitably to be wrong and then to have to catch up lost ground. [...] The time has come to commit our friends, to fortify them and to bind them clearly on our side – otherwise they will fall helter-skelter into the other camp making friends with the Power of Evil because there seems to be no Power of Good. And we are capable of being a Power of Good if only we will play our part and show some guts.[80]

In a sobering reply he was warned that even though the FO understood how demanding and exasperating conditions in Sofia were, the strength of expression in some of his recent telegrams had 'prejudiced important officials against, rather than in favour of his recommendations'.[81] Indeed, FO officials found themselves beyond the stage of avoiding action so as simply not to stir Soviet sensitivities. By their own admission, more than ever they faced the difficulty of devising actions, which would have a real effect. That is why without entertaining hopes for implementing the Moscow decision, the FO clung to its phraseology. Unable to find a substitute for the Moscow agreement, the FO was loath to admit failure.[82]

Despite his frequent reminders that 'the first element of success in Bulgaria was to have a foreign policy and stick to it', Houstoun-Boswall himself found it intricate to recommend a definite course of action in the spring of 1946.[83] He agreed with the Southern Department that the general aim of British policy in the Balkan satellites should be 'to strengthen and encourage the anti-Communist elements'.[84] And yet, he comprehended the Southern Department's serious difficulty at this moment 'to think of any action to be really effective in checking the spread of Communism and Totalitarianism'.[85] The only possibility appearing remotely plausible at the moment was the relaunching of negotiations between the Bulgarian prime minister Georgiev and the opposition.[86]

The earliest opportunity for such an advance presented itself at the end of June 1946, when in Paris Molotov agreed that Soviet troops were going to withdraw from Bulgaria within ninety days after the signature of the peace treaty.[87] For Great Britain there was the distinct danger of finding itself in a situation in which to get rid of the Soviet army, it might be forced to recognize the Bulgarian government without approving of it. Thus, even a partial success towards the implementation of the Moscow communiqué might render the approaching recognition of the Bulgarian government more palatable.

This was endorsed by the readiness of the Bulgarian opposition to moderate its demands for participation in the government. The British representatives in Sofia began thinking that the mere presence of the opposition in the government would be psychologically and politically valuable for it.[88]

The FO was eager to pressure the Bulgarian Communists directly through Vassil Kolarov, who headed the Bulgarian peace delegation in Paris. The British foreign secretary had been advised by senior civil servants to show a very stiff attitude, not only criticizing internal conditions in Bulgaria but above all repudiating the 'monstrously impudent' Bulgarian territorial and financial claims against Greece.[89] However, when Bevin received Kolarov on 29 June 1946, Greek issues were hardly raised. As soon as Kolarov had mentioned Bulgarian disappointment at not being recognized, he was told that the British government would not even discuss recognition until negotiations with the opposition were resumed. Bevin insisted that the opposition had been given onerous terms which had precipitated the breakdown of the Moscow decision. He also pointed out that the persecution of the opposition press and the behaviour of the militia showed that there was no political freedom in Bulgaria. Kolarov helplessly repeated the official Bulgarian line that the opposition was to blame for the breakdown of the talks as it had imposed the impossible demand of dissolving the assembly. He stated that there would be fresh elections in September and promised that if the opposition cooperated the government would also seek accommodation with it.[90]

British diplomats and civil servants concluded that the deliberately cold attitude and plain speaking of the foreign secretary had impressed the Bulgarian delegation and shocked the Bulgarian government. This was seen as a stimulus for the Bulgarian government to initiate a settlement with the opposition to which end Britain's main task would be to remain equally steadfast until a genuine reconstruction of the government.[91] Britain even became uncharacteristically eager to encourage similar US firmness. Bevin wrote to Byrnes informing him about the talk with Kolarov and suggesting a new attempt to implement the Moscow decision. In his subsequent conversation with Kolarov, the US secretary of state essentially confirmed the British views.[92]

Not for the first time did similar analysis of the circumstances lead US and British policy makers to different recommendations. The US State Department surmised that the Bulgarian side would be so eager for an immediate conclusion of the peace treaty that it would willingly make reasonable offers to the opposition. Until then the United States should refuse to recognize the Bulgarian government or to sign the peace treaty with Bulgaria. Following this logic, the State Department issued a declaration on the Byrnes–Kolarov talks repeating that the United States could not have normal relations with the current Bulgarian government.[93]

While the US strategy was to warn of nonrecognition so as to drive the Bulgarian Communists towards acceptance of opposition members in the government, Britain's aim was almost the opposite. For the FO, resumption of negotiations could bring at least limited participation of the opposition in the executive which could then be taken as a sufficient basis for the recognition of the Bulgarian government. Recognition would make the signature of the peace treaty possible and three months later all Soviet troops could be out of Bulgaria, thus relieving the pressure on the Eastern Mediterranean. This prospect was so appealing to the British government that Bevin had suggested to Kolarov that the British representative in Sofia should mediate between the government and the opposition. In addition, the foreign secretary hinted that in view of the new elections, Britain would advise the opposition to withdraw some of its demands. This constituted the first official admission that Britain carried some influence with the opposition and was willing to use it. Houstoun-Boswall had already ascertained that the opposition was ready to modify its conditions for taking up office. It had dropped its requirements for the dissolution of the National Assembly and for obtaining the Ministry of Justice. It still insisted on two opposition deputy ministers for the Ministry of the Interior, equal participation of supporters of all parties in the militia as well as general political amnesty for offences committed after September 1944. Communicating with opposition leaders, British observers concluded that the non–Fatherland Front parties realized that they faced one of their last chances to enter the executive before the new elections in the autumn. On their part, British experts felt they should not press the opposition too much lest it came to suspect it was being urged to accept too little and backed out.[94]

Simultaneously, the FO found it necessary to bring the Bulgarian question to the attention of the Soviet government. The foreign secretary chose to approach Moscow alone, without asking for a supportive US move.[95] On 12 July 1946, Bevin brought up the subject of Bulgarian recognition in a conversation with Molotov and Vyshinski and suggested that both sides use their influence with the government and opposition respectively. Bevin informed Molotov that the Bulgarian opposition was ready to drop the demand for the dissolution of the assembly but in exchange its remaining demands had to be met by the government. Without acknowledging the right of the opposition to put forward any claims at all, Molotov agreed that the recognition of Bulgaria was an outstanding question which should be resolved before the signature of the peace treaty. His words left little doubt in the British delegation that the Soviet Union was well aware of the link between recognition and the peace treaty and was anxious to improve the international status of Bulgaria.[96]

In the summer of 1946, British senior officials showed unprecedented willingness to deal with the Bulgarian question quickly and efficiently. For the first time they were prepared to accept openly the role of mediators in Bulgarian internal affairs so as to facilitate the compromise between government and opposition. Most uncharacteristically, Britain even approached the Soviet Union to speed up some form of implementation of the Moscow agreement, which the FO had long held to be unrealistic.

This practical British involvement in Bulgaria occurred at a moment when it seemed that Britain could draw substantial strategic benefits in the form of complete Soviet evacuation from the country. British strategists considered that an agreement on Soviet withdrawal from Bulgaria would alleviate pressure on the Eastern Mediterranean and especially Turkey, which had been directly threatened by the Soviet Union earlier in 1946. It also meant that the Soviet Union would commit itself not to continue its actions in Iran from where it was refusing to withdraw, causing a major international dispute.[97]

All this was acknowledged as a real concession on the part of the Soviet Union at a time when its actions in the Middle East and Eastern Europe had helped to magnify its expansionist image. Even though it was becoming rapidly obvious that a more resolute British foreign policy to check unilateral Soviet actions was required, the British government was unwilling to forego any possibility of collaborating with Soviet Russia on international decisions. In this sense, Bulgaria was an opportune case: British interest in it was not sufficient to justify an Anglo–Soviet clash. Once again it provided a testing ground for minor compromises on both sides.

Recognition without conditions

In mid-July 1946, Houstoun-Boswall reported a most urgent appeal from the opposition to Britain and the United States for assistance to put an end to the reign of Communist terror in Bulgaria. To the British representative, it seemed that while agreeing to seek a compromise in Bulgaria, Molotov had privately given Kolarov full Soviet backing for the elimination of the opposition from Bulgarian political life.[98]

Given that British representatives in Bulgaria could move outside the capital only with difficulty, they were able to send to London a surprisingly accurate picture of the state of Bulgarian politics. As official encounters were rarely enlightening, the British mission relied on overt or covert adversaries of the regime for detailed information. Throughout the latter half of 1945 and the beginning of 1946, the FO had to consider its attitudes to the problem of Bulgarian recognition on the background of accumulating news of Communist-backed arrogance and violence towards opponents of Communist rule across the country. Despite plans for the resumption of talks between the Bulgarian government and the opposition, British experts could not overlook the constantly increasing lawless behaviour of the Bulgarian authorities.

The renewed offensive against the opposition in Bulgaria had begun just after the November 1945 elections and was stepped up after the January 1946 failure of talks based on the Moscow agreement. Verbal and physical assaults on the opposition had not even stopped during the short-lived government attempts for dialogue with it. The accelerated clamp down on the opposition was initiated by the Communist Politburo, which in early 1946 postulated that no actions against the interests of the Communist Party were to be tolerated. Accordingly, repressive laws[99] were adopted which could be used by the Communist-controlled militia and courts of justice to maltreat, imprison and intern any real or imagined opponents of the regime.[100] A succession of political trials followed in the second half of 1946, beginning with the sentencing to death *in absentia* of the exiled G. M. for treason. In this and subsequent trials, attacks against Petkov increased in number and gravity. Social Democrat leaders such as Pastuhov and Lulchev and Agrarians such as Assen Stamboliiski were subjected to violence by the authorities. The well-known journalists Tsveti Ivanov and Trifon Kunev, who criticized the regime in the Social Democrat paper *Svoboden Narod*, were also convicted. Simultaneously, the interior minister imposed arbitrary bans on opposition newspapers for publishing allegedly anti-Soviet and anti-Yugoslav articles. All this created an ominous atmosphere in which accusations and sentences of members of anti-Communist organizations abounded. This happened to the infamous Internal Macedonian Revolutionary Organization led by Ivan Mihailov and the phantom Tsar Krum Secret Military Organization – both for a range of 'terrorist activities' and 'anti-Government conspiracies'.[101]

The aim of the Communist Party was to eliminate the opposition by portraying its actions as harmful to the national interests: the CC literally ordered Interior Minister Yugov to 'give details' for this.[102] Moreover, there can be little doubt that the actions of the Bulgarian Communists were known and approved by the Soviet government. The January 1946 onslaught on the opposition was triggered by the Communist Politburo immediately after Vyshinski had proclaimed that negotiations with the non-FF parties were futile. On 29 June 1946, the day Kolarov met Bevin in Paris, the Politburo gathered in the presence of Marshal Tolbukhin, the head of the Allied Control Commission and commander in chief of the Third Ukrainian Front, to deliberate on the need to 'cleanse' the army and remove from government the Zveno leader War Minister Velchev.[103] In the summer of 1946, several delegations of high-ranking Bulgarian Communists consulted with Stalin about the Bulgarian political situation. The Soviet leader was especially interested in the army and militia, probably wanting to know whether they would be a reliable support for the Bulgarian regime after the withdrawal of the Soviet forces. Stalin personally oversaw the changes in the Bulgarian cabinet, insisting however that in view of the worsening international status of Bulgaria Georgiev should by all means be retained as prime minister but should be induced to distance himself from the right wing of his party, Zveno.[104] The intensifying persecution of non-Communists occurred with at least the Kremlin's acquiescence, if not encouragement. The only recorded case of Soviet displeasure was Pastuhov's arrest on tactical grounds: instead of helping make a martyr of the old and feeble Social Democrat, the Bulgarian Communists were told to target Petkov.[105]

Of the numerous violent incidents reported by the British mission in Sofia, Pastuhov's imprisonment stirred the Foreign Office the most and provoked the handing of a rare *note verbale* to the Bulgarian government. It expressed not only the British government's disapproval of the particular case but also protested against the lack of civil liberties, and especially of freedom of the press in Bulgaria. The Bulgarian reply stuck to mere diplomatic formalities, after which Britain showed no taste for sustaining action in this or further similar cases.[106] Witnessing the steady Communist advance, Foreign Office observers were convinced daily that the situation in Bulgaria after the Moscow decision was only changing for worse. They entertained no illusion that British interference could bring but the slightest and temporary political improvement. Already in June 1946, Geoffrey Warner of the Southern Department admitted that he saw no way to help the opposition and therefore had no hope that it would succeed.[107]

The FO considered that the position of the British government regarding Bulgaria had been expressed unequivocally on a number of occasions and was therefore well known to Bulgaria's rulers. The latter had had sufficient time and opportunity for compromise and since they had not offered any, no further British action was expedient. The FO stood by this view even when in May 1946 the Bulgarian opposition sent a new appeal to Britain and the United States drawing attention to the aggravated political situation. After a similar letter from the Romanian opposition, the British government had raised the issue with the Soviet government and failed to progress, leading to the conclusion that protests in the Bulgarian case would hardly make any headway either.[108] British observers recognized the difficult task of the Bulgarian opposition, and doubted that any direct British encouragement would be justified. The FO advised Bevin not to send Petkov a message of encouragement despite Houstoun-Boswall's request. The political representative was instructed simply to convey the 'general agreement of HMG with the opposition's views' and explain that for precisely this reason the Bulgarian government had not been recognized.[109] So stark did the picture in Bulgaria look to British experts that even Houstoun-Boswall, still convinced of the daily strengthening of the opposition, at this moment appreciated the need to await developments quietly rather than to undertake doomed haphazard actions.[110]

As the FO perceived the situation in Bulgaria to be rapidly deteriorating, it recognized the necessity to formulate a clear course of action to be implemented steadily. By the end of July 1946, the predominant opinion of FO officials was that from the British perspective it was best to grant recognition to the Bulgarian government at the first suitable opportunity, as it had become useless to tie their hands by publicly adhering to the Moscow decision which they knew was no longer relevant. Since they foresaw no chances to induce the entry of the Bulgarian opposition into the government, it was logical to pay less attention to Bulgarian internal affairs.[111]

In the internal Southern Department discussion on Bulgarian recognition in August 1946, there were not many dissenting voices like that of the newcomer to the FO Bulgarian desk R. P. Pinsent. He argued that even with the Red Army out of Bulgaria, the chances that the next elections would be free were extremely slim. Already the Communist hold over the country was judged to be so complete that it would not make much difference whether Soviet troops were physically present. For the proponents of this line the question was, 'Is it worth making an evident climb down involving a severe loss of prestige in order to gain an illusory advantage?'. Even Pinsent conceded that refusal of recognition, apart from its distinct moral satisfaction, would yield few practical advantages.[112] Houstoun-Boswall reached the peak of frustration when he claimed that 'HMG [...] have decided to swallow the rape of Bulgaria by the Communists' and challenged the FO at least to display 'guts and honesty to tell the world beforehand just what we are doing'.[113] Putting aside violent emotions brought by the need 'to stand by impotently and watch events', he made an attempt at arguing with the sober FO decision with equally rational calculations. He tried to prove that even according to the most optimistic estimate, ratification was logistically unlikely before December 1946, which then pushed the departure of Soviet troops to the end of March 1947. Therefore he pleaded that Britain's decision to recognize Bulgaria should not be announced so far in advance.[114]

The Soviet military withdrawal from Bulgaria was for the FO the only noticeable benefit in the extremely unsatisfactory state of affairs. It was estimated that as the withdrawal was not in the strict Soviet interest, Britain should secure it while the USSR was still willing to make the compromise. In the late summer of 1946, the Southern Department worried whether it had double-guessed Soviet thinking correctly, wondering if Stalin might have committed himself to withdrawal in the knowledge that the West would not recognize the Bulgarian government soon. The British military mission in

Bulgaria reported a strong Soviet military presence on the Turkish border and fortification of the Bulgarian–Greek border. As always, this added to British fears of an invasion of Greece and once again pointed to the need to speed up the removal of the Red Army from the southern Balkans.[115]

This indeed was the most pressing argument for diplomatic recognition of the Bulgarian government. For Britain, Soviet withdrawal was judged to be the only positive development in the Balkans outside Greece. If recognition of the Bulgarian regime was the price, it should be paid without imposing any further conditions. The adoption of this logic by the FO signified the final point of an important reversal of priorities in British policy towards Bulgaria which had begun with the realization that recognition could actually bring the initially unforeseen advantage of Soviet military withdrawal from bases threatening the Eastern Mediterranean.

The one hindrance to the fulfilment of Britain's resolution to grant recognition to the Bulgarian government came from the United States. At the beginning of August 1946 the State Department was considering a new representation to Moscow to urge again the Bulgarian Communists to include the opposition in office.[116] In addition, on 28 August 1946 the secretary of state received the Bulgarian prime minister Kimon Georgiev in Paris and warned him that unless the situation was remedied there would be no peace treaty with Bulgaria as the US Senate would refuse to ratify it. Georgiev retorted that in the circumstances of exclusive Soviet influence his government was the best there could be in Bulgaria. He made it clear that the only way the Bulgarian government could comply with the US demands was with Soviet agreement, so the US efforts should be directed to Moscow. The US officials, including Barnes, urged Georgiev to start acting on the US proposal immediately and to summon the opposition to Paris to begin negotiations. For a moment it looked as if this was going to happen, as on 31 August the Bulgarian delegation in Paris handed Barnes a memorandum stating its readiness to start negotiations with the opposition and accepting the mediation of US representatives. Three days later Georgiev shifted his ground completely, telling the US delegation he 'could not do what was politically impossible'.[117]

The FO judged State Department officials to be 'subdued and chastened' by their experience in Paris.[118] Moreover, it was satisfied that it had rightly declined to support any US démarche in Moscow, of which nothing positive had come. FO officials were also horrified that their US counterparts had nearly succeeded in putting them precisely in the position they wished to avoid. Their attitude to the latest US move was mixed: some civil servants hoped that the US representation would have some slight effect which would provide an opportunity to grant recognition to the Bulgarian government.[119] When on 30 August 1946 Byrnes approved recognition in principle, the FO breathed with relief that eventually the United States was coming round to the British point of view. Another more cynical thought began creeping into British reasoning: since Bulgarian behaviour was so deplorable, it seemed expedient to recognize the government before it committed yet another offence.[120]

Looking for opportunities to grant recognition

The longer British officials looked at the Bulgarian government, the firmer their belief became that it should be granted recognition if not before, then at the time of the signing of the peace treaty. Towards the middle of August 1946, the FO began scrutinizing events with the purpose of finding at least some positive developments which could justify the extension of diplomatic relations. Its hopes were pinned on the forthcoming elections to the Grand National Assembly, for which the referendum for a republic was going to be a dress rehearsal.

The issue of the abolition of the Bulgarian monarchy was a matter of indifference to the British government. Wartime plans had dismissed the Bulgarian ruling dynasty as more or less irrelevant as it had earned little sympathy from British statesmen. The FO was convinced of the widespread republicanism of the Bulgarian people and entertained no illusions that a republic would bring Bulgaria closer to the Soviet model and facilitate the creation of a federation with Yugoslavia. Indeed, as a result of the political violence following the coup of 9 September 1944, there remained no groups or individuals in Bulgaria prepared to declare pro-monarchist feelings and thus openly challenge the government's determination to abolish the monarchy. Even the opposition was well known for its republican convictions and had difficulty in distinguishing itself from the FF on the question of the form of the state. While urging a pro-republican vote, the opposition objected to the referendum in principle as such a method was not provided for by the existing constitution.[121]

The referendum took place on 8 September 1946 with a turnout of over ninety-one per cent. Almost ninety-six per cent of the votes were in favour of a republic. On 15 September 1946 the National Assembly proclaimed Bulgaria to be a 'people's republic'.[122] Not unexpected, this provoked little official reaction from London and Washington. Exclusive attention was directed towards the elections for a Grand National Assembly, which were scheduled for 28 October 1946.

Although British observers could not realistically expect the Grand National Assembly to influence radically political developments in Bulgaria, they followed closely the electoral campaign. The opposition parties united in the Federation of Urban and Rural Labour, launching a strong electoral campaign.

They engaged intensely with the Communists and reported in their newspapers the full extent of the terror campaign unleashed by the authorities. The FO did not preoccupy itself with details of the pre-electoral campaign in Bulgaria but focused instead on the fact that the new Grand National Assembly could provide the desired opportunity for recognition. The main British concern was that some inopportune US action would delay the signature of the peace treaty. The State Department was contemplating withdrawal of the US military mission from Bulgaria as a sign of utmost displeasure with political developments. British officials in London were strongly opposed to the idea, mainly because they were convinced it would have no effect on the Bulgarian government while at the same time denying the West an important source of information and intelligence.[123]

The greater British anxiety was that Secretary Byrnes saw no reason why the treaty with Bulgaria had to be signed as soon as it was ready. To British civil servants he did not seem to be convinced of the importance of getting the Soviet troops out of the country.[124] On the whole, US specialists analysed the Bulgarian situation from the perspective of democratic principles, pointing to the nonimplementation of either the Yalta Declaration or the Moscow decision. That is why they still hoped that as a result of Byrnes' conversation with Georgiev, the Bulgarian elections were not going to be 'too unjust'.[125] Moreover, in the light of the violent election campaign, the US government was extremely reluctant to extend recognition to the Bulgarian government.[126]

Senior Foreign Office civil servants like Sargent had been pressing for discussion and coordination of the whole policy towards the satellite countries with their US colleagues. They were worried that the US government might go in the opposite direction from the British and become so committed to a policy of nonrecognition as not to be able to sign the peace treaty at all.[127] While these matters were briefly touched upon at a meeting between Bevin and Byrnes in Paris on 4 October 1946, their resolution was left to the ordinary diplomatic channels.[128]

Britain's views were most extensively outlined in a letter from Bevin to Byrnes of 7 October 1946. For the FO, the latest talks with Georgiev in Paris showed that serious modification of the present Bulgarian policy could not be expected. For Britain, there seemed no alternative but to resign itself to 'recognising the present government or one similarly controlled by Communists'. This course was not seen as satisfactory but was pragmatic. Even though for the British government it was technically possible to sign a peace treaty with an unrecognized government, its inclination was to simplify things by granting the Bulgarian government recognition at the time of signature.[129]

The State Department appreciated British moderation and agreed not to withdraw the US mission from Bulgaria. It began to consider the possibility of signing the peace treaty with Bulgaria even though it was still firmly opposed to granting the Bulgarian regime formal recognition. In a last attempt to influence the Bulgarian government, on 24 October 1946 Byrnes sent a letter to Georgiev reminding him that the future international status of Bulgaria depended on the conduct of the elections. Simultaneously, in order to demonstrate US interest, Barnes and the new head of the US military mission General Robertson were authorized to propose a full ACC meeting in relation to the forthcoming elections. Wishing to refute any impression that it was condoning the terror perpetrated by the authorities, the US mission requested from the Bulgarian government a full report on recent events and insisted on visiting concentration camps and prisons, including a visit to the arrested former war minister Velchev.[130]

The FO instructed the British representative in Sofia to support the US move. Nevertheless, British officials deplored the wide range of US demands and strove to limit them. The demand for prison inspection was judged to be especially unfortunate as it might turn into a precedent for reciprocal Soviet demands in Greece, which would be unpalatable to Britain. It seemed difficult to alter the active US approach but the FO hoped that by going along, it would be in a better position to prevent more undesirable steps.

On 23 October 1946 at a meeting of the ACC, the US representatives put forward comprehensive measures to ensure freedom and fairness of elections. The most important proposal was for opposition controllers at each polling booth. Ostensibly, the circumstances resembled those of August 1945, when elections were postponed upon joint US and British insistence. In this instance, however, Biryuzov refused to consider what he termed 'interference in Bulgaria's internal affairs'.[131] His words echoed those of Vyshinski, who days earlier had mentioned in a speech in Paris that no interference would be allowed in Bulgaria where there was 'no place for Petkov or Lulchev'.[132] The US retreated, but continuing to look for ways to improve the situation in Bulgaria, Byrnes contemplated discussing it directly with Molotov and Vyshinski at the forthcoming Council of Foreign Ministers in New York. He believed he could get the Soviet Union 'to order the Bulgarian Communists to show some degree of co-operation with the Opposition'. Alternatively, he suggested placing the matter of Bulgarian elections on the agenda of the General Assembly of the United Nations.[133]

Apart from thinking that the proposed moves would be 'utterly useless', most FO officials discerned a hardening of the US approach. Even more worrying was the fact that Biryuzov's behaviour in Bulgaria and Vyshinski's declarations in Paris indicated that the Soviet Union too was becoming less flexible.

The FO could accept that the time for identical British and US actions and strictly coordinated initiatives in Bulgaria had passed. Simultaneously, it worried that the moderate British approach was being sidelined.[134]

The only reason attention continued to be paid to the elections was because they would demonstrate the strength of the opposition and indicate the chances for a compromise with the ruling Communists.[135] Without British knowledge, in June 1946 Stalin gave instructions about the electoral tactics of the Bulgarian Communists. He approved the preservation of the FF, in which, however, the Communists 'should do everything possible to be the first party'. If the Communists could not secure at least forty per cent on the common FF electoral lists they should run on their own.[136] In addition, Stalin made it clear that it was important that the Bulgarian opposition should not boycott the ballot again. He saw it as natural that after the elections the government would not include the opposition. But it was crucial for the FF's image not to be seen as dismissing the possibility of negotiations for a coalition government prematurely.[137]

In public, Communist leaders stood for calm and orderly elections, but their pronouncements revealed that they were planning severe measures against the opposition. Dimitrov called for restraining the militia until the elections but he also claimed that the opposition was preparing evil acts of provocation which the militia were ready to prevent.[138]

On the eve of the elections, the United Opposition asked Great Britain and the United States to intervene again in favour of postponing the elections. This action had little but propaganda value, as the most the British and US governments could do was to protest to the Bulgarian and Soviet governments regarding the improper conduct of the electoral campaign. Indeed, they had already done so without any obvious effect. From Britain's perspective, it remained to watch the Bulgarian situation carefully and find a suitable moment to discard responsibility for it – by granting recognition to the Bulgarian government.

Despite its unfavourable position, the United Bulgarian Opposition secured more than a quarter of the vote – 28.4 per cent – and returned 99 deputies to the Grand National Assembly. The Fatherland Front had 365 deputies. The new government was formed without the opposition and contained a bigger number of Communists than the previous one. For the FO, the mere presence of the opposition in parliament seemed to open prospects for altering the course of events in the country. This could be a justification for active abandoning of the policy of nonrecognition on Britain's part.

On 12 November 1946, the House of Commons debated the peace treaties with the former Axis satellites. The FO minister of state Hector McNeil criticized the methods used by the Bulgarian government to obtain a parliamentary majority and expressed profound doubts that the results of the elections truly reflected the wishes of the Bulgarian people. But he was unable to state clearly what methods the British government planned to employ in place of nonrecognition in order to register disapproval of the Bulgarian regime.[139] After the debate there were voices at the FO suggesting that it was better to leave the Bulgarians guessing as to when exactly Britain would extend diplomatic relations.[140] Captain Raynold Blackburn, a Conservative MP, put forward to the FO the idea of 'conditional and gradual recognition' in exchange for strictly formulated concessions on the part of the Bulgarians. This was swiftly discarded as inappropriate.[141]

These few isolated cases of attention to Bulgaria did nothing to alter the official view that recognition should be accorded at the time of the signing of the peace treaty. The decision taken in principle by the FO was reaffirmed by the advice of its legal expert, G. G. Fitzmaurice; in fact, he insisted that from a legal point of view, HMG had already recognized the Bulgarian government. As the British government had sent representatives to Bulgaria, a *de facto* recognition had essentially been granted, which carried almost all the legal consequences. In international practice this differed from a *de jure* recognition, which implied political attitude and, if it was extended, meant that Britain was satisfied with the proper credentials of the regime in Bulgaria. Unsure whether a *de jure* recognition was necessary to bring the state of war to an end, the legal adviser admitted that the whole 'recognition business' had fallen into 'a terrible mess causing endless tangles'. After weeks of confusing interdepartmental memoranda, the FO arrived at the conclusion that it 'would not be legally impossible' to sign or ratify a peace treaty with a government which was only recognized *de facto*, as was the case with the Bulgarian government.[142]

With the end of the Paris Peace Conference approaching, it was clear that the signing of the peace treaty with Bulgaria was also near. This increased the desire of the Foreign Office to get the 'whole muddle' of Bulgarian recognition out of the way.[143] The issue was no longer of securing political or even strategic advantages for Britain; the only practical benefit appeared to be the closure of a confusing and at times embarrassing question for British foreign policy. There were signals that for political and practical reasons even the US State Department was beginning to reconcile itself to the approaching recognition of the Bulgarian regime.[144]

While officials in London were elaborating on a number of legal and technical details, noticeable deterioration of the Bulgarian political situation was reported at the beginning of 1947. It had become obvious that the Bulgarian Communists were intent on eliminating the opposition unaffected by the withdrawal of the Red Army. The British representative in Sofia wrote that, without doubt, in the persecution of opponents the Bulgarian government 'makes use of torture as a method of interrogation, maintains concentration camps and is in general the most barbaric of all totalitarian regimes in Eastern Europe'.[145] Boyd Tollinton, acting head of the British mission, believed that the prospect of the departure of the Red Army from Bulgaria had resulted in a drive to stamp out all effective opposition. Even Dimitrov, already Bulgarian prime minister and acting minister of foreign affairs, had stated in the Bulgarian parliament that the opposition would be dealt with in a month. Tollinton wrote that far from enabling more normal political life to be established in Bulgaria, the signature of the peace treaty would become the occasion 'for an additional attempt to fix a totalitarian grasp upon further aspects of Bulgarian life with the two-fold object of settling the Soviet hand on the country and of preventing Western influence of any chance of reviving'. He recommended that as a sign of disapproval the British government should not appoint a minister plenipotentiary to Sofia, but instead send just another political representative to act as an observer. In Tollinton's opinion, the last weapon Britain possessed was the power to deny Bulgaria trade, making it the price for certain political concessions. His gravest doubts were that soon there would be no democratic elements in Bulgaria, despite the courage opposition leaders continued to show.[146]

At the beginning of February 1947, just before the signing of the peace treaty, Dimitrov made an ostensible show of good will towards the opposition. He stated in the assembly that 'certain collaboration is possible and necessary', while also continuing to insist that the opposition was slandering the government and the FF as well as encouraging the dissatisfied elements in the country. This proclamation of moderation was immediately obscured by Dimitrov's words that he could throw the opposition out of parliament 'within an hour' and that the Communists were under obligation 'to bridle the opposition'.[147]

The Southern Department judged the moderating elements in Dimitrov's speech to be 'sickeningly insincere'. On the other hand, the very proclamation of the need for compromise with the opposition was seen as a sign that Britain's attitude still counted for something with the Bulgarian government. But it was to be expected that until recognition was granted not only by Britain but also the United States, the Bulgarian Communists would be on their best behaviour.[148] Some FO officials like D. Colville were amazed that some of the articles in the opposition press had been allowed to appear at all, which would not have been possible in Yugoslavia, Romania or Poland.[149]

On 10 February 1947, the peace treaty with Bulgaria was signed. On 11 February 1947, the British representative wrote to Dimitrov informing him that HMG had decided to recognize the Bulgarian government *de jure* even if he also made it clear that the Bulgarian government was not considered to be representative of the people's wishes. On 12 February, the Bulgarian government replied expressing satisfaction with the recognition and intention of fulfilling the requirements of the peace treaty. John Sterndale-Bennett was appointed minister plenipotentiary in Sofia, while Professor Nikola Dolapchiev became the Bulgarian minister in London.

The United States Senate ratified the peace treaty with Bulgaria only in June 1947, against the strongly worded advice of the US representative in Sofia, who likened the Soviet nonfulfilment of the Yalta agreements to the behaviour of Germany in the prelude to the First and Second World Wars. President Truman used the occasion of the ratification to voice strong dissatisfaction over the violation of civil liberties in Bulgaria.[150] The delay and the simultaneous criticism, however, produced no effect on the situation in Bulgaria and, more embarrassingly for the US government, coincided with the arrest of Petkov. This signified the start of a new wave of terror aimed at eliminating anyone who challenged the Communist-dominated government before the withdrawal of the Soviet army from Bulgaria. The very development which according to British policy makers could alleviate political tension in Bulgaria had the opposite effect.

Nikola Petkov was accused of 'fomenting disorder and sabotage to induce foreign powers to intervene in Bulgarian affairs'. The prosecution named no particular foreign country, but the official press freely linked the accused with Britain and the United States. Petkov's case stirred Western public opinion.[151]

If this did not send a clear signal to the Communists that neither Britain nor the United States intended to become seriously involved in Bulgaria, the quasi measures taken at the proclamation of Petkov's death sentence did. Instead of threatening to suspend relations with Bulgaria, as recommended by their diplomats, both governments protested to the Soviet chairman of the ACC and discussed whether to invite the Soviet side to a tripartite discussion of the case. Shortly before Petkov's execution in September 1947, a desperate appeal was made by the two Western powers to the veteran Communist Vassil Kolarov, then president of the republic. All actions met with the reply that the trial and sentence were an internal matter. Dimitrov went as far as stating that Petkov's sentence 'might have been commuted but for foreign intervention and attempts to dictate in ultimatum fashion'.[152] This pronouncement only confirmed Sterndale-Bennett's words that 'guilty connection between ourselves and the accused is [...] just as likely to be assumed from silence as it is from official intervention'.[153] Even though British officials were certain that Petkov's execution had been decided in advance of any British and US moves, Dimitrov's statement was interpreted as an unconcealed warning for future cases. It aimed at putting the Western powers on the defensive. It was obvious that steps undertaken to alleviate the plight of the accused in subsequent trials would inevitably be regarded as aggravating circumstances. Every suggestion for action on the part of the FO would be weighed against the possibility of unwittingly victimizing the accused further.[154]

British and US recognition did not improve the international reputation of the Bulgarian government but was used to boost the latter's internal standing and to some degree facilitated the consolidation of the regime. Without the fear that they might incur the intervention of Britain and the United States, the Bulgarian Communists were unrestrained against political opponents. To those Bulgarian politicians who were familiar with Stalin's reassurance that Bulgaria would eventually be recognized, the Soviet leader's words to a Bulgarian delegation in early 1946 must have seemed almost prophetic:

> Why are you so worried about that? If the opposition does not want to enter [the government], it is possible that they will not recognize you immediately. But the time for the preparation of the peace treaty is short. In about two or three months they are going to recognize you. [...] We were not recognized for twelve years and nevertheless we survived. [...] If Petkov thinks that because of him Britain and America are going to go to war with us, he is gravely mistaken.[155]

* * *

For almost half a year after the November 1945 elections Britain had practically accepted that free elections 'in harmony with the Yalta agreement' were not possible in Bulgaria. It believed that the future of its influence in the country lay with the fortunes of the anti-Communists and therefore its main efforts had been directed towards securing more favourable conditions for the opposition. The crucial question Britain faced was how to facilitate the entry of non-FF politicians into the government, which would then become more representative of popular opinion.

Subscribing to the Moscow decision, Britain realized that it could not implement its views unless it stood up firmly to the Soviet Union. Although willing to take issue with the Soviet government on different occasions, London was not ready for open confrontation and instead had to scale down British demands. The impression of British vulnerability was not helped by the frequent lack of synchrony between the two Western Allies even though there was hardly any meaningful disagreement between them. This was exploited by the Bulgarian Communists for their own propaganda and diplomatic purposes.

Part Three

Consolidation of the Cold War Frontline: 'We Are Supporting Certain Principles'*

---

* J. H. Watson, FO minute, 6 August 1947, cited in V. Rothwell, *Britain and the Cold War 1941–1947* (London: Cape, 1982), 388.

Chapter Six

BRITISH ACCEPTANCE OF COMMUNIST RULE IN BULGARIA

The conclusion of the peace treaties with Germany's ex-satellites marked the intensification of the controversy between the Soviet Union and its Western Allies regarding Eastern Europe. Disagreements focused on the undemocratic nature of the emerging regimes. Britain and the United States believed the violent methods used by the local Communists to be not only condoned, but actually inspired by the Soviet government and Communist Party. This was judged to be true to the greatest degree of the Bulgarian government.

British policy makers did not dispute the place of Bulgaria in the postwar Soviet zone of interest. Although earlier conflicts over the area had marked some of the lowest points in relations with the Soviet Union, in early 1947 the overall importance of Eastern Europe in British foreign policy had visibly diminished. By then, the British government had adopted the view that little was to be gained from clashes over long-foreseen faits accomplis. In the case of Bulgaria, throughout the armistice period the British search for compromises on specific problems failed to improve relations in general. This approach had yielded unpalatable results: in addition to seeing the Soviet Union assert its power in Bulgaria, the Foreign Office began worrying that the Soviet leaders perceived British mildness as a sign of weakness.

Britain's continued watchfulness of Bulgaria was justified by the notion of the country as a testing ground for the lengths to which the Soviet Union would go to safeguard control of its areas of interest. British aspirations regarding Bulgaria were dominated by the need to devise a course of firm and successful actions, which would have a definite impact on political events in the country. Britain explored a range of diplomatic, cultural and economic means to revitalize its influence and above all retard the pace of Communization of Bulgaria.

Background of British Policy to Bulgaria

In the postwar period, British policy towards Bulgaria was elaborated predominantly in the context of Anglo-Soviet relations. The Foreign Office scrutinized each prospective action regarding the country in the light of its possible effect on the behaviour of the Soviet Union, not only in Bulgaria itself but also in the whole adjoining region. British officials were sensitive to Soviet Russia's capacity for retaliation outside its zone, should it perceive any British actions as intended to curtail Soviet superiority in Eastern Europe. This had been clearly demonstrated in the negotiations over the Bulgarian peace treaty.[1] In the first half of 1946, Soviet reluctance to withdraw troops from Iran and suspected preparation for an attack on Turkey had confirmed the strong British fear of Soviet pressure on the Middle East.[2] Such considerations forced British strategists to pay greater than usual attention to Bulgaria, which could provide military bases for Soviet aggression.

From March 1946 to June 1947, British military planners undertook a comprehensive effort to outline the strategic position of the British Commonwealth resulting from the end of the world war. A range of issues were examined, including possible enemy diplomacy, strategy and warfare. The various studies commissioned by the Chiefs of Staff repeated one conclusion, namely that the main threat for Great Britain and its overseas territories would come from Soviet aggression in any area adjacent to the Soviet sphere. The underpinning assumption was that the Soviet Union would continue to pursue a policy of expansion by all means short of war. Any political or military vacuum created by reduced British commitment in territories of strategic importance for Britain would in due course be penetrated by the Soviet Union and add to the latter's war-making capability. As it was difficult to predict the risks Stalin would be willing to undertake, the chance of a new war was not as remote as it had seemed immediately after the end of the most recent conflict.[3] In the eyes of most British military experts, the Soviet Union's double motivation – Russian nationalistic desire to seize foreign lands coupled with a militant Communist ideology committed to the destruction of capitalism worldwide – increased the threat to British long-term strategic interests.

None of the papers produced by various government departments responsible for war planning forecast an imminent danger from the Soviet Union. British analysts believed the Soviet leadership needed to overcome the exhaustion of the war, rebuild the economy and consolidate its gains in Eastern Europe before it could afford a breakdown of relations with the West. On the whole, British policy makers looked upon Soviet military power as 'a source of unease, rather than a direct threat'.[4]

Stalin's insatiable security demands and the belligerent public pronouncements of Soviet statesmen caused grave concern to the British government. Striving to acquire influence over its adjacent territories, the USSR created an international atmosphere of animosity and uncertainty, which itself increased the risk of an accidental war.[5] Even if the Soviet government itself was not prepared to engage in armed hostilities with its erstwhile Allies, British observers suspected it of backing Communists everywhere with material and propaganda help. Overzealous local Communists, in particular those in Yugoslavia and Bulgaria, were obviously involved in supporting the Greek left-wing guerrillas. Most British officials found it hard to believe that this was not sanctioned by Moscow.[6] Communist solidarity across the Balkans was a sufficient reminder of how vulnerable to outside pressure Britain's position in the Mediterranean was.

In British postwar military strategy the importance of the Mediterranean could not be overestimated. It was vital for imperial sea and air communications. It constituted the first line of defence of Great Britain, which could not be secured from a Western base only. The region was at the centre of British strategic planning against the USSR as its continuous reinforcement would be an instrumental advantage at the start of any future war.[7] Even though the overall British aim was to prevent military conflict, Britain's diplomatic strength against the Soviet Union could not be maintained without proper military reinforcement.[8]

The diplomatic perspective

In 1946–47, at the time of the final British preparations for the conclusion of the peace treaty with Bulgaria and the recognition of the existing Bulgarian government, the Foreign Office thoroughly re-examined British relations with the Soviet Union. The re-evaluation had been spurred on by Frank Roberts's dispatches in March 1946.[9] It was crucial for the formulation of British policy towards the small Eastern European satellites, including Bulgaria. Echoing many of the issues addressed by the military planners, the diplomatic discourse naturally centred on the political dimensions of the unfolding international conflict and sought political means to reinforce the British position. Among the most influential FO papers with particular relevance to Eastern Europe was a long memorandum entitled 'The Soviet Campaign against This Country and Our Response to It', produced in April 1946 by Christopher Warner, head of the FO Northern Department.[10] Altogether, FO studies confirmed both the premises and the conclusions of the military authorities' analysis.

Internal FO documents and exchanges with diplomats serving abroad disclose that British officials had little direct evidence of Soviet thinking, relying mainly on clues from specific actions. In Bulgaria the Soviet Union appeared to be exerting ruthless control, coupled with the native Communists' emulation of Soviet domestic policies. On the one hand, this supported the assumption that the same pattern would be followed across the Soviet zone. On the other, the southward Soviet pressure on Turkey and Iran and the virulent anti-West propaganda campaign could not but be seen by the British government as a prelude to attempts at increasing Soviet influence in the Middle East and the Eastern Mediterranean, leading gradually to takeovers similar to those in the Soviet zone. Churchill's words at Fulton, that nobody knew the limits to Soviet 'expansive and proselytising tendencies' reflected the growing concerns of the British government.[11]

The FO experienced difficulties in determining whether ideology or realpolitik was the leading trend in Soviet foreign policy. It was impossible to ignore increasing pronouncements by top Soviet politicians about the inevitability of the clash between world Communism and capitalism. For Roberts, this fundamental Marxist principle guided Soviet long-term strategic thinking, thus aggravating the danger of 'a modern equivalent of the religious wars of the sixteenth century' in which the opposing philosophies would struggle for domination of the world.[12] Soviet revolutionary proselytism was all the more disconcerting since it championed military superiority and could lead to behaviour not much different from that of centuries-long Russian imperialism. This could transform militant Communism into an aggressive foreign-policy course which threatened on an equal scale the security of the British Empire and the democratic principles upheld by Britain.

Uncertain as to whether Marxism was the predominant motive of Soviet external policy, the FO as a whole inclined to the view that Soviet Russia could be the only future aggressor against Britain. In British estimates, the Soviet Union would certainly use the implicit threat of its vast military potential for obtaining political influence over the areas of its interest despite the possibility of a clash with the West. There was no doubt either that the Soviet Union was employing the international Communist movement for achieving its strategic goals. As the military balance in Europe favoured the USSR, Soviet actions in Eastern Europe and claims outside it were seen by the FO as attempts to profit from the unsettled postwar condition of the continent. In such a fluid situation, however, British experts judged that a substantial possibility of miscalculation existed.[13]

Once convinced of the reality of the Soviet threat, Whitehall officials looked for effective resistance against it. The first principle of British defence was that no territories should be evacuated voluntarily as this would always result in Soviet attempts to extend influence in direct or indirect ways through the local Communists parties. In response to Soviet propaganda, Britain should point out the value of freedom, democracy and political tolerance in stark opposition to physical violence and psychological terror. Sargent suggested that one possible counterattack would be for the United Nations to indict the Soviet government for establishing a reign of terror in Eastern Europe. Most important of all, victory in any future conflict with the USSR depended on the state of the British economy, which should be strong and viable.[14]

Contemplating the worst possible outcome, the FO did not disregard the search for some *modus vivendi* with the Soviet Union. Despite pointing out the imperialist aspects of Soviet foreign policy, Roberts advocated the acceptance of the virtually existing spheres of interest. He recommended that Britain should insist on reciprocity but simultaneously not shy away from the establishment of cultural and trade links with the Soviet Union. Warner was not opposed to the idea that, if the USSR concentrated on its own sphere in Eastern Europe, Britain should be more careful with measures against it. However, all British analysts insisted on demonstrating British determination never to abandon the Mediterranean.[15]

The FO was keen to keep open channels of communication with the Soviet Union: at the last Council of Foreign Ministers in London in December 1947 opinions were exchanged on East European matters.[16] Even so, most officials understood the futility of this approach, which was moreover reminiscent of appeasement: concessions just vanished in a bottomless pit of demands. Thomas Brimelow, a Soviet specialist at the Northern Department noted, 'If we were to pursue a policy of appeasement, our concessions would be accepted without gratitude and used against us. We must therefore be firm. On the other hand, if we are actively hostile, we merely confirm the rulers of the Soviet Union in their belief that we hate and fear them, and we accelerate the deterioration of relations.'[17] This echoed the thoughts of some US experts such as Charles Bohlen at the State Department, who contended that Bolshevik ideology paid no attention to 'what the capitalist countries did; the mere fact that they were capitalist made them the object of continuous hostility on the part of the Soviet rulers'.[18] Gradually, a tougher attitude to the Soviet Union was formulated in both Britain and the United States.

This new line of thinking in the FO was reflected in public pronouncements made by British political leaders. In June 1947, in the parliamentary debate on foreign policy, Bevin admitted that confidence and trust were lacking in relations with the Soviet Union. He claimed that the British government had not, and was not, supporting 'any party or movement in any country' which was hostile to the legitimate Soviet interests. Simultaneously, he unambiguously criticized the Soviet Union for not allowing its satellites to have political and commercial ties with the West. He also rebuked the Soviet Union for 'giving the impression [...] that it is satisfied with no Government however democratically elected and however well-intentioned which is not subservient to Soviet aims and indeed dominated by Communists'.[19]

A most effective criticism of Soviet behaviour in Eastern Europe was voiced by the British prime minister, Clement Attlee. In January 1948, he publicly summed up the perception of the Soviet threat as 'imperialism in a new form – ideological, economic and strategic – which threatens the welfare and the way of life of other nations in Europe'.[20] This formed the basis of the Foreign Office 'Bastion' position paper of July 1948, which summarized the considered opinion of all departments dealing with the USSR and Eastern Europe. Its point of departure was the assumption that 'from secure entrenchment in Eastern Europe the Russians are now seeking to infiltrate Western and Southern Europe'. The preferred Soviet tactic was to probe for a weak spot along the Western line, to find and to penetrate it causing 'the whole line to collapse'.[21] Concurrent Soviet actions in Eastern Europe contributed to such British understanding of Soviet policy.

The decision to take a firm stand against Soviet aggression was translated mostly into anti-Communist propaganda. It was also reflected in the uncompromising attitude towards the Soviet Union taken by Britain at the United Nations forums. Above all, it was the main stimulus to participate in the strengthening of the defence of Western Europe and to try to draw the United States closer to European affairs.[22] In purely British–Soviet relations there were still friendly gestures, most notably the new trade agreement signed at the end of 1947 and Soviet consent to the incorporation of the Dodecanese Islands into Greece.[23]

Soviet behaviour contained indications that once it had gained control over territories considered essential in terms of security, the Soviet Union could afford to display flexibility. Stalin recognized and in most cases was ready to accept the limits imposed on Soviet ambitions by the interests of his former Allies. In the countries of the Soviet zone he did not contemplate compromises. The British and US influence was to be curtailed to the absolute minimum, particularly in Bulgaria, which was a vital link in the Soviet zone and occupied a strategic location in the Balkans. With the willing collaboration of the Bulgarian Communist leaders, the country was a suitable ground for the speedy implementation of a new Soviet-dominated political model. The Bulgarian government became increasingly aggressive both in actions at home and foreign policy pronouncements towards the end of 1947. Since its political moves were synchronized with the Kremlin, they provided good indications of Soviet policy and thinking. Any British reaction to events in Bulgaria had to be considered in the light of the impact this would have on relations with the Soviet Union.

Anglo-Bulgarian Relations in the Aftermath of the Peace Treaty

With the ratification of the peace treaty Bulgaria regained legal sovereignty and most European states established diplomatic relations with it. The Allied Control Commission terminated its activities. The Soviet Union withdrew all troops from Bulgaria by mid-December 1947. The normalization of Bulgaria's international status enabled the Bulgarian Communists to concentrate on internal developments, triggering brutal attacks on the opposition. Nothing characterized the Communists' drive to eliminate all active opponents better than the vicious treatment of the Agrarian leader Petkov, who was arrested in parliament just days before the United States granted recognition to the Bulgarian government. This happened against the background of noticeable deterioration of relations between Bulgaria and the West; the latter was portrayed in official Bulgarian propaganda as offering moral and material support to the opposition. At the same time, lacking even the flawed machinery of the ACC, the British and US governments had to find new ways of influencing Bulgaria's rulers.

In late 1947 and especially at the beginning of 1948, John Sterndale-Bennett, the newly appointed British minister in Sofia, reported increasingly strident defiance of the Bulgarian government regarding Britain and the United States. He noted that 'not a speech is made by a Bulgarian politician which does not include an attack upon us both and yet it is us who are held up as warmongers'.[24] The tone was set and maintained by the most prominent Bulgarian Communists, who were most closely connected to the Soviet government. In two speeches at the turn of 1947, Prime Minister Dimitrov accused 'the imperialists' of employing 'diplomatic pressure, intrigues, threats, blackmail' in order 'to hinder the peaceful development and creative construction of Bulgaria'. He also stated that those who wished Bulgaria ill supported 'the remnants of the exploiting circles' as represented by the opposition. Dimitrov saw the ultimate proof of his allegations in the international campaign against Petkov's execution.[25] Kolarov, newly appointed as foreign minister, added that Britain and the United States were demonstrating 'a flagrant disregard' of their treaty obligations by refusing to support Bulgaria's application for membership of the United Nations.[26]

The Bulgarian Communists perceived their open hostility towards the West as a legitimate response to the proclamation of the Truman Doctrine and the Marshall Plan. By trumpeting the alleged imperialist schemes for intervention in the countries with 'people's democracy', they effectively undermined in advance any Western interest in Eastern European affairs. This reflected the Soviet Union's own profoundly altered attitude towards its former Allies. In the latter half of 1947, Soviet propaganda against 'the Anglo-Americans' noticeably gained momentum, ceasing to differentiate publicly between the two governments and their policies. The newly gained confidence of the Bulgarian Communists was also rooted in developments affecting the whole emerging Soviet bloc. The founding conference of the Communist Information Bureau (Cominform) in September 1947 mildly criticized the Bulgarian Communist Party for following a 'vague and hesitant' course and not showing sufficient strength in dealings with the Bulgarian 'bourgeoisie, church and opposition'. In direct consequence to these observations, on 14 October 1947 the CC of the BCP resolved to 'destroy completely' the opposition.[27]

Observing the final elimination of opposition

British officials in Sofia were aware that since their seizure of power the Communists had never really abstained from meddling in the internal affairs of the other political parties. They had simply mitigated their interference until the conclusion of the peace treaty essentially gave them a free hand.[28]

The British representative in Sofia discerned the first sign of the treatment that awaited the opposition in the closing down of various anti-government newspapers: the move eliminated the single most effective means for disseminating non-Communist views. Sterndale-Bennett pointed out that 'the suppression of the Opposition press is only one symptom of a general move aiming at complete disintegration of the Opposition'. His understanding of the situation generated no suggestion as to how to convey to the Bulgarian authorities the British government's displeasure at the violation of civil freedoms in Bulgaria. It was even more challenging to plan measures for stopping the Communist advance as a whole.[29]

This difficulty was aggravated by the fact that many of the remaining opposition activists were discredited in Soviet-style political show trials which routinely unveiled 'Anglo-American' conspiracies. In February 1948 the Agrarian Gichev and in the following November the Social Democrat Lulchev were both sentenced for inciting economic sabotage and armed resistance against the regime. The government prosecutor maintained that both had acted on the instructions of the British and US political representatives.[30] Sterndale-Bennett, who had followed the judicial proceedings as closely as possible, concluded that the trials specifically aimed at discrediting Great Britain and the United States as a measure to isolate them from any contact with nongovernment political organizations.[31]

Having effectively disposed of their adversaries, the Communists turned the state security apparatus against all organizations which were hostile to the regime and had foreign contacts, and were therefore seen as potential centres of anti-Communist activities. This was the rationale behind the trial in February 1949 of fifteen evangelical pastors accused of espionage and currency offences, in which an unprecedented number of Western correspondents and missionaries were specifically implicated by name. In addition, former and serving British and US diplomats were linked to the allegations of the pastors. The FO in conjunction with the State Department expressed concern about the violation of the human rights of the accused and the improper conduct of the trial. The Bulgarian government used this as further proof of guilty association.[32]

By this time all foreign schools, colleges and courses maintained by foreign governments, as well as all religious missions in Bulgaria, had been closed down.[33] In early 1948, the English Speaking League was among the first to disappear, immediately followed by the British Council.[34] Sterndale-Bennett concluded that in Bulgaria 'anything British is a matter of suspicion and anything which is both cultural and British attracts the special attention of the militia'.[35]

Attacks against the Western missions

With the closure of the foreign cultural and educational institutions, the diplomatic missions remained the only sign of Western presence in Bulgaria, presenting the next targets of repression. A succession of trials of Bulgarians working for foreign institutions took place in the middle of 1948. The most publicized was that of Yuli Genov, a long-term employee of the British Legation. Together with three journalists, who had all worked for opposition newspapers and had maintained links with Britain, he was arrested on charges of 'activities against the security of the state'.[36] Seeing in the accusations an attempt to implicate the British Legation, the British representative was extraordinarily concerned as the arrested 'did obtain information, which [was] passed on to the Legation'. Nothing more than 'the usual political gossip' had been passed in 'the usual informal way', but in the current political climate it was 'sufficient for a charge of espionage through an organised spy ring'.[37] Genov's case was reviewed by the Communist Politburo, which instructed the judges to pass a 'ruthless' sentence.[38] Accordingly, Genov was sentenced to twelve and a half years of rigorous imprisonment.[39] This took place over a background of intimidation and mistreatment by the militia of numerous Bulgarian residents who had any personal or business connections with the West. On one occasion, the British minister learned that a British citizen living in Bulgaria had been told by a Bulgarian official 'that Bulgaria was now against England'.[40]

Links with the West were hindered further by the constantly changing and increasing restrictions on the movement of diplomatic personnel.[41] By 1949, the border regions, especially those to the south, were practically sealed off for the staff of foreign missions. In addition to official restrictions, the Bulgarian Foreign Ministry went to incredible lengths to block even leisure journeys.[42] More importantly, the work of the British and US Legations was impeded by an upsurge of accusations against diplomatic personnel. In August 1948, shortly after the expulsion of the US vice consul Donald Ewing, the British pro-consul Jack Adams was declared *persona non grata*.[43] Months of efforts to find out the reasons for this drastic measure revealed the enormity of Adams' offences as having given 'from time to time [...] presents, including chocolates, to Bulgarian friends with the implication that this was in return for information with which they had supplied him'.[44] In March 1949, the Bulgarian government made it known that the first secretary of the British Legation Denis Greenhill was not welcome in Bulgaria. Once again, no official explanation was supplied; privately the expulsion was connected to Greenhill's past naming in the pastors' trial as someone who had recruited the accused for the British intelligence services.[45]

Greenhill's expulsion brought British retaliation against Bogomil Todorov, the third secretary of the Bulgarian Legation in London. This led to the declaration in July 1949 that the third secretary of the British Legation in Sofia John Blakeway was *persona non grata*. Then Boris Temkov, the Bulgarian press attaché in London was sent home, and in September 1949 the British minister was forced to withdraw the assistant military attaché Major B. G. Merivale-Austin in a case of pure reprisal.[46]

The cycle of expulsions was becoming disadvantageous for the British Legation in Bulgaria as it was causing loss not only of prestige but also of experienced officers. Significantly, a relatively short series of reprisals would bring Britain up against the question of whether to expel the head of the Bulgarian Legation in London. In August 1949, the new British minister in Sofia, Paul Mason, suggested that Britain should retaliate directly against the Soviet government, as he was convinced that the actions of the Bulgarian government were incited by the USSR. The FO dismissed this suggestion on the grounds that reprisals against the Soviet Union would inflict exactly the same problems as those against Bulgaria. Moreover, similar developments were taking place in Hungary and Romania. Retaliation against the Soviet Union would imply that the satellites were not treated as independent states, a concept which in itself logically required the withdrawal of missions.[47]

Most British officials recognized the futility of the expulsions but considered that the Bulgarian government would interpret any sign of reconciliation as nervousness and weakness on the British side. The dilemma the FO had to resolve was 'whether to continue [a] tit-for-tat policy with the risk that it will end in a complete rupture of relations, or whether to climb down and let ... opponents win a moral victory'. Bevin himself supported a policy of full retaliation. In a telegram to Sofia he explained that he was 'prepared to face the consequences [...] even to the point of expelling the Bulgarian chargé d'affaires', which would mean the breaking off of diplomatic relations.[48]

The prevailing opinion in the FO was that the satellites would be only too glad to break off diplomatic relations with Britain if Britain could be made to appear responsible. Unlike Hungary, Bulgaria would not even lose trade with Britain. What Britain would miss if its missions were withdrawn from Eastern Europe was receiving 'from time to time [...] a scrap of information, which throws light on Soviet intentions'.[49] The FO had often pointed out that probably the most useful function of its personnel in Bulgaria was to collect information about developments behind the Iron Curtain, especially in view of Bulgaria's proximity to the Eastern Mediterranean. As the Soviet Union was universally suspected of having designs on that region, it was vital for Britain to gather data on the Bulgarian armed forces 'which might be useful and should be passed on to the Greeks and Turks'.[50]

In a lengthy discussion about breaking off relations with Bulgaria, US experts agreed as to the usefulness of Sofia as 'a listening post', but nevertheless believed that the balance of advantage was in favour of a break. British analysts drew the opposite conclusions. For one, the British minister in Sofia believed that if the Bulgarian government was anxious to get rid of his US colleague, 'it would be a mistake to play prematurely into its hands'.[51] The Southern Department accepted the minister's logic as it envisaged that both the British and US governments stood to lose more than they would gain from a rupture of relations with Bulgaria.

> This seems to be [...] one of these occasions [...] in which the same solution to a problem happens to suit both sides. The Soviet Government might well wish us to maintain our missions in the satellite countries [...] but it does not follow that it must therefore be in our interest to withdraw them. On the contrary, they will continue to be useful so long as they are able to obtain some inkling about what is going on behind the Iron Curtain. Our experience with Albania demonstrates the disadvantage of having no diplomatic mission in a satellite country.[52]

The Search for Effective British Policy towards Bulgaria

In such an atmosphere of fierce intolerance to all real and potential internal opponents as well as deep-seated hostility to the Western powers by the radicalized Bulgarian Communist Party, the British government had to formulate a policy towards Bulgaria. It had to be consistent with its dealings elsewhere in the Soviet zone and also fit in with British–Soviet relations.

Contemporary British documents pertaining to Bulgaria contain little more than general policy objectives which applied to most Eastern European satellites. The British government desired to preserve interest in the region, but the priority was ensuring against strategic threats from that direction. This was most pertinent in the case of Bulgaria, which bordered the British Eastern

Mediterranean zone of influence. Britain wanted to restore economic links with the Soviet bloc, as trade could prove an opening for other contacts. Yet attempts at maintaining some political and economic presence in Bulgaria should not obliterate the fact that it had been a war enemy and was becoming a front line of the Soviet zone. The British government was adamant that Bulgaria should fulfil prudently all its treaty obligations, resolving to require from it no less than the Soviet Union would from Italy, for instance.[53]

Simultaneously, the British attitude to Bulgaria was conditioned by traditional views of the country's Russophilia. In mid-1947, in the parliamentary debate on foreign policy, Christopher Mayhew, the FO minister of state, claimed that the Bulgarian government was 'entirely Communist-dominated and entirely subservient to Russia'. In his opinion, the prevailing pro-Russian feelings of the population would make Soviet domination more acceptable to the Bulgarian people than in other Eastern European countries.[54]

With no illusions about the course of Bulgarian development, the FO was still careful that Britain should not look intent on confrontation. The policy it was trying to formulate did not envisage active political intervention to change the nature of the Bulgarian regime. British government officials would only commit themselves to watching the situation closely and pressing the Bulgarian government to fulfil its peace treaty obligations. Shortly after ratification, the peace treaty remained almost the only point of diplomatic and political dialogue between Bulgaria and Great Britain. Instead of being an instrument of British policy, the insistence on adherence to the peace treaty became a policy objective in its own right. This was shaped by two separate issues: Bulgarian lack of respect for human rights and failure to reorganize the army.

Dealing with the political trials

Already in September 1947, the Foreign Office realized that it would 'not be able physically to prevent the [Bulgarian government] from evading such of their treaty obligations as Communist policy demands'.[55] Shortly after the ratification of the treaties with the ex-satellites, in the House of Lords debate Lord Vansittart suggested that in view of the persistent violations by the Soviet puppet regimes the treaties should be reconsidered and possibly even repudiated.[56] This was hardly a realistic demand, especially since the FO had decided to recognize the Communist-controlled governments after long and painful deliberations.

The need to react to particular developments inside the Communist bloc had been championed by most Western representatives since the armistice period. Among them Sterndale-Bennett in Sofia had 'long clamoured for action', often in relation to specific instances of violation of human rights.[57] His successor Mason was also dissatisfied with the mild British reaction to the numerous charges of British espionage plots mentioned in most trials. He tried to explain to his superiors that the typical British 'refusal to be drawn and to pass over with silent contempt obviously baseless charges' was totally inadequate when dealing with Communists, who regarded silence 'as an admission or at least as proving inability to deny'.[58] Both diplomats recommended that the British government should adopt the US government's approach of putting on record every single case in which it disapproved of the conduct of the Bulgarian government. While agreeing to prior consultation with the State Department, the FO preferred to examine each case on its own merits. Eastern European specialists in London claimed that it was neither necessary to have the same approach to all the countries in the region, nor useful to get involved in constant friction.[59]

British reluctance to challenge the Bulgarian authorities was rooted in the realization that such efforts were bound to have minimal effect. Moreover, the Foreign Office was eager to avoid any suspicions of double-dealing in the Balkans, which would aggravate relations with the Soviet Union. This rationale was defeated by the fact that the implication of Britons in the trials of anti-Communists continued despite official British self-restraint. To some extent, the FO hesitated between adopting a high moral stance and a thoroughly realistic, almost cynical one. This generally accounted for a wait-and-see attitude, often taken to the point when delay made late reaction superfluous and irrelevant. One example was Kolarov's speech blaming Britain and the United States for not abiding by their treaty obligations. This spurred a strongly worded US note of protest. The British Legation in Sofia was unanimously in favour of a similar move, while the FO United Nations Department was categorically against it. The Southern Department tried to satisfy both by not ruling out a protest in principle but deferring it for a number of tactical reasons.[60]

The FO's vacillating manner was further demonstrated in internal memoranda aiming to clarify outstanding issues. At the beginning of January 1948, Geoffrey Wallinger, head of the Northern Department, noted that 'the trend is towards toughness'.[61] He was convinced that after Dimitrov's recent shocking statements, public and parliamentary opinion favoured swift and firm dealing with Bulgaria. He saw numerous indications from all Eastern European countries 'that toughness may at least have the effect of delaying moves by the Communists to speed their plans of consolidation'.[62] This theory was not applied: at precisely the same time, Sterndale-Bennett's appeals for vociferous criticism of the Bulgarian government were ignored. The rather strange logic for such lack of response was that 'there will be plenty of chances later to go to town on some Bulgarian incident'.[63]

The FO hesitated mainly as to whether British censure of particular actions of the Bulgarian authorities should be extended into a general offensive against the regime. Article 2 of the peace treaty obliged the Bulgarian government to observe human rights and could justify attempts to stop the Communist advance. Such a course would affect all Eastern European countries, signalling an assault on the Soviet model as a whole. Sterndale-Bennett was among the staunchest advocates of this initiative. He repudiated the British government's narrow legalistic view of the treaties, which revealed British uncertainty.[64] The British minister in Sofia was not deterred even by the memory of Petkov's execution as he believed British protests had been made 'in full realisation of the risk that [they] might not help him personally'.[65]

Occasionally, FO specialists agreed that Britain should not become apathetic just because it could not give the people concerned any effective assistance; yet their prevailing inclinations were on the side of patience and caution. From the local perspective this could only be perceived as unwittingly helping to strengthen the Bulgarian government and diminish British prestige in the country. It could not impress the Bulgarian authorities; neither could it win the respect of the dissidents.[66] If anything, the FO was growing more convinced that any involvement, for example insisting for mitigation of Genov's sentence, could become a source of potential embarrassment.[67] By the time of Traicho Kostov's trial in late 1949, after the Communists had started purges within their own party, the British representatives refrained even from demanding access to the courtroom. The FO wished to avoid the impression that it was 'unduly concerned' about the charges.[68]

Donald Heath, the US ambassador in Sofia, was as active as his British colleague in trying to impress his superiors with the need to protest vigorously against all treaty violations. This would disabuse both the Bulgarian and Soviet governments of their belief that their actions in Eastern Europe provoked no interest in the West.[69] The high point of US involvement in Bulgaria after the conclusion of the peace treaty was a stiff aide-memoire handed to Kolarov on 23 September 1948 which was unequivocally critical of the behaviour of the Bulgarian government from the very moment Sofia had signed the peace treaty:

> The Bulgarian Government has prosecuted a systematic and ruthless campaign to obliterate democratic opposition in direct disregard of fundamental principles of freedom. [...] Through abuse of the instrumentalities of political power and subversion of judicial process the Bulgarian Government has subjected substantial numbers of Bulgarian people whose only crime was a belief in the rights of man, to involuntary servitude, banishment, concentration camps, imprisonment, torture

and execution. It has obliterated the Opposition party and by means of terror stifled free expression.[70]

Not only did the Bulgarian government claim a clean record in its reply but it also complained that the great powers had taken no concerted action under Article 35 to exercise their right to advise and enlighten the Bulgarian government in the interpretation of the peace treaty. Sterndale-Bennett approved of the tone of the US representation and called for immediate British support. He believed that the Bulgarian government's militancy was in substance a reflection of Soviet policy. The latter appeared not 'in the least concerned about protests to the [Soviet] Orbit countries as long as they do not interfere with the main line of Soviet policy'.[71] He further sought to impress on the FO that in such circumstances, British silence would 'lower the morale of Bulgarian Opposition and encourage the impertinence of the authorities'. Instead, he thought it necessary to reinforce swift and blunt occasional protests with a more principled long-term approach. For the moment, however, British diplomats in Sofia could only repeat the need for consistent acceptance, observation and control of treaty obligations assumed by both sides under Article 2.

In January 1949, Mayhew proclaimed in the House of Commons that 'the record of the present Bulgarian Government [...] shows that their interpretation of human freedom is so different from ours as to make any form of protest quite unavailing'.[72] This conviction had been formed by the time of the Lulchev trial in 1948. While initially keen to continue with the handing of notes of protest to the Bulgarian government, the FO could foresee nothing but sterile diplomatic exchanges. Unlike US foreign policy officials, the FO experts never really contemplated applying the machinery of the peace treaty for the resolution of arguments with the Bulgarian authorities.[73]

Article 36 of the peace treaty with Bulgaria detailed the procedure for the handling of disputes between the signatories about the interpretation and implementation of the treaty. As this involved the participation of the Soviet Union expectations of its effectiveness were minimal.[74] The FO believed that the first attempt to enforce the treaty through the dispute machinery should be a 'specific, solid-ground case'. It should be related to military or economic clauses, rather than 'something so indefinite as infringement of human rights'.[75]

Sterndale-Bennett was naturally disconcerted by the irresolute attitude of Whitehall. He lamented that officials in London were 'hypnotised by the legal difficulties and overlooking the psychological aspect' and warned that the excessive caution of the British government could be seen as lack of confidence and determination. In his view, the treaty gave Britain a lever with respect to the satellite countries which was not available in the case of the Soviet Union itself. Such advantage should be used consciously with the aim of throwing Communists 'off their balance' and embarrassing them wherever it was practicable. The British minister in Sofia saw this as the only way 'to give hope to people who otherwise see none [and] keep alive the core of potential resistance to Communists. [...] It is precisely by broadening the moral, as opposed to the purely material, basis of our stand against the Communist offensive that we are most likely in the long term to defeat it.'[76]

The FO, however, was moving in exactly the opposite direction to its representative in Bulgaria. It assured him that it too was thinking about how 'to expose to the world the tyrannical and menacing policy' of the Kremlin-directed Communist parties throughout Europe. Even so, it concluded that the Soviet orbit should be treated as a whole: the puppet governments should be openly branded as Moscow's agents, rather than merely unrepresentative and tyrannical. Thus, a clear distinction would be drawn between ordinary people in the satellites and their Communist rulers. Furthermore, while condemning the behaviour of local Communist parties, Britain's main target would be the USSR.[77]

These intentions showed that the British government was effectively ceasing to attach much importance to the peace treaties. By the time of Lulchev's trial, it had become 'the fixed policy of HMG not to invoke the treaty'.[78] The logical extension of such an approach was that even protests on specific cases became undesirable. Bevin wrote to the British minister in Sofia explaining that, instead of referring to Article 2, the British government was going to seek opportunities for exposing publicly Bulgaria's treatment of human rights.[79]

In the two years following the signing of the peace treaty, Britain sent seven protests to the Bulgarian government against violations of Article 2 and the Universal Declaration of Human Rights.[80] The sober conclusion was that these official communications had produced no result and the British government had to face the fact that it possessed no means of enforcing respect for human rights in Soviet-dominated states. Even worse, any attempt to do so merely demonstrated and emphasized the ineffectiveness of the treaty machinery to deal with violations. It also advertised British impotence to achieve results in the Soviet zone.[81]

Publicizing the 'Bulgarian atrocities'

The British Legation followed closely the series of political trials in Bulgaria in 1947–48. Concern about the allegations against British citizens was combined with careful observation of the ominous proceedings, which revealed the nature of the Communist regime. This contributed towards the ongoing analysis of the process of establishing the Soviet system in Eastern Europe, which could be then employed in education and propaganda.

As British officials were looking for effective methods of influencing the Bulgarian regime without engaging in direct clashes, they were acutely aware of a double disadvantage: they could be both presented in a confrontational light and exposed to possible rebuff. When in January 1948, Wallinger urged adoption of a more offensive policy he had in mind above all intensified propaganda.[82] The idea had been encouraged by diplomats in the field and taken up by a number of Southern Department members. They considered that vigorous publicity of the unsightly events in Bulgaria would make up to some extent for British inability to implement the peace treaty with the country.

> One fundamental fact which is clear to us and public opinion is that it is not possible to prevent the Bulgarian Government and others in the Soviet Orbit from behaving as they wish. We may, by means of successful publicity, and by means of keeping the flame of liberty alight, i.e. by pressure of public opinion outside and inside Bulgaria – be able to modify the actions of these Governments to some very slight extent. [...] We cannot hope [...] to enforce the Treaty on Bulgaria. What we can do is to make the most effective use of the Treaty for publicity purposes.[83]

The British representatives in Sofia were especially keen on collaborating with the BBC Overseas Service, whose programmes were judged to have a big impact on listeners in Bulgaria. Daily contacts with the Communist authorities provided possible topics for press and radio features. Sterndale-Bennett was extremely glad when Georgi Dimitrov's boisterous speeches at the start of 1948 were noticed by the BBC and interpreted as proof that Petkov's execution and the treatment of anti-Communists had been motivated by political vengeance. The speeches were turned into real political news – they were quoted on the BBC Bulgarian transmissions, used for several newspaper editorials and finally formed the basis for an 'inspired' parliamentary question.[84]

The most important result from such a media campaign in Britain was the clear embarrassment of the Bulgarian Communist leadership, whose actions and statements for domestic consumption were now being widely circulated abroad.[85] Reports from Sofia confirmed that the appearance of materials in the Western media was the one weapon which deeply affected the Bulgarian government, touching it 'on the raw'. Prominent disclaimers were published in Bulgarian national newspapers in attempts to counter the Western publications. At the time of Lulchev's trial, the Bulgarian Ministry of Justice summoned a special foreign-press conference in order to give a comprehensive official 'explanation'.[86]

Even when the pressure of international public opinion was believed to have a significant impact on the Bulgarian government, it was of little help to the defendants.[87] The FO worried lest publicity should do more personal harm than good to the accused. It was exceedingly reluctant to circulate freely diplomatic reports from Bulgaria, preferring to show the dispatches in confidence to selected journalists who could be trusted to weave them into articles. Whitehall officials hoped to develop 'a system for ordering feature articles and [...] place these in the appropriate journals'.[88] Such an approach, however, was not to the liking of the British press and radio. The media handled information coming directly from the FO with care, generally regarding it as being adapted to government interests and therefore partial. The FO often found even the government-funded BBC European Service scrupulously objective and reluctant to broadcast what it considered to be undiluted propaganda. Yet, as news editors preferred to rely on their own correspondents, rather than use ready diplomatic information, they were subject to the many hindrances the Bulgarian authorities posed to the entry of journalists into the country. Additionally, most trials were conducted *in camera* leaving the media with the feeling that their people had travelled in vain.[89]

By far the greatest impediment to what the FO saw as adequate publicity of Bulgarian developments was the low British public interest towards the country. Consequently, the BBC tended to include information about it in pieces dealing with the Soviet satellites in general. The FO complained that it was almost impossible to 'sell' material from Bulgaria to the diplomatic correspondents of the newspapers.[90] In response, British diplomatic representatives who felt frustrated by the meagre coverage occasionally berated the Southern Department for not 'organising better publicity'. In relation to the Social Democrats' trial in mid-1948, Sterndale-Bennett wrote that 'public apathy [lay] very largely in the hands of the governments concerned and the main object of the British government's action should surely be to awake public interest'.[91]

The British Legation in Sofia received the greatest blow during Gichev's trial in early 1948. It had managed to secure the right for foreign observers to be present in court, but no British journalist was willing to report.[92] When even the foreign secretary enquired about press coverage, the FO confessed to the futility of its attempts to induce various papers to send reporters for the trial: 'Their men are wasted in that they can only send straight reports such as the news agencies supply and are unable, owing to censorship and/or physical danger, to provide any worthwhile comment until they have passed through the Curtain.'[93]

In addition to problems related to professional principles and pragmatic concerns, a range of political difficulties affected the work of reporters in

Eastern Europe. The FO worried that British media attention could expose the government's actions abroad in an undesirable light. It would not be difficult for journalists to notice that Britain's attitude to foreign trials was not the same everywhere. It would be embarrassing for the government to answer questions about why it sent observers to Polish trials and not to Greek, and why it was willing to answer parliamentary questions about Polish and Bulgarian trials but not about those in Greece or Spain.[94]

The FO feared that the increased publicity it favoured would bring greater public scrutiny of British policy, which could then backfire. The government could be accused of not following up its propaganda with sufficiently tough concrete measures towards the Communist bloc. The FO faced a dilemma on publicity, similar to its earlier predicament regarding official protests to the Bulgarian government. British foreign policy experts had no illusions that while a bolder policy had inherent propaganda value, publicity was presently receiving so much attention because it remained one of the few means of exerting pressure on the Communist regime in Bulgaria. It was necessary because it signified continued British interest in Bulgarian developments. If British attempts to make the peace treaty work had come to no avail, then the continuous disregard of the Bulgarian government for its international obligations should be exposed at every suitable opportunity.[95]

The controversial issue of publicity was complicated further when Sargent became anxious 'that the number of protests being made to the satellites and given to the press was too great and was beginning to look ridiculous'. Contrary to the Southern Department's carefully elaborated logic that where protests had no effect, publicity would work, he suggested that it was 'all right to protest' as long as less publicity followed.[96] Sargent's influential opinion rapidly changed the FO's perspective of the link between action and propaganda. Since diplomatic notes had no meaningful consequences and media coverage merely advertised defeat, both methods came to be considered undesirable. Towards the end of 1948, the general feeling at the department was that 'ineffectual protests' should be restrained so as not to publicly display Britain's 'inability to enforce the Treaty'.[97]

Publicity was essential but not sufficient, unless closely linked to a well-rounded approach towards the Bulgarian regime. To have any effect on the course of events in Bulgaria, Britain needed to combine international exposure of the methods of the Bulgarian authorities with political action which would secure implementation of the peace treaty. This was where the scheme faltered: it did nothing about violations of the human rights provisions beyond just calling attention to them. It even refused to admit openly that the question was related to the very essence of the political system, and that this was too broad an issue to be dealt with by the limited machinery of the treaty.

Economic relations with Bulgaria

While experiencing difficulties in the formulation of precise and enforceable policy towards Bulgaria, the Foreign Office was equally unprepared for dealing with British–Bulgarian economic relations. The general state of affairs between the two countries rendered the prospect of normal trade exchanges not only unlikely but also highly controversial, and throughout 1948 the British side strove to clarify the basic principles that should govern this sphere.

Since interest in trade with Bulgaria was determined neither by a strong tradition nor a sound economic rationale, the question had distinct political undertones. The international political climate made each country look upon the approaches of the other with suspicion. The Bulgarian government seemed eager to trade but feared that Britain would impose severe conditions for compensation of the property of Allied citizens nationalized after 9 September 1944. The British government insisted that Bulgaria should resume payment of its external prewar debt, which was unilaterally suspended in March 1948. Bulgaria should also reach agreement with the foreign holders of prewar Bulgarian government bonds. Until this was done in December 1948, trade was conducted on an ad hoc basis. This involved protracted negotiations between the two sides, long and complicated coordination between the various British governmental departments dealing with 'trade with the enemy', as well as painful communication with the multitudinous Bulgarian state enterprises which took 'until Doomsday' to make up their minds.[98]

As on other subjects, the views of the British representative in Bulgaria and of the FO differed. Sterndale-Bennett recommended a consistent course for the conclusion of a trade agreement which would guard British economic interest. He warned that unless forced to commit itself to specific terms, Bulgaria would continue to obtain supplies from Britain without reciprocal legal binding. His reasoning also questioned the long-term effects of British–Bulgarian trade. Bulgarian purchases in 1948 exceeded export threefold in value and consisted mainly of machines, wool, chemicals, medicines and rubber, all supplies that undoubtedly could contribute to the collectivization of agriculture and support industry. Significantly, Bulgaria was buying from the West only goods not secured by its long-term agreement with the Soviet Union.[99]

The alternative view was that since Britain was not in a position to affect internal Bulgarian policy, or for that matter the policy of any of the satellites, some trade 'might whet the [Bulgarian] appetite'. Unless the desired items were included in the British list of controlled exports, it would seem unwise to refuse the business, especially since Britain was rarely the only exporter. Britain could even make buying easy without itself buying anything from Bulgaria, who – like other satellites – would soon be in need of sterling earnings and then prepared to sign a trade agreement. If, as a result, Bulgaria became to any extent dependent on the UK, this could be turned into a useful political weapon.[100]

The gravest British doubt regarding trade with Bulgaria sprang from scepticism that 'the Bulgarians had anything of exceptional value'. At the beginning of 1949, the Ministry of Food wrote to the Foreign Office that it had 'really no interest [and] saw little prospect of trade'. The biggest potential Bulgarian export was tobacco, but the FO ruled out purchases, categorically refusing to allow Bulgarian tobacco to compete with Greek and Turkish even if the latter 'cost a little more'.[101] Such attitude echoed prewar concerns, showing little change of the link between politics and trade when it came to choosing between Bulgaria and its southern Balkan neighbours.

The unyielding British attitude proved justified. While hesitating about its economic approach to Bulgaria, Britain had turned down Bulgarian requests for licences for import in the spring and summer of 1949. As a result the Bulgarian government conceded that there should be a general agreement not only on trade but also on issues related to debt and compensations.[102] This, however, did not alter the ambiguous British conduct. Unwittingly, the FO and the Board of Trade made sure that Britain accrued no significant economic advantages which could be used to exert political influence on the Bulgarian authorities.

Even in economic relations, the FO was more interested in propaganda rather than in actual trade. Already in January 1947, in a special memorandum Mayhew promoted the idea of putting 'Communism in Eastern Europe on the defensive vis-à-vis Social Democracy not only politically but in terms of living standards'. He proposed publicizing the idea that Eastern Europe was being exploited by the Soviet Union. This was discussed at a special meeting chaired by Gladwyn Jebb, then head of the FO Reconstruction Department, which decided that such an argument was too broad and easily disputed. Instead, it was more useful to concentrate on concrete topics with relatively short-term implications. Attention should focus on the great expenses incurred by the Soviet troops in occupied countries and on Soviet acquisition of former German and Italian assets in Eastern Europe. Simultaneously, the Communist parties' lack of economic competence should be continuously exposed.[103]

The International Dimension

As the British government had little practical interests in Bulgaria, it stumbled over the task of how to translate its disapproval of Bulgarian Communism into specific foreign policy measures. By the end of 1948, the need to react to internal Bulgarian developments was dominated by moral and ideological elements. This was in sharp contrast to the FO's unwillingness to get involved in actions, which were known to produce little effect inside Bulgaria and merely drew attention to British helplessness. Still, Britain refused to dissociate itself completely from Bulgaria on account of the broader significance of events there. Not only was the consolidation of the Communist regime indicative of developments across Eastern Europe, but it had well-defined Balkan dimensions.

Bulgarian involvement in the Greek Civil War

Throughout the Second World War British attention to Bulgaria had been dominated by Bulgarian occupation of Greek and Yugoslav territories. Postwar relations between Bulgaria and its neighbours remained a critical factor for the British position regarding the country. British foreign-policy experts could point to numerous evidence of continuing Bulgarian irredentist ambitions. The original FF government had reiterated its wartime predecessors' demands for Greek Thrace, or at the minimum, an Aegean outlet. This objective was common to all Bulgarian political parties, remaining a foreign-policy priority for Petkov's Agrarians and Lulchev's Social Democrats even after they walked out of the coalition with the Communists. From Britain's perspective such claims to Greek territory were all the more dangerous for coinciding with Soviet interests in the Balkans. British military and political analysts, in agreement with the US government, had concluded that securing a presence at the Straits had been among the prime objects of Soviet manoeuvres in the Middle East in the spring of 1946.[104]

As Greece stood in the first line of defence of the Eastern Mediterranean, its ongoing civil war made its position especially precarious in Britain's eyes. It was widely assumed that the Greek Communists were receiving moral and material support from the Soviet Union. If successful, they could provide Stalin with the double advantage of establishing another Communist regime in the Balkans and acquiring vital strategic positions. The FO Southern Department was certain that the Soviet Union planned to obtain control of Greece or at least to diminish sufficiently British and US influence there: 'Communist control of Greece would not place the Commonwealth in mortal danger but it would seriously jeopardise [...] chances of defending vital areas, turn Turkey's flank, weaken Italy's strategic position and threaten communications through the Mediterranean.'[105]

The British government's concern was that unofficial Bulgarian involvement in the Greek Civil War was a key instrument for the realization of such a Soviet design in addition to potentially benefitting Bulgaria territorially.

The civil war was most acute in northern Greece and the Athens government constantly provided the FO with evidence that the Bulgarian Communist authorities were arming, training and sheltering Greek guerrillas, leading to regular armed clashes on the Bulgarian–Greek border. The tension did not recede after the conclusion of the peace treaty with Bulgaria, which the Greek government also signed.[106]

The British government acknowledged that Bulgarian assistance to the Greek rebels was not as crucial as that afforded by Yugoslavia and Albania. Even so, it was an important contribution to the cause of spreading Communism and disrupted the fragile balance of power in the Balkans.[107] British observers were convinced that Bulgarian state-organized help to the Greek Communists was carried on in close coordination with the Soviet Union. This derived from the assumption that as a rule Moscow actively supported and directed foreign Communists and was overtly confirmed by Soviet diplomatic actions and public pronouncements castigating British involvement in Greece. Similarly, Bulgarian Communist leaders' open hostility to Britain only served to solidify the British belief in a Soviet-led initiative for comprehensive aid to the KKE, the Greek Communist Party. Therefore, British observers dwelled little on occasions showing Soviet conciliation regarding Greece, for instance agreeing to the formation of the Commission of Investigation of Greek Frontier Incidents.[108] In fact, unsuspected to the British government in May 1947, in a personal meeting with the Greek Communist leader Nichos Zachariades, Stalin was extremely reserved as to the wisdom of providing money, equipment and weapons to the Greek Partisans.[109] By January 1948, the Soviet leader had grown completely disillusioned with the KKE, warning that the Soviet Union would not come to Yugoslavia's rescue if the latter inflicted war with Britain and the United States because of supporting the Greek guerrillas.[110] No such caution is known to have been directed to the Bulgarian Communists, who – with Stalin's knowledge – had set up a whole secret organization for aid to their Greek comrades.[111]

The FO understood that the proclamation of the Truman Doctrine and the Marshall Plan would be additional stimuli for Soviet determination to win over Greece with the help of its northern neighbours.[112] The changing disposition of forces in South Eastern Europe had an impact on the role of Bulgaria. While it was 'a springboard towards Turkey and Greece', from the opposite standpoint it was also 'an important link which, if broken, might seriously weaken the whole Soviet chain'.[113]

British representatives in Bulgaria suggested that what they believed to be Soviet intervention in Greece could be effectively deterred only by matching military measures undertaken jointly by Britain and the United States.[114] In agreement with Heath, Sterndale-Bennett recommended determined action to stop the progress of the Communists in Greece. For the two diplomats, resolute common Anglo-American action carried less danger of precipitating an open war than allowing Soviet subversion in Greece to continue and eventually spill over into Turkey. The latter effect would occur if Britain and the United States only remonstrated verbally.[115] With some hesitation, the FO Southern Department acknowledged the value of Sterndale-Bennett's recommendations and in the late spring of 1948 started to explore the possibility of applying diplomatic pressure on Moscow both directly and through the United Nations. Preliminary efforts were however cut short by Bevin, who totally disagreed that this was the time or place for a 'showdown' with the USSR.[116]

Any British offensive against what was considered to be the Soviet involvement in the Balkans had to be backed by a real show of force. Greece offered such a possibility, as the international influence of the Soviet Union would be seriously undermined by curtailing the advance of the Greek Communists. This would have the supplementary effect of frustrating the consolidation of Communism in Bulgaria. Any British military initiative in northern Greece would alert the Bulgarian leaders as to their vulnerability caused by the proximity to Greece and Turkey. Although somewhat unstable, Britain's position in these two countries in 1947 and 1948 could theoretically be used as a point from which to apply pressure on the southern flank of the Soviet zone.

For this, however, Britain possessed neither the military capability nor the necessary political will. In the immediate postwar period, its government was intent on restricting military commitments overseas, which also affected armed forces in the Balkans. Accordingly, the British government looked into possibilities of reducing the cross-border tensions created by the Greek Civil War and abstained from directly challenging the perceived Soviet contribution to it. In consequence, the Soviet hold across Eastern Europe was affected.

The danger of a Danubian federation

Britain's concern about Bulgarian interference in the Greek Civil War had a corollary in the question of a Bulgarian–Yugoslav federation. The idea for closer national cooperation among the countries seceding from the Ottoman Empire had existed in Balkan political thinking since the late eighteenth century. In the interwar years it was promoted by leftist political circles as a solution to the bitter rivalries on the peninsula, and was eventually adopted by the Bulgarian Communist Party.[117]

Towards the end of the Second World War, the Foreign Office too had contemplated the possibility of a Balkan federation but had come up against the Soviet veto in Moscow in October 1943. When the postwar Bulgarian and Yugoslav governments revived the idea, Britain faced a completely different geopolitical situation. The appearance of a large state with a predominantly Slav population would certainly change drastically the balance of forces in the region, all the more so in view of the Communist-dominated governments in both Yugoslavia and Bulgaria. With these willing channels of Soviet influence at the core of the proposed South Slav federation, Britain's position in the Balkans would suffer profoundly.

In January 1945, after official Bulgarian declarations calling for the speedy establishment of a federation, the British government was quick to send notes to the Bulgarian, Yugoslav and Soviet governments, voicing disagreement with the proposal. Britain did not oppose the planned institution of a separate Macedonian unit in the federal Yugoslav state but warned that it would not recognize any transfer of territory from Bulgaria to Yugoslavia hinted at by official Bulgarian statements. The British warning was firmly reiterated at the Yalta Conference.[118] Britain's stance reflected concern that the discussed unification of Yugoslav (Vardar) and Bulgarian (Pirin) Macedonia, within Yugoslavia or as a federal entity in its own right, would undoubtedly raise the question of the status of the Greek – that is, Aegean – part of Macedonia.

Britain's uneasiness regarding Macedonia was exacerbated by the existing fears about Bulgarian and Yugoslav involvement on the side of the Greek guerrillas. FO position papers and internal communications show that it did not underestimate the traditionally strong attachment to Macedonia for any Bulgarian regime, including the Communist. The strength of the latter, in turn, would bear directly on the vitality of any Danubian scheme. British officials suspected that unfulfilled Bulgarian territorial demands could be linked with those of Yugoslavia, which was vigorously supporting the Greek guerrillas.

It was the logical connection between the aspirations of the Greek Partisans and the Bulgarian–Yugoslav plans that made the British government extremely watchful of any notion of changes in the southern Balkan region. The Greek Communists were known to be fighting for 'Free Greece'. The worst scenario Britain envisaged was that the Partisans' efforts could concentrate on Greek Macedonia with Bulgarian and Yugoslav backing. In 1947–48 the KKE talked of detaching Aegean Macedonia from Greece, admitting that this could only succeed with the assistance of the 'people's democracies' to the north.[119] If Greek Macedonia effectively seceded from the Athens government, it would not be difficult to set up a 'Free Macedonia' by the addition of territory from Bulgaria and Yugoslavia. Such a possibility looked all the more realistic when considered against the background of the Bulgarian authorities' concurrent promotion of a 'Macedonian nation' in the Pirin region as part of the project for a Bulgarian–Yugoslav federation. It would solve a number of existing irredentist and ideological problems: nationalist Bulgarian and Serbian ambitions towards Macedonia would be satisfied, while the Greek Communists could join established Communist regimes.

Above all, from the British perspective the federation idea would present considerable danger to the independence and integrity of Greece. If a large Communist Slav state took shape in the south of the Balkans, the Soviet orbit would be extended to the Aegean, thus disrupting British plans for the reinforcement of the Mediterranean. Greece would be reduced to impotence and Turkey severed from Europe. For Britain therefore, the importance of the preservation and strengthening of Greek legitimacy was such that the FO thought it prudent to prevent the Macedonian question from even becoming a subject of international discussion.[120]

Britain's consideration of the Macedonian question steered clear of any judgement of the validity of the claims of either Bulgaria, Serbia or Greece as to the ethnic composition of Macedonia. The nationalist controversy had for decades marred relations in the Balkans but was of little genuine interest per se to the British government. The latter was of course acutely aware of the political passions these issues always inflamed in Greece and the neighbouring countries. After the Second World War, Britain refused to become entangled in the ongoing debate as to the existence and origins of any 'Macedonian nation' as opposed to the mere mixture of populations of different religious and ethnic character.[121] For practical purposes Britain looked upon Macedonia mostly in geographic terms, evaluating its strategic importance in the shifting Balkan equilibrium. As Britain could neither influence the substance of the Bulgarian–Yugoslav negotiations after 1945, nor secure territorial alterations to the Greek advantage, it firmly supported the status quo regarding Macedonia – that is, its division between Bulgaria, Yugoslavia and Greece.

Looking for means to fortify Britain's Eastern Mediterranean flank, British officials understood that the Soviet Union was undoubtedly going to do the same on the edges of its sphere. In the light of this, Britain was bound to reconsider the importance of Bulgaria, which bordered two countries forming a vital link in Britain's strategic defence plan. British specialists had no doubt that Stalin monitored and in fact guided the progress of the federation idea. They were certain that Stalin would not fail to understand that the creation of a large state at the centre of the Balkans would naturally increase the apprehension of the neighbouring countries and so offset some of the advantages of the establishment of a pro-Soviet Communist formation.[122] Keeping abreast of the Bulgarian and Yugoslav governments' plans for a South Slav federation would give Britain another indication of the overall aims of the Soviet Union and the lengths to which it proposed to pursue them.

In the two years between the British note of 1945 opposing the federation and the conclusion of the peace treaty, the Bulgarian government was careful not to provoke further British protests on the subject. This did not mean, however, that the goal had been cancelled: it was simply postponed. Meanwhile, the government was implementing internal measures which would smooth the prospective union with Yugoslavia. The unconcealed plan was to establish a customs union after the ratification of the peace treaty, then an alliance with Yugoslavia and Albania, and finally a federation. In some unguarded statements, Bulgarian Communists even called for rapprochement with Greece, where they envisaged the establishment of 'a democratic regime'. This alerted Britain to the fact that indeed Bulgaria and Yugoslavia were poised to unify into one state stretching between the Black and Adriatic seas, which could then form the nucleus of an even larger Balkan federation.[123] For Britain this constituted a design for unprecedented Communist territorial, economic and ultimately strategic gains in the Aegean. This spelt the undisguised danger of Greece's eventual engulfment in the Soviet sphere.

After the recognition of the Bulgarian government, Great Britain had no means of influencing the course of events regarding a Balkan federation. All it could do was to observe the process from outside and try to judge how fast it could be completed. Diplomatic reports from across Eastern Europe suggested that the federation's launch was not as imminent as some declarations of Bulgarian statesmen suggested. Sterndale-Bennett's growing impression in January 1948 was that in Bulgaria itself the 'formality of a federation even with Yugoslavia may still be in doubt and formation of a larger confederation even more so'. In Sofia it was apparent that for various reasons the question was receding into the background. There had been speculation about the personal rivalry between Dimitrov and Tito, the latter displaying the air of 'a prospective purchaser coming to inspect the estate with a view to taking it over' during his visit in Sofia. Another difficulty related to Macedonia, as it seemed to the British minister that Bulgaria was not really prepared to see the Pirin region detached except in exchange of territorial compensation in the Aegean.[124] Nothing in Prague, Bucharest or Budapest, or for that matter Belgrade, made the British representatives in these cities consider the idea of a federation practical or think that Yugoslavia was seriously contemplating it.[125] Still, the available information was often confusing and the substance of the propaganda had not changed much.[126]

The vague British perception that progress towards a Balkan federation had been halted was not based on any firm evidence, and even less on knowledge of the changing Soviet position. It was known that leading Bulgarian and Yugoslav Communists had been summoned to Moscow shortly after the signing of the Bulgarian–Yugoslav Agreement for Friendship and

Cooperation in Bled (Yugoslavia) on 1 August 1947. British observers however had no information about the talks with the Soviet leadership, and even less of the severe Soviet criticism of the noisy publicity with which the agreement had been concluded. Stalin condemned the wide scope of the document, which touched on a number of political, economic and cultural issues – and equally, the fact of its signing before the ratification of the peace treaty. Most importantly, Stalin pointed out that the precipitate actions of the two governments gave 'the reactionary Anglo-American elements' a pretext to increase their military intervention in Greek and Turkish affairs.[127]

Stalin's angry reaction to continued open Bulgarian and Yugoslav adherence to a Balkan federation reached an unprecedented level in early 1948. On 17 January 1948, Dimitrov spoke to journalists about, among other questions, the federation, stating that the idea should be left to mature, but a first step would be a customs union. Adding that when it finally went ahead, the envisaged federation might include Greece, he provoked an immediate international outcry.[128]

The Kremlin reacted swiftly: on 24 January Dimitrov received a ciphered telegram that his interview was 'judged by the Moscow friends as harmful'. It was considered to be undermining the 'new democracies' and above all giving a winning card to Britain and the United States, who could construe Dimitrov's inopportune words as an example of aggressive Soviet plans. The Soviet message underlined that such grand designs, propagated by a well-known activist of the international Communist movement, might serve as an excuse for closer alignment of Britain, the United States and Western Europe against Communism worldwide.[129] Adding insult to injury, the private reproach was supplemented by a public rebuke in *Pravda*, which wrote that the Soviet leadership did not subscribe to 'problematic and fantastic federations and confederations'.[130] The final blow to Dimitrov was dealt on 10 February 1948 when Stalin presided over a tripartite Bulgarian–Yugoslav–Soviet meeting at the Kremlin. He castigated the Bulgarian prime minister for making sweeping statements without higher authorization. Stalin repeated that Dimitrov's declarations made easier the creation of the Western bloc. He was especially irritated by the possibility that friends and foes alike could think that it was all a Soviet idea.[131]

The FO was quick to grasp that the setting up of a broad federation would make it extremely difficult for the Soviet Union to condemn plans for Western European integration.[132] However, this was not viewed as the primary reason for the Soviet change of attitude regarding federation. British experts had little information on which to base their analysis convincingly and could only speculate about Stalin's reluctance to deal with an extraordinarily strong South Slav state which might spur centrifugal tendencies in the Soviet bloc.

Retrospective interpretations of Stalin's motives were precipitated by the open Soviet–Yugoslav split later in 1948. What became immediately obvious, however, was that the Bulgarian Communist leadership was not in a position to take independent decisions about Bulgaria's external or internal affairs. The quick dropping of plans for a Bulgarian–Yugoslav federation demonstrated clearly that even the most long-standing items on the Bulgarian Communists' agenda could be overturned at the Kremlin's insistence. If Britain needed proof that the Bulgarian Communists' loyalty to the Soviet Union stood above commitment to any specific actions, it could hardly have received a more convincing one.[133]

This trend was only reaffirmed by the founding in September 1947 of the Cominform, which undertook the coordination of the activities of nine Communist parties. This practically subordinated them to the Soviet Communist Party and, through it, to the interests of the Soviet state. The leading objective of the Cominform was the acceleration of the revolutionary transformation of the countries of Eastern Europe on the Soviet model. The Cominform's first meeting confirmed the validity of Marxist–Leninist postulates about the inevitable clash between Communism and capitalism.[134]

The establishment of the Cominform had relatively little impact on British attitudes to Bulgaria. The new organization was immediately seen as a Soviet instrument for exporting Communism and consolidating the Soviet position in Eastern Europe through the national Communist parties. The development marked a new phase in the evolution of the Communist bloc, only reinforcing existing British assumptions about the Soviet Union's aggressive foreign policy. It also increased British understanding of the Soviet Union's political and strategic objectives. As Bulgaria's role in the Cominform was in line with British expectations, it confirmed the FO's belief that the Bulgarian Communist Party was set on emulating faithfully the Soviet model. As British government circles had long accepted the advent of Communism in Bulgaria, this brought no active British reaction.[135]

Observation of the military clauses of the peace treaty

Britain had one supplementary objection to the establishment of a Danubian federation, namely that it would lead to the formal disappearance of Bulgaria as a separate object of international law. If the Bulgarian state no longer existed as such, its economic, military and moral obligations under the peace treaty would be nullified. In view of Yugoslavia's Allied status, the new joint state could refuse to assume the responsibilities of the former Bulgarian government.[136] This would entail serious consequences for British interests in the Balkans, once again pertaining to the Greek issue. As a federal unit, Bulgaria could continue providing help to the Greek Communist guerrillas; combining resources with Yugoslavia would pose a greater threat to the existence of Greece than the sum of the two separately.

Even as the federation question was fading during the unfolding Tito–Stalin dispute in 1948, Britain was distinctly aware of Bulgaria's military capabilities. To limit these the British government could only insist on due observation of the restrictions the peace treaty imposed on the Bulgarian army. Britain had abstained from enforcement of human rights observation in Bulgaria, but this did not preclude it from contesting the latter's fulfilment of the military clauses of the peace treaty.

In March 1948, the Bulgarian minister of defence, Georgi Damyanov, declared that the country had complied with the military articles of the treaty, something Britain was in a position to challenge formally. Carefully compiled British information showed that although Bulgaria had indeed cut down its armed forces, it was increasing the activities of paramilitary organizations, including the militia, the border guards, and even sports clubs. To prove or refute such suspicions Britain needed to inspect the Bulgarian army, above all in border areas which for some time had been practically sealed off for foreigners. British demands to that effect were justified by the assertion that proper verification and acceptance of the official Bulgarian statement could only be brought by examination.[137]

Earlier US attempts to inspect the southern Bulgarian border had been ignored or obstructed by the Bulgarian government. The latter had declined to give assistance, claiming that it was only obliged to respond to demands emanating from all three Allied powers, and the USSR had not supported the US initiative.[138]

At the end of January 1948, Britain had agreed to participate in another US-led joint attempt at border inspection. The diplomatic notes requesting a tour of the borders were to be based on the relevant Article 12 of the peace treaty and not to mention alleged Bulgarian involvement in the Greek situation. The FO also agreed to back the State Department in declaring a dispute with the Bulgarian government under Article 36 in case of renewed Bulgarian obstruction.[139] In their response, for the first time the Bulgarian authorities did not dispute Britain's and the United States' right of inspection but again insisted on a similar Soviet approach, which was not forthcoming.[140]

Nonetheless, a last-moment British reversal ruined the endeavour. The British Legation in Italy insisted that any action in the Balkans be postponed until after the Italian elections, scheduled for 18 April 1948, and Bevin swiftly agreed. The embarrassed FO was left with the task of explaining to the State Department that 'the balance of advantages' had been reconsidered in an attempt 'to co-ordinate [...] overall policy [...] without undue regard for Treaty enforcement for its own sake'.[141] The change provoked a strongly worded warning from Sterndale-Bennett that

> in countries like Bulgaria we are unlikely to achieve effective results and therefore it is easy to argue that implementation here is of academic value which should be subordinated to practical considerations in Italy. This is false reading because the importance in Bulgaria is not in concrete results but in psychological stand – whenever we try to soft-pedal the Communists are jubilant and our stock goes down in other quarters.[142]

In June 1948, the question of inspection of the Bulgarian border was briefly revived in both Britain and the United States. This time Bevin dismissed it, claiming that it was not 'wise to intensify a quarrel now while we have so much on our hands in Germany'.[143] This attitude was maintained in the face of streaming Greek grievances on border incidents as well as over restitution of Greek property and war reparations. Greece continuously pressed the British and US governments to implement those provisions of the peace treaty dealing with Bulgarian failure to fulfil its obligations. Invariably, the Greek government was firmly told that Britain was not in the position to uphold the Greek claims against Bulgaria.[144]

British anxiety that Bulgaria 'will simply treat the Treaty as a joke'[145] was confirmed by the Bulgarian government's attitude to the special commission set up in December 1947 by the United Nations to investigate Bulgarian–Greek border incidents (UNSCOB). The commission was to look into the Greek government's allegations that the Bulgarian regime was helping the Greek Communist guerrillas. Initially, Bulgaria showed signs of cooperating with the United Nations only to refuse categorically to admit the commission into the country, stating that it had been established illegally and infringed Bulgarian sovereignty.[146] Simultaneously, Kolarov practically confirmed some of the accusations against Bulgaria, stating that it was right to let in refugees from 'the terror of Greece' and unwittingly admitting the occurrence of frontier incidents.[147] Without British knowledge, Molotov had informed Dimitrov that the USSR was no longer in favour of the UNSCOB and advised the Bulgarian government to refuse the Commission right of entry to the country.[148]

British reluctance to bring the Bulgarian government to task about non-observation of its military obligations partially derived from the belief that Bulgaria could not pose an imminent military threat to Greece. Intelligence from the spring of 1948 testified that despite the gradual re-equipping of the Bulgarian army with Soviet help, the state of training was backward and the general efficiency very low. Some units were judged to be potentially able to stage guerrilla-style operations in Greece, but the army as a whole could not be considered modern or efficient by European standards.[149] Such arguments showed that British policy planners distinguished between the perceived ambitions of the Bulgarian government and the practical ability to fulfil them. They were guided by realities and considered it inappropriate to immerse Britain in disputes from which little tangible improvements would follow. The nuisance value of the incidents on the Bulgarian–Greek border was not judged sufficient to justify the initiation of the lengthy and unpromising procedure envisaged by the peace treaty.

Non-admission to the United Nations

The impossibility of implementing the peace treaty had a long-term effect on the international situation of Bulgaria, most notably in terms of the Bulgarian application for admission to the United Nations Organization (UNO). On two separate occasions, in September 1947 and April 1948, the UN Security Council reviewed new candidates. The British delegation abstained from voting on Hungary's and Romania's applications on account of these countries' abuse of human rights. Britain, however, pointedly voted against Bulgaria's application, arguing that apart from constantly violating human rights, the Bulgarian government had deliberately flouted the authority of the UN Security Council over the dispute with Greece.[150]

The Foreign Office foresaw unwanted consequences of its vote against Bulgarian UN membership. Any argument against the entry of Bulgaria into the UNO could be used *mutatis mutandis* by the Soviet government regarding Italy's application. This might easily happen, as the Italian government had criticized the Soviet attitude to Italy's admission in a form milder but similar to statements made by Kolarov. The FO understood that 'it would, to say the least of it, be difficult [...] to maintain that the Italian government had carried out effectively every single provision of the Italian peace treaty, [...] but rather we wish to wink an eye at some [...] occasional failures'.[151]

On a more practical basis, the FO treated the matter of admissions to the UNO as distinct from that of the implementation of the human rights clauses of the peace treaty. Whitehall officials had long acknowledged that they could do next to nothing to force the Bulgarian government, or any other totalitarian government, to observe human rights. The British government, however, possessed effective instruments to bar Bulgaria's entry into the UNO.[152]

British officials realised that the Bulgarian candidacy for the United Nations could succeed only as a part of some general understanding between the Soviet Union on the one hand and Britain and the United States on the other. To this, Bulgaria's, or the other satellites', domestic record would not be relevant. Such a possibility in turn reinforced British reluctance to act decisively on developments inside the country as protests might prejudice the UNO negotiations. The FO for instance reasoned that the Lulchev trial provided an admirable occasion for launching an attack on the Bulgarian government without touching on Bulgarian eligibility for the UNO. The two questions were, however, very closely linked and the logical implication of any indictment would also clearly go against the Bulgarian application.[153] The conclusion was that since a compromise on Bulgarian admission could not be thoroughly excluded, the protest on the human rights issue should be forestalled. Moreover, the FO reasoned that if Bulgaria's application was rejected, a protest would become superfluous, whereas in the unlikely event of Bulgaria being admitted, a protest 'would only be irrelevant'. Therefore, experts in London concluded that no protest should be undertaken before the outcome of the membership talks in Paris was known. The Foreign Office was anxious to avoid 'looking silly', which could happen if, 'having let off steam', it eventually concluded a deal with the Soviet Union.[154]

No agreement was reached in 1948 and in early 1949 Britain reverted to the policy of public condemnation of the totalitarian regimes of the Soviet satellites. But the momentum for protests to the individual governments had been lost. The new approach was to criticize the Soviet orbit countries at international forums, most notably the United Nations, towards which they aspired. In the spring of 1949, the UN General Assembly discussed the trials of the Bulgarian pastors and church leaders in other Communist-controlled countries. Despite strong Soviet opposition, the assembly expressed deep concern at the alleged violations of human rights. As a result, the UNO brought the question before the International Court of Justice in the Hague. Great Britain together with the United States was a protagonist of the prosecution. Britain's statement on the case was careful to emphasize concern not with the substance of the allegations but only with the steps that should be taken to investigate them.[155]

The hearings at The Hague were a protracted affair. In April 1950, the court confirmed the validity of those articles in the peace treaty which related to the settlement of disputes.[156] When the satellite states refused to comply, the court admitted that it was powerless to take the case further.[157] This amounted to official international acknowledgement of what the FO had long maintained internally – the treaty procedure had become unworkable and the possibilities of recourse and settlement had been exhausted.

Pursuing the case further, in 1951 the UN General Assembly invited its members to submit evidence of breaches of the human rights clauses of the Paris peace treaties. The British government constructed its first case against Bulgaria, presenting as evidence the Bulgarian constitution, the Law for the Ban and Dissolution of the Bulgarian Agrarian Union of Petkov, the general elections law and the local elections law.[158] Subsequently, the same was done for Hungary and Romania.[159] Nevertheless, in March 1951 when the question of human rights appeared on the agenda of the imminent four-power talks, a Foreign Office expert wrote: 'I do rather view with dismay the prospect of flogging again the dead horse of human rights in the satellites. There is frankly nothing that we can do about it here, it merely exasperates the local governments and it makes it much more difficult for us to establish any kind of reasonable relations with them.'[160]

* * *

After the signing of the peace treaty with Bulgaria, the British government found it almost impossible to devise a policy which would reflect Britain's general strategic goals and achieve concrete results in the country. Already during the armistice the British government had become aware of the discrepancy between its proclaimed commitment to democratic ideals and the practical inability to defend those who supported such ideals in the Soviet-dominated area. After 1947, the Foreign Office attempted to follow a middle course, protesting against infringements of human rights in Bulgaria but simultaneously refraining from invoking the treaty machinery. This seemingly lopsided method was undertaken after initial disputes with the Bulgarian government had produced no effect but had only demonstrated British political and diplomatic impotence.

Britain concentrated on reinforcing the countries which remained outside Soviet control, mainly on preventing any potential conflict with Greece's and Turkey's Communist neighbours and on speedy economic recovery to immunize these two countries against Communist penetration. Britain realistically accepted that the Soviet Union would act with parallel policies to secure and consolidate its own sphere of influence. In such circumstances, the best Britain could hope for in Bulgaria was 'to keep the flame of liberty alight [...] by demonstrating our own vitality' and 'following events here with close attention'.[161]

As few proposals for action to secure British moral leadership stood up to scrutiny, doubt settled over the whole rationale of an active policy, which itself could easily serve as an excuse for increased Soviet hostility. This posed the question of whether it made sense to take any interest in Bulgaria, which was small and of secondary importance in global terms. Yet developments in Bulgaria illuminated larger trends in the Soviet zone and could indicate Soviet intentions in the new borderlines of the Cold War. Against the background of such soul searching in the Foreign Office, the British representatives in Bulgaria were driven to near desperation by their status of silent observers. Their very presence in the country became a constant reminder of the futile position of Britain vis-à-vis the Soviet Union in this part of Europe.

CONCLUSION

In the final years of the Second World War and the armistice period, British foreign policy was truly global in extent and one of the active formative elements in the emerging postwar order. Despite the constraints imposed on it by the rising strength of its two wartime Allies, the United States and the Soviet Union, and economic decline, Britain's wartime performance and its traditional role in diplomacy determined its continuing significance in world affairs. The study of Britain's involvement with a small power on the border of core British interest provides an interesting perspective into the process of readjustment to the new postwar realities; it illuminates Britain's long-term priorities and the principles underlying its international conduct.

As British postwar planning for Bulgaria started in earnest in the latter half of the war, it was interlinked with military objectives regarding the country and the surrounding area. It had to take into consideration the concurrent disposition of armed forces and the prospects of cooperation with local political actors. Further, British policy makers drew heavily on experiences from the interwar period, projecting past developments onto future models of relations. The external resemblance between Britain's attitudes and approaches to Bulgaria before and after the war was underpinned by the essentially stable nature of Britain's strategic and political interests in the region.

The interval between 1943 and 1949 was the longest single historical period when Britain consistently manifested interest towards Bulgaria. Britain became engaged in a host of military and political problems arising from Bulgaria's participation in the Second World War and bearing upon Bulgaria's place in postwar Europe. This was unusual, especially in comparison to the interwar period, when Britain had treated Bulgaria, at best, with indifference and had given it little genuine encouragement to reconsider its growing attachment to Germany. It was also in striking contrast to the second half of the twentieth century, when Britain saw Bulgaria as the most obedient satellite of Soviet Russia, almost refusing to look at Bulgaria as a sovereign country. Conversely, Bulgaria underwent a radical political transformation in the years 1943–49 – to which British policy contributed. The interaction of Bulgarian domestic transition and British foreign policy illustrates the role of the variety of internal and external forces that placed the country in the emerging Soviet bloc. When analysed in conjunction with other regional examples, it acquires larger historical relevance to the onset of the Cold War in South Eastern Europe.

* * *

While the Second World War was still raging, Britain's attention to Bulgaria focused on the necessity to secure the latter's withdrawal from the neighbouring territories it had occupied. British military strategists had judged this to be essential for the weakening of the Axis hold in the Balkan Peninsula. Accordingly, under the coordination of the Foreign Office a triple policy was designed consisting of special operations, propaganda and strategic bombing.

Sabotage and subversion, carried out by the SOE, were hindered not only by a series of mishaps but above all by inadequate prewar preparations. The biggest problem arose from the fact that there was little genuine local resistance willing to cooperate with – let alone be guided by – Britain. Although well organized and benefitting from the exiled Bulgarian politicians' insights, British wartime propaganda to Bulgaria suffered from an overwhelmingly negative character. British official broadcasting from London and émigré channels in the Middle East condemned Bulgaria's adherence to the Tripartite Pact without offering any genuine inducement for the reversal of Bulgaria's conduct. Aware that nationalist ambitions were the principal factor for Bulgaria's choice of allies, the British government did not offer the one encouragement that might have pushed Bulgaria to turn against Germany, that of indicating that the Bulgarian territorial question might be reassessed in the future. Moreover, it even refused to guarantee Bulgaria's continued independence after the war. The bombing of Bulgaria, undertaken jointly with the United States and with Soviet consent, caused physical destruction and administrative and economic chaos. Yet, the air raids fell short of their principal goal, namely forcing the Bulgarian government to capitulate to the Allies.

The narrow effects of British military and propaganda activities in Bulgaria in 1943–44 were related to the abandonment of the Balkan front strategy strenuously propagated by British commanders and politicians while planning the Allied war effort in Europe. Indeed, the proponents of the idea, including Churchill, were motivated chiefly by military expediency rather than the political advantages military presence in the Balkans would have afforded Britain. Such a conclusion is also confirmed by Britain's preparedness to lend assistance to the most radical wartime opposition elements in Bulgaria, the Communists, as long as they were seen to contribute to the downfall of Bulgaria's pro-German regime and thus to the defeat of the Axis in the Balkans.

CONCLUSION

The precedence of military exigencies over the elaboration of long-term political objectives resulted in one of the enduring features of British foreign policy towards Bulgaria in the mid-1940s, namely the lack of consistent political planning regarding that country. The British government fully appreciated Bulgaria's central strategic position: influence in the country could facilitate any British aspirations to predominate in the adjoining region and seriously strengthen the traditionally important British positions in the Eastern Mediterranean. The one British political initiative this logic produced was the proposal that Bulgaria joined a Balkan federation. The timing, national composition or form of government were never clearly stipulated, but most British Balkan experts thought that the idea provided the only opportunity for Britain to secure a lasting role in the whole of the Balkan Peninsula. It was precisely this view that made the Soviet Union practically veto the Balkan federation idea in October 1943.

Contemplating possibilities for British involvement in Bulgaria, the FO realistically faced the fact of its limited capabilities to influence Bulgaria's internal or external policies. British military and political planners did not underestimate the traditional Russian links with Bulgaria and the variety of methods with which the Soviet Union could determine the country's behaviour. Therefore, the British government did not shy away from attempting to involve Soviet Russia in the effort of forcing Bulgaria out of the war. Although specific Anglo-Soviet cooperation was negligible as far as Eastern Europe was concerned, the British government – when it was informed – generally approved of the independent political and diplomatic pressure the Soviet Union applied on Bulgaria throughout 1944. Even though the Soviet declaration of war on Bulgaria of 5 September 1944 caught Britain unawares, the latter did not hesitate to readjust the armistice terms and to join fresh Soviet-led negotiations with Bulgaria. For Britain, the sudden Soviet intervention was controversial but did not justify a clash with the Soviet Union. To a degree, it was Britain's passivity and even confusion as to the Soviet actions regarding Bulgaria, along with willingness to be seen to accommodate its Soviet Ally, that allowed Soviet troops to occupy Bulgaria unimpeded.

The greatest deal of attention the country received was at the time of Churchill's visit to Moscow in October 1944. On that occasion, the British prime minister offered Stalin 75 percent influence in Bulgarian affairs; later Molotov extracted from Eden as much as 80 percent. The 'percentages deal' was a prime illustration of Britain's precarious position regarding Bulgaria. Despite its debatable nature and the different interpretations it has provoked, it constituted a practical understanding between two great powers where their interests in the Balkans overlapped to some extent. The agreement embodied a realistic assessment of Britain's own restricted role in Bulgaria and signalled that Britain did not intend to challenge Soviet dominance there. The 'percentages formula' was a device for satisfying Soviet aspirations in the Balkans and preserving vital British interests in the Eastern Mediterranean. At the same time, it could provide a zone of 'mixed' influence so as to allow space for negotiation and cooperation.

Only after the conclusion of the 'percentages agreement' were the armistice terms for Bulgaria finally settled, allotting Britain relatively small participation in the Allied Control Commission for Bulgaria, a body under Soviet command. Significantly for the British government, however, this was the first moment since relations had been broken off in March 1941 when it had a direct official presence in Bulgaria. The British delegation in the ACC provided adequate analysis of the political scene and Soviet activities in Bulgaria. It became an important participant in the discussion and formulation of British policy towards Bulgaria; its experiences and advice also contributed to the elaboration of British attitudes to the Soviet Union.

In 1944-45, Britain found it desirable to increase contacts with Bulgaria and insist on the practical implementation of political freedom and democracy. It had not perceived the zones of influence as completely sealed off but now interpreted Soviet behaviour in Bulgaria to aim at such an effect. By mid-1945 the FO was able to observe the growing tension in Bulgarian domestic politics caused by the Bulgarian Communists' endeavours to establish full control over the coalition Fatherland Front government as well as infiltrate the whole national and local administration. This coincided with similar developments in the rest of the Soviet-occupied lands and the widening of the cracks in the Grand Alliance with regard to other issues of war and reconstruction. The British government could not but suspect that these concurrent processes were linked and signalled a hardening of Soviet policies, which became all the more threatening a prospect since the Soviet Union was identified as the most possible future enemy. Therefore, the Bulgarian Communists' attempts at political monopoly coupled with increased Soviet dictate over the country's internal developments and relations with the outside world spelt for Britain the establishment of a Soviet stronghold too close to the focal points of British Balkan strategy. Exclusively controlled by the Soviet Union, Bulgaria could become a springboard for the spread of Communism in Europe and for the undermining of British power in the Eastern Mediterranean. Contacts between the Bulgarian and Greek Communists, renewed if occasional Soviet attention to Greece and the menacing Soviet attitude towards Turkey in late 1945 and 1946 could not but confirm such apprehensions.

Britain therefore associated itself with the anti-Communist political groups which emerged in Bulgaria in the spring and summer of 1945, mainly the Agrarians of Nikola Petkov and the Social Democrats of Krustyo Pastuhov.

Being careful not to appear to be urging anti-Soviet behaviour, British political representatives in Bulgaria encouraged the opposition's stand against the dictatorial manner of the Communists and insisted on the upholding of democratic principles in Bulgarian government and politics. These efforts culminated in British support for the postponement of the Bulgarian general elections in August 1945 as demanded by the opposition. The postponement remained the most important victory of Britain and the United States in Bulgaria for the whole period under review. True as it is, that the initiative was taken by the members of the two Western Missions without full authorization from their superiors, it showed that firmness and an active attitude paid off. For once, the local British representatives were vindicated in their long-neglected recommendations of decisive and timely actions in Bulgaria coupled with strong representations in Moscow.

The postponement of the elections was, however, an isolated incident, which the British government had not fully sanctioned in advance and was not prepared to repeat for fear of antagonizing unduly the Soviet Union. Since the subsequent November 1945 elections were carried out in an atmosphere not much different than that in August, the postponement had no other lasting effect than to make the Bulgarian Communists and the Soviet Union more acutely aware of the dangers of joint British and US pressure. As overall Communist dominance was not challenged and Soviet control remained at least as firm as before, Britain's boldest effort brought only temporary marginal achievements.

As confrontation had the dual effect of revealing British weakness and antagonizing the Soviet Union, it resulted in continuous scaling down of British demands as to the democratic standards to be observed by the Bulgarian government. This in turn indicated British vulnerability, bringing renewed Communist onslaughts and increasingly isolating Britain from the Bulgarian political scene. In 1946, after the failure of the Moscow decision for the reconstruction of the Bulgarian government, Britain's main preoccupation became how to grant a speedy recognition to the Bulgarian regime. Understanding that such an act would only support the Bulgarian Communists' claim for legitimacy, the FO also realized that to oppose it could not alter the political direction of the Bulgarian government. After prolonged soul-searching and much disagreement with the United States, the British government finally adopted the view that the very conclusion of the peace treaty with Bulgaria in February 1947 amounted to a *de jure* recognition. In this, Britain focused on the advantage of the withdrawal of Soviet troops from Bulgaria which Moscow had pledged in the event.

Already in 1946, Britain steadily moved towards a passive policy in Bulgaria. After the signing of the peace treaty with Bulgaria, the British government experienced substantial difficulties as to what course to adopt towards internal Bulgarian developments. The problem lay in the near impossibility to devise a policy which would coordinate Britain's general strategic goals of maintaining strong influence in the Southern Balkans and keeping hostility to the Soviet Union to a minimum, and achieve concrete results of undermining the Communists' strength in Bulgaria. Prolonged interdepartmental discussions of the possibilities to take Bulgaria to task in front of the international community for not observing various articles of the peace treaty remained but intellectual and legalistic exercises. In practice, without any open supporters inside the country, Britain reverted to the type of negative policy towards Bulgaria it had displayed in the latter stages of the Second World War. Having recognized the near impossibility to assert the little interest it had left in Bulgaria, Britain effectively treated the country as a Soviet dependency. In 1949 as relations were frozen at the lowest point, the British Legation acted more and more as a monitor of the consolidation and Sovietization of the Bulgarian regime.

* * *

The analysis of British involvement with Bulgaria in the latter stages of the Second World War and the first years afterwards adds historical detail and substance to the understanding of the origins of the Cold War in one of the zones of its earliest controversies. This incorporates not only the view from the high level of Britain's relations with its wartime Allies, but the much less explored actions and initiatives 'on the ground'. Among the principal conclusions to be highlighted is that of the importance of historical experience and precedent. The long-term historical approach reveals that while military exigencies stimulated the search for active Allied engagement with Bulgaria, the legacy of the past hindered it in relation to both concept and deeds. It was the lack of a solid historical foundation of the relationship with Bulgaria that made it difficult to identify political actors willing to work with Britain for the promotion of its interests, resulting in isolated contacts and ineffective political and military schemes. The 'negative' planning created little sympathy to the British cause among Bulgarian elites and allowed Bulgarian factors to use it to their own gain during the war and the armistice. Simultaneously, it signalled to the Soviets little concern for Bulgaria's future on the part of Britain, perceived to be in line with erstwhile attitudes. Thus, Britain was placed at a serious disadvantage when it was time to look beyond the conduct of the war and negotiate Bulgaria's position in the peaceful settlement.

Further, it is most productive to evaluate the evolution of British policy to Bulgaria and its contribution to the growing inter-Allied tensions while looking at the broad and complex regional framework. The country was part of several overlapping zones, the boundaries of which altered in relation to dynamic military, political and diplomatic developments. It is evident from the plans for knocking Bulgaria out of the war and the idea of a Balkan federation that for Britain Bulgaria was mostly significant as a Balkan power, bordering areas of long-standing British patronage. However, with the advance of the Red Army, the country was increasingly linked with and compared to the Soviet-occupied countries in Eastern and Central Europe. However, as soon as Bulgaria was identified to fall outside the perimeter of solid British interest, the latter was threatened by the growing power of the Bulgarian Communists and the augmented capability to put militarily pressure on the Eastern Mediterranean.

Even within its Eastern European context Bulgaria did not at any point assume the importance of Poland for instance, over which Britain was prepared to go to considerable disputes with the Soviet Union. When compared to the extent of British involvement in the neighbouring Greece and Turkey, attention to Bulgaria acquires marginal proportions. This is also clearly illustrated by the low level of decision making regarding Bulgaria. Most issues were resolved by the Southern Department of the Foreign Office with rare intervention by the foreign secretary. On very few specific occasions were matters related to Bulgaria presented to the cabinet, and then mostly in an informative capacity. Only at highly exceptional moments – most conspicuously the 'percentages agreement' and the Balkan front strategy – did the British prime minister devote attention to Bulgaria. Conversely, one of the most successful events in the course of British relations with Bulgaria, that of the August 1945 election postponement, occurred on the initiative of the British representatives in Bulgaria even without proper consultation with the FO.

Neither the low priority accorded to Bulgaria, nor the predominantly ineffective outcome of Britain's attempts to give some practical dimension of its objectives should be construed as lack of interest. It is useful to employ the notion of misunderstandings and missed opportunities when explaining British actions regarding Bulgaria. Although postwar planning had clearly foreseen increased Soviet interest in the country, the lack of urgency displayed by the British in the handling of the Bulgarian peace feelers of the late summer of 1944, and the failure to appreciate the Soviet detachment from these, demonstrates that British diplomats were unable to seize the moment to secure a more substantial say on the terms of the armistice with Bulgaria. This situation supports the thesis that to a great degree the logic of Soviet behaviour was not well understood. In contrast, Stalin was much more skilful in turning such openings to his advantage and subsequently did not surrender the acquired positions,[1] as evident from the manner in which the Western representatives were marginalized in the working of the ACC. Moreover, pronounced British willingness to avoid confrontation on numerous occasions when Allied agreements had been violated is also likely to have encouraged the Communists. Such reading of early Cold War tactics also confirms the view that on most occasions Soviet initial cooperation in due time turned it into a zero-sum game.[2] In Bulgaria, evidence for this is provided by the Moscow decision, which was reached so as to meet challenges to the legitimacy of the government but was soon used by the Soviets and local Communists to exclude any pro-Western elements from power.

Finally, a case can be made of the secondary role played by ideology with regards to tensions and clashes over Bulgaria. In the course of the war, British thinking about Bulgaria envisaged almost completely strategic objectives: the advances of the Bulgarian Communists were considered in terms of enhancing the Soviet proximity and pressure on the Mediterranean Straits – which Soviet moves elsewhere in the region, such as Turkey and Iran, seemed to confirm. British concerns for democracy in Bulgaria as reflected in the armistice agreement were offset by the Stalin–Churchill deal. When voiced later at the time of Yalta and Potsdam, it was with some ambiguity, while moves to assert them were more often than not preconditioned on the desire not to exacerbate Soviet hostility. Britain was not so much committed to democracy in the country as it was watchful of the use of Communism as an instrument of promoting Soviet strategic gains in areas adjacent to the recognized Soviet zone.

The most significant and stable feature of British policy towards Bulgaria was the realization that Britain had no practical means of matching either the traditional Russian influence or the advantages that sprang from the Soviet occupation of the country in 1944–47. The British government conceded predominance in Bulgarian affairs to the Soviet Union, as long as this was not used for anti-British purposes. British involvement in Bulgarian internal developments was reluctant, inconsistent and ineffective: recognition of the dominant Soviet position did not bring clear disavowal of the British interest; opposition to the Soviet Union did not rule out practical British acquiescence with Soviet actions; moral support for the Bulgarian anti-Communists found little outward demonstration. Finally, Britain's predicament in Bulgaria was exemplified in its inability to stand firmly behind a policy of disinterest and detachment.

NOTES

Introduction

1 Although not comprehensive, the following chapters in the most recent collaborative overview delineate the geography and the complexity of the problem: N. Naimark, 'The Sovietisation of Eastern Europe, 1944–1953', and S. Rajak, 'The Cold War in the Balkans, 1945–1956', in *The Cambridge History of the Cold War, Volume One: Origins*, ed. O. A. Westad and M. Leffler (Cambridge: Cambridge University Press, 2010), 175–220. More detailed and discursive presentations are found in A. Varsori and E. Calandri, eds, *The Failure of Peace in Europe, 1943–48* (Basingstoke: Palgrave, 2002) and F. Gori and S. Pons, eds, *The Soviet Union and Europe in the Cold War, 1943–53* (Basingstoke: Macmillan Press, 1996).
2 J. L. Gaddis, 'The Emerging Post-revisionist Synthesis on the Origins of the Cold War', *Diplomatic History* 7, no. 3 (July 1983): 171–90.
3 J. L. Gaddis, *The United States and the Origins of the Cold War 1941–1947* (New York: Columbia University Press, 1972); J. L. Gaddis, *Russia, the Soviet Union and the United States* (Chichester: Wiley, 1978); J. L. Gaddis, *We Now Know: Rethinking Cold War History* (Oxford: Clarendon Press, 1997); V. Mastny, *Russia's Road to the Cold War* (New York: Columbia University Press, 1979); V. Mastny, *The Cold War and Russian Insecurity* (New York: Oxford University Press, 1996).
4 Mastny, *Russia's Road*.
5 G. Bennett, ed., *The End of War in Europe 1945* (London: HMSO, 1996), 204, 238.
6 Gaddis, *We Now Know*, 289.
7 J. Haslam, *Russia's Cold War: From the October Revolution to the Fall of the Wall* (New Haven, CT: Yale University Press, 2011), 1–18.
8 V. Zubok, *A Failed Empire: The Soviet Union in the Cold War from Stalin to Gorbachev* (Chapel Hill: University of North Carolina Press, 2007), 7–21.
9 V. O. Pechatnov, 'The Big Three of Soviet Foreign Policy: New Documents on Soviet Thinking about Post-War Relations with the United States and Great Britain', Working Paper no. 13, Cold War International History Project: Woodrow Wilson International Center for Scholars, July 1995, 17; D. Reynolds, ed., *The Origins of the Cold War in Europe: International Perspectives* (New Haven, CT: Yale University Press, 1994), 60; G. Roberts, 'Ideology, Calculation and Improvisation: Spheres of Influence and Soviet Foreign Policy 1935–1945', *Review of International Studies* 25, no. 4 (October 1999): 655–73.
10 G. Roberts, *Stalin's Wars: From World War to Cold War, 1939–1953* (New Haven, CT: Yale University Press, 2006), 23–9, 245–9.
11 M. Leffler, *For the Soul of Mankind: The United States, the Soviet Union and the Cold War* (New York: Hill and Wang, 2007).

12 M. Trachtenberg, *A Constructed Peace: The Making of the European Settlement, 1945–1963* (Princeton, NJ: Princeton University Press, 1999), 3–15.
13 R. Garson, 'Churchill's "Spheres of Influence": Rumania and Bulgaria', *Survey* 24, no. 3 (summer 1979): 144–58; J. M. Siracusa, 'The Meaning of TOLSTOY: Churchill, Stalin and the Balkans, Moscow, October 1944', *Diplomatic History* 2, no. 4 (fall 1979): 443–63; G. Ross, 'Foreign Office Attitudes to the Soviet Union 1941–1945', *Journal of Contemporary History* 16, no. 3 (July 1981): 521–40; W. F. Kimball, 'Naked Reverse Right: Churchill, Roosevelt and Eastern Europe from TOLSTOY to Yalta and a Little Beyond', *Diplomatic History* 9, no. 1 (winter 1985): 1–24; G. H. Holdich, 'A Policy of Percentages? British Policy and the Balkans after the Moscow Conference of October 1944', *International History Review* 9, no. 1 (February 1987): 28–47; W. Kimball, 'Anglo-American War Aims, 1941–43: The First Review; Eden's Mission to Washington', in *The Rise and Fall of the Grand Alliance, 1941–1945*, ed. A. Lane and H. Temperley (Basingstoke: Macmillan, 1995): 1–21; G. Roberts, 'Ideology, Calculation and Improvisation'; J. Kent, 'British Post-war Planning for Europe 1942–1945', in *Failure of Peace*, 40–48.
14 E. Barker, *The British between the Superpowers, 1945–1950* (Basingstoke: Macmillan, 1983), 60–62.
15 A. Deighton, ed., *Britain and the First Cold War* (Basingstoke: Macmillan, 1989); A. Deighton, 'The "Frozen Front": The Labour Government, the Division of Germany and the Origins of the Cold War 1945–1947', *International Affairs* 63, no. 3 (summer 1987): 449–64.
16 A. Deighton, 'Britain and the Cold War, 1945–1955', in *Cambridge History*, 112–32; K. Larres, *Churchill's Cold War: The Politics of Personal Diplomacy* (New Haven, CT: Yale University Press, 2002), 110–19.
17 Haslam, *Russia's Cold War*, 18.
18 M. Folly, *Churchill, Whitehall and the Soviet Union, 1940–45* (Basingstoke: Macmillan, 2000); D. Carlton, *Churchill and the Soviet Union* (Manchester: Manchester University Press, 1999); K. Larres, *Churchill's Cold War*.
19 M. Kitchen, *British Policy towards the Soviet Union during the Second World War* (Basingstoke: Macmillan, 1986); V. Rothwell, *Britain and the Cold War 1941–1947* (London: Cape, 1982). A similar line is followed by G. Warner, 'From Ally to Enemy: British Relations with the Soviet Union, 1941–48', in *Diplomacy and World Power: Studies in British Foreign Policy, 1890–1950*, ed. M. Dockrill and B. McKercher (Cambridge: Cambridge University Press, 1996), 221–43.
20 J. Kent, 'The British Empire and the Origins of the Cold War', in *Britain and the First Cold War*, 165–83.
21 E. Barker, *Truce in the Balkans* (London: Percival Marshall, 1948); E. Barker, *Macedonia: Its Place in Balkan Politics* (London: RIIA, 1950); E. Barker, *British Policy in South-East Europe in the Second World War* (Basingstoke: Macmillan, 1976); E. Barker et al., eds, *British Political and Military Strategy in Central-Eastern and Southern Europe in 1944* (Basingstoke: Macmillan, 1988).
22 Bennett, *The End of War; The Rise and Fall; The Soviet Union and Europe*; N. Naimark and L. Gibianskii, eds, *The Establishment of Communist Regimes in Eastern Europe, 1944–1949* (Boulder, CO: Westview Press, 1997).
23 B. Arcidiacono, 'Great Britain, the Balkans and the Division of Europe, 1943–45', in *Failure of Peace*, 93–103.
24 M. M. Boll, *Cold War in the Balkans: American Policy towards Bulgaria 1943–1947* (Lexington: University Press of Kentucky, 1984).

25 C. E. Black, 'The Start of the Cold War in Bulgaria: A Personal View', *Review of Politics* 41, no. 2 (April 1979): 163–202; J. E. Horner, 'Traicho Kostov: Stalinist Orthodoxy in Bulgaria', *Survey* 24, no. 3 (summer 1979): 135–42; J. E. Horner, 'The Ordeal of Nikola Petkov and the Consolidation of Communist Power in Bulgaria', *Survey* 28, no. 2 (summer 1984): 75–83. A few articles on the ACC in Bulgarian are mainly narratives containing numerous technical details: S. Pintev, 'Nachalna deinost na Suyuznata Kontrolna Komisia v Bulgaria, oktomvri 1944–januari 1945', *Istoricheski Pregled* 35, no. 4/5 (1979): 196–203; S. Pintev, 'SSSR, SASht i Velikobritania i Moskovskoto primirie s Bulgaria, septemvri–oktomvri 1944', *Izvestia na Bulgarskoto Istorichesko Druzhestvo* 32 (1978): 241–59.

26 V. Dimitrov, *Stalin's Cold War: Soviet Foreign Policy, Democracy and Communism in Bulgaria, 1941–48* (Basingstoke: Palgrave Macmillan, 2008).

27 A. Prazmowska, *Civil War in Poland, 1942–1948* (Basingstoke: Palgrave Macmillan, 2004).

28 E. Hazard, *Cold War Crucible: United States Foreign Policy and the Conflict in Romania, 1943–1952* (Boulder, CO: East European Monographs, 1996); G. Mitrovich, *America's Strategy to Subvert the Soviet Bloc, 1947–1956* (Ithaca, NY: Cornell University Press, 2000); P. Grose, *America's Secret War behind the Iron Curtain* (New York: Houghton Mifflin, 2000); R. Aldrich, *The Hidden Hand: Britain, America and Cold War Secret Intelligence* (London: John Murray, 2001).

29 The definitive Soviet-period work is V. G. Trukhanovskii, *Vneshyaya politika Anglii v period Vtoroy mirovoy voinyi 1939–1945gg.* (Moscow: Progress Publishers, 1970). For Bulgarian versions see G. Gunev and I. Ilchev, *Winston Churchill i Balkanite* (Sofia: Izdatelstvo na OF, 1984); for comparison see S. Rachev, *Anglo-Bulgarian Relations during the Second World War 1939–1944* (Sofia: Sofia Press, 1981) and S. Rachev, *Churchill, Bulgaria i Balkanite* (Sofia: Sotri, 1995).

30 G. Daskalov, *Bulgaria i Gurtsia: Ot razriv kum pomirenue 1944–1964gg.* (Sofia: Universitetsko Izdatelstvo 'Sv. Kliment Ohridski', 2004).

31 E. Kalinova, *Sledvoennoto desetiletie na bulgarskata vunshna politika (1944–1955g.)* (Sofia: Polis, 2003); I. Baeva and E. Kalinova, *Bulgarskite prehodi 1939–2005* (Sofia: Paradigma, 2006); J. Baev, *Balkanite v sistemata za evropeyska sigurnost v godinite na Studenata voina* (Sofia: Izdatelstvo Damian Yakov, 2010).

32 M. E. Pelly et al., eds, *Documents on British Policy Overseas* (hereafter *DBPO*), ser. 1, vol. 6, Eastern Europe, August 1945–April 1946 (London: HMSO, 1991).

33 G. Ross, ed., *The Foreign Office and the Kremlin: British Documents on Anglo-Soviet Relations 1944–1945* (Cambridge: Cambridge University Press, 1985).

34 F. L. Loewenheim et al., eds, *Roosevelt and Churchill: Their Secret Wartime Correspondence* (New York: Barrie and Jenkins, 1975).

35 US Department of State, *Foreign Relations of the United States* (hereafter *FRUS*), 1943–1955 (Washington, DC, 1961–1985).

36 M. M. Boll, *The American Military Mission in the Allied Control Commission for Bulgaria 1944–1947* (Boulder, CO: Columbia University Press, 1985).

37 *The Trial of Nikola D. Petkov, August 5–15, 1947: Records of the Judicial Proceedings* (Sofia: Ministry of Information and Arts, 1947); *The Trial of Traicho Kostov and His Group* (Sofia: Press Department, 1949); *Ustanovyavane i ukrepvane na narodnodemokratichnata vlast septemvri 1944–may 1945* (Sofia: Izdatelstvo na BAN, 1969); *Vunshna politika na Narodna Republika Bulgaria: Sbornik ot dokumenti i materiali v dva toma 1944–1962* (Sofia: Durzhavno Izdatelstvo 'Nauka i Izkustvo', 1970).

38 Its full name was the Bulgarian Workers' Party (Communists) but BCP will be used hereafter.
39 V. Toshkova et al., eds, *Bulgaria: Nepriznatiyat protivnik na Tretiya Raih* (Sofia: Izdatelstvo na MO 'Sv. Georgi Pobedonosets', 1995); L. Ognyanov et al., eds, *Narodna demokratsiya ili diktatura* (Sofia: Literaturen Forum, 1992).
40 D. Sirkov et al., eds, *Georgi Dimitrov: Dnevnik 9 mart 1933–6 fevruari 1949* (Sofia: Universitetsko Izdatelstvo 'Sv. Kl. Ohridski', 1997).
41 L. B. Valev et al., eds, *Sovetsko–Bolgarskie otnosheniya i svyazi, 1944–1948gg.: Documenti i materiali* (Moscow: Nauka, 1981); N. S. Lebedev et al., eds, *Comintern i Vtoraya Mirovaya Voina*, 2 vols (Moscow: Pamyatniki Istoricheskoy Myisli, 1994, 1997); T. V. Volokitina et al., eds, *Vostochnaya Evropa v dokumentah rossiyskih arhivov 1944–1953*, vol. 1, *1944–1948* (Moscow: Sibirskiy Hronograf, 1997).

Chapter One: Bulgaria in British Postwar Planning

1 E. Barker, *Britain in a Divided Europe* (Basingstoke: Macmillan, 1971), 11; G. Kennan, *Russia and the West under Lenin and Stalin* (London: Hutchinson, 1961); G. Kennan, 'The X Article', in *Caging the Bear: Containment and the Cold War*, ed. C. Gati (Indianapolis: Bobbs-Merrill, 1974), 9–23; H. Ragsdale, ed., *Imperial Russian Foreign Policy* (Cambridge: Cambridge University Press, 1993), 211–46; A. Cohen, *Russian Imperialism* (London: Praeger, 1996), 48–56
2 G. Jebb, *The Memoirs of Lord Gladwyn* (London: Weidenfield & Nicolson, 1972), 113–19.
3 M. L. Miller, *Bulgaria during the Second World War* (Stanford, CA: Stanford University Press, 1975), 53–62.
4 HS5/180, SOE memorandum, 7 June 1943; FO371/37152, R6704, Howard to Barker, 28 June 1943.
5 R. T. Shannon, *Gladstone and the Bulgarian Agitation, 1876* (Hassoks: Harvester Press, 1963); A. P. Saab, *Gladstone, Bulgaria and the Working Classes, 1856–1878* (Cambridge, MA: Harvard University Press, 1991).
6 E. Barker, *British Policy in South-East Europe in the Second World War* (Basingstoke: Macmillan, 1976), 134.
7 W. S. Churchill, *The Second World War*, vol. 4 (London: Cassell, 1950), 433.
8 W. H. McNeill, *America, Britain and Russia: Their Co-operation and Conflict 1941–1946* (London: Johnson Reprint, 1970), 221, 304–5.
9 H. Macmillan, *The Blast of War 1939–1945* (Basingstoke: Macmillan, 1967), 503.
10 H. L. Stimson and M. Bundy, *On Active Service in Peace and War* (New York: Harper & Bros, 1947), 437.
11 W. D. Leahy, *I Was There* (London: Victor Gollanz, 1950), 191; Lord Ismay, *The Memoirs of General the Lord Ismay* (London: Heinemann, 1960), 287, 323; Macmillan, *Blast of War*, 190–91, 503–4. American secretary of war H. L. Stimson was among the few who believed in Churchill's sincerity: Stimson and Bundy, *On Active Service*, 437, 447.
12 M. Howard, *Grand Strategy*, vol. 4, part 1 (London: HMSO, 1966), 275.
13 S. Deringil, *Turkish Foreign Policy in the Second World War: An 'Active' Neutrality* (Cambridge: Cambridge University Press, 1989), 133–65.
14 Sir E. L. Woodward, *British Foreign Policy in the Second World War*, vol. 2 (London: HMSO, 1971), 273.

NOTES 205

15 Miller, *Bulgaria*, 7.
16 I. Dimitrov, *Anglia i Bulgaria 1938–1941: v navecherieto na Vtorata svetovna voina* (Sofia: Izdatelstvo na OF, 1983), 15–16; Sir G. Rendel, *The Sword and the Olive: Recollections of Diplomacy and the Foreign Service 1913–1954* (London: Murrey, 1957), 141–44; Deringil, *Turkish Foreign Policy*, 24.
17 FO371/24873, R43, BoT to FO, 1 June 1940, R1697, MEW to FO, 6 February 1940; FO371/24882, R5681–R7795, Sofia to FO, May–October 1940; D. Kaiser, *Economic Diplomacy and the Second World War: Germany, Britain, France and Eastern Europe 1930–1939* (Princeton, NJ: Princeton University Press, 1980), 170–95.
18 Barker, *British Policy*, 8, 57.
19 FO371/24862, R939, Rendel to FO, 12 January 1940; FO371/37151, R5372, Rose minute (hereafter minutes will be indicated by the name of the author only), 18 June 1943; Miller, *Bulgaria*, 30; Dimitrov, *Anglia i Bulgaria*, 22.
20 FO371/24869, R3730, Rendel to FO, Clutton, 17 March 1939.
21 US Department of State, *FRUS*, 1943, vol. 1 (Washington, DC, 1961), 489, British Embassy Washington aide-memoire, 6 April 1943.
22 FO371/37153, R11655, Soviet aide-memoire, 29 October 1943.
23 FO371/37002, N1246, Kuibyshev to FO, 16 January 1943.
24 FO371/37153, R2129, Eden brief, 9 March 1943.
25 FO371/37153, R11655, Sargent, 24 July 1943.
26 FO371/37248, R9396, Romanos to Laskey, 28 September 1943, R9740, Eden brief, October 1943.
27 FO371/37158, R5885, Clutton to Helm, 10 July 1943, FORD paper, 13 July 1943; Woodward, *British Foreign Policy*, vol. 4., 109, 110, 117.
28 *FRUS* 1943, vol. 1, 493, State Department (hereafter State) to FO, 28 April 1943.
29 FO371/37173, R974, Rendel to Sargent, 1 February 1943.
30 FO371/37157, R1592, Clark Kerr to FO, 20 February 1943.
31 Howard, *Grand Strategy*, vol. 3, part 1, 273; G. Swain, 'Stalin's Wartime Vision of the Post-war World', *Diplomacy and Statecraft* 7, no.1 (March 1996): 78–9.
32 FO371/37173, R974, Rendel to Sargent, 1 February 1943.
33 Ibid.
34 V. Rothwell, *Britain and the Cold War 1941–1947* (London: Cape, 1982), 113; E. Barker, 'Problems of the Alliance: Misconceptions and Misunderstandings', in *British Political and Military Strategy in Central-Eastern and Southern Europe in 1944*, ed. E. Barker et al. (Basingstoke: Macmillan, 1988), 45–6.
35 FO371/36991, N983, radio intercept, 8 February 1943; D. Dilks, 'British Political Aims in Central, Eastern and Southern Europe', in *British Political and Military Strategy*, 24.
36 FO371/37158, R5885, FORD paper, 2 July 1943; Woodward, *British Foreign Policy*, vol. 4, 83.
37 FO371/37158, R12535, Southern Department to Eden, 3 December 1943.
38 FO371/43583, R8542, FO memorandum, 30 May 1944.
39 D. Sirkov et al., eds, *Georgi Dimitrov: Dnevnik 9 mart 1933–6 fevruari 1949* (Sofia: Universitetsko Izdatelstvo 'Sv. Kl. Ohridski', 1997), 235–437; M. M. Boll, *Cold War in the Balkans: American Policy towards Bulgaria 1943–1947* (Lexington: University Press of Kentucky, 1984), 55; K. Muraviev, *Subitiya i hora: Spomeni* (Sofia: Bulgarski Pisatel, 1992), 341, 413.
40 A. M. Filitov, 'V komissiyah Narcomindela', in *Vtoraya Mirovaya Voina: Aktualnye voprossyi*, ed. O. A. Rzhshevskyi (Moscow: Nauka, 1995), 55.
41 Filitov, 'V komissiyah', 57.

42 O. Pechatnov, 'The Big Three of Soviet Foreign Policy: New Documents on Soviet Thinking about Post-War Relations with the United States and Great Britain', Working Paper no. 13, Cold War International History Project: Woodrow Wilson International Center for Scholars, July 1995, 7
43 Filitov, 'V komissiyah', 61.
44 Swain, 'Stalin's Wartime Vision', 73; Pechatnov, 'The Big Three', 22–23.
45 Filitov, 'V komissiyah', 57.
46 Filitov, 'V komissiyah', 57; Pechatnov, 'The Big Three', 3; J. Haslam, 'Soviet War Aims', in *The Rise and Fall of the Grand Alliance, 1941–1945*, ed. A. Lane and H. Temperley (Basingstoke: Macmillan, 1995), 23–4.
47 FO371/43646, R9092, Warner, 7 June 1944.
48 J. Kent, *British Imperial Strategy and the Cold War in the Middle East* (London: Leicester University Press, 1994), 17–18; Dilks, 'British Political Aims', 22–3, 28–9.
49 FO371/43646, R9092, FO memorandum, 7 June 1944.
50 Ibid.
51 Ibid.
52 Ibid.
53 Barker, 'Problems of the Alliance', 45–7.
54 Kent, *British Imperial Strategy*, 14.
55 FO371/43646, R9092, FO memorandum, 7 June 1944.
56 Ibid.
57 M. Kitchen, *British Policy towards the Soviet Union during the Second World War* (Basingstoke: Macmillan, 1986),106–9.
58 FO371/36991, N4574, Wilson paper, 25 July 1943.
59 Ibid.
60 Ibid.; FO371/36991, N499, Preston memorandum, 21 October 1942.
61 FO371/36992, N4531, Bruce Lockhart paper, 9 August 1943.
62 FO371/36992, N4717, Cripps to Eden, 10 August 1943.
63 Cited in Kitchen, *British Policy*, 117.
64 FO371/37173, R6753, Rendel to Eden, 21 July 1943.
65 Ibid., Sargent to Craigie draft, August 1943.
66 FO371/37173, R974, Rendel to Sargent, 1 February 1943.
67 FO371/37173, R6753, Rose, 6 August 1943; FO371/37153, R10192, draft brief, 4 October 1943.
68 FO371/37152, R6499, PWE directive, 19 August 1943, R7451; Barker–Howard correspondence, 9–19 August 1943, R9332; Barker–Howard correspondence, 5, 8 October 1943, R9601, R1226, PWE directives, 3 November 1943, 3 December 1943.
69 FO371/37248, R9740, Eden brief, October 1943.
70 FO371/37151, R6037, Eden to Halifax, 27 July 1943.
71 FO371/37153, R10192, draft brief, 4 October 1943.
72 FO371/77151, R6037, Howard, 22 July 1943.
73 *FRUS* 1943, vol. 1, 492–3, FO to State, 28 April 1943.
74 FO371/37173, R974, Rendel to Sargent, 1 February 1943.
75 FO371/37152, R8169, PWE directive, 3 September 1943.
76 V. Toshkova, 'SASht i izlizaneto na Bulgaria ot Tristranniya Pakt, yuni–septemvri 1944g.', *Istoricheski Pregled* 35, no. 4/5 (1979): 206.
77 FO371/77151, R6037, Clutton, 18 July 1943, Howard, 22 July 1943.
78 Ibid.

79 Ibid., Eden to Halifax, 27 July 1943.
80 FO371/37153, R10192, draft brief, 4 October 1943.
81 Dr Georgi M. Dimitrov was a Bulgarian Agrarian leader, popularly known in Bulgaria by his initials, G. M., in order to be distinguished from his namesake, the Communist Georgi Dimitrov.
82 FO371/37173, R587, Rendel to Sargent, 18 January 1943.
83 K. Larres, *Churchill's Cold War: The Politics of Personal Diplomacy* (New Haven, CT: Yale University Press, 2002), 79–86.
84 FO371/37156, R1310, research papers, R2729, McCartney paper, 22 March 1943.
85 TsDA–AMVnR, f. 176, op. 15, a.e. 48, l. 149, 173, Ankara to Sofia, 6 February 1943, a.e. 49, l. 24, Ankara to Sofia, 12 February 1943; FO371/37179, R5081, Cadogan–Jovanovic conversation, 4 June 1943. This is not mentioned in Deringil, *Turkish Foreign Policy*, 133–66, nor in D. Livanios, 'Bulgar–Yugoslav Controversy over Macedonia and the British Connection, 1939–1949', DPhil dissertation, University of Oxford, 1995.
86 FO371/36992, N4906, FO memorandum, 10 August 1943.
87 K. Sainsbury, *The Turning Point* (Oxford: Oxford University Press, 1985), 88–90; C. Hull, *The Memoirs of Cordell Hull* (New York: Macmillan, 1948), 1298.
88 FO/37031, N6921, Moscow Conference proceedings, 19–30 October 1943.
89 J. Haslam, *Russia's Cold War: From the October Revolution to the Fall of the Wall* (New Haven, CT: Yale University Press, 2011)
90 FO371/43583, FO memorandum, 30 May 1944.

Chapter Two: Getting Bulgaria Out of the War

1 N. West, *The Story of SOE: Britain's Wartime Sabotage Organisation* (London: Hodder & Stoughton, 1992), 20–21; M. R. D. Foot, *SOE 1940–1946* (London: BBC Publications, 1986); D. A. T. Stafford, *Britain and European Resistance 1940–1945* (Basingstoke: Macmillan, 1979); B. Sweet-Escott, *Baker Street Irregular* (London: Methuen, 1963). Most of these mention operations in Bulgaria only in passing.
2 HS5/181, D/H2 to D/H1, 28 October 1940.
3 Ibid.; J. Amery, *Approach March* (London: Hutchinson, 1973), 175. The links of the Protoguerovists with the Bulgarian Communists are revealed in P. Semerdjiev, *BKP: Makedonskiyat vupros i VMRO* (Detroit: Macedono-Bulgarian Institute, c. 1990), 60, 84.
4 HS5/181, D/H2 to D/H1, 28 October 1940.
5 G. Rendel, *The Sword and the Olive: Recollections of Diplomacy and the Foreign Service* (London: Murrey, 1957), 178; C. Moser, *Dimitrov of Bulgaria: A Political Biography of Dr George M. Dimitrov* (Ottawa, IL: Caroline House, 1979), 169–70.
6 HS5/183, Lord Glenconner to Dr G. M. Dimitrov, September 1941.
7 HS5/183, SOE communications, SOE to FO, September 1941; K. Todoroff, *Balkan Firebrand* (Chicago: Ziff-Davis, 1943), 312–13.
8 HS5/180, special report: April–September 1943, 1 October 1943; HS5/190, D/H2, 28 September 1944; K. Young, ed., *The Diaries of Sir Robert Bruce Lockhart*, vol. 2, *1939–1965* (Basingstoke: Macmillan, 1980), 115; Moser, *Dimitrov*, 159.
9 FO371/37151, R3420, Momchilov to Sargent, 10 April 1943.
10 S. Rachev, *Churchill, Bulgaria i Balkanite* (Sofia: Sotri, 1995), 157; FO371/37151, R3420, Momchilov to Sargent, 10 April 1943; R3952, Momchilov to Sargent, 30 April 1943; FO371/37152, R10716, Momchilov to Sargent, 24 October 1943.

11 Moser, *Dimitrov*, 159; E. Barker, *British Policy in South-East Europe in the Second World War* (Basingstoke: Macmillan, 1976), 214.
12 FO371/37155, R817, Matsankiev memorandum, 12 January 1943, R4215, Barker to Southern Department, 8 May 1943; FO371/43589, R7421, Momchilov to Southern Department, March 1944; FO371/43586, R7482, Momchilov to Howard, 10 May 1944.
13 FO371/37153, R5322 and HS5/180, Major Boughey to Howard, 16 June 1943, 21 June 1943; FO371/43587, R2808, SOE plan, 4 February 1944.
14 HS5/180, memorandum on Bulgaria, 7 June 1943.
15 FO371/37153, R8978, Sargent, Rose, 13 September 1943; Barker, *British Policy*, 215.
16 The accusation was initially publicized by the Bulgarian Partisan leader General Slavcho Trunski in *Rabotnichesko Delo*, 26 November 1947. It was tirelessly repeated by Bulgarian Communist historiography and resurfaced much later in E. P. Thompson, *Beyond the Frontier: The Politics of a Failed Mission* (Woodbridge: Merlin Press, 1997).
17 HS5/185, DH/V to CD, 27 February 1943.
18 H. De Santis, *The Diplomacy of Silence: The American Foreign Service, the Soviet Union and the Cold War 1933-1947* (Chicago: Chicago University Press, 1980), 108; US Department of State, *FRUS*, 1944, vol. 3 (Washington, DC, 1962), vol. 3, 317, Berry to Hull, 25 March 1944.
19 Foot, *SOE*, 145-7; N. Beloff, *Tito's Flawed Legacy* (London: Gollanz, 1985), 89-93.
20 HS5/180, memorandum on Bulgaria, 7 June 1943; Rachev, *Churchill*, 193.
21 HS5/180, Bulgaria situation report, March 1944.
22 FO371/43579, R724, Talbot-Rice to Howard, 14 January 1944, R3645, BLO report, 21 February 1944, R3646, BLO reports, 23 February 1944.
23 Postwar Western historiography accepted these numbers as opposed to the hugely inflated ones put forward by the Bulgarian Communists after September 1944: J. D. Bell, *The BCP from Blagoev to Zhivkov* (Stanford, CA: Hoover Institute Press, 1986), 63.
24 The first communications from the BLOs in Bulgaria claimed that the Partisans numbered in the 'several thousands', but later they were reported at about twelve thousand: FO371/43587, R2808, SOE plan, 4 February 1944. The lower figure is confirmed by a communication to Tito stating a total of around two thousand eight hundred Partisans: AMVR, OB15513, vol. 4, 1.32; D. Daskalov, *Zhan suobshtava: Zadgranichnoto Byuro i antifashistkata borba v Bulgaria 1941-1944* (Sofia: Universitetsko Izdatelstvo 'Sv. Kl. Ohridski', 1991), 187. An even smaller figure (2,180) is quoted in Dimitrov's diary: D. Sirkov et al., eds, *Georgi Dimitrov: Dnevnik 9 mart 1933-6 fevruari 1949* (Sofia: Universitetsko Izdatelstvo 'Sv. Kl. Ohridski', 1997), 414.
25 FO371/43587, R2808, Force 133 appreciation, 4 February 1944.
26 HS5/180, situation report, March 1944.
27 FO371/43654, R4736, Lord Moyne memorandum, 8 March 1944; FO371/43655, R10986, 9th meeting of AFHQ Political Committee, 16 May 1944.
28 T. Dragoicheva, *Povelya na dulga*, vol. 3 (Sofia: Partizdat, 1980), 495-6; *Rabotnichesko Delo*, 26 November 1947; N. S. Lebedev et al., eds, *Comintern i Vtoraya Mirovaya Voina*, 2 vols (Moscow: Pamyatniki Istoricheskoy Myisli, 1994, 1997), 425, 443.
29 FO371/43579, R3646, Steel to Howard, 24 February 1944.
30 FO371/43587, R2808, SOE plan, 4 February 1944; FO371/43585, R6050, FO to Cairo, 9 April 1944; FO371/43586, R9693, Clutton, 21 June 1944.
31 FO371/43579, R12750, Lord Moyne to FO, 15 August 1944.
32 J. R. Deane, *The Strange Alliance* (London: John Murray, 1947), 27-33.

33 M. M. Boll, 'US Plan for a Post-war Pro-Western Bulgaria: A Little-Known Wartime Initiative in Eastern Europe', *Diplomatic History* 7, no. 2 (spring 1983): 125–30.
34 M. M. Boll, *Cold War in the Balkans: American Policy towards Bulgaria 1943–1947* (Lexington: University Press of Kentucky, 1984), 11, 15–16, 28; Barker, *British Policy*, 118–20.
35 B. F. Smith, *Sharing Secrets with Stalin: How the Allies Traded Intelligence 1941–1945* (Lawrence: University Press of Kansas, 1996), 188; HS5/173, FO to SOE Cairo, 9 July 1944.
36 E. Barker, *Churchill and Eden at War* (Basingstoke: Macmillan, 1976), 274; V. Mastny, *Russia's Road to the Cold War* (New York: Columbia University Press, 1979), 97–8; FO371/43587, R781, Balfour to FO, 13 January 1944; FO371/43579, R775, Talbot-Rice to Dew, 4 January 1944; Daskalov, *Zhan*, 196.
37 HS5/179, report on Bulgaria, 1 March 1943.
38 *Comintern i Vtoraya Mirovaya Voina*, 72–80.
39 Bell, *The BCP*, 58; Daskalov, *Zhan*, 184–5; *Georgi Dimitrov: Dnevnik*, 258–82.
40 M. Issussov, *Stalin i Bulgaria* (Sofia: Universitetsko Izdatelstvo 'Sv. Kl. Ohridski', 1991); Daskalov, *Zhan*; *Comintern i Vtoraya Mirovaya Voina*, 175.
41 E. L. Valeva, 'Kurs na vooruzhennuyu bor'bu bolgarskogo naroda: Perviyie partizanyi (yun' 1941g.–fevral' 1943g.)', in *Dvizheniya soprotivleniya v stranah Tsentral'noy i Yugo-vostochnoy Evropy 1939–1945*, ed. V. V. Mar'ina (Moscow: Radiks, 1995), 211–14.
42 Daskalov, *Zhan*, 281; Rachev, *Churchill*, 234; *Comintern i Vtoraya Mirovaya Voina*, 12.
43 Bell, *The BCP*, 6.
44 All were Soviet subjects and most were operatives of the NKVD.
45 Bell, *The BCP*, 59; Valeva, 'Kurs', 221–2.
46 Rachev, *Churchill*, 206.
47 I. Dimitrov, *Ivan Bagryanov: Tsaredvorets, politik, durzhavnik* (Sofia: Akademichno Izdatelstvo 'Prof. Marin Drinov', 1995), 65–6.
48 HS5/180, SOE memoranda, 19 March – 6 April 1944.
49 C. Barnett, 'Anglo-American Strategy in Europe', in *The Rise and Fall of the Grand Alliance, 1941–1945*, ed. A. Lane and H. Temperley (Basingstoke: Macmillan, 1995), 175–87.
50 V. Rothwell, *Britain and the Cold War 1941–1947* (London: Cape, 1982), 201.
51 Barker, *British Policy*, 124; D. Dilks, 'British Political Aims in Central, Eastern and Southern Europe', in *British Political and Military Strategy in Central-Eastern and Southern Europe in 1944*, ed. E. Barker et al. (Basingstoke: Macmillan, 1988), 28; J. Kent, *British Imperial Strategy and the Cold War in the Middle East* (London: Leicester University Press, 1994), 9; E. Barker, *Churchill and Eden at War* (Basingstoke: Macmillan, 1978), 282; T. Campbell and G. C. Herring, eds, *The Diaries of Edward R. Stettinius, Jr. 1943–1946* (New York: New Viewpoints, 1975), 214.
52 Rachev, *Churchill*, 184.
53 Stimson, H. L., and M. Bundy, *On Active Service in Peace and War* (New York: Harper, 1947), 428–43; Boll, *Cold War*, 11; Barker, *British Policy*, 115–18; Rothwell, *Britain*, 211.
54 FO371/43655, R9612, 13th meeting of AFHQ Political Committee, 6 June 1944; Dilks, 'British Political Aims', 28; J. Erickson, 'Stalin, Soviet Strategy and the Grand Alliance', in *The Rise and Fall*, 151; Barker, *British Policy*, 124; E. Barker, 'Problems of the Alliance: Misconceptions and Misunderstandings', in *British Political and Military Strategy*, 40–53; C. Kennedy-Pipe, *Stalin's Cold War: Soviet Strategies in Europe 1943–1956* (Manchester: Manchester University Press, 1995), 41; J. Harvey, ed., *The War Diaries of Oliver Harvey* (London: Collins, 1978), 324; Stimson and Bundy, *On Active Service*, 447.
55 Barker, *British Policy*, 112; Rothwell, *Britain*, 109.

56 FO 37173, R5514, *Observer*, excerpt, 20 June 1943; FO371/43587, R2808, Force 133 appreciation, 4 February 1944.
57 AMVnR, f. 176, op. 15, a.e. 48, l. 167–8, Ankara to Sofia, 5 February 1943.
58 AMVnR, f. 176, op. 15, a.e. 59, l. 35, Madrid to Sofia, 31 May 1943, l. 82, 7 July 1943, Budapest to Sofia, a.e. 60, l. 37, Berlin to Sofia, 24 July 1943, l. 75, Bucharest to Sofia, 27 July 1943, a.e. 67, l. 5, Budapest to Sofia, 11 October 1943.
59 Rachev, *Churchill*, 158–60, 221.
60 FO371/43587, R2241, Clutton, 11 February 1944; Barker, *British Policy*, 115, 122; M. L. Miller, *Bulgaria during the Second World War* (Stanford, CA: Stanford University Press, 1975), 115; Deane, *Strange Alliance*, 19, 41–2, 148.
61 M. Percival, 'British–Romanian Relations, 1944–1965', PhD thesis, University of London, 1997, 16.
62 Barker, *British Policy*, 121; Miller, *Bulgaria*, 169; Young, *Diaries*, 285.
63 Boll, *Cold War*, 17; Miller, *Bulgaria*, 166.
64 FO371/37161, R12382, Air Ministry to Washington, DC, 20 October 1943.
65 FO371/37161, R12382, Air Ministry to Commander-in-Chief Middle East, 26 October 1943, Sargent minute, 26 October 1943.
66 FO371/37161, R12466, PWE memorandum, undated.
67 HS5/173, FORD memorandum, 25 January 1944.
68 FO371/43587, R2808, Force 133 appreciation, 10 February 1944.
69 Boll, *Cold War*, 23; AIR9/462, Cairo to Resident Minister Algiers, 28 January 1943.
70 HS5/180, Bulgaria situation report, 23 February 1944.
71 AIR9/462, Air Ministry to AFHQ Algiers, 4 April 1944.
72 FO371/37161, R12382, Moscow to FO, 23 October 1943, PM to Eden, 24 October 1943; FO371/43589, R7420, Clutton, Sargent, 22 March 1944; Barker, *British Policy*, 216–18; Boll, *Cold War*, 22.
73 FO371/43587, R2160, Resident Minister Algiers to FO, 1 February 1944, R2333, FO to Washington, DC, 12 February 1944.
74 Young, *Diaries*, 284–5.
75 AMVnR, f. 176, op. 15, a.e. 77, l. 90, 28 March 1944, Stockholm to Sofia; Miller, *Bulgaria*, 111–13; Boll, *Cold War*, 9; Rachev, *Churchill*, 227.
76 AMVnR, f. 176, op. 15, a.e. 48, l. 84–7, Ankara to Sofia, 8 January 1944.
77 FO371/37173, R5514, *Observer*, excerpt, 20 June 1943.
78 FO371/43646, R4242, SOE Cairo review, 4 March 1944; FO371/43657, R4608, Lord Selbourne, 10 March 1944.
79 FO37/37151, R6037, Halifax to Eden, 6 July 1943.
80 FO371/43596, R3421, FO to Algiers, 5 March 1944; FO371/43583, R67485, Clutton, 4 April 1944, Howard, 6 April 1944.
81 FO371/43588, R3558, Lord Killearn to FO, 4 March 1944, R3897, Sargent, 22 March 1944.
82 FO371/43587, R2808, Force 133 appreciation, 4 February 1944.
83 Young, *Diaries*, 302, 309.
84 *FRUS* 1944, vol. 3, 300, Washington, DC to Moscow, 10 February 1944; 302, Roosevelt to Churchill, 25 February 1944; 310, Stettinius to Winant, 4 March 1944; 311, MacVeagh to Hull, 7 March 1944; 307, Istanbul to Hull, 3 March 1944; Rachev, *Churchill*, 225; Miller, *Bulgaria*, 170–72.
85 Boll, *Cold War*, 12–18.
86 FO371/43587, R2537, Clark Kerr to FO, 21 February 1944, R2160, FO to Moscow, 12 February 1944, R2161, Lord Killearn to FO, 9 February 1944, R2331, FO to Washington, DC, 12 February 1944.

NOTES

87 AMVnR, f. 176, op. 15, a.e. 68, l. 6–7, Bern to Sofia, 30 October 1943, l. 29, Moscow to Sofia, 29 October 1943, l. 21, Stockholm to Sofia, 2 November 1943, l. 56, Madrid to Sofia, 6 November 1943, l. 67, Madrid to Sofia, 10 November 1943, l. 74, Berlin to Sofia, 11 November 1943, a.e. 69, l. 101–2, Army Staff to Foreign Ministry, 16 November 1943.
88 G. Mishkov, ed., *Dnevnikut na Purvan Draganov: Bivsh minister na vunshnite raboti ot 12 yuni do 1 septemvri 1944* (Sofia: VIK 'Sv. Georgi Pobedonosets', 1993), 12.
89 AMVnR, f. 176, op. 15, a.e. 75, l. 15, Ankara to Sofia, 18 March 1944.
90 Rachev, *Churchill*, 233.
91 Dimitrov, *Ivan Bagryanov*, 64–8, 73–4; *Dnevnikut na Purvan Draganov*, 39, 54.
92 Dimitrov, *Ivan Bagryanov*, 71–3; Boll, *Cold War*, 39.
93 Daskalov, *Zhan*, 182; Dimitrov, *Ivan Bagryanov*, 62.
94 *Hansard*, vol. 402, 2 August 1944, cols 1483–4.
95 S. Moshanov, *Moyata missiya v Cairo* (Sofia: Bulgarski Pisatel, 1991), 242; *Dnevnikut na Purvan Draganov*, 68.
96 Miller, *Bulgaria*, 182; Moshanov, *Moyata missiya*, 225–404.
97 Moshanov, *Moyata missiya*, 233–4, 237–8, 261.
98 Rachev, *Churchill*, 260–65; Dimitrov, *Ivan Bagryanov*, 79–81.
99 Rachev, *Churchill*, 278; Moshanov, *Moyata missiya*, 289–90.
100 Moshanov, *Moyata missiya*, 302–4. There is a hint of this in Balabanov's message of 2 September 1944 in AMVnR, op. 176, op. 15, a.e. 87, l. 73; *FRUS* 1944, vol. 3, 380, Berry to Hull, 30 August 1944; V. Toshkova, 'SASht i izlizaneto na Bulgaria ot Tristrannia Pakt, iuni–septemvri 1944', *Istoricheski Pregled* 4, no. 5 (1979): 213.
101 AMVnR, f. 176, op. 15, a.e. 87, l. 83, Ankara to Sofia, 4 September 1944.
102 Rachev, *Churchill*, 280.
103 Toshkova, 'SASht i izlizaneto', 214.
104 Boll, *Cold War*, 45; Moshanov, *Moyata missiya*, 319, 321, 345–8.
105 Moshanov, *Moyata missiya*, 325–6; 339, 349; Rachev, *Churchill*, 283.
106 TsPA, f. 146, op. 4, a.e. 235, Moshanov to Dimitrov, 10 December 1947; Moshanov, *Moyata missiya*, 224. This is not confirmed by the record of the conversation sent by Yakovlev to Moscow: T. V. Volokitina et al., eds, *Vostochnaya Evropa v dokumentah rossiyskih arhivov 1944–1953gg*, vol. 1, 1944–1948 (Moscow: Sibirskiy Hronograf, 1997), 105–9.
107 Mastny, *Russia's Road*, 97–8.
108 FO371/43588, R3181, Sargent to Eden, 21 February 1944.
109 Earl of Avon, *The Eden Memoirs: The Reckoning* (London: Cassell, 1965), 459.
110 FO371/43579, R729, PRB Stockholm to Southern Department, 8 January 1944, R6168, Last to Rose, 12 April 1944; FO371/43583, R4126, FO memorandum to PID, 8 March 1944, R5382, Angora to FO, 3 April 1944; *FRUS* 1944, vol. 3, 318, Berry to Hull, 25 March 1944; K. Muraviev, *Subitiya i hora: Spomeni* (Sofia: Bulgarski Pisatel, 1992), 349, 351, 377.
111 Mastny, *Russia's Road*, 199.
112 I. Dimitrov, ed., Bogdan Filov, *Dnevnik* (Sofia: Izdatelstvo na OF, 1990), 625, 659, 665.
113 *FRUS* 1944, vol. 3, 313–15, Winant–Hull correspondence, 13, 17 March 1944, 316–17, Hull–Harriman correspondence, 17, 19 March 1944; Boll, *Cold War*, 32.
114 AMVnR, f. 176, op. 15, a.e. 78, p. 80, Ankara to Sofia 6 March, 20 May 1944.
115 Barker, *British Policy*, 219.
116 *Dnevnikut na Purvan Draganov*, 2; Rachev, *Churchill*, 255, 259.
117 AVPRF, f. 06, op. 6, no. 241, p. 23, l. 124–5, Molotov–Clark Kerr conversation, 20 August 1944.
118 *FRUS* 1944, vol. 3, 355, Stettinius to Winant, Harriman to Hull, 12 August 1944, 356, Winant to Hull, 14 August 1944.

119 Barker, *British Policy*, 220–22; Rachev, *Churchill*, 276, 280; Dimitrov, *Ivan Bagryanov*, 83; Moshanov, *Moyata missiya*, 310. Mastny thinks Gussev's withdrawal from the EAC signified a desire to get Bagryanov under the Soviet wing in return for subservience: *Russia's Road*, 200.
120 Miller, *Bulgaria*, 192.
121 Toshkova, V., *Bulgaria v balkanskata politika na SASht, 1939–1944* (Sofia: Izdatelstvo 'Nauka i Izkustvo', 1985).
122 AMVnR, f. 176, op. 15, a.e. 83, l. 10, Stockholm to Sofia, 3 August 1944, a.e. 87, l. 29, 46, Ankara to Sofia, 1 September, 31 August 1944.
123 Mastny, *Russia's Road*, 199–200; Rachev, *Churchill*, 268; Dimitrov, *Ivan Bagryanov*, 83.
124 Muraviev, *Subitiya*, 361, 387, 413; G. Swain, 'Stalin's Wartime Vision of the Post-war World', *Diplomacy and Statecraft* 7, no.1 (1996): 85.
125 *FRUS* 1944, vol. 3, 398, Steinhart to Hull, 6 September 1944.
126 Boll, *Cold War*, 57–60.
127 *Nepriznatiyat protivnik*, 19; G. Chakalov, *Ofitser za svruzka* (Sofia: Lari, 1993), 25.
128 Dimitrov, *Ivan Bagryanov*, 78; *Nepriznatiyat protivnik*, 18.
129 Ibid., 21, 31; Rachev, *Churchill*, 281, 286.
130 Rachev, *Churchill*, 294; Moshanov, *Moyata missiya*, 358.
131 AVPRF, f. 06, op. 6, no. 242, p. 23, l. 62–4, Molotov–Harriman–Clark Kerr correspondence, 6 September 1944; FO371/43583, R14080, Clark Kerr to FO, 6 September 1944; *FRUS* 1944, vol. 3, 397, Harriman to Hull, 5 September 1944, 401–2, Harriman to Hull, 7 September 1944.
132 Boll, *Cold War*, 27.
133 De Santis, *Diplomacy of Silence*, 109.
134 AIR9/461, PWE to COS, 16 April 1944.
135 *FRUS* 1944, vol. 3, 351–2, Berry to Hull, 21 July 1944.
136 FO371/43585, R17441, Clutton, 3 February 1944.
137 FO371/43596, R3421, FO to Algiers, 5 March 1944; FO371/43583, R67485, Clutton, 4 April 1944, Howard, 6 April 1944, R7443, Lord Moyne to FO, 9 May 1944.
138 FO371/43583, R8327, Eden to Clark Kerr, 26 May 1944.
139 FO371/43586, R13699, Lord Killearn to FO, 29 August 1944.
140 *FRUS* 1944, vol. 3, 381, Berry to Hull, 30 August 1944.
141 Ibid., Harriman to Hull, 26 August 1944, 377, Winant to Hull, 29 August 1944; Sir H. Knatchbull-Hugessen, *Diplomat in Peace and War* (London: John Murray, 1949), 204; Moshanov, *Moyata missiya*, 298–9.
142 FO371/43584, R15149, Clerk Kerr to Molotov, 29 August 1944, R15150, Clerk Kerr to Molotov, 4 September 1944.
143 FO371/43583, R13685, Eden to Clark Kerr, 31 August 1944, R13963, Lord Moyne to FO, 4 September 1944, R14012, FO to Moscow, 5 September 1944; *FRUS* 1944, vol. 3, 395, British Embassy Washington to State, 4 September 1944.
144 *FRUS* 1944, vol. 3, 361, British Embassy aide-memoire to State, 20 August 1944; Kennedy-Pipe, *Stalin's Cold War*, 45.
145 FO371/43584, R14275, Clerk Kerr to FO, 9 September 1944.
146 FO371/43584, R14137, McDermott, 8 September 1944, Clutton, 9 September 1944.
147 *FRUS* 1944, vol. 3, 392, Steinhart to Hull, 2 September 1944.
148 Muraviev, *Subitiya*, 381.
149 FO371/43586, R9693, Sargent, 22 June 194.

Chapter Three: The Principles of British Postwar Policy towards Bulgaria

1 Sir Winston Churchill, *The Second World War*, vol. 6 (London: Cassell, 1954), 197–9; Earl of Avon, *The Eden Memoirs: The Reckoning* (London: Cassell, 1965), 482–3; C. Hull, *The Memoirs of Cordell Hull* (New York: Macmillan, 1948), 1252–8; E. R. Stettinius, *Roosevelt and the Russians: The Yalta Conference* (London: Jonathan Cape, 1950), 20–22; C. Bohlen, *Witness to History 1929–1969* (London: Weidenfeld & Nicolson, 1973), 163–5; A. Harriman and E. Abel, *Special Envoy to Churchill and Stalin 1941–1946* (New York: Random House, 1975), 356–8; J. Harvey, ed., *The War Diaries of Oliver Harvey* (London: Collins, 1978), 359. The British interpreter at the meeting did not refer to the deal: A. H. Birse, *Memoirs of an Interpreter* (London: Michael Joseph, 1967), 170. One of the Russian interpreters mentioned Churchill's proposal but denied the conclusion of a deal: V. Berezhkov, *History in the Making: Memoirs of World War II Diplomacy* (Moscow: Progress, 1984), 369–74.
2 The Russian records are in AVPRF, f. 6, op. 6, p. 23, no. 228, and in the Archive of the President of the Russian Federation (APRF), f. 45, op. 1, no. 282. The Russian record of the Churchill–Stalin conversation of 9 October 1944 has been put into an English translation in O. A. Rzheshevsky, 'Soviet Policy in Eastern Europe (1944–1945): Liberation or Occupation? Documents and Commentary', lecture at St Antony's College, Oxford, April 1995. The British records are in PREM3, 66/7, FO181, 990/2 and FO371/43601 and have been published in J. M. Siracusa, 'The Meaning of TOLSTOY: Churchill, Stalin and the Balkans, Moscow, October 1944', *Diplomatic History* 3, no. 4 (fall 1979): 443–63.
3 Churchill's account (Churchill, *Second World War*, vol. 6, 197–9), has been quoted by many historians: H. Feis, *Churchill, Roosevelt, Stalin* (Princeton, NJ: Princeton University Press, 1967), 448–9; A. Resis, 'The Churchill-Stalin Secret "Percentages" Agreement on the Balkans, Moscow, October 1944', *American Historical Review* 83, no. 2, (April 1978): 368–9; Siracusa, 'The Meaning', 443–4.
4 FO371/43601, R16315, Eden to FO, 10 October 1944.
5 PREM3, 66/7, 177, Strang and Sargent to Eden, 11 October 1944, 176, Eden to Sargent, 12 October 1944; Resis, 'The Churchill–Stalin Secret', 371.
6 PREM3, 66/7, Churchill to Hopkins, 12 October 1944; FO371/43647, R16426, Churchill to Hopkins, 11 October 1944.
7 H. Feis, *Churchill, Roosevelt, Stalin: The War They Waged and the Peace They Sought* (Oxford: Oxford University Press, 1957), 340.
8 Siracusa, 'The Meaning', 447.
9 Rzheshevsky, 'Soviet Policy', 7.
10 PREM3, 66/7, Eden to Sargent, 12 October 1944; P. G. H. Holdich, 'A Policy of Percentages? British Policy in the Balkans after the Moscow Conference of October 1944', *International History Review* 9, no. 1 (February 1987): 31–2.
11 Churchill, *Second World War*, vol. 6, 203–4.
12 Siracusa, 'The Meaning', 448, 450.
13 Resis, 'The Churchill–Stalin Secret', 373–4.
14 Ibid., 376–7.
15 The Russian record attributes this phrase to Eden: Rzheshevsky, 'Soviet Policy', 7.
16 W. F. Kimball, 'Naked Reverse Right: Churchill, Roosevelt and Eastern Europe from TOLSTOY to Yalta and a Little Beyond', *Diplomatic History* 9, no. 1 (winter 1985): 2.

17 V. Rothwell, *Britain and the Cold War 1941–1947* (London: Cape, 1982), 127; Feis, *Churchill*, 349.
18 FO371/43636, R11461, PM to Eden, 1 August 1944; FO371/72194, R5413, FO paper on British and Soviet interests in the Balkans, 10 August 1943; J. O. Iatrides, ed., *Ambassador McVeagh Reports: Greece 1933–1947* (Princeton, NJ: Princeton University Press, 1980), 572; W. H. McNeill, *America, Britain and Russia: Their Co-operation and Conflict 1941–1946* (London: Johnson Reprint, 1970), 390; E. Barker, *British Policy in South-East Europe in the Second World War* (Basingstoke: Macmillan, 1976), 139; S. G. Xydis, 'The Secret Anglo–Soviet Agreement on the Balkans of 9 October 1944', *Journal of Central European Affairs* 15, no. 3 (October 1955): 257, 259. At the same time the Soviets increased their attention to Turkey: S. Deringil, *Turkish Foreign Policy during the Second World War: An 'Active' Neutrality* (Cambridge: Cambridge University Press, 1989), 175–6.
19 Earl of Avon, *Eden Memoirs*, 459.
20 FO371/43646, R9092, FO paper and Eden memorandum, 7 June 1944.
21 K. Sainsbury, *The Turning Point* (Oxford: Oxford University Press, 1985), 53–61; Earl of Avon, *Eden Memoirs*, 412, 417.
22 Sir Curtis Keeble, *Britain and the Soviet Union, 1917–1989* (Basingstoke: Macmillan, 1990), 188–9.
23 K. G. M. Ross, 'The Moscow Conference of October 1944 (Tolstoy)', in *British Political and Military Strategy in Central-Eastern and Southern Europe in 1944*, ed. E. Barker et al. (Basingstoke: Macmillan, 1988), 68.
24 Earl of Avon, *Eden Memoirs*, 459.
25 FO371/43636, Churchill to Eden, May–October 1944; Harvey, *War Diaries*, 344, 348.
26 G. Ross, 'Foreign Office Attitudes to the Soviet Union 1941–1945'. *Journal of Contemporary History* 16, no. 3 (July 1981): 521–40.
27 J. Haslam, *Russia's Cold War: From the October Revolution to the Fall of the Wall* (New Haven, CT: Yale University Press, 2011), 22–4.
28 Hull, *Memoirs*, 253–8.
29 Rothwell, *Britain*, 128; Earl of Avon, *Eden Memoirs*, 460.
30 Resis, 'The Churchill–Stalin Secret', 375; Barker, *British Policy*, 143; R. Garson, 'Churchill's "Spheres of Influence": Rumania and Bulgaria', *Survey* 24, no. 3 (summer 1979): 144–5, 153–6.
31 FO371/43601, R16186, Eden, 6 October 1944, R16586, Eden to Sargent, 15 October 1944; Earl of Avon, *Eden Memoirs*, 483.
32 FO371/43601, R16547, Sargent to Eden, 11 October 1944; Holdich, 'A Policy', 45, interprets this as criticism by the Foreign Office.
33 Harvey, *War Diaries*, 363.
34 D. Dilks, ed., *The Diaries of Sir Alexander Cadogan O. M. 1938–1945* (London: Cassell, 1971), 672.
35 K. Young, ed., *The Diaries of Sir Robert Bruce Lockhart*, vol. 2, 1939–1965 (Basingstoke: Macmillan, 1980), 360.
36 Harvey, *War Diaries*, 363, 368.
37 Garson, 'Churchill's "Spheres"', 145.
38 Xydis, 'The Secret', 263.
39 Resis, 'The Churchill–Stalin Secret', 375.
40 Xydis, 'The Secret', 256.
41 Holdich, 'A Policy'; C. Kennedy-Pipe, *Stalin's Cold War: Soviet Strategies in Europe, 1943 to 1956* (Manchester: Manchester University Press, 1995), 47.

42 Garson, 'Churchill's "Spheres"'.
43 Holdich, 'A Policy', 37–42.
44 G. Roberts, *Stalin's Wars: From World War to Cold War, 1939–1953* (New Haven, CT: Yale University Press, 2006), 219–25; Haslam, *Russia's Cold War*, 22–4.
45 V. Mastny, 'Soviet Plans for Post-war Europe', in *The Failure of Peace in Europe, 1943–48*, ed. A. Varsori and E. Calandri (Basingstoke: Palgrave, 2002), 59–75.
46 D. Sirkov et al., eds, *G. Dimitrov: Dnevnik 9 mart 1933–6 fevruari 1949* (Sofia: Universitetsko Izdatelstvo 'Sv. Kl. Ohridski', 1997), 443.
47 Earl of Avon, *Eden Memoirs*, 482–3.
48 FO371/43613, R13392, FORD paper, 24 August 1944; FO371/43600, R15270, Laskey, 26 September 1944; FO371/43649, R20431, Leeper to FO, 11 November 1944.
49 FO371/43613, R13392, FORD paper, 24 August 1944; US Department of State, *FRUS*, 1944, vol. 3 (Washington, DC, 1962), vol. 3, 343, proposed terms, 17 June 1944.
50 V. Toshkova, *Bulgaria v balkanskata politika na SASht, 1939–1944* (Sofia: Izdatelstvo 'Nauka i Izkustvo', 1985), 39.
51 Holdich, 'A Policy', 30.
52 Feis, *Churchill*, 441.
53 S. Rachev, *Churchill, Bulgaria i Balkanite* (Sofia: Sotri, 1995), 305, 309, 316.
54 FO371/43600, R15274, Papandreou to Leeper, 1 September 1944.
55 FO371/43602, R18455, Athens to FO, 13 November 1944; FO371/43649, R20431, Leeper to FO, 19 November 1944.
56 Toshkova, *Bulgaria*, 23.
57 Ibid., 39.
58 Toshkova, *Bulgaria*, 31; Rachev, *Churchill*, 315–23.
59 FO371/43599, R14799, Earle (WCO) to Sargent, 16 September 1944; FO371/43647, R14858, FO to Moscow, 17 September 1944; FO371/43647, R15409, Joint Intelligence Sub-committee report, 19 September 1944.
60 Earl of Avon, *Eden Memoirs*, 482.
61 Siracusa, 'The Meaning', 454–5.
62 Holdich, 'A Policy', 31.
63 Earl of Avon, *Eden Memoirs*, 482.
64 FO371/43601, R16433, Eden to Sargent, 11 October 1944, R14688, Sargent to Eden, 12 October 1944; FO371/43647, R16458, Eden to Sargent, 12 October 1944; T. V. Volokitina et al., eds, V*ostochnaya Evropa v dokumentah rossiyskih arhivov 1944–1953gg.*, vol. 1, 1944–1948 (Moscow: Sibirskiy Hronograf, 1997), 73–5.
65 Resis, 'The Churchill–Stalin Secret', 380.
66 FO371/43589, R11992, Sargent and Clutton, 28 July 1944, Eden to PM, 10 August 1944; FO371/43649, R21989, Sargent memorandum, 5 December 1944.
67 Xydis, 'The Secret', 264.
68 *Georgi Dimitrov: Dnevnik*, 441–2.
69 V. Zubok and C. Pleshakov, *Inside the Kremlin's Cold War from Stalin to Khrushchev* (Cambridge, MA: Harvard University Press, 1996), 92–3.
70 A. Resis, ed., *Molotov Remembers: Inside Kremlin Politics; Conversations with Felix Chuev* (Chicago: Ivan R. Dee, 1993), 65.
71 TsPA, f. 1, op. 7, a.e. 23, Kostov to Dimitrov, 8 October 1944, a.e. 30, Kostov to Dimitrov, 12 October 1944; L. Ognyanov et al., eds, *Narodna demokratsiya ili diktatura*, (Sofia: Literaturen Forum, 1992), 10, 12; *Ustanovyavane i ukrepvane na narodnodemokratichnata vlast septemvri 1944–may 1945* (Sofia: Izdatelstvo na BAN, 1969), 45, 133.

72 *Georgi Dimitrov: Dnevnik*, 440.
73 FO371/43601, R16315, Eden to FO, 11 October 1944; FO371/43649, R19241, Eden memo, 21 November 1944; W. R. Roberts, *Tito, Mihailović and the Allies 1941–45* (Durham, NC: Duke University Press, 1987), 270.
74 Lord Strang, *Home and Abroad* (London: Andre Deutsch, 1956), 201.
75 Sainsbury, *The Turning*, 69–75.
76 Lord Strang, *Home*, 205.
77 FO371/43590, R14123, Howard to Earle, 7 September 1944; *FRUS* 1944, vol. 3, 367–70, Winant to Hull, 25 August 1944.
78 FO371/43598, R13528, FO memorandum, 29 August 1944; FO371/43597, R13778, Eden, 30 August 1944; FO371/43600; R15276, Strang to Eden, 21 September 1944; FO371/43599, R14505, Gussev to Strang, 9 September 1944.
79 FO371/43590, R13641, COS committee meeting, 25 August 1944.
80 Lord Strang, *Home*, 224–5.
81 M. M. Boll, *Cold War in the Balkans: American Policy towards Bulgaria 1943–1947* (Lexington: University Press of Kentucky, 1984), 31–5, 46; C. E. Black, 'The Start of the Cold War in Bulgaria: A Personal View', *Review of Politics* 41, no. 2 (April 1979), 170.
82 Toshkova, *Bulgaria*, 29–30; Boll, *Cold War*, 47–51.
83 Black, 'The Start', 165.
84 Ibid., 170–71; Boll, *Cold War*, 49–51.
85 Barnes, M. 'The Current Situation in Bulgaria', lecture at the National War College, Washington, DC, 3 June 1947, 7.
86 Ibid., 10.
87 Resis, 'The Churchill–Stalin Secret', 377–8, 381–3; Siracusa, 'The Meaning', 457–61.
88 FO371/43601, R16444, WO to BMM Bulgaria, 13 October 1944, R16586, Eden to Sargent, 15 October 1944; FO371/43591, R18888, Eden to Molotov, 15 October 1944; *FRUS* 1944, vol. 3, 461–4, Winant to Hull, 11 and 18 October 1944.
89 Black, 'The Start', 167; E. Barker, 'British Policy towards Romania, Bulgaria and Hungary 1944–1946', in *Communist Power in Europe 1944–1949*, ed. M. McCauley (Basingstoke: Macmillan, 1977), 201–3; M. M. Boll, 'Reality and Illusion: The Allied Control Commission for Bulgaria as a Cause for the Cold War', *East European Quarterly* 17, no. 1 (1984): 422.
90 FO371/43600, R15158, Clerk Kerr to FO, 23.9.1944.
91 Siracusa, 'The Meaning', 456.
92 E. Hazard, (*Cold War Crucible: United States Foreign Policy and the Conflict in Romania, 1943–1952* (Boulder, CO: East European Monographs, 1996), 59)) claims that the 'percentages deal' immediately created difficulties for Western personnel on the ground; S. Pintev, 'Nachalna deinost na Suyuznata Kontrolna Komisia v Bulgaria, oktomvri 1944–januari 1945', *Istoricheski Pregled* 35, no. 4/5 (1979): 198.
93 FO371/43602, R17355, Armistice agreement with Bulgaria, 28 October 1944; *FRUS* 1944, vol. 3, 481, Kennan to Washington, DC, 28 October 1944; M. M. Boll, ed., *The American Military Mission in the Allied Control Commission for Bulgaria 1944–1947* (Boulder, CO: Columbia University Press, 1985), 5.
94 Kennedy-Pipe, *Stalin's Cold War*, 48, 61–6.
95 Kimball, 'Naked Reverse Right', 16–24.
96 Boll, *American Military Mission*, 7.
97 A. Heller and F. Feher, *From Yalta to Glasnost* (Oxford: Blackwell, 1990), 7; G. Alperovitz, *Atomic Diplomacy: Hiroshima and Potsdam* (London: Secker & Warburg, 1966), 148.

98 Kennedy-Pipe, *Stalin's Cold War*, 54; J. L. Gaddis, *We Now Know: Rethinking Cold War History* (Oxford: Clarendon Press, 1997), 15.
99 Harvey, *War Diaries*, 373, 377.
100 F. Roberts, *Dealing with Dictators: The Destruction and Revival of Europe 1930–1970* (London: Weidenfeld & Nicolson, 1991), 73–5; Feis, *Churchill*, 547.
101 D. S. Clemens, *Yalta* (New York: Oxford University Press, 1970), 258–62.
102 G. Jebb, *The Memoirs of Lord Gladwyn* (London: Weidenfeld & Nicolson, 1972), 153–4.
103 B. Kovrig, *Of Walls and Bridges: The United States and Eastern Europe* (New York: New York University Press, 1991), 19; K. Schwabe argues that Yalta was unenforceable but provided the West with a moral right: 'The US and Europe from Roosevelt to Truman', in *The Failure*, ed. Varsori and Calandri, 17–39.
104 Rothwell, *Britain*, 363.
105 L. Saiu, *The Great Powers and Romania, 1943–1947* (Boulder, CO: Columbia University Press, 1992), 83–91.
106 FO371/48123, R4072, Howard, 5 March 1945, Sargent, 6 March 1945.
107 FO371/47883, N8674, Clerk Kerr to FO, 10 July 1945; M. Percival, 'British–Romanian Relations, 1944–1965', PhD thesis, University of London, 1997, 51–5.
108 Saiu, *The Great Powers*, 95–6.
109 K. A. Hamilton, *The Quest for the Modus Vivendi: The Danubian Satellites and Anglo–Soviet Relations 1945–46*, Occasional Papers, no. 4 (London: FCO Historical Branch, 1992), 5–7; Ross, *Foreign Office*, 60, 210–17.
110 Keeble, *Britain*, 198; G. Ross, ed., *The Foreign Office and the Kremlin: British Documents on Anglo-Soviet Relations 1944–1945*, (Cambridge: Cambridge University Press, 1985), 210–17.
111 Bohlen, *Witness to History*, 175–6; Kennedy-Pipe, *Stalin's Cold War*, 51.
112 Ibid., 79; Alperovitz, *Atomic Diplomacy*, 134–6.
113 R. S. Dinardo, 'Glimpse of an Old World Order? Reconsidering the Trieste Crisis of 1945', *Diplomatic History* 21, no. 3 (fall 1997): 365–81.
114 H. S. Truman, *Memoirs* (New York: Doubleday, 1955), 382–6; Bohlen, *Witness to History*, 234.
115 Boll, *Cold War*, 139–40.
116 M. Issussov, *Stalin i Bulgaria* (Sofia: Universitetsko Izdatelstvo 'Sv. Kl. Ohridski', 1991), 87; G. Roberts, *Stalin's Wars: From World War to Cold War, 1939–1953* (New Haven, CT: Yale University Press, 2006), 278, 296 takes the view that the Western leaders glossed over the issues in Bulgaria and Romania.

Chapter Four: Observing the Establishment of Communist Rule in Bulgaria

1 J. Mendelsohn, ed., *Covert Warfare: The OSS–NKVD Relationship, 1943–1945* (New York: Garland, 1989), doc. 64, OSS Cairo to Secretary of State, 25 September 1944, doc. 66, US Army Forces Cairo to War Department, 26 September 1944.
2 Black, C. E, 'The Start of the Cold War in Bulgaria: A Personal View', *Review of Politics* 41, no. 2 (April 1979): 171–5; M. M. Boll, 'Reality and Illusion: The Allied Control Commission for Bulgaria as a Cause for the Cold War', *East European Quarterly* 17, no. 4 (January 1984): 426.
3 RTsHIDNI, f. 17, op. 128, a.e. 750, l. 16, Kostov report, 26 January 1945.
4 M. Barnes, 'The Current Situation in Bulgaria', lecture at the National War College, Washington, DC, 3 June 1947, 9.

5 FO371/48644, U827, Sofia to FO, FO minutes, 3–8 February 1945; FO371/48166, R3192, Sofia to FO, FO minutes, 13–20 February 1945.
6 P. Semerdjiev, *Narodniyat sud v Bulgaria 1944–1945g. Komu i zashto e bil neobhodim* (Jerusalem: Macedonian-Bulgarian Institute, 1997), 406; R. J. Crampton, *A Short History of Modern Bulgaria* (Cambridge: Cambridge University Press, 1987), 149. By comparison, contemporary unpublicized Communist documents admitted to a total of 1,590 death sentences for political crimes, of which 199 had been carried during what they called the 'fascist rule' in 1923–44: AVPRF, f. 74, op. 26, p. 16, no. 6, l. 116, MID note, 21–2 December 1944.
7 L. Ognyanov et al., eds, *Narodna demokratsiya ili diktatura* (Sofia: Literaturen Forum, 1992), 29.
8 FO371/48644, U827, Sofia to FO, FO minutes, 3–8 February 1945; FO371/48166, R3192, Sofia to FO, FO minutes, 13–20 February 1945.
9 NA, RG220, entry 108, box 90, OSS report, 30 December 1944; J. D. Bell, *The Bulgarian Communist Party from Blagoev to Zhivkov* (Stanford, CA: Hoover Institute Press, 1986), 82; R. J. Crampton, *Eastern Europe in the Twentieth Century* (London: Routledge, 1994), 223; S. M. Max, *The United States, Great Britain, and the Sovietization of Hungary, 1945–1948* (Boulder, CO: Columbia University Press, 1985), 33–9.
10 FO371/48123, R4072, Howard, 5 March 1945.
11 FO371/48123, R4072, Houstoun-Boswall to FO, 28 February 1945.
12 G. Lundestad, *The American Non-Policy towards Eastern Europe 1943–1947* (Oslo: Universitetsforlaget, 1978), 232–3; M. M. Boll, *Cold War in the Balkans: American Policy towards Bulgaria 1943–1947* (Lexington: University Press of Kentucky, 1984), 94–5.
13 FO371/48123, R6011, Halifax to FO, 30 March 1945.
14 AVPRF, f. 74, op. 27, p. 17, no. 18, l. 29, MID to Roberts, May 1945; FO371/48124, R8082, Roberts to FO, 6 May 1945; Lundestad, *American Non-Policy*, 197–205.
15 Ognyanov, *Narodna*, 34.
16 FO371/48124, R6239, Houstoun-Boswall to FO, 4 April 1945.
17 FO371/48124, R6081, US Embassy London to FO, 31 March 1945, Churchill, 3 April 1945, Clerk Kerr to Molotov, 12 April 1945.
18 FO371/48123, R4072, Howard, 5 March 1945, Sargent, Cadogan, 6 March 1945, Eden, 8 March 1945.
19 FO371/48124, R6239, Williams, 9 May 1945.
20 FO371/48128, R12876, Houstoun-Boswall to FO, 31 July 1945; FO371/48159, R11158, Houstoun-Boswall to FO, 29 June 1945.
21 FO371/48159, R11158, Stewart, 1 July 1945.
22 FO371/48122, R3785, FO to Angora, 3 April 1945.
23 FO371/48219, R5063, Sargent memorandum, 13 March 1945.
24 FO371/48123, R4072, Sargent, 6 March 1945.
25 FO371/48219, R5063, Sargent memorandum, 13 March 1945.
26 RTsHIDNI, f. 17, op. 128, a.d. 750, l. 16–17, Kostov report, 26 January 1945; TsPA, f. 146, op. 4, a.e. 182, p. 3, Kostov to Dimitrov, 2 June 1945.
27 TsPA, f. 146, op. 4, a.e. 174, Kostov to Dimitrov, 9 February 1945.
28 RTsHIDNI, f. 17, op. 128, a.d. 758, l. 21, Vassilev to Dimitrov, 10 February 1945; D. S. Clemens (*Yalta* (New York: Oxford University Press, 1970), 268–70) claims that before Potsdam Stalin favoured free elections in Eastern Europe.
29 FO371/48128, R11987, Houstoun-Boswall to FO, 11 July 1945.
30 Ognyanov, *Narodna*, 34.
31 G. Dimitrov, *Izbrani suchineniya*, vol. 6 (Sofia: Partizdat, 1972), 212–13.
32 V. Dimitrov, 'The Cominform and the Bulgarian Communist Party: Embarking on a New Course?', paper presented at the Ninth International Colloquium 'L'Unione Sovietica e l'Europa nella Guerra Fredda (1943–1953)', Cortona, Italy, September 1994, 5.

33 C. Moser, *Dimitrov of Bulgaria: A Political Biography of Dr George M. Dimitrov* (Ottawa, IL: Caroline House, 1979), 224–32.
34 FO371/48223, R12235, Stewart, 18 July 1945.
35 FO371/48128, R12711, Houstoun-Boswall to FO, 31 July 1945.
36 FO371/48128, R12711, Stewart, 20 July 1945; FO371/48128, R12711, FO to Sofia, 28 July 1945.
37 FO371/48223, R12235, TERMINAL briefs, 30 June 1945.
38 FO371/48128, R12616, Houstoun-Boswall to FO, 26 July 1945.
39 Ognyanov, *Narodna*, 35–6.
40 FO371/48128, R12347, Houstoun-Boswall to FO, 21 July 1945.
41 FO371/48129, R13862, Houstoun-Boswall to FO, 17 August 1945.
42 FO371/48129, R13863, Houstoun-Boswall to FO, 17 August 1945, Stewart, 18 August 1945.
43 FO371/48128, R12616, Stewart, 27 July 1945.
44 FO371/48128, R12711, FO to Sofia, 28 July 1945.
45 FO371/48223, R13696, Dixon, 14 August 1945.
46 J. O. Iatrides, ed., *Ambassador McVeagh Reports: Greece 1933–1947* (Princeton, NJ: Princeton University Press, 1980), 691–4; P. J. Stavrakis, *Moscow and Greek Communism 1944–1949* (Ithaca, NY: Cornell University Press, 1989), 84–94.
47 FO371/48128, R13766, Washington, DC to FO, 15 August 1945.
48 US Department of State, *FRUS*, 1945 (Washington, DC, 1963), 295, Byrnes to Barnes, 18 August 1945.
49 FO371/48129, R13862, Houstoun-Boswall to FO, 17 August 1945.
50 FO371/48128, R13766, Stewart, 15 August 1945.
51 FO371/48129, R13863, Houstoun-Boswall to FO, 17 August 1945.
52 FO371/48129, R13863, Stewart, 18 August 1945.
53 FO371/48128, R13548, Stewart, 12 August 1945.
54 FO371/48128, R13548, FO to Moscow, 20 August 1945.
55 FO371/48129, R14209, BMM to WO, 22 August 1945.
56 Boll, *Cold War*, 146.
57 FO371/48129, R14209, BMM to WO, 22 August 1945.
58 AVPRF, f. 74, op. 27, no. 18, p. 17, l. 30, Kirsanov to MID, 22 August 1945.
59 FO371/48129, R14328, BMM to FO, 23 August 1945.
60 FO371/48129, R14209, FO to Washington, DC, 24 August 1945.
61 FO371/48129, R14365, BMM to FO, 24 August 1945.
62 Ibid.
63 FO371/48129, R14356, BMM to WO, 25 August 1945, R14436, Houstoun-Boswall to FO, 27 August 1945; M. Mackintosh, 'Stalin's Policies towards Eastern Europe, 1939–1948: The General Picture', in *The Anatomy of Communist Takeovers*, ed. T. T. Hammond and R. Farrell (New Haven, CT: Yale University Press, 1975), 239–40.
64 FO371/48131, R17892, Houstoun-Boswall to FO, 12 October 1945.
65 FO371/48129, R14329, BMM to WO, 24 August 1945.
66 FO371/48131, R17892, Houstoun-Boswall to FO, 12 October 1945.
67 Ibid.
68 FO371/48129, R14329, Stewart, 25 August 1945, FO to Sofia, 25 August 1945; A. Lane and K. Hamilton, 'Britain and Eastern Europe', in *Europe within the Global System, 1938–1960: Great Britain, France, Italy and Germany from Great Powers to Regional Powers*, ed. M. Dockrill (Bochum: Universitätsverlag 'Dr N. Brockmeyer', 1995).
69 FO371/48129, R15115, Lawford to Sargent, Hayter to Lawford, 28 August 1945.

70 FO371/48129, R14437, Houstoun-Boswall to FO, 27 August 1945; FO371/48130, R14591, Houstoun-Boswall to FO, 28 August 1945.
71 FO371/48130, R14591, Stewart, Sargent, 30 August 1945, Cadogan, 31 August 1945.
72 FO371/48129, R14437, FO to Washington, DC, 31 August 1945.
73 Ibid.
74 *FRUS* 1945, vol. 4, 314, Barnes to State, 28 August 1945.
75 Ibid., 317, Barnes to State, 3 September 1945.
76 FO371/48131, R16061, Houstoun-Boswall to FO, 19 September 1945.
77 FO371/48131, R17057, Stewart, 9 October 1945.
78 FO371/48131, R15717, Stewart, 25 September 1945.
79 FO371/48131, R16832, Houstoun-Boswall to FO, 22 September 1945.
80 FO371/48131, R16308, Houstoun-Boswall to FO, 23 September 1945.
81 FO371/48131, R15511, Houstoun-Boswall to FO, 11 September 1945.
82 FO371/48131, R15519, Houstoun-Boswall to FO, 12 September 1945.
83 *Narodno Zemedelsko Zname*, no. 41, 28 September 1945.
84 M. Issussov, *Stalin i Bulgaria* (Sofia: Universitetsko Izdatelstvo 'Sv. Kl. Ohridski', 1991), 33.
85 TsPA, f. 1, op. 7, a.e. 52, l. 1, Dimitrov to Kostov, 18 October 1945; *Ustanovyavane i ukrepvane na narodnodemokratichnata vlast septemvri 1944–may 1945* (Sofia: Izdatelstvo na BAN, 1969), 214; L. Ognyanov, *Durzhavno-politicheskata sistema v Bulgaria, 1944–1948* (Sofia: BAN, 1993), 75.
86 Ognyanov, *Durzhavno-politicheskata sistema*, 79.
87 Dimitrov, 'The Cominform', 6.
88 FO371/48131, R15519, Houstoun-Boswall to FO, 12 September 1945.
89 FO371/48131, R17057, Houstoun-Boswall to FO, 5 October 1945; TsPA, f. 1, op. 7, a.e. 351, l. 1, Kostov to Dimitrov, 31 May 1945; *FRUS* 1945, vol. 4, 316, Barnes to State, 30 August 1945.
90 FO371/48131, R17057, Stewart, 9 October 1945.
91 FO371/48131, R17254, Houstoun-Boswall to FO, 10 October 1945.
92 FO371/48132, R18371, Houstoun-Boswall to FO, 27 October 1945.
93 FO371/48130, R15267, Houstoun-Boswall to FO, 8 September 1945.
94 FO371/48131, R17254, Houstoun-Boswall to FO, 10 October 1945.
95 Ibid.
96 FO371/48131, R16061, Stewart, 25 September 1945.
97 FO371/48131, R17057, Stewart, 9 October 1945.
98 FO371/48131, R16660, Stewart, 2 October 1945.
99 FO371/48131, R17703, Houstoun-Boswall to FO, 17 October 1945.
100 FO371/48132, R18146, Washington, DC to FO, 24 October 1945.
101 M. Etheridge and C. E. Black, 'Negotiating on the Balkans', in *Negotiating with the Russians*, ed. R. Dennett and J. E. Johnson (Boston: World Peace Foundation, 1951), 185.
102 Etheridge, 'Negotiating', 191; Black, 'The Start', 187.
103 TsPA, f. 146, op. 4, a.e. 192, l. 3–4, Kostov to Dimitrov, 22 October 1945.
104 Black, 'The Start', 189; FO371/48194, R19201, Washington, DC to FO, 12 November 1945.
105 TsPA, f. 146, op. 4, a.e. 192, l. 3–4, Kostov to Dimitrov, 22 October 1945.
106 Ibid.
107 Etheridge, 'Negotiating', 192.
108 FO371/48132, R18750, Houstoun-Boswall to FO, 3 November 1945; Black, 'The Start', 189.

109 TsPA, f. 146, op. 4, a.e. 192, l. 4, Kostov to Dimitrov, 22 October 1945.
110 RTsHIDNI, f. 17, op. 128, a.e. 759, l. 70–77, Ehrenburg draft article 19–22 October 1945.
111 FO371/48194, R19324, Moscow to FO, 14 November 1945.
112 FO371/48132, R18348, Houstoun-Boswall to FO, 26 October 1945.
113 TsPA, f. 146, op. 4, a.e. 192, l. 4, Kostov to Dimitrov, 22 October 1945; FO371/48132, R18371, Houstoun-Boswall to FO, 27 October 1945.
114 FO371/48132, R18899, FO to Washington, DC, 10 November 1945.
115 FO371/48132, R18750, Stewart, 5 November 1945, Williams, 6 November 1945.
116 FO371/48194, R9168, Washington, DC to FO, 12 November 1945.
117 FO371/48132, R18899, Washington, DC to FO, 7 November 1945.
118 FO371/48132, R20247, Moscow Embassy to FO, 20 November 1945.
119 FO371/48132, R18899, Williams, 8 November 1945; FO371/48194, R19327, Sargent, Dixon, 16 November 1945.
120 FO371/48132, R18899, Williams, 8 November 1945.
121 FO371/48131, R17623, Stewart, 17 October 1945.
122 TsPA, f. 1, op. 7, a.e. 393, l. 2, Kostov to Dimitrov, 5 July 1945.
123 FO371/48194, R19324, Moscow to FO, 14 November 1945.
124 FO371/48194, R19326, Sofia to FO, 15 November 1945; T. Kostadinova, *Bulgaria 1879–1946: The Challenge of Choice* (Boulder, CO: East European Monographs, 1995), 86.
125 FO371/48132, R18348, Houstoun-Boswall to FO, 26 October 1945.
126 FO371/48194, R19327, Washington to FO, R19201, Stewart, 14 November 1945.
127 FO371/48194, R19201, Williams, 14 November 1945.
128 FO371/48194, R19201, Sargent, 15 November 1945.
129 FO371/48194, R19327, Sargent, Dixon, 16 November 1945.
130 Ognyanov, *Narodna*, 45–7.
131 FO371/48132, R19440, US Embassy to Sargent, 16 November 1945, R 19454, BMM to WO, 16 November 1945.
132 FO371/48132, R18348, Houstoun-Boswall to FO, 26 October 1945.
133 FO371/48132, R19498, Houstoun-Boswall to FO, 17 November 1945.
134 FO371/48194, R19541, Sofia to FO, 17 November 1945.
135 FO371/48194, R19541, FO to Sofia, 23 November 1945.
136 Kostadinova, *Bulgaria*, 88.
137 FO371/48132, R19781, Houstoun-Boswall to FO, 20 November 1945.
138 FO371/48132, R19781, Stewart, 23 November 1945.
139 FO371/48194, R20177, Sofia to FO, 29 November 1945.
140 FO371/48194, R20451, Sofia to FO, 3 December 1945.
141 FO371/48194, R20177, Sofia to FO, 29 November 1945.
142 FO371/48194, R20830, Clark Kerr to FO, 12 December 1945.
143 FO371/48194, R20451, Williams, 6 December 1945, Sargent, 7 December 1945, R20830, FO draft to Houstoun-Boswall, December 1945.

Chapter Five: Recognizing the Bulgarian Communist Regime

1 L. B. Valev et al., eds, *Sovetsko–Bolgarskie otnosheniya i svyazi, 1944–1948gg.: Documenti i materiali* (Moscow: Nauka, 1981), 112–13.

2 M. E. Pelly et al., eds, *DBPO*, ser. 1, vol. 6, Eastern Europe, August 1945–April 1946 (London: HMSO, 1991), 245–6, Sargent to Houstoun-Boswall, 26 November 1945.
3 US Department of State, *FRUS*, 1945, vol. 4 (Washington, DC, 1963), 384, Barnes to Byrnes, 17 November 1945.
4 *FRUS* 1945, vol. 4, 396–7, Barnes to Byrnes, 26 November 1945, 398, Stoychev–Reber conversation, 27 November 1945.
5 TsPA, f. 1, op. 5, a.e. 5, l. 4–6, Kostov's speech, 12 December 1945.
6 L. Ognyanov et al., eds, *Narodna demokratsiya ili diktatura* (Sofia: Literaturen Forum, 1992), 47.
7 L. E. Davis, *The Cold War Begins: Soviet–American Conflict over Eastern Europe* (Princeton, NJ: Princeton University Press, 1974), 33
8 According to the Turnovo Constitution, a Grand Assembly had double the number of deputies of an Ordinary Assembly. It could alter the constitution and make other important decisions, e.g., ratify peace treaties.
9 *FRUS* 1945, vol. 4, 378, Etheridge to Byrnes, 14 November 1945.
10 *FRUS* 1945, vol. 4, 410–11, Barnes to Byrnes, 13 December 1945.
11 Etheridge, *Negotiating*, 201.
12 Davis, *The Cold War*, 328–31.
13 *FRUS* 1946, vol. 6, 47, Byrnes to Barnes, 12 January 1946, 64, Byrnes to Cohen, 31 January 1946.
14 M. Issussov, *Stalin i Bulgaria* (Sofia: Universitetsko Izdatelstvo 'Sv. Kl. Ohridski', 1991), 40–41; V. Dimitrov, 'The Failure of Democracy in Eastern Europe and the Emergence of the Cold War, 1944–1948: A Bulgarian Case Study', DPhil thesis, Cambridge, 1996, 324–8.
15 TsPA, f. 146, op. 6, a.e. 1028, l. 1–2, Dimitrov at Politburo, 27 December 1945.
16 TsPA, f. 147, op. 2, a.e. 56, l. 1–8, Kolarov's notebook, 29 March 1946.
17 L. Ognyanov, *Durzhavno-politicheskata sistema v Bulgaria, 1944–1948* (Sofia: BAN, 1993), 92.
18 AVPRF, f. 74, op. 28, no. 19, p. 20, l. 1, Byrnes's statement, 9 January 1946.
19 *FRUS* 1946, vol. 6, 48, Acheson to Barnes, 12 January 1946; C. E. Black, 'The Start of the Cold War in Bulgaria: A Personal View', *Review of Politics* 41, no. 2 (April 1979), 192.
20 J. L. Gaddis, *The United States and the Origins of the Cold War 1941–1947* (New York: Columbia University Press, 1972), 276.
21 A. Adamthwaite, 'Britain and the World, 1945–9: The View from the Foreign Office', *International Affairs* 61, no. 2 (spring 1985): 245.
22 RTsHIDNI, f. 17, op. 128, a.e. 759, l. 121, CC of BCP secret letter to CC of VCP(b), 30 December 1945.
23 TsPA, f. 147, op. 2, a.e. 56, l. 1–8, Kolarov's notebook, 29 March 1946; *FRUS* 1946, vol. 6, 48, Acheson to Barnes, 12 January 1946; Black, 'The Start', 192; RTsHIDNI, f. 17, op. 128, a.e. 759, l. 121, CC of BCP secret letter to CC of VCP(b), 30 December 1945, 30 December 1945; TsPA, f. 146, op. 6, a.e. 1028, l. 1–2, 27 December 1945, Dimitrov at Politburo.
24 AVPRF, f. 74/074, op. 27, no. 8, p. 16, l. 57–68, various communications, December 1945.
25 TsPA, f. 146, op. 4, a.e. 983, l. 4–5, cabinet information, 4 January 1946.
26 *FRUS* 1946, vol. 6, 46, Barnes to Byrnes, 4 January 1946.
27 TsPA, f. 146, op. 4, a.e. 983, l. 5, cabinet information, 4 January 1946.

NOTES

28 Ognyanov, *Durzhavno-politicheskata sistema*, 94.
29 *FRUS* 1946, vol. 6, 55–7, Kennan to Byrnes, 15 January 1946.
30 TsPA, f. 147, op. 2, a.e. 1033, l. 1, Kolarov's notebook, 27 January 1946.
31 Issussov, *Stalin i Bulgaria*, 41.
32 Ognyanov, *Durzhavno-politicheskata sistema*, 95.
33 TsPA, f. 147, op. 2, a.e. 1033, l. 2, Kolarov's notebook, 27 January 1946; *FRUS* 1946, vol. 6, 50, Barnes to Byrnes, 13 January 1946; Issussov, *Stalin i Bulgaria*, 42–3; *Narodna demokratsiya*, 52–5.
34 *FRUS* 1946, vol. 6, 48, Barnes to Byrnes, 12 January 1946; Ognyanov, *Durzhavno-politicheskata sistema*, 96.
35 *FRUS* 1946, vol. 6, 56, Kennan to secretary of state, 15 January 1946.
36 TsPA, f. 146, op. 6, a.e. 1032, l. 3–4, Dimitrov in Foreign Affairs Parliamentary Commission, 9 February 1946.
37 RTsHIDNI, f. 17, op. 128, a.e. 94, l. 29, DII bulletin, 15 January 1946 – the official representatives of Britain and the US are named as members of the respective intelligence services.
38 FO371/58512, R538, FO to Sofia, 10 January 1946; FO371/58513, R1732, Washington, DC to FO, 1 March 1946.
39 *FRUS* 1946, vol. 6, 60, Barnes to Byrnes, 18 January 1946, 66, 86, Byrnes to Barnes, 2 February 1946, 23 March 1946.
40 FO371/58513, R1732, Washington, DC to FO, 1 March 1946.
41 *FRUS* 1946, vol. 6, 67, Cohen to Byrnes, 2 February 1946.
42 FO371/58512, R1011, FO to Sofia, 26 January 1946; *FRUS* 1946, vol. 6, 63, Barnes to Byrnes, 30 January 1946.
43 FO371/58513, R1101, FO to Sofia, 22 January 1946, R1432, Moscow to FO, 28 January 1946; R1362, Hayter, 31 January 1946.
44 *FRUS* 1945, vol. 4, 403, Barnes to Byrnes, 3 December 1945.
45 FO371/58512, R538, FO to Sofia, 10 January 1946.
46 *FRUS* 1945, vol. 4, 405–6, Winant to Byrnes, 7 December 1945.
47 FO371/58513, R1269, Sofia to FO, 24 January 1946, R1832, Sofia to FO, 4 February 1946.
48 FO371/58513, R1788, Sofia to FO, 1 February 1946.
49 *FRUS* 1946, vol. 6, 65, 71, Byrnes to Cohen, 31 January, 5 February 1946.
50 *FRUS*, 1946, vol. 6, 75, Cohen to Byrnes, 16 February 1946, 78, Barbour–Stoychev conversation, 22 February 1946; FO371/58515, R3848, Washington, DC to FO, 6 March 1946.
51 FO371/58514, R3167, R3208, R3254, R3519, R3624, Sofia–FO correspondence, 26 February–7 March 1946.
52 *FRUS* 1946, vol. 6, 78, Novikov to Byrnes, 7 March 1946; Ognyanov, *Durzhavno-politicheskata sistema*, 97–8.
53 *FRUS* 1946, vol. 6, 85, Barnes to Byrnes, 13 March 1946.
54 FO371/58515, R4217, Sofia to FO, 16 March 1946.
55 FO371/58514, R3733, FO to Gussev, 22 March 1946; FO371/58515, R4520, R4611, R4612, Houstoun-Boswall to FO, 12, 24 March 1946.
56 FO371/58515, R4216, Sofia to FO, 14 March 1946.
57 FO371/58515, R4611, Sofia–FO correspondence, 24–6 March 1946.
58 FO371/58512, R625, Williams, 12 January 1946.
59 *FRUS* 1946, vol. 6, 87, Barnes to Byrnes, 25 March 1946; Ognyanov, *Durzhavno-politicheskata sistema*, 99.

60 FO371/58515, R4575, Sofia to FO, 16 March 1946.
61 TsPA, f. 147, op. 2, a.e. 56, l. 48, Kolarov's notebook, 28 March 1946.
62 FO371/58515, R4794, Sofia to FO, 26 March 1946; *FRUS* 1946, vol. 6, 91, Byrnes to Barnes, 26 March 1946; Ognyanov, *Durzhavno-politicheskata sistema*, 99.
63 FO371/58515, R4855, R4904, R4906, Washington, DC–FO–Sofia, 27–28 March 1946.
64 Issussov, *Stalin i Bulgaria*, 45.
65 Ibid., 45–6.
66 TsPA, f. 147, op. 2, a.e. 56, l. 46–47, Kolarov's notebook, 29 March 1946; *FRUS* 1946, vol. 6, 93, Barnes to Byrnes, 29 March 1946; M. Padev, *Dimitrov Wastes No Bullets: Nikola Petkov, the Test Case* (London: Eyre & Spottiswoode, 1948), 44.
67 FO371/58515, R4942, Sofia to FO, 28 March 1946; FO371/558516, R4952, Sofia to FO, 29 March 1946; *FRUS* 1946, vol. 6, 95–6, Barnes to Byrnes, 29 March 1946.
68 FO371/58515, R4941, Sofia to FO, 28 March 1946; FO371/58516, R5197, Sofia to FO, 1 April 1946.
69 Ognyanov, *Durzhavno-politicheskata sistema*, 100.
70 FO371/58516, R4992, Williams, 1 April 1946.
71 FO371/58516, R4952, Sofia to FO, 29 March 1946.
72 FO371/58516, R5250, Sofia to FO, 2 April 1946, Warner, 6 April 1946.
73 A. Dallin, 'Stalin and the Prospects of Post-war Europe', in *The Soviet Union and Europe in the Cold War, 1943–1953*, ed. F. Gori and S. Pons (London: Macmillan, 1996), 188.
74 De Santis, H., *The Diplomacy of Silence: The American Foreign Service, the Soviet Union and the Cold War 1933–1947* (Chicago: Chicago University Press, 1980), 170–78.
75 *DBPO*, ser. 1, vol. 6, 315–44; P. Boyle, 'The British Foreign Office View of Soviet-American Relations 1945–1946', *Diplomatic History* 3, no. 3 (summer 1979): 310; F. Roberts, *Dealing with Dictators: The Destruction and Revival of Europe 1930–1970* (London: Weidenfield & Nicolson, 1991), 107–11.
76 G. Warner, 'From "Ally" to Enemy: Britain's Relations with the Soviet Union, 1941–1948', in *The Soviet Union and Europe*, 301.
77 Boyle, 'The British Foreign Office', 314.
78 V. Rothwell, *Britain and the Cold War 1941–1947* (London: Cape, 1982), 398–402; E. Mark, 'The War Scare of 1946 and Its Consequences', *Diplomatic History* 21, no. 3 (1997): 383–415.
79 FO371/58518, R6586, Houston-Boswall letter, 17 April 1946.
80 Ibid.
81 FO371/58521, R103365, R 11018, Houstoun-Boswall–FO correspondence, 9–24 July 1946.
82 FO371/58518, R6586, Hayter, 9 May 1946.
83 FO371/58518, R6586, Houston-Boswall to FO, 17 April 1946.
84 FO371/58518, R6586, Williams, 9 May 1946.
85 FO371/58518, R6586, Warner, 15 May 1946.
86 FO371/58517, R6066, FO brief, 1 April 1946.
87 *FRUS* 1946, vol. 6, 106, Barnes to Byrnes, 21 June 1946.
88 FO371/58520, R9326, Houstoun-Boswall to FO, 22 June 1946.
89 FO371/58520, R9547, Sargent, 26 June 1946, Henniker-Major, 27 June 1946.
90 FO371/58520, R9547, Bevin–Kolarov meeting, 29 June 1946; TsPA, f. 147, op. 2, a.e. 1044, l. 44–45, Byrnes–Kolarov and Bevin–Kolarov meetings, 28 June 1946.
91 FO371/58520, R8277, Houstoun-Boswall to FO, 1 June 1946.
92 *FRUS* 1946, vol. 6, 110–11, Caffery to Acheson, 1 July 1946.
93 FO371/58521, R10784, Washington, DC to FO, 20 July 1946.
94 FO371/58521, R9677, Houstoun-Boswall to FO, 29 June 1946.

95 FO371/58521, R10186, Marjoribanks to Hayter, 8 July 1946; *FRUS* 1946, vol. 6, 110, Bevin to Byrnes, 1 July 1946.
 96 FO371/58521, R10430, FO to Sofia, 18 July 1946; FO371/58522, R11273, Marjoribanks, 15 July 1946.
 97 G. Roberts, *Stalin's Wars: From World War to Cold War, 1939–1953* (New Haven, CT: Yale University Press, 2006), 311; De Santis, *The Diplomacy*, 170–72.
 98 FO371/58521, R10430, Houston-Boswall to FO, 12 July 194
 99 Law for Defence of the People's Power (April 1946), Law for Control of the Army (July 1946) and Law for Mobilization of Idlers and Loafers (August 1946).
100 Z. Tsvetkov, *Sudut nad opozitsionnite lideri* (Sofia: Kupessa, 1991), 10–11.
101 Ognyanov, *Durzhavno-politicheskata sistema*, 102–12.
102 Ibid., 102.
103 Issussov, *Stalin i Bulgaria*, 47.
104 D. Sirkov, et al., eds, *Georgi Dimitrov: Dnevnik 9 mart 1933–6 fevruari 1949* (Sofia: Universitetsko Izdatelstvo 'Sv. Kl. Ohridski', 1997), 533; Dimitrov, 'The Failure', 358–60, 373–6.
105 RTsHIDNI, f. 17, op. 128, a.e. 887, l. 20, Konstantinov note, 9 March 1946; Issussov, *Stalin i Bulgaria*, 43.
106 FO371/58515, R6455, FO communications, 5–19 March 1946.
107 FO371/58519, R8277, Houstoun-Boswall to FO, 1 June 1946, Warner, 5 June 1946.
108 FO371/58518, R7331, Houstoun-Boswall to FO, 9 May 1946, FO to Sofia, 28 May 1946, Warner, 23 May 1946; *FRUS* 1946, vol. 6, 101, Barnes to Byrnes, 8 May 1946.
109 FO371/58517, R6066, FO brief, 1 April 1946.
110 FO371/58515, R6456, Houstoun-Boswall to FO, 16 April 1946.
111 FO371/58524, R12682, FO draft to Byrnes, 28 August 1946.
112 FO371/58523, R11992, FO minutes, 13–31 August 1946.
113 FO371/58523, R11992, Houston-Boswall to Hayter, 5 August 1946.
114 Ibid.
115 FO371/58524, R12707, R13920, R14821, Sofia to FO and WO, 26 August , 28 September 1946.
116 FO371/58522, R11299, FO minutes, July 1946; FO371/58523, R11992, FO minutes, August 1946.
117 FO371/58583, R12904, R12993, R13031, R113283, Paris–FO–Sofia correspondence, 1–5 September 1946.
118 FO371/58583, R13283, Paris to Sofia, 5 September 1946.
119 FO371/58524, R12682, Warner, Dixon, 29–30 August 1946.
120 FO371/58524, R12682, Warner, 17 August 194. The Turnovo Constitution stipulated that the form of the state could only be altered by a Grand National Assembly. This could only be summoned by the monarch and in the present instance nine years had to pass before the king would come of age.
121 Ognyanov, *Durzhavno-politicheskata sistema*, 120–21.
122 Ibid., 122; for details on the referendum see: T. Kostadinova, *Bulgaria 1879–1946: The Challenge of Choice* (Boulder, CO: East European Monographs, 1995), 90–92.
123 FO371/58525, R14052, US Embassy London to FO, 16 September 1946, R14543, Houstoun-Boswall to FO, 1 October 1946, R14715, Paris to Sofia, 4 October 1946; FO371/58585, R14912, FO to Washington, DC, 7 October 1946, R15340, British Embassy Washington aide-memoire to State, 9 October 1946.
124 FO371/58585, R15464, Warner, 12 October 1946.
125 FO371/58525, R15254, Warner (Paris) to FO, 13 October 1946.

126 FO371/58526, R15583, Washington, DC to FO, 23 October 1946.
127 FO371/58585, R14912, Sargent to Bevin, 1 October 1946.
128 FO371/58525, R14932, Paris to Sofia, 4 October 1946.
129 *FRUS* 1946, vol. 6, 152, Acheson to US delegation Paris, 9 October 1946.
130 FO371/58524, R12444, Houstoun-Boswall to FO, 21 August 1946, R12544, Houstoun-Boswall to FO, 21 August 1946, FO to UK delegation Paris, 30 August 1946; FO371/58525, R14052, Williams, 16 September 1946.
131 FO371/58526, R15609, Tollinton to FO, 24 October 1946; FO371/58525, R14268, Houstoun-Boswall to Warner, 16 September 1946.
132 FO371/58525, R15254, Warner to FO, 13 October 1946.
133 FO371/58527, R16212, Tollinton to FO, 7 November 1946.
134 FO371/58527, R16212, FO to Washington, DC, 14 November 1946, Colville, 11 November 1946.
135 FO371/58519, R8277, FO minutes, 5–11 June 1946.
136 *Georgi Dimitrov: Dnevnik*, 528; Issussov, *Stalin i Bulgaria*, 46.
137 Issussov, *Stalin i Bulgaria*, 50–51.
138 Tsvetkov, *Sudut*, 19.
139 FO371/58527, R16584, House of Commons debate extracts, 12 November 1946.
140 FO371/58528, R17083, Washington, DC to FO, 18 November 1946, Colville, 3 December 1946.
141 FO371/66912, R1558, Blackburn to McNeil, 21 January 1947.
142 FO371/58526, R15583, FO minutes, 26 October–22 November 1946.
143 FO371/58526, R15583, FO to UK delegation New York, 22 October 1946, R15948, FO to Washington, DC, 6 November 1946.
144 FO371/66912, R1315, Lord Inverchapel to FO, 29 January 1947, Colville, 1 February 1947.
145 FO371/66912, R62, Colville, 4–22 January 1947.
146 FO371/66912, R1461, Tollinton to FO, 31 January 1947.
147 *Otechestven Front*, 12 February 1947.
148 FO371/66929, R2083, Colville, 12 February 1947, Williams, 18 February 1947.
149 FO371/66905, R1014, Tollinton to FO, 10 January 1947.
150 De Santis, *The Diplomacy*, 180–81.
151 *FRUS* 1947, vol. 4, 164, notes; J. E. Horner, 'The Ordeal of Nikola Petkov and the Consolidation of Communist Power in Bulgaria', *Survey* 28, no. 2 (summer 1984): 77; Padev, *Dimitrov Wastes No Bullets*, 151–3.
152 Horner, 'The Ordeal', 82–3.
153 FO371/72137, R12767, Sterndale-Bennett to FO, 11 November 1948.
154 FO371/72138, R13034, Sterndale-Bennett to FO, 17 November 1948.
155 Tsvetkov, *Sudut*, 1.

Chapter Six: British Acceptance of Communist Rule in Bulgaria

1 FO371/47883, R13784, Molotov–Bevin conversation, 23 September 1945; FO371/47883, N15702, Roberts to Bevin, 31 October 1945.
2 P. Boyle, 'The British Foreign Office View of Soviet-American Relations 1945–1946', *Diplomatic History* 3, no. 3 (summer 1979): 316; A. Adamthwaite, 'Britain and the World,

1945–9: The View from the Foreign Office', *International Affairs* 61, no. 2 (spring 1985): 227; R. Smith and J. Zametica, 'The Cold Warrior: Clement Attlee Reconsidered, 1945–7', *International Affairs* 61, no. 3 (1985): 240.

3 J. Lewis, *Changing Direction: British Military Planning for Post-war Strategic Defence, 1942–1947* (London: Sherwood Press, 1988), 243–9, 316–34.
4 Sir Curtis Keeble, *Britain and the Soviet Union, 1917–1989* (Basingstoke: Macmillan, 1990), 218.
5 Lewis, *Changing*, 295–6.
6 FO371/47883, N8674, Clerk Kerr to FO, 10 July 1945, N15702, Roberts to Bevin, 31 October 1945.
7 Lewis, *Changing*, 285–7.
8 Ibid., 292; Keeble, *Britain*, 219.
9 US Department of State, *FRUS*, 1945 (Washington, DC, 1964) 1946, vol. 4, 696–709, Kennan to Byrnes, 22 February 1946; K. M. Jensen, ed., *Origins of the Cold War: The Novikov, Kennan and Roberts 'Long Telegrams' of 1946* (Washington, DC: United States Institute of Peace Press, 1993), 17–32; Keeble, *Britain*, 213–14; F. Roberts, *Dealing with Dictators: The Destruction and Revival of Europe 1930–1970* (London: Weidenfeld & Nicolson, 1991), 107–11.
10 M. E. Pelly et al., eds, *DBPO*, ser. 1, vol. 6, Eastern Europe, August 1945–April 1946 (London: HMSO, 1991), 345–52; V. Rothwell, *Britain and the Cold War 1941–1947* (London: Cape, 1982), 255–60.
11 J. P. Morray, *From Yalta to Disarmament: Cold War Debate* (New York: MR Press, 1961), 41–9; C. E. Bohlen, *Witness to History* (New York: Norton, 1973), 271.
12 *DBPO*, 305–11, 315–32; Roberts, *Dealing*, 107–11.
13 Rothwell, *Britain*, 269; Lewis, *Changing*, 257–63.
14 Rothwell, *Britain*, 265.
15 Ibid., 247–57.
16 Keeble, *Britain*, 210–11.
17 Rothwell, *Britain*, 277.
18 Bohlen, *Witness*, 271.
19 FO371/66966, R8719, Bevin speech, 27 June 1947.
20 Keeble, *Britain*, 220.
21 FO371/72196, R10197, 'Bastion' memorandum, 20 July 1948.
22 Ibid.; E. Barker, *Britain in a Divided Europe* (Basingstoke: Macmillan, 1971), 64–96.
23 Rothwell, *Britain*, 262–3; Keeble, *Britain*, 216.
24 FO371/72143, R278, Sterndale-Bennett to FO, 2 January 1948.
25 *Rabotnichesko Delo*, 31 December 1947, 13 January 1948.
26 FO371/72135, R10432, Greenhill to FO, 8 September 1948.
27 L. Ognyanov, *Durzhavno-politicheskata sistema v Bulgaria, 1944–1948* (Sofia: BAN, 1993), 191–5.
28 FO371/72160, R8341, Sterndale-Bennett to FO, 29 June 1948.
29 FO371/66907, R9439, Sterndale-Bennett to FO, 10 July 1947.
30 Ognyanov, *Durzhavno-politicheskata sistema*, 194–5; FO371/72131, R1754, Lord Inverchapel to FO, 6 February 1948; FO371/72132, R2120, US press release, 6 February 1948, R3592, Sofia to FO, FO minutes, 13 March 1948; FO371/72138, R12957, Sterndale-Bennett to FO, 16 November 1948.
31 FO371/72137, R12731, R12788, Sterndale-Bennett to FO, 10, 12 November 1948; FO371/72138, R12957, Sterndale-Bennett to FO, 16 November 1948.

32 H. Devedjiev, *Stalinisation of the Bulgarian Society 1949–1953* (Philadelphia: Dorrance, 1975), 61–73; FO371/78300, R2523, FO brief, 2 March 1949; FO371/78298, R1916, BBC Monitoring Service, 10 February 1949.
33 FO371/72134, R9168, Greenhill to FO, 3 August 1948.
34 FO371/72129, R1274, Sterndale-Bennett to FO, 23 January 1948.
35 FO371/72130, R3686, Sterndale-Bennett to FO, 18 May 1948, FO minute 31 May 1948.
36 FO371/72129, R86, Sterndale-Bennett to FO, 30 December 1947; FO371/72131, R1427, FO minutes, 31 January–19 February 1948.
37 FO371/72131, R1427, Sterndale-Bennet to FO, 31 January 1948, Conquest, 9 March 1948.
38 Ognyanov, *Durzhavno-politicheskata sistema*, 209.
39 FO371/72130, R6140, Sterndale-Bennett to FO, 15 May 1948.
40 FO371/72143, R3003, Sofia to FO, 25 February 1948; FO371/72130, R9170, Sterndale-Bennett to FO, 31 July 1948.
41 FO371/72136, R11745, Sterndale-Bennett to FO, 14 October 1948.
42 FO371/78289, R631–R11390, Sofia to FO, January–August 1949.
43 FO371/72130, R9593, Greenhill to FO, 16 August 1948.
44 FO371/72137, Dunnet to FO, 21 September 1948, Sterndale-Bennett to FO, 20 October 1948.
45 FO371/78261, R2702, Sofia to FO, 9 March 1949; D. Greenhill, *More by Accident* (York: Wilton 65, 1992), 64–6.
46 FO371/78264, R7323, Mason to FO, 29 July–1 August 1949, R7811, Bateman, 11 August 1949; FO371/78265, R8724, Mason to FO, 8 September 1949.
47 FO371/78264, R7576, Mason to FO, 3 August 1949.
48 FO371/78311, R9881, FO minutes, 5 October 1949.
49 Ibid.
50 FO371/72175, R1536, Wallinger, 17 December 1947, Watson to WO, 6 February 1948.
51 FO371/78250, R11468, Sofia to FO, 9 December 1949.
52 FO371/78251, R11704, FO to Washington, DC, 22 December 1949.
53 FO371/66971, R1879, FO information, 31 January 1947; FO371/66974, R8796, Campbell, 2 July 1947.
54 FO371/66965, R8719, Bevin draft speech, 27 June 1947.
55 FO371/66976, R12522, FO to Washington, DC, 13 September 1947.
56 FO371/66979, R14882, House of Lords debate, 5 November 1947.
57 FO371/72154, R4837, Peck, 26 April 1948.
58 FO371/78251, R11682, Mason to FO, 19 December 1949.
59 FO371/66978, R14041–R14568, FO–Washington, DC, Sofia correspondence, October–November 1947.
60 FO371/72136, R11007, FO to US Embassy, 24 September 1948, Wallinger, 23 September 1948.
61 FO371/72129, R1837, Sterndale-Bennett to FO, 20 December 1947, Wallinger, 24 December 1947–2 January 1948.
62 FO371/72131, R641, FO to Sterndale-Bennett, 20 January 1948.
63 FO371/72163, R2305, FO minutes, December 1947–February 1948.
64 FO371/72170, R2582, Sterndale-Bennett to FO, 14 February 1948, R2367, Sterndale-Bennett to FO, 18 February 1948.
65 FO371/72130, R6140, Greenhill to FO, 15 May 1948.
66 FO371/72136, R11410, Greenhill to FO, 4 October 1948, R11745, Porter, 10 October 1948.

67 FO371/72130, R5099, Sterndale-Bennett to FO, 22 April 1948, R5098, FO minutes, 22 April 1948.
68 FO371/78249, R11420, FO to Sofia, 8 December 1949.
69 FO371/72136, R11007, US Embassy London to FO, 22 September 1948.
70 *FRUS* 1948, vol. 6, 375, Heath to secretary of state, 23 September 1948; FO371/72136, R11012, R11050, Dunnett to FO, 24 September 1948.
71 FO371/72136, R11326, Greenhill to FO, 2 October 1948; FO371/72136, R11672, Sterndale-Bennett to FO, 13 October 1948.
72 FO371/78292, R1234, FO draft, 10 February 1949.
73 FO371/72130, R5098, Sykes, 23 April 1948; FO371/72170, R59, R2582, FO minutes, 7 January 1948, 8–16 March 1948, R3967, Washington, DC to FO, 26 March 1948.
74 FO371/66972, R4928, Hoyer–Miller, 14 April 1947.
75 FO371/66982, R16687, Warner–Hickerson conversation, 18 December 1947.
76 FO371/72168, R5205, Sterndale-Bennett to Wallinger, 3 April 1948.
77 FO371/72168, R5205, Wallinger to Sterndale-Bennett, 24 April 1948.
78 FO371/72139a, R13568, Bateman, 20 November 1948.
79 FO371/72138, R13231, FO to Sofia, 30 November 1948.
80 FO371/78290, R6783, Sofia to FO, 7 July 1949.
81 FO371/78300, R2487, FO brief, 3 March 1949.
82 FO371/72129, R1837, Sterndale-Bennett to FO, 20 December 1947, Wallinger, 24 December 1947–2 January 1948.
83 FO371/66980, R15859, Bevin memorandum for cabinet, 24 November 1947; FO371/72167, R3320, FO to Sterndale-Bennett, 20 March 1948.
84 FO371/72131, R637, Sterndale-Bennett to FO, 14 January 1948.
85 FO371/72139a, R13675, Greenhill to FO, 4 December 1948.
86 FO371/72138, R13231, FO to Sofia, 30 November 1948; FO371/72139a, R13675, Greenhill to FO, 4 December 1948.
87 FO371/72130, R5097, FO minutes, 5 April 1948.
88 FO371/72133, R8342, McDermott, 29 July 1948, Talbot de Malahide, 21 August 1948.
89 FO371/72143, R279, Bateman to Sterndale-Bennett, 6 February 1948.
90 FO371/72135, R10406, Wallinger, Watson, Stannarel, 4 September 1948.
91 FO371/72134, R9096, Sterndale-Bennet to FO, 30 July 1948.
92 FO371/72132, R5337, FO minutes, 3 May 1948.
93 FO371/72131, R1861, Bevin, Wallinger, 9–11 February 1948.
94 FO371/72200, R13066, Peck, Bateman, 20–25 November 1948.
95 FO371/72170, R2367, Sterndale-Bennett to FO, 18 February 1948; FO371/72138, R13231, FO to Sofia, 30 November 1948.
96 FO371/72170, R2307, Wallinger, 9 February 1948.
97 FO371/72139a, R13568, Talbot de Malahide, 18 November 1948.
98 FO371/72135, R10432, Watson, 17 September 1948; FO371/72158, R5861, *note verbale*, 31 March 1948, 3 May 1948.
99 FO371/78227, R946, Porter, 17 February 1949.
100 FO371/78331, R833, conversation between the British Embassy Washington and the State Department Office of European Affairs, 15 January 1949.
101 FO371/78334, R1280, Ministry of Food to FO, 1 February 1949.
102 FO371/78277–8, FO minutes and letters, 29 December 1948–13 October 1949.
103 FO371/65975, N7438, FO minutes, 9 June 1947; FO371/65947, N4247, Mayhew memorandum, 10 January 1947, EID paper, 23 January 1947.

104 E. Mark, 'The War Scare of 1946 and Its Consequences', *Diplomatic History* 21, no. 3 (fall 1997): 383–415.
105 FO371/72196, R10197, 'Bastion' memorandum, 20 July 1948.
106 V. Bozhinov, *Zashtita na natsionalnata nezavissimost na Bulgaria 1944–1947* (Sofia: Izdatelstvo na BAN, 1962), 214.
107 FO371/72154, R4837, Sterndale-Bennett to FO, 14 April 1948.
108 P. Stavrakis, *Moscow and Greek Communism 1944–1949* (Ithaca, NY: Cornell University Press, 1989), 138–43.
109 V. Zubok and C. Pleshakov, *Inside the Kremlin's Cold War from Stalin to Khrushchev* (Cambridge, MA: Harvard University Press, 1996), 127–8; A. Ulunian, 'Grazhdanskaya voina v Gretsii i Bolgaria', in *Bulgaria v sferata na suvetskite interesi*, ed. V. Toshkova (Sofia: AD 'Prof. Marin Drinov', 1998), 140–50.
110 RTsHIDNI, f. 17, op. 128, a.e. 1160, l. 59–62, CC of KKE to CC of Yugoslav Communist Party, 22 December 1947; M. Djilas, *Conversations with Stalin* (New York: Harcourt, 1962), 182; Zubok and Pleshakov, *Inside the Kremlin's Cold War*, 135.
111 RTsHIDNI, f. 17, op. 128, a.e. 279, l. 149–55, Kostas to CC of BCP, 15 August 1947.
112 Rothwell, *Britain*, 361.
113 FO371/72143, R279, Sterndale-Bennett to FO, 3 January 1948.
114 Ibid.
115 FO371/72154, R4836, Sterndale-Bennett to FO, 14 April 1948.
116 FO371/72154, R4837, Wallinger, Bateman, 27 April 1948.
117 P. Semerdjiev, *BKP, Makedonskiyat vupros i VMRO* (Detroit, MI: Macedono-Bulgarian Institute, 1994), 27–45; M. Lalkov, *Ot nadezhdata kum razocharovanieto* (Sofia: Vek 22, 1994), 44–70.
118 Lalkov, *Ot nadezhdata*, 215; D. Livanios, 'Bulgar–Yugoslav Controversy over Macedonia and the British Connection, 1939–1949', DPhil dissertation, University of Oxford, 1995, 208–15.
119 H. Howard, 'Greece and Its Northern Neighbours 1948–1949', *Balkan Studies* 7, no. 8 (1966/67): 10.
120 FO371/66985, R10224, Cooper–Menemencioglu conversation, 8 July 1948, FO aide-memoire to state, 21 July 1948; FO371/72341, R2745, Sargent, 23 February 1948; Rothwell, *Britain*, 255.
121 Yugoslav and Bulgarian views on 'the Macedonian nation' are discussed in Lalkov, *Ot nadezhdata* and R. Nation, 'A Balkan Union? Southeastern Europe in Soviet Security Policy, 1944–8', in *The Soviet Union and Europe in the Cold War, 1943–53*, ed. F Gori and S. Pons (Basingstoke: Macmillan, 1996), 127, 131.
122 FO371/72162, R730, Sofia to FO, 9 January 1948, R771, Belgrade to FO, 17 January 1948, R1084, Sofia to FO, 23 January 1948.
123 Lalkov, *Ot nadezhdata*, 209–21.
124 FO371/66985, R10224, British aide-memoire to state, 21 July 1947; FO371/72162, R484, Sofia to FO, 8 January 1948.
125 FO371/72162, R52, Belgrade to FO, 27 December 1947, R740, Bucharest to FO, 16 January 1948.
126 FO371/66958, R10530–R16486, Sofia, Moscow, Belgrade to FO, July–November 1947.
127 L. Gibianskii, 'The Soviet–Yugoslav Conflict and the Soviet Bloc', in *The Soviet Union and Europe*, 228–9.
128 Nation, 'A Balkan Union?', 135.

129 Gibianskii, 'The Soviet–Yugoslav Conflict', 234–5.
130 FO371/72162, R1349, translation of *Pravda* excerpt, Moscow to FO, 29 January 1948.
131 M. Issussov, *Stalin i Bulgaria* (Sofia: Universitetsko Izdatelstvo 'Sv. Kl. Ohridski', 1991), 68–72; Djilas, *Conversations*, 173–5.
132 FO371/72162, R1391, Sterndale-Bennett to FO minutes, 29 January 1948, R1777, Paris to FO, 6 February 1948.
133 FO371/66475, R11554, Roberts to FO, 6 October 1947, FO minutes, 7 October 1947; FO371/66993, R13461, R13625, FO minutes, 6 October 1947 (the Cominform is referred to as 'the new Comintern'); Gibianskii, 'The Soviet–Yugoslav Conflict', 221–41.
134 A. Di Biaggio, 'The Marshall Plan and the Founding of the Cominform June–September 1947', in *The Soviet Union and Europe*, 212–18; N. Yegorova, 'From the Comintern to the Cominform: Ideological Dimensions of the Cold War Origins (1945–1948)', paper presented at the 'New Evidence on Cold War History' conference, Moscow, January 1993.
135 FO371/66993, R13889, Watson, 20 October 1947.
136 FO371/72162, R95, FO memorandum, 23 December 1947, R700, Fitzmaurice, 31 October 1947.
137 FO371/72138, R13328, FO to Sofia, 22 December 1948.
138 FO371/72166–72169, FO communications and minutes, 26 February–27 May 1948.
139 FO371/72165, R1177, Washington, DC, FO correspondence, 26–31 January 1948.
140 FO371/72165, R1733, R1746, R1747, Sterndale-Bennett to FO, 5, 7 February 1948; FO371/72166, R2045, *note verbale*, 7 February 1948, R2098, Sterndale-Bennett to FO, 13 February 1948, R2432, Sterndale-Bennett to FO, 19 February 1948, R2858, Bevin brief, 26 February 1948, R2995, Levyitchkin to US Embassy, 18 February 1948.
141 FO371/72168, R4468, FO aide-memoire to state, 3 April 1948.
142 FO371/72166, R2727, Sterndale-Bennett to FO, 27 February 1948.
143 FO371/72169, R6473, R6698, R7333, R7580, FO minutes, 1–30 June 1948.
144 FO371/72171–2, FO notes, February–March 1948; FO371/78439, R4257, R7926, Greek Embassy memoranda, 20 April–12 August 1949.
145 FO371/66981, R16308, Watson, 15 December 1947.
146 *Rabotnichesko Delo*, 31 December 1947.
147 FO371/72136, R11012, R11050, Dunnett to FO, 24 September 1948.
148 Issussov, *Stalin*, 100–103.
149 FO371/72156, R4744, Green memorandum, 30 March 1948.
150 FO371/78332, R4631, Grant, 6 April 1949.
151 FO371/72136, R11323, Brown, 29 September 1948.
152 FO371/72136, R11410, Greenhill to FO, Wallinger, 4 October 1948.
153 FO371/72139a, R13568, Talbot de Malahide, 18 November 1948.
154 FO371/72136, R11745, FO minutes, 18 October–2 November 1948.
155 FO371/87464, R1072/3, FO press release, 27–8 February 1950.
156 FO371/87464, R1072/4, Registrar of International Court to Bevin, 30 March 1950.
157 FO371/87464, R1072/8, FO minutes, 5 April–27 June 1950,
158 FO371/87464, R1072/16, FO minutes, 18 March–3 November 1950; FO371/95004, R1072/10, FO brief for UN secretary general, August 1951.
159 FO371/95003, R1072/4–5, FO reports on human rights in Bulgaria, Romania, Hungary, November 1950–May 1951.

160 FO371/95006, R1073/4, Mason to FO, 30 March 1951.
161 FO371/72143, R279, Sterndale-Bennett to FO, 3 January 194.

Conclusion

1 This pattern is commented on in M. Leffler, *For the Soul of Mankind: The United States, the Soviet Union and the Cold War* (New York: Hill and Wang, 2007), 30–35.
2 V. A. Zubok, *Failed Empire: The Soviet Union in the Cold War from Stalin to Gorbachev* (Chapel Hill, NC: University of North Carolina Press, 2007), 18–19.

BIBLIOGRAPHY

I. Primary Sources

1. Unpublished

Archive of the Bulgarian Ministry of Foreign Affairs, Sofia:
 Political Department 1943–56.
Archive of the Bulgarian Ministry of Internal Affairs, Sofia:
 British Military Missions.
Archive of the Foreign Ministry of the Russian Federation, Moscow:
 Allied Control Commission for Bulgaria, Bulgarian Desk 1944–49,
 Molotov, Vyshinski.
Central Communist Party Archive, Sofia, Bulgaria:
 Central Committee, Georgi Dimitrov, Traicho Kostov, Vassil Kolarov.
Russian Centre for the Preservation and Study of Documents
on Modern History, Moscow:
 Department of International Information of the CC of the VKP(B)
National Archives, Kew, Richmond, UK:
 FO371, general political correspondence 1943–49.
 HS5, SOE in the Balkans.

2. Published

Boll, M. M., ed. *The American Military Mission in the Allied Control Commission for Bulgaria 1944–1947.* Boulder, CO: Columbia University Press, 1985.
Pelly, M.E., et al., eds. *Documents on British Policy Overseas*, ser. 1, vol. 6, Eastern Europe, August 1945–April 1946. London: HMSO, 1991.
Elliot, D., ed. *Documents on International Affairs.* Oxford: Oxford University Press, 1954.
Etzold, T. H., and J. L. Gaddis, eds. *Containment: Documents on American Policy and Strategy 1945–1950.* New York: Columbia University Press, 1978.
Foreign Office. *Weekly Political Intelligence Summaries (October 1939–November 1947).* London: Milwood, 1983.
Lebedev, N. S., et al., eds. *Comintern i Vtoraya Mirovaya Voina* [The Comintern and the Second World War], 2 vols. Moscow: Pamyatniki Istoricheskoy Myisli, 1994, 1997.
Loewenheim, F. L., et al., eds. *Roosevelt and Churchill: Their Secret Wartime Correspondence.* London: Barrie & Jenkins, 1975.
Mendelsohn, J., ed. *Covert Warfare: The OSS–NKVD Relationship, 1943–1945.* New York: Garland, 1989.
Ministry of Foreign Affairs of the USSR. *Stalin's Correspondence with Churchill, Attlee, Roosevelt and Truman, 1941–1945*, 2 vols. London: Lawrence & Wishart, 1958.

Ognyanov, L., et al., eds. *Narodna demokratsiya ili diktatura* [People's democracy or dictatorship]. Sofia: Literaturen Forum, 1992.
Ross, G., ed. *The Foreign Office and the Kremlin: British Documents on Anglo–Soviet Relations 1944–1945*. Cambridge: Cambridge University Press, 1985.
The Trial of Nikola D. Petkov, August 5–15, 1947: Records of the Judicial Proceedings. Sofia: Ministry of Information and Arts, 1947.
The Trial of Traicho Kostov and His Group. Sofia: Press Department, 1949.
Toshkova, V., et al., eds. *Bulgaria: Nepriznatiyat protivnik na Tretiya raih* [Bulgaria: The unrecognized enemy of the Third Reich]. Sofia: Izdatelstvo na MO 'Sv. Georgi Pobedonosets', 1995.
US Department of State. *American Foreign Policy 1950–1955: Basic Documents*. Washington, DC: 1957.
———. *Foreign Relations of the United States [FRUS], 1943–1955*. Washington, DC, 1961–85.
Ustanovyavane i ukrepvane na narodnodemokratichnata vlast septemvri 1944–may 1945 [Establishment and consolidation of the people's democratic rule, September 1944–May 1945]. Sofia: Izdatelstvo na BAN, 1969.
Valev, L. B., et al., eds. *Sovetsko–Bolgarskie otnosheniya i svyazi, 1944–1948g.: Documenti i materiali* [Soviet–Bulgarian relations and links, 1944–1948: Documents and materials]. Moscow: Nauka, 1981.
Volokitina, T. V., et al., eds. *Vostochnaya Evropa v dokumentah rossiyskih arhivov 1944–1953g.* [Eastern Europe in Russian archives 1944–1953], vol. 1, *1944–1948*. Moscow: Sibirskiy Hronograf, 1997.
Vunshna politika na Narodna Republika Bulgaria: Sbornik ot dokumenti i materiali [Foreign Policy of the People's Republic of Bulgaria: Documents and Materials], vol. 1, *1944–1962*. Sofia: Durzhavno Izdatelstvo 'Nauka i Izkustvo', 1970.

II. Literature

1. Diaries and memoirs

Acheson, D. *Present at the Creation*. New York: W. W. Norton, 1969.
Amery, J. *Approach March: A Venture in Autobiography*. London: Hutchinson, 1973.
The Earl of Avon. *The Eden Memoirs: The Reckoning*. London: Cassell, 1965.
Berezhkov, V. *History in the Making: Memoirs of World War II Diplomacy*. Moscow: Progress, 1982.
Birse, A. H. *Memoirs of an Interpreter*. London: Michael Joseph, 1967.
Biryuzov, S. S. *Surovye Gody* [Harsh years]. Moscow: Nauka, 1966.
Bohlen, C. E. *Witness to History*. New York: Norton, 1973.
Byrnes, J. F. *All in One Lifetime*. New York: Harper, 1958.
———. *Speaking Frankly*. London: William Heinemann, 1947.
Chakalov, G. *Offitser za svruzka* [Liaison officer]. Sofia: Lari, 1993.
Churchill, Sir Winston. *The Second World War*, vols 3, 5, 6. London: Cassell, 1948–54.
Deane, General J. R. *The Strange Alliance: The Story of American Efforts at Wartime Co-operation with Russia*. London: Murray, 1947.
Dalton, H. *The Fateful Years: Memoirs 1939–1945*. London: F. Muller, 1957.
Dilks, D., ed. *The Diaries of Sir Alexander Cadogan O. M. 1938–1945*. London: Cassell, 1971.
Dimitrov, I., ed. *Bogdan Filov: Dnevnik* [Diary]. Sofia: Izdatelstvo na OF, 1990.
Djilas, M. *Conversations with Stalin*. New York: Harcourt, 1962.
Greenhill, D. *More by Accident*. York: Wilton 65, 1992.

Harriman, A., and E. Abel. *Special Envoy to Churchill and Stalin 1941–1946.* London: Hutchinson, 1976.
Harvey, J., ed. *The War Diaries of Oliver Harvey.* London: Collins, 1978.
Hull, C. *The Memoirs of Cordell Hull.* New York: Macmillan, 1948.
Ismay, Lord. *Memoirs.* London: Heinemann, 1960.
Jebb, G. *The Memoirs of Lord Gladwyn.* London: Weidenfield & Nicolson, 1972.
Kazassov, D. *Burni godini: 1918–1944* [Years of turmoil: 1918–1944]. Sofia: Narodna pechatnica, 1949.
―――. *Vidyano i prezhivyano* [What I saw and lived through]. Sofia: Izdatelstvo na OF, 1969.
Kennan, G. F. *Memoirs.* Boston: Atlantic Monthly/Little, Brown, 1967.
Knatchbull-Hugessen, Sir H. *Diplomat in Peace and War.* London: John Murrey, 1949.
Leahy, W. D. *I Was There.* London: Victor Gollanz, 1950.
Maclean, F. *Eastern Approaches.* London: Cape, 1949.
Macmillan, H. *The Blast of War 1939–1945.* Basingstoke: Macmillan, 1967.
Mishkov, G., ed. *Dnevnikut na Purvan Draganov: Bivsh ministur na vunshnite raboti ot 12 yuni do 1 septemvri 1944* [The diary of Purvan Draganov: Foreign minister from 12 June to 1 September 1944]. Sofia: Voenno-izdatelski kompleks 'Sv. Georgi Pobedonosets', 1993.
Moshanov, S. *Moyata missiya v Cairo* [My mission in Cairo]. Sofia: Bulgarski Pisatel, 1991.
Muraviev, K. *Subitiya i hora: Spomeni* [Events and people: Memoirs]. Sofia: Bulgarski Pisatel, 1992.
Nicolson, H. *Diaries and Letters 1939–1945.* New York: Atheneum, 1967.
Rendel, Sir G. *The Sword and the Olive: Recollections of Diplomacy and the Foreign Service 1913–1954.* London: Murrey, 1957.
Resis, A., ed. *Molotov Remembers: Inside Kremlin Politics; Conversations with Felix Chuev.* Chicago: Ivan R. Dee, 1993.
Roberts, F. *Dealing with Dictators: The Destruction and Revival of Europe 1930–1970.* London: Weidenfield & Nicolson, 1991.
Sirkov, D., et al., eds. *Georgi Dimitrov: Dnevnik 9 mart 1933–6 fevruari 1949* [Diary 3 March 1933–6 February 1949]. Sofia: Universitetsko Izdatelstvo 'Sv. Kl. Ohridski', 1997.
Stettinius, E. R. *Roosevelt and the Russians: The Yalta Conference.* London: Jonathan Cape, 1950.
Stimson, H. L., and M. Bundy. *On Active Service in Peace and War.* New York: Harper, 1947.
Stoynev, A., et al., eds. *Dimiter Mihalchev: Mezhdu filosofiyata i zhivota; Dokumenti 1904–1946* [Dimiter Mihalchev: Between philosophy and life; Documents 1904–1946]. Sofia: Universitetsko Izdatelstvo 'Sv. Kl. Ohridski', 1997.
Strang, Lord. *Home and Abroad.* London: Andre Deutsch, 1956.
Sweet-Escott, B. *Baker Street Irregular.* London: Methuen, 1963.
Truman, H. S. *Memoirs.* New York: Doubleday, 1955.
Young, K., ed. *The Diaries of Sir Robert Bruce Lockhart*, vol. 2, *1939–1965*. Basingstoke: Macmillan, 1980.
Znepolska, M., ed. *Dencho Znepolski: Posmurtna Izpoved* [Dencho Znepolski: Posthumous confession]. Sofia: Izdatelska kushta 'Hristo Botev', 1997.

2. Historiography

i) Books

Aldrich, R. *The Hidden Hand: Britain, America and Cold War Secret Intelligence.* London: John Murray, 2001.
Alperovitz, G. *Atomic Diplomacy: Hiroshima and Potsdam.* London: Secker & Warburg, 1966.

Apor, B., et al., eds. *The Sovietization of Eastern Europe: New Perspectives on the Postwar Period.* Washington, DC: New Academia Publishing, 2008.
Baev, J. *Balkanite v sistemata za evropeyska sigurnost v godinite na Studenata voina* [The Balkans in the European security system during the years of the Cold war]. Sofia: Izdatelstvo Damian Yakov, 2010.
Baeva, I., and E. Kalinova. *Bulgarskite prehodi 1939–2005* [Bulgarian transitions 1939–2005]. Sofia: Paradigma, 2006.
Barker, E. *Truce in The Balkans.* London: Percival Marshall Company, 1948.
_____. *Macedonia: Its Place in Balkan Politics.* Basingstoke: Macmillan, 1950.
_____. *Britain in a Divided Europe.* Basingstoke: Macmillan, 1971.
_____. *British Policy in South-East Europe in the Second World War.* Basingstoke: Macmillan, 1976.
_____. *Churchill and Eden at War.* Basingstoke: Macmillan, 1978.
_____. *The British between the Superpowers 1945–1950.* Basingstoke: Macmillan, 1983.
_____., et al., eds. *British Political and Military Strategy in Central-Eastern and Southern Europe in 1944.* Basingstoke: Macmillan, 1988.
Bell, J. D. *The Bulgarian Communist Party from Blagoev to Zhivkov.* Stanford, CA: Hoover Institute Press, 1986.
Beloff, N. *Tito's Flawed Legacy.* London: Golancz 1985.
Bennett, G., ed. *The End of War in Europe 1945.* London: HMSO, 1996.
Black, C. E., ed. *Challenge in Eastern Europe.* New Brunswick, NJ: Rutgers University Press, 1954.
Boll, M. M. *Cold War in the Balkans: American Policy towards Bulgaria 1943–1947.* Lexington: University Press of Kentucky, 1984.
Bozhinov, V. *Zashtita na natsionalnata nezavissimost na Bulgaria, 1944–1947* [Protection of Bulgaria's national independence, 1944–1947]. Sofia: Izdatelstvo na BAN, 1962.
Brown, J. F. *Bulgaria under Communist Rule.* London: Pall Mall Press, 1970.
_____. *Eastern Europe under Communist Rule.* Durham, NC: Duke University Press, 1988.
Carlton, D. *Churchill and the Soviet Union.* Manchester: Manchester University Press, 1999.
Clemens, D. S. *Yalta.* New York: Oxford University Press, 1970.
Cohen, A. *Russian Imperialism.* London: Praeger, 1996.
Crockatt, R. *The Fifty Years War.* London: Routledge, 1994.
Craig, G., and F. L. Loewenheim. *The Diplomats 1939–1979.* Princeton, NJ: Princeton University Press, 1994.
Crampton, R. J. *A Short History of Modern Bulgaria.* Cambridge: Cambridge University Press, 1987.
Crampton R. J. *Eastern Europe in the Twentieth Century.* London: Routledge, 1994.
Davis, L. E. *The Cold War Begins: Soviet–American Conflict over Eastern Europe.* Princeton, NJ: Princeton University Press, 1974.
Daskalov, G. *Bulgaria and Gurtsia: Ot razriv kum pomirenue 1944–1964gg.* [Bulgaria and Greece: From rupture to rapprochement, 1944–1964]. Sofia: Universitetsko Izdatelstvo 'Sv. Kl. Ohridski', 2004.
Daskalov, D. *Zhan suobshtava: Zadgranichnoto byuro i antifashistkata borba v Bulgaria 1941–1944g.* [Zhan Reports: The foreign bureau and the antifascist struggle in Bulgaria 1941–1944]. Sofia: Universitetsko Izdatelstvo 'Sv. Kl. Ohridski', 1991.
Deighton, A., ed. *Britain and the First Cold War.* Basingstoke: Macmillan, 1989.
Dellin, L. A. D. *The Communist Party of Bulgaria.* New York: Columbia University Press, 1979.
De Santis, H. *The Diplomacy of Silence: The American Foreign Service, the Soviet Union and the Cold War 1933–1947.* Chicago: Chicago University Press, 1980.

Deringil, S. *Turkish Foreign Policy during the Second World War: An 'Active' Neutrality*. Cambridge: Cambridge University Press, 1989.
Dimitrov, I. *Anglia i Bulgaria 1939–1941* [Britain and Bulgaria 1939–1941]. Sofia: Izdatelstvo na OF, 1983.
_____. *Ivan Bagryanov: Tsaredvorets, politik, durzhavnik* [Ivan Bagryanov: Courtier, politician, statesman]. Sofia: Akademichno Izdatelstvo 'Prof. Marin Drinov', 1995.
_____. *Burzhoaznata opozitsiya 1939–1944* [The bourgeois opposition 1939–1944]. Sofia: Izdatelska kushta 'Hristo Botev', 1997.
Dimitrov, V. *Stalin's Cold War: Soviet Foreign Policy, Democracy and Communism in Bulgaria, 1941–48*. Basingstoke: Palgrave Macmillan, 2008.
Dockrill, M., and B. McKercher, eds. *Diplomacy and World Power: Studies in British Foreign Policy, 1890–1950*. Cambridge University Press, 1996.
Dunnett, R., and J. E. Johnson, eds. *Negotiating with the Russians*. Boston: World Peace Foundation, 1951.
Dutton, D. *Anthony Eden: A Life and a Reputation*. London: Arnold, 1997.
Feis, H. *Churchill, Roosevelt, Stalin: The War They Waged and the Peace They Sought*. Oxford: Oxford University Press, 1957.
Folly, M. *Churchill, Whitehall and the Soviet Union, 1940–45*. Basingstoke: Macmillan, 2000.
Foot, M. R. D. *SOE 1940–1946*. London: BBC Publications, 1986.
Frankel, J. *British Foreign Policy 1945–1973*. Oxford: Oxford University Press, 1975.
Gaddis, J. L. *The United States and the Origins of the Cold War 1941–1947*. New York: Columbia University Press, 1972.
_____. *Russia, the Soviet Union and the United States*. Chichester: Wiley, 1978.
_____. *We Now Know: Rethinking Cold War History*. Oxford: Clarendon Press, 1997.
Gardner, L. C. *Spheres of Influence: The Partition of Europe from Munich to Yalta*. London: John Murray, 1993.
Gati, C., ed. *Caging the Bear: Containment and the Cold War*. Indianapolis: Bobbs-Merrill, 1974.
_____., ed. *The International Politics of Eastern Europe*. New York: Praeger, 1976.
Gilbert, M. *Road to Victory: Winston Churchill 1941–1945*. London: Heinemann, 1986.
Gori, F., and S. Pons, eds. *The Soviet Union and Europe in the Cold War, 1943–53*. Basingstoke: Macmillan, 1996.
Grigorova, Z., et al., eds. *Balkanite v mezhdunarodnite otnosheniya, 1944–1948* [The Balkans in international relations, 1944–1948]. Sofia: Izdatelstvo na BAN, 1984.
Grose, P. *America's Secret War behind the Iron Curtain*. New York: Houghton Mifflin, 2000.
Gunev, G. *Kum brega na svobodata ili za Nikola Petkov i negovoto vreme* [Towards the shore of freedom or on Nikola Petkov and his times]. Sofia: Informatsionno Obsluzhvane na AD, 1992.
Gunev, G., and I. Ilchev. *Winston Churchill i Balkanite* [Winston Churchill and the Balkans]. Sofia: Izdatelstvo na OF, 1984.
Hammond, T. T., ed. *Witnesses to the Origins of the Cold War*. Seattle: University of Washington Press, 1982.
Hammond, T. T., and R. Farrell, eds. *The Anatomy of Communist Takeovers*. New Haven, CT: Yale University Press, 1975.
Harbutt, F. J. *The Iron Curtain, Churchill, America and the Origins of the Cold War*. Oxford: Oxford University Press, 1986.
Hasanli, J. *Stalin and the Turkish Crisis of the Cold War, 1945–1953*. Lanham, MD: Lexington Books, 2011.
Haslam, J. *Russia's Cold War: From the October Revolution to the Fall of the Wall*. New Haven, CT: Yale University Press, 2011.

Hathaway, R. M. *Ambiguous Partnership: Britain and America 1944–1947*. New York: Columbia University Press, 1981.
Hazard, E. *Cold War Crucible: United States Foreign Policy and the Conflict in Romania, 1943–1952*. Boulder, CO: East European Monographs, 1996.
Heller, A., and F. Feher. *From Yalta to Glasnost*. Oxford: Basil Blackwell, 1990.
Heuser, B. *Western Containment Policies in the Cold War: The Yugoslav Case*. London: Routledge, 1989.
Iatrides, J. O., ed. *Ambassador MacVeagh Reports: Greece, 1933–1947*. Princeton, NJ: Princeton University Press, 1980.
Issussov, M., ed. *Mezhdunarodni otnosheniya i vunshna politika na Bulgaria sled Vtorata svetovna voina* [International relations and Bulgarian foreign policy after the Second World War]. Sofia: Izdatelstvo na BAN, 1982.
———. *Stalin i Bulgaria* [Stalin and Bulgaria]. Sofia: Universitetsko Izdatelstvo 'Sv. Kl. Ohridski', 1991.
Jensen, K. M., ed. *Origins of the Cold War: The Novikov, Kennan and Roberts Long Telegrams of 1946*. Washington, DC: US Institute of Peace, 1991.
Johnson, S. *Agents Extraordinary*. London: Hale, 1975.
Kaiser, D. *Economic Diplomacy and the Second World War: Germany, Britain, France and Eastern Europe 1930–1939*. Princeton, NJ: Princeton University Press, 1980.
Kalinova, E. *Sledvoennoto desetiletie na bulgarskata vunshna politika (1944–1955g.)* [The postwar decade of Bulgarian foreign policy]. Sofia: Polis, 2003.
Katsikas, S., ed., *Bulgaria and Europe: Shifting Identities*. London: Anthem Press, 2011.
Keeble, Sir Curtis. *Britain and the Soviet Union, 1917–1989*. Basingstoke: Macmillan, 1990.
Kennan, G. *Russia and the West under Lenin and Stalin*. London: Hutchinson, 1961.
Kennedy-Pipe, C. *Stalin's Cold War: Soviet Strategies in Europe, 1943 to 1956*. Manchester: Manchester University Press, 1995.
Kent, J. *British Imperial Strategy and the Cold War in the Middle East*. London: Leicester University Press, 1994.
Kertesz, S. D., ed. *The Fate of Eastern Europe: Hopes and Failures of American Foreign Policy*. Notre Dame, IN: Notre Dame University Press, 1956.
Kitchen, M. *British Policy towards the Soviet Union during the Second World War*. Basingstoke: Macmillan, 1986.
Kolko, G. *The Politics of War: Allied Diplomacy and the World Crisis 1943–1945*. London: Weidenfield & Nicolson, 1969.
Kovrig, B. *Of Walls and Bridges: The United States and Eastern Europe*. New York: New York University Press, 1991.
Kostadinova, T. *Bulgaria 1879–1946: The Challenge of Choice*. Boulder, CO: East European Monographs, 1995.
Kuniholm, B. R. *The Origins of the Cold War in the Near East*. Princeton, NJ: Princeton University Press, 1980.
Lalkov, M. *Ot nadezhdata kum razocharovanieto: Ideayata za federatsiyata na balkanskiya yugoiztok, 1944–1948g.* [From hope to disappointment: The idea of federation in the southeastern Balkans, 1944–1948]. Sofia: IK Vek 22, 1994.
Lane, A., and H. Temperley, eds. *The Rise and Fall of the Grand Alliance, 1941–1945*. Basingstoke: Macmillan, 1995.
Larres, K. *Churchill's Cold War: The Politics of Personal Diplomacy*. New Haven, CT: Yale University Press, 2002.
Leffler, M. *For the Soul of Mankind: The United States, the Soviet Union and the Cold War*. New York: Hill and Wang, 2007.

BIBLIOGRAPHY

Lendvai, P. *Eagles in Cobwebs: Nationalism and Communism in the Balkans.* New York: Doubleday, 1969.
Lewis, J. *Changing Direction: British Military Planning for Post-war Strategic Defence 1942–1947.* London: Sherwood Press, 1988.
Lundestad, G. *The American Non-policy towards Eastern Europe 1943–1947.* Oslo: Universitetsforlaget, 1978.
Mar'ina, V. V. *Dvizheniya soprotivleniya v stranah Tsentral'noy i Yugo-vostochnoy Evropyi 1939–1945* [The resistance movements in Central and South Eastern Europe 1939–1945]. Moscow: Radiks, 1995.
Mastny, V. *Russia's Road to the Cold War.* New York: Columbia University Press, 1979.
———. *The Cold War and Russian Insecurity.* New York: Oxford University Press, 1996.
Max, S. M. *The United States, Great Britain, and the Sovietization of Hungary, 1945–1948.* Boulder, CO: Columbia University Press, 1985.
McCauley, M., ed. *Communist Power in Europe 1944–1949.* Basingstoke: Macmillan, 1977.
McNeill, W. H. *America, Britain and Russia: Their Co-operation and Conflict 1941–1946.* London: Johnson Reprint, 1970.
Miller, M. L. *Bulgaria during the Second World War.* Stanford, CA: Stanford University Press, 1975.
Mitrovich, G. *America's Strategy to Subvert the Soviet Bloc, 1947–1956.* Ithaca, NY: Cornell University Press, 2000.
Morray, J. P. *From Yalta to Disarmament: Cold War Debate.* New York: MR Press, 1961.
Moser, C. *Dimitrov of Bulgaria: A Political Biography of Dr George M. Dimitrov.* Ottawa, IL: Caroline House, 1979.
Naimark, N., and L. Gibianskii, eds. *The Establishment of Communist Regimes in Eastern Europe, 1944–1949.* Boulder, CO: Westview Press, 1997.
Ognyanov, L. *Durzhavno-politicheskata sistema na Bulgaria 1944–1948g.* [State and political system in Bulgaria]. Sofia: Izdatelstvo na BAN, 1993.
Oren, N. *Bulgarian Communism: The Road to Power, 1934–1944.* Ann Arbor, MI: University Microfilms, 1971.
———. *Revolution Administered. Agrarianism and Communism in Bulgaria.* Baltimore: Johns Hopkins University Press, 1973.
Perlmutter, A. *FDR and Stalin.* Columbia: University of Missouri Press, 1993.
Pintev, S. *Bulgaria v britanskata diplomatsiya, 1944–1947g.* [Bulgaria in British diplomacy]. Sofia: AI 'Prof. Marin Drinov', 1998.
Plokhy, S. M. *Yalta: The Price of Peace.* New York: Viking, 2010.
Prazmowska, A. *Civil War in Poland, 1942–1948.* Basingstoke: Palgrave Macmillan, 2004.
Rachev, S. *Anglia i suprotivitelnoto dvizhenie na Balkanite* [Britain and the resistance movements in the Balkans]. Sofia: Izdatelstvo na BAN, 1982.
———. *Churchill, Bulgaria i Balkanite 1939–1945g.* [Churchill, Bulgaria and the Balkans]. Sofia: Sotri, 1995.
Ragsdale, H., ed. *Imperial Russian Foreign Policy.* Cambridge: Cambridge University Press, 1993.
Resis, A. *Stalin, the Politburo, and the Onset of the Cold War, 1945–1946.* Pittsburgh: University of Pittsburgh, Center for Russian and East European Studies, 1988.
Reynolds, D., ed. *The Origins of the Cold War in Europe: International Perspectives.* New Haven, CT: Yale University Press, 1994.
Reynolds, D., et al., eds. *Allies at War: The Soviet, American and British Experience 1939–1945.* Basingstoke: Macmillan, 1994.
Roberts, G. *Stalin's Wars: From World War to Cold War, 1939–1953.* New Haven, CT: Yale University Press, 2006.

Roberts, W. R. *Tito, Mihailović and the Allies 1941–45.* Durham, NC: Duke University Press, 1987.
Rothschild, J. *The Communist Party of Bulgaria.* New York: Columbia University Press, 1959.
Rothwell, V. *Britain and the Cold War 1941–1947.* London: Cape, 1982.
Rzhshevskyi, O. A., ed. *The Second World War: Current Issues.* Moscow: Nauka, 1995.
Sainsbury, K. *The Turning Point.* Oxford: Oxford University Press, 1985.
Saiu, L. *The Great Powers and Romania, 1943–1947.* Boulder, CO: Columbia University Press, 1992.
Saville, J. *The Politics of Continuity: British Foreign Policy and the Labour Government 1945–1946.* London: Verso, 1993.
Semerdjiev, P. *Sudebniyat protsess sreshtu Nikola Petkov prez 1947* [The trial of Nikola Petkov in 1947]. Paris: Fondatsiya A. Stamboliiski / N. Petkov / Dr G. M. Dimitrov, 1987.
———. *BKP, Makedonskiyat vupros i VMRO* [The BCP, the Macedonian question and the IMRO]. Detroit: Macedono-Bulgarian Institute, 1994.
———. *Narodniyat sud v Bulgaria 1944–1945g.: Komu i zashto e bil neobhodim* [The people's court in Bulgaria 1944–1945: Who needed it and why]. Jerusalem: Macedonian-Bulgarian Institute, 1997.
Seton-Watson, H. *The East European Revolutions.* Boulder, CO: Westview Press, 1985.
Smith, F. B. *Sharing Secrets with Stalin: How the Allies Traded Intelligence, 1941–1945.* Lawrence, KA: University Press of Kansas, 1996.
Stavrakis, P. *Moscow and Greek Communism 1944–1949.* Ithaca, NY: Cornell University Press, 1989.
Stafford, D. A. T. *Britain and European Resistance 1940–1945.* Basingstoke: Macmillan, 1979.
Thomas, H. *Armed Truce: The Beginnings of the Cold War, 1945–46.* London: Sceptre, 1988.
Todorov, N., ed. *Velikite sili i Balkanite v novo i nai-novo vreme* [The great powers and the Balkans in modern times]. Sofia: Izdatelstvo na BAN, 1985.
Toshkova, V. *Bulgaria v balkanskata politika na SASht, 1939–1944* [Bulgaria in the US Balkan Policy, 1939–1944]. Sofia: Izdatelstvo 'Nauka i Izkustvo', 1985.
———, ed. *Bulgaria v sferata na suvetskite interesi* [Bulgaria in the sphere of Soviet interests]. Sofia: AD 'Prof. Marin Drinov', 1998.
Trachtenberg, M. *A Constructed Peace: The Making of the European Settlement, 1945–1963.* Princeton, NJ: Princeton University Press, 1999.
Tsvetkov, Z. *Sudut nad opozitsionnite lideri* [The trials of opposition leaders]. Sofia: Kupessa, 1991.
Varsori, A., and E. Calandri, eds. *The Failure of Peace in Europe, 1943–48.* Basingstoke: Palgrave, 2002.
Vassilev, V. A., ed. *Bulgaro–angliiski otnosheniya v novo i nai-novo vreme* [Bulgarian–British relations in modern times]. Sofia, Izdatelstvo na BAN, 1987.
Volokitina, T. V., et al., eds. *Narodnaya Demokratiya: Mif ili real'nost?* [People's democracy: Myth or reality?]. Moscow: Nauka, 1993.
West, N. *Secret War: The Story of SOE Britain's Wartime Sabotage Organisation.* London: Hodder & Stoughton, 1992.
Westad, O. A., et al., eds. *The Soviet Union and Eastern Europe 1945–1989.* New York: St Martin's Press, 1994.
Westad, O. A., and M. Leffler, eds. *The Cambridge History of the Cold War*, vol. 1, *Origins.* Cambridge: Cambridge University Press, 2010.
Woodward, Sir E. L. *British Foreign Policy in the Second World War*, vols 2, 3. London: HMSO, 1971.
Wolfe, T. W. *Soviet Power and Europe 1945–1970.* Baltimore: Johns Hopkins Press, 1970.
Zubok, V. *A Failed Empire: The Soviet Union in the Cold War: From Stalin to Gorbachev.* Chapel Hill, NC: University of North Carolina Press, 2007.
Zubok, V., and C. Pleshakov. *Inside the Kremlin's Cold War from Stalin to Khrushchev.* Cambridge, MA: Harvard University Press, 1996.

ii) Articles

Adamthwaite, A. 'Britain and the World, 1945–1949: The View from the Foreign Office'. *International Affairs* 61, no. 2 (spring 1985): 223–5.
Black, C. E. 'The Start of the Cold War in Bulgaria: A Personal View'. *Review of Politics* 41, no. 2 (April 1979): 163–202.
Boll, M. M. 'A Little-Known American Initiative for Post-war Bulgaria'. *Diplomatic History* 7, no. 2 (spring 1983): 117–38.
———. 'Reality and Illusion: The Allied Control Commission for Bulgaria as a Cause for the Cold War'. *East European Quarterly* 17, no. 4 (January 1984): 417–35.
———. 'Pro-Monarchist and Pro-Moscovite: The Transformation of the Bulgarian Army 1944–1948'. *East European Quarterly* 20, no. 4 (January 1987): 409–28.
Boyle, P. G. 'The Foreign Office View of Soviet–American Relations 1945–1946'. *Diplomatic History* 3, no. 3 (summer 1979): 307–20.
Deighton, A. 'The "Frozen Front": The Labour Government, the Division of Germany and the Origins of the Cold War, 1945–7'. *International Affairs* 63, no. 3 (summer 1987): 449–64.
Hamilton, K. A. 'The Quest for the Modus Vivendi: The Danubian Satellites and Anglo-Soviet Relations 1945–46'. Occasional Papers no. 4. FCO Historical Branch: London, April 1992.
Howard, H. 'Greece and Its Northern Neighbours 1948–1949'. *Balkan Studies* 7, no. 8 (1966/67): 1–26.
Holdich, P. G. H. 'A Policy of Percentages? British Policy and the Balkans after the Moscow Conference of October 1944'. *International History Review* 9, no. 1 (February 1987): 28–47.
Horner, J. E. 'Traicho Kostov: Stalinist Orthodoxy in Bulgaria'. *Survey* 24, no. 3 (summer 1979): 135–42.
———. 'The Ordeal of Nikola Petkov and the Consolidation of Communist Power in Bulgaria'. *Survey* 28, no. 2 (summer 1984): 75–83.
Gaddis, J. L. 'The Emerging Post-revisionist Synthesis on the Origins of the Cold War'. *Diplomatic History* 7, no. 3 (July 1983): 171–90.
Garson, R. 'Churchill's "Spheres of Influence": Rumania and Bulgaria'. *Survey* 24, no. 3 (summer 1979): 144–58.
Kimball, W. F. 'Naked Reverse Right: Churchill, Roosevelt and Eastern Europe from TOLSTOY to Yalta and a Little Beyond'. *Diplomatic History* 9, no. 1 (winter 1985): 1–24.
Marantzidis, N. 'The Greek Civil War (1944–1949) and the International Communist System.' *Journal of Cold War Studies* 15, no. 4 (fall 2013): 25–54.
Mark, E. 'Charles E. Bohlen and the Acceptable Limits of Soviet Hegemony in Eastern Europe: A Memorandum of 18 October, 1945'. *Diplomatic History* 3, no. 2 (spring 1979): 201–13.
———. 'American Policy towards Eastern Europe and the Origins of the Cold War, 1941–1946: An Alternative Interpretation'. *Journal of American History* 68, no. 2 (September 1981): 313–33.
———. 'The War Scare of 1946 and Its Consequences'. *Diplomatic History* 21, no. 3 (summer 1997): 383–416.
———. 'Revolution by Degrees. Stalin's National-Front Strategy for Europe, 1941–1947'. Working paper no. 31, Cold War International History Project, Woodrow Wilson International Center for Scholars, Washington, DC, February 2001.

Max, S. M. 'Cold War on the Danube: The Belgrade Conference of 1948 and Anglo-American Efforts to Reinternationalize the River'. *Diplomatic History* 7, no. 1 (winter 1983): 57–77.
Messer, R. L. 'Paths Not Taken: The United States Department of State and Alternatives to Containment 1945–1946'. *Diplomatic History* 1, no. 3 (summer 1977): 297–319.
Miller, J. E. 'Taking Off the Gloves: The US and the Italian Elections 1948'. *Diplomatic History* 7, no. 1 (winter 1983): 35–56.
Pavlowitch, S. K. 'Out of Context: The Yugoslav Government in London 1941–1945'. *Journal of Contemporary History* 16, no. 1 (January 1981): 89–118.
Pechatnov, V. O. 'The Big Three of Soviet Foreign Policy: New Documents on Soviet Thinking about Post-war Relations with the United States and Britain'. Working paper no. 13, Cold War International History Project, Woodrow Wilson International Center for Scholars, Washington, DC, July 1995.
Pechatnov, V. O., translated by V. Zubok. '"The Allies are Pressing on You to Break Your Will...": Foreign Policy Correspondence between Stalin and Molotov and Other Politburo Members, September 1945–December 1946'. Working paper no. 26, Cold War International History Project, Woodrow Wilson International Center for Scholars, Washington, DC, September 1999.
Perovic, J. 'The Tito-Stalin Split: A Reassessment in Light of New Evidence'. *Journal of Cold War Studies* 9, no. 2 (spring 2007): 32–63.
Pintev, S. 'Nachalna deinost na Suyuznata Kontrolna Komisia v Bulgaria, oktomvri 1944–yanuari 1945' [The initial activities of the Allied Control Commission in Bulgaria, October 1944–January 1945]. *Istoricheski Pregled* 35, no. 4/5 (1979): 196–203.
Pintev, S. 'SSSR, SASht i Velikobritania i Moskovskoto primirie s Bulgaria, septemvri-oktomvri 1944' [The USSR, the USA and Great Britain and the armistice with Bulgaria, Moscow, September–October 1944]. *Izvestia na Bulgarskoto Istorichesko Druzhestvo* 32 (1978): 241–59.
Resis, A. 'The Churchill–Stalin Secret "Percentages" Agreement on the Balkans, Moscow, October 1944'. *American Historical Review* 73, no. 2 (April 1978): 368–87.
Roberts, G. 'Ideology, Calculation and Improvisation: Spheres of Influence and Soviet Foreign Policy 1935–1945'. *Review of International Studies* 25, no. 4 (October 1999): 655–73.
Ross, G. 'Foreign Office Attitudes to the Soviet Union 1941–1945'. *Journal of Contemporary History* 16, no. 3 (July 1981): 521–40.
Siracusa, J. M. 'The Meaning of TOLSTOY: Churchill, Stalin and the Balkans, Moscow, October 1944'. *Diplomatic History* 2, no. 4 (fall 1979): 443–63.
Smith, R., and J. Zametica. 'The Cold Warrior: Clement Attlee Reconsidered, 1945–7'. *International Affairs* 61, no. 2 (spring 1985): 237–52.
Swain, G. 'Stalin's Wartime Vision of the Postwar World'. *Diplomacy and Statecraft* 7, no. 1 (March 1996): 73–96.
Toshkova, V. 'SASht i izlizaneto na Bulgaria ot Tristrannia Pakt, iuni–septemvri 1944' [The USA and the detachment of Bulgaria from the Tripartite Pact, June–September 1944]. *Istoricheski Pregled* 4, no. 5 (1979): 204–17.
Trachtenberg, M. 'The United States and Eastern Europe in 1945: A Reassessment'. *Journal of Cold War Studies* 10, no. 4 (fall 2008): 94–132.
Traikov, V. 'Bulgarskata podgotovka za Parizhkata mirna konferentsiya' [Bulgarian preparation for the Paris Peace Conference]. *Makedonski Pregled* 20, no. 1 (1997): 23–38.

Westad, O. A. 'The New International History of the Cold War: Three (Possible) Paradigms'. *Diplomatic History* 24 (2000): 551–65.
Xydis, S. G. 'The Secret Anglo–Soviet Agreement on the Balkans of 9 October 1944'. *Journal of Central European Affairs* 15, no. 3 (October 1955): 248–71.

3. Unpublished

Barnes, M. 'The Current Situation in Bulgaria'. Lecture at the National War College, Washington, DC, 3 June 1947.
Economides, S. 'The International Implications of the Greek Civil War'. PhD dissertation, LSE, 1990.
Dimitrov, V. 'The Cominform and the Bulgarian Communist Party: Embarking on a New Course?' Paper presented at the Ninth International Colloquium 'L'Unione Sovietica e l'Europa nella Guerra Fredda (1943–1953)', Cortona, Italy, 23–4 September 1994.
_____. 'The Failure of Democracy in Eastern Europe and the Emergence of the Cold War, 1944–1948: A Bulgarian Case Study'. DPhil dissertation, University of Cambridge, 1996.
Gibianskii, L. 'Sovetsko–Yugoslavskii konflikt i sovetskii blok' [The Soviet–Yugoslav conflict and the Soviet bloc]. Paper presented at the Ninth International Colloquium 'L'Unione Sovietica e l'Europa nella Guerra Fredda (1943–1953)', Cortona, Italy, 23–4 September 1994.
_____. 'Problems of East European International Political Structuring in the Period of the Formation of the Soviet Bloc'. Paper presented at the Cold War International History Project conference 'New Evidence on Cold War History', Moscow, January 1993.
Livanios, D. 'Bulgar–Yugoslav Controversy over Macedonia and the British Connection, 1939–1949'. DPhil dissertation, University of Oxford, 1995.
Nation, C. R. 'A Balkan Union? Southeastern Europe in Soviet Security Policy, 1944–1948'. Paper presented at the Ninth International Colloquium 'L'Unione Sovietica e l'Europa nella Guerra Fredda (1943–1953)', Cortona, Italy, 23–4 September 1994.
Percival, Mark L. 'British–Romanian Relations 1944–1967'. PhD dissertation, University of London, March 1997.
Rzheshevsky, O. A. 'Soviet Policy in Eastern Europe (1944–1945): Liberation or Occupation? Documents and Commentary'. Lecture at St Antony's College, Oxford, April 1995.
Stefanides, I. 'The United States, Great Britain and Greece 1949–1952'. PhD dissertation, LSE, 1989.
Yegorova, N. I. 'From the Comintern to the Cominform: Ideological Dimensions of the Cold War Origins 1945–1948'. Paper presented at the Cold War International History Project conference 'New Evidence on Cold War History', Moscow, January 1993.

INDEX

Allied Control Commission (ACC)
    Bulgaria 4, 8, 10, 74, 97, 130, 144
  British participation in 92, 196
  composition of 88
  establishment of 86–90
  involvement in elections of 108–9, 150
  periods of activity of 88
  Soviet domination of 84, 92, 100, 130
  termination of 164
  Western membership of 84, 98
Adams, Jack 168
Adana 51
Adrianopolis 21
Adriatic Sea 22, 50, 185
Aegean Greece 82, 97, 183
Aegean Sea 22, 34, 184
  Bulgarian access to 23, 25, 35, 81, 128, 180, 185
    Etheridge views of 117
Aegean Thrace 83
  Bulgarian claims in 85–6, 184, 185
  Bulgarian Communist delegation to 82–4
  Bulgarian occupation of 16, 81, 83
  Bulgarian withdrawal from 62, 85, 97
Africa 44, 49, 51
Agrarians 64, 102, 180
  British support for opposition 112–13, 196
  collaborating with British in resistance to Axis 39
  dissolution of 191
  Etheridge proposals regarding 115, 117
  factions collaborating with Communists 126
  in joint electoral lists with Communists 103
  negotiations for reorganisation of government 111–12, 130
  participation in Fatherland Front government 99
  splits within 103–4
  wartime British attitude to 41, 45, 68
  violence against 144, 165–6
  see also BANU
Agreement for Friendship and Cooperation between Bulgaria and Yugoslavia 185–6
Albania 169
  assistance to Greek rebels by 181
  in Balkan federation 185
Albanian declaration 32
Alexander, General Sir Harold 18
Allies 4, 10, 33, 57, 63–6, 81, 83, 95, 111, 194, 198
  armistice approaches to, Bulgarian 58–60
  attention to Balkans by 18, 49–50, 92
  bombing Bulgaria by: *see* bombing: Bulgaria
  calling upon Bulgaria to leave Axis 21, 31, 40
  conditions for armistice with Bulgaria 31, 56–7, 84, 87
  cooperation among 6, 86, 91, 134
  efforts to enlist Turkey 73
  lack of unity among 28–9, 35, 47, 77, 132, 134–5, 138
  opposition letters to missions of 104, 119
  postwar tensions among 67, 127, 139, 159, 161, 164–5
  representation in ACC 87
  views on Bulgaria 2
  wartime negotiations among 10

Western 22, 24–5, 47, 64, 66, 87, 89, 93, 113
  appeal in trial of Nikola Petkov 154
  armistice talks with 66, 68, 84, 86–9
  and Balkan front 50
  Bulgarian links with 54–5
  and Bulgarian opposition 113, 132
  Communist views of 130, 169
  consultation / friendly relations with Soviet Union 62–3, 97
  controversy with Soviet Union 12, 132, 159, 161,
  demands on Bulgaria 57
  differences / lack of coordination regarding Bulgaria 106, 132, 155
  and elections in Bulgaria 100
  exclusion from decisions on Eastern Europe 29
  participation in ACC 87, 89
  and recognition of Bulgarian government 126
  strategy regarding Soviet Union 67, 93, 129
American College Sofia 59
American Military Mission in the Allied Control Commission for Bulgaria 1944–1947, The (Boll) 10
Andreichin, Georgi 47
Anglo-Soviet treaty 22, 34
Ankara 54–5, 59, 65
Arab states 34
Arcidiacono, Bruno 8
armistice treaty (with Bulgaria) 81, 84, 87
army:
  British 28, 58, 60, 80, 82
  Bulgarian 38, 41, 45, 53, 65, 85, 103, 144–5, 170, 189–90
    British contacts with 41
    conspiracy in 41
    exiles contacting 40
    fighting Germany 83, 86
    occupying neighbouring territories 17, 81–2
    peace treaty restrictions on 87, 188
    withdrawal from occupation of 52, 59, 63, 65, 76, 83–5, 87, 89, 97
  Soviet: *see* Red Army
  US 50, 56

Attlee, Clement: criticism of Soviet behaviour 163
Axis 16, 18–19, 49, 54, 128
  Bulgarian engagement with 16–17, 40, 42, 62
  detaching Bulgaria from 21, 31–2, 36–7, 50, 54–6, 59, 69
  presence in Balkans of 17, 73, 194
  resistance against 38
  satellites of 53, 128, 151
  subversion against 49, 78
  troops of 62

Baev, Jordan 10
Baeva, Iskra 10
Bagryanov, Ivan 48, 58–9, 63–4, 67
Balkan Affairs Committee 45
Balkan Allied Force 44
Balkan Entente 20
Balkan (con)federation 7, 33, 35, 121, 148, 182, 185, 188, 199
  British opposition to 183–5
  British plans for 32–4, 195
  Churchill favouring 33
  Communist project for 185
  Georgi Dimitrov's interview on 186
  Soviet dismissal of 34–5
  Stalin and 186–7
Balkan front: *see* Balkans: Allied offensive on
Balkan Peninsula: *see* Balkans
Balkans 1, 15, 41, 55–9, 73, 114–15, 182
  Allied offensive on 7, 17–18, 20, 49–52
  Axis hold of 17, 194
  British interest in 16, 28–30, 34, 42, 73–97, 122, 126–9, 134–5, 147, 161, 195, 171, 183–4, 188, 194–6, 198
  Bulgarian role in 3, 10, 15, 127, 164, 181
  Communist influence 26, 69
  German occupation and withdrawal: *see* Germany: withdrawing troops
  'percentages agreement' for: *see* 'percentages agreement'
  Soviet policy in 3, 8, 12, 21–7, 26, 36, 56, 62, 76–8, 86–90, 121, 126–7, 180, 182, 195–6
  see also Stalin, Joseph: policy in Balkans

special operations in: *see* OSS; SOE
strategic importance of 15–16, 73
US interest 127–9
Baltic republics 25, 33
BANU 33
see also Agrarians
Bari 44,
Barker, Elisabeth 7–8, 40, 50
Barnes, Maynard 88, 105, 110, 115, 136, 147, 150
 approval of Etheridge mission by 115, 127
 and postponement of elections 107
 views on 'percentages agreement' of 88
'Bastion' position paper 164
BBC 21, 175–6
Belgrade 185
Bern 55
Bevin, Ernest 110, 112, 119, 145, 168, 174, 188
 and Bulgarian recognition 149
 opposition to confrontation with Soviets 135, 182, 189
 support for diplomatic expulsions 168
 talks with Kolarov 141–2, 144
 view of Soviets 109, 129, 163
Big Three: *see* Allies
Biryuzov, General Sergey 98, 107–11, 150
Black Sea 1, 15, 48, 51, 185
 bombing of ports on 53
 Soviet control of 76, 80
 Soviet naval bases on 81
Black, Cyril 115
Black, Floyd 59
Blackburn, Captain Raynold 152
Blakeway, John 168
Bled 186
Board of Trade 11, 179
Bohlen, Charles 163
Boll, M. M. 8, 10
Bolshevik ideology 163
Bolshevik Party 48, 102
Bolshevik Revolution 2, 5
Bolshevization 22
bombing:
 Bulgaria 10, 52–6
  coordinated with Partisans 53
  as part of Allied strategy 55–6, 194

 Soviet concurrence for 53–4
 stopping 54, 62
 Romania 52–3
border:
 Bulgarian–Greek 10, 81–2, 181–2, 190
 Greek 82–3, 147, 189
 Turkish 34, 39, 147
 southern Bulgarian 81, 188–9
Boris III, King 40
 British attitude to 31–2
 death of 30–31, 41, 52, 57
Bozhilov, Dobri 57, 62
Brimelow, Thomas 163
British Council 167
British Liaison Officers (BLOs) 43
Bruce Lockhart, Robert 29
Bucharest 9, 93, 185
Budapest 185
Bulgarian Communist Party (BCP):
 see Communists, Bulgarian
Burgas 22
Burov, Atanas 61
Byrnes, James 110, 149
 and Etheridge mission 114, 116, 127
 and Moscow decision 128–9, 141
 and recognition of Bulgarian government 106, 147, 150

'Cabinet of Affairs', Bulgarian 108, 111
Cadogan, Sir Alexander 79
Cairo 57, 60
 SOE in 39, 43–5
 armistice mission in, Bulgarian 59–60, 63–4, 66, 68–9
Carpathian mountains 29
Calandri, Elena 8
Casablanca Conference 5, 55
Central Powers 18
Cheshmedzhiev, Grigor 126
Chiefs of Staff:
 British 40, 77, 88, 139
  bombing Bulgaria 52
  invasion of South East Europe 17
  attitude to SOE 37, 40
  view of Soviet Union 139, 160
 Combined: signature of armistice 89
 US Joint 46, 88
  and invasion of South-East Europe 50

and unconditional surrender 55
Churchill, Sir Winston 7, 10, 13, 28, 47,
    57, 71, 92, 195, 200
  accusations of Bulgaria 52, 59
  and bombing Bulgaria 53–4
  concern for Soviet advances 26
  devising 'percentages agreement': see
    'percentages agreement'
  favouring invasion of Balkans: see
    Balkans: Allied offensive on
  favouring Balkan federation: see Balkan
    (con)federation: Churchill favouring
  Fulton speech of 139, 162
  suspicious of Soviet intentions 90, 94–6
claims, Bulgarian territorial 17, 22, 81
  British views on 33, 141, 180, 184
  US attitude to 81
  Stalin's support of 85
  see also Aegean Thrace; Macedonia
Clark Kerr, Sir Archibald 63, 65–6, 68,
    117, 121
Cold War 3, 45
  British role in 198–200
  historiography of 5–10
  place of Bulgaria in origins of 4, 192,
    194, 198
Colville, David 153
Communist Information Bureau
  (Cominform) 165, 187
Communists:
  Bulgarian 9, 82, 113, 121, 142, 197
  aiming for political monopoly 196
  attacks against opposition by 134,
    152–3, 165
  attitude to Greece of 185
  British views of 146, 162–3, 171, 174
  British dealings with 196–200
  concessions to opposition by 115,
    126, 136
  criticism by Cominformburo of 165–6
  directed from Moscow during war 48, 61
  and elections 100, 103, 115, 122
  hostility to Western representatives 98,
    102, 105, 125, 165–7, 171
  in wartime resistance: see Partisans:
    Bulgarian
  increasing political role towards end of
    war 60, 69
  interference in other parties 103, 126,
    130, 166
  interpretation of Moscow decision
    112, 130
  involvement in coup of 9 September
    1944 65
  key positions in Fatherland Front
    government 99
  preparation for elections for Grand
    National Assembly 151
  proposal for firm treatment of
    174, 189
  purges within 172
  remaining outside last war
    government 64
  resistance of 149
  resisting Western pressure 118
  Soviet directives and support for
    112–13, 127–9, 137, 139, 144–5,
    151, 159, 187
  staging political trials 166
  temporary restraint of 153–5
  territorial views of 85–6
  treatment of Petkov by 165
  US pressure on 147, 150
  vengeance of 99
  views of Etheridge mission: see
    Etheridge mission: Communist
    views of
  Western rebuke of 106, 141
  Greek: see Greece: Communist
    Partisans in
  international 10, 23, 26–7, 80, 110,
    161, 181
Communization:
  of Bulgaria 3, 138, 159
  of Balkans 26, 51
  of Europe 6
  see also Sovietization
cordon sanitaire 35
'Council of Europe' 33
Council of Foreign Ministers:
  London (September 1945) 112, 114
  London (December 1947) 163
  Moscow (December 1945) 8, 119,
    126–8
  New York (October 1946) 150
  Paris (April 1946) 139

INDEX

Craiova agreement 86
Crane, General John 108
Cripps, Sir Stafford 29
Czechoslovakia 3, 7

Damyanov, Georgi 188
Danube 22, 29, 50, 60, 63, 65, 69
Danubian federation: *see* Balkan (con) federation
Dardanelles 22
  see also Straits, Mediterranean
Daskalov, Georgi 10
Davies, Mostyn 41, 45
Declaration of Liberated Europe: *see* Yalta Declaration
Decree for the Amendment of Electoral Law (1945) 111
Decree for the Protection of the People's Power (1945) 99
Dedeagatch 22, 82, 117
Defense Committee: bombing of Bulgaria 52
Deighton, Anne 7
democracy/ democratic freedoms
  in Bulgaria 122, 134
    British uncertainty about 98–102, 122
    demanded by opposition 104
    importance for Britain of 34, 162, 196, 200
    relation to security 36, 125, 134, 200
    lacking before elections 108, 119
    historical obstacles 90, 102
    Soviet views of 24, 91, 108
    violation of 166
    Western policy regarding 6
  in Eastern Europe 128, 162
Department of International Information (DII) of CC of Bolshevik Party 48, 102, 116
Department of State, US 10, 31, 56, 88, 104, 108, 110, 115, 132–3, 137–8, 149–150, 163
  bound by Yalta Declaration 100
  concerns about violation of human rights 166
  differences with Foreign Office 88, 101, 104, 147, 171, 189

diplomatic notes to Bulgarian government: see diplomatic notes to Bulgaria: US
  and Etheridge mission 117
  'long-range plan' for Bulgaria 32, 46
  mediation between government and opposition 147
  opposing spheres of influence 78, 96
  resumption of relations with Bulgaria 105–6, 141
  and second postponement of elections in Bulgaria 116
Dimitrov, Dr G. M. 45, 68
  accusations of treason of 103
  Communist campaign against 103
  death sentence of 144
  discussion with Greek and Yugoslav exiles 33
  involvement with SOE 39, 41, 68
  political asylum of 103–4
Dimitrov, Georgi 12, 83, 85, 95, 116, 118, 189
  accusations of imperialists 165, 171
  censured by Stalin 186
  communication with Stalin 23, 128, 137
  diary of 11
  and elections 118, 120
  and Etheridge mission 115–16
  and Moscow decision 129, 132, 137
  Moshanov's letter to 60
  pronouncement on Petkov's sentence 154, 165
  rivalry with Tito 185
  speeches commented on BBC 175
  treatment of opposition 151, 153
  warning of British policy 45
Dimitrov, Vesselin 9
diplomatic notes to Bulgaria:
  British 135, 145, 173, 177, 185, 188
  Etheridge recommending 118
  US 105–6, 119–20, 135, 171
Dobrudja 20, 32
Documents on British Policy Overseas 10
Dodecanese islands 164
Dolapchiev, Professor Nikola 154
Donovan, Colonel William 46, 56–7
  see also Department of State, US: 'long-range plan' for Bulgaria

Draganov, Purvan 40, 58–9, 63
Dubrovnik 22
Dulles, Allen 55

EAM–ELAS 82–3
  see also resistance: Greek
Eastern Front 51, 53, 62
'Eastern Question' 2, 15
Eden, Sir Anthony 22–3, 30–31, 35, 40, 53, 68, 86
  anxiety regarding Soviet ambitions 26, 61, 77
  endorsing cooperation with Soviets 28
  involvement in 'percentages agreement' 74–5, 79, 81–2, 84, 88–9, 95
  views on Balkan federation 34
  views on Bulgaria 32, 67, 78
Ehrenburg, Ilya 116
elections 91–3, 136, 141, 191, 155
  Bulgarian:
    boycott of 115, 151
    British interest in conduct of 98, 142–4, 150–52, 155
    British involvement in 98–125, 197
    conduct of 120–21,
    Communist violations of 151
    for Grand National Assembly: *see* Grand National Assembly
    US views of 116, 127–8, 133–4, 150–51
    postponement of 108–14, 151
    Stalin's views on 112, 128, 151
  Greek 135
  Italian 188
electoral law, Bulgarian (1945) 102, 104–6, 108, 110–12, 130
English Speaking League 167
Entente 54
Etheridge, Mark: *see* Etheridge mission
Etheridge mission 114–15, 119, 122
  British views of 117–18
  Communist views of 115–16
  final report of 127
  meeting Bulgarian politicians 115–17
  recommending second postponement of Bulgarian elections 115
  talks in Moscow 116
Europe:

Eastern 11–12, 15, 19, 53, 75
  British interest in 22–3, 26–30
  in Cold-War historiography 3–10
  Red Army in: *see* Red Army: advance in Europe 24–27
  Soviet influence in Soviet policy in:
    see Bulgarian Communists: Soviet support for; 'percentages agreement'; Stalin; Yalta Conference
  Western 51, 92,164, 186
  see also Allies: Western
European Advisory Commission (EAC) 84, 86–8
Ewing, Donald 168
expulsions, diplomatic 138, 168

Failure of Peace in Europe, 1943–48, The (Varsori and Calandri) 8
Fatherland Front 65, 67, 82–3, 99, 102, 112, 125, 131
  Communist role in 43, 196
  involvement with anti-Axis resistance 43
  opposition compromise with 136–7, 142
  participating in elections 103–4, 120, 151
  proposed reconstruction of 115–16
  in wartime Soviet propaganda 67
Federation of Urban and Rural Labour 148
First World War 2, 15, 18, 81, 154
Fitzmaurice, G. G. 152
foreign minister:
  British 74, 76, 79, 89, 119, 142, 199
    see also Eden, Sir Anthony; Bevin, Earnest
  Bulgarian 58–9, 63, 17, 126, 134–5, 153, 165
    see also Draganov, Purvan; Kolarov, Vassil; Stainov, Petko
  Soviet 74, 76, 95, 100
    see also Molotov, Vyacheslav
  Turkish 34, 60
    see also Menemencioglu, Numan
Foreign Ministry, Bulgarian: *see* Ministry of Foreign Affairs, Bulgarian
Foreign Office and the Kremlin: British Documents on Anglo-Soviet Relations, The (Ross) 10

INDEX

Foreign Office Research Department (FORD) 11, 33
France 50
Free and Independent Bulgaria Committee 39

G. M.: *see* Dimitrov, Dr G. M.
Gaddis, John Lewis 5
Ganev, Venelin 111
Geneva 55
Genov, Yuli 167, 172
Georgiev, Kimon 116, 126, 140, 145, 150
  meeting Byrnes 147, 149
  meeting Stalin 131
  readiness to negotiate with opposition 111, 136–7, 147
  talks with Etheridge 115
Germany 2, 16, 31, 74, 85, 86, 88, 95, 102, 140, 154, 159, 189, 193
  Bulgarian alliance with 16–21, 31
  detaching Bulgaria from 4, 37–8, 45, 50–64, 68–9, 81, 83, 194
    Soviet pressure towards 59–64
  position in Balkans of 50–53, 55
  resistance against: *see* resistance: anti-Axis wartime
  withdrawing troops 35, 52, 64
Girginov, Alexander 61, 112
Glenconner, Lord 39
government-in-exile:
  Bulgarian 33, 39–40
  Czechoslovak 29
  Greek 33, 37, 55, 83
  Yugoslav 20–21, 33, 37, 55, 92
Grand Alliance 2, 4, 196
Grand National Assembly, Bulgaria 127, 148–9, 151
great powers 66, 173
  British strategy regarding 2, 3, 7, 16, 90
  compromise and cooperation of 74–5, 97, 132, 136, 195
  engagement with Bulgaria 9
  see also Allies: cooperation; 'percentages agreement'
Greece 64, 84, 92, 98, 111, 117, 128, 141, 164, 177, 189
  British commitment to 2, 8, 16, 28, 37, 67, 77, 180, 199
  British help for resistance in 20–21
  Bulgarian influence on 22, 26–7
  Bulgarian withdrawal from: *see* army: Bulgarian: withdrawal from occupation
  civil war in 82, 90–92, 180–83
  Communist Partisans in 42, 183
  effect of Balkan federation on 31, 35, 184–6, 188
  external Communist support for 82, 160, 180–81, 190
  government-in-exile: *see* government-in-exile: Greek
  'percentages agreement' for: *see* 'percentages agreement': and British concerns for Greece
  Soviet attitude to 61, 83, 180–81, 196
  Soviet intelligence in 84
  Soviet pressure on 77, 93, 105, 109, 126, 147, 150
Greenhill, Denis 168
guerrillas: *see* resistance
  Communist: *see* Partisans
Gussev, Fyodor 62, 67–8, 85, 87–8

Hague 191
Hamburg 52
Hanover 52
Harriman, Averell 65, 105
Harvey, Oliver 79, 91
Haslam, Jonathan 5–6
Hazard, Elizabeth 9
Heath, Donald 172, 181
historiography 4, 9, 53, 80, 107
Hopkins, Harry 75
House of Commons 13, 59, 80, 133, 151, 173
  see also Parliament: British
House of Lords 170
  see also Parliament: British
Houstoun-Boswall, William 100, 114, 139, 145–6
  advising firmness regarding Communists 118, 120–21, 133–6
  concerns about elections 103–4, 111
  contacts with opposition 104–5, 113, 136, 142–3

involvement in postponement of
    elections 108–9
sceptical of US action 101
support for Etheridge proposals 117
views of Communist objectives in
    Bulgaria 120
see also political representatives in Bulgaria
Howard, Douglas 31–2, 101
human rights 173–4, 190–92
    violation of, Bulgarian 167, 170–71,
        177, 188
    prescribed in peace treaty 172
Hungary 3, 105, 168–9
    application to UN 190
    see also UN
    British action against 190, 192
    case against in UN 192
    priority for bombing 53
    in 'percentages agreement' 74, 76, 84
    see also 'percentages agreement'
    Soviet influence in 90, 94

imperialism:
    Anglo-American, agent of 104
    Russian 6, 162–3
intelligence services:
    British 37, 51, 139, 149, 168
    Soviet 47–8
Interior Ministry, Bulgarian: *see* Ministry of
    Interior, Bulgarian
Internal Macedonian Revolutionary
    Organisation (IMRO) 144
    Protoguerovist wing of: *see*
        Protoguerovists
independence, Bulgarian 1, 21, 23, 38, 61,
    63, 108, 164, 189
    British wartime views on 30–32, 194
International Court of Justice 191
invasion:
    of Balkans: *see* Balkans: Allied offensive on
    of Soviet Union, Nazi 42, 49
Iran 6, 139, 143, 160–61, 200
Italy 18, 29, 44, 47, 52, 60, 170, 188–9
    admission to UN 190
    in Churchill–Stalin discussions 76
    possible Soviet retaliation in 92–3
    as precedent for Bulgarian ACC 89
    strategic position of 49, 180
Ivanov, Tsveti 144

Jadwin, Colonel 56–7
Jebb, Gladwyn 16, 179
    see also FORD
Joint Intelligence Committee 139
Joint Planning Staff 82
Justice ministry: *see* Ministry of Justice,
    Bulgarian

Kalinova, Evgenia 10
Kavalla 22, 82
Kazanluk 53
Kennan, George 94, 138–9
Kent, John 8
Kirsanov, Stepan 107–8
Kisselov, Georgi 58
Kitchen, Martin 7
Knatchbull-Hugessen, Sir Hughe
    59, 68
Kolarov, Vassil 12, 154, 172, 189–90
    accusations against Western allies 165, 171
    calling for annexation of Greek
        territory 86
    support by Molotov 143
    talk with Bevin 141–2, 144
    views of Moscow decision 129
Kostov, Traicho 12, 116, 126, 137, 172
    accusations against British
        representatives 102
    attitude to Greek Civil War 83
    views of Etheridge mission 117–18
Kosturkov, Stoyan 112
Kremlin, the 10, 24, 174
    Bulgarian Communists' coordination
        with 145, 164
    criticism of Dimitrov 186
    superiority over Bulgarian
        Communists 187
    see also Stalin; Soviet government
Kunev, Trifon 144
Kuyumdjiiski, Angel 56–7

Lavrishchev, Alexander 61–2
Law for Labour Educational Institutions
    (1945) 99
Law for the Ban and Dissolution of the
    Bulgarian Agrarian Union 191
Leffler, Melvyn 6
Lend-Lease 39
Litvinov, Maxim 24

'Ljubljana Gap' 5
'long telegram' 138
  see also Kennan, George
'long-range plan' for Bulgaria: see also
  Department of State, US: 'long-range plan for Bulgaria'
Lulchev, Kosta 112, 150, 173–5, 180
  negotiating after Moscow decision 131
  subject to violence 144, 166
  British attitude to 191

Macedonia 86, 183
  Aegean, occupation of 16
  autonomy of 31–2
  British views on 183–5
  Bulgarian interest in 184–5
    see also Pirin
  Bulgarian withdrawal from 64
  Greek Partisans' attitude to 183
  Yugoslav part of 81, 86
    see also Vardar
'Macedonian nation' 183–4
MacVeagh, Lincoln 60
Maisky, Ivan 24
Marshall Plan 165, 181
Mason, Paul 168, 171
Mastny, Vojtech 5
Matsankiev, Dimiter 40
Mayhew, Christopher 170, 173, 179
McNeil, Hector 151
Mediterranean Sea 18, 35, 49, 97, 180
  British positions in 96, 134, 161, 163, 184
  Soviet threat to 84–5, 125, 127, 129
  Eastern 27, 49, 54, 142–3, 180
    British interest / influence in 8, 15–17, 25, 28, 36–7, 80, 170, 184, 195–6
    importance of Bulgaria regaring 1–2, 95, 169, 195, 199
    Soviet interest in / presence near 15, 26, 28, 126, 129, 147, 162
    see also Straits, Mediterranean
Menemencioglu, Numan 34
  see also foreign minister, Turkish
Merivale-Austin, Major B. G. 168
Middle East 1, 16, 18, 46–7, 63, 76, 121
  British interests in 3, 8, 15
  Bulgarian émigrés in 33, 39, 194
  SOE work from 41, 43, 45, 51
  Soviet threat to 125–6, 129, 143, 160, 162, 180
Middle Eastern Command 53
Mihailov, Ivan 144
Mihov, General Nikola 4
Micklethwaite-Miller, Major 83
military landings, Allied:
  in Balkans 50
  on Greek coast 82
  in Sicily 41
  in southern France 50–51
  see also Overlord
Military League 38–9, 41
military missions to Bulgaria:
  Allied 89
  British 41–3, 68, 82, 103, 146
  US 8, 10, 56, 149, 150
militia, Bulgarian 104, 144, 151, 188
  persecution of opposition by 113, 141
  reorganisation of 116, 142
  suspicions towards British institutions by 167
Ministry of Foreign Affairs:
  Bulgarian 12, 130, 167
  Soviet 24, 30, 63
Ministry of Justice, Bulgarian 142, 175
Ministry of Internal Affairs:
  Bulgarian 12, 142
  Soviet 47
  see also NKVD
Ministry of Food, British 179
Molotov, Vyacheslav 24, 63, 65–6, 68, 128, 189
  accusation against Britain 81
  advising Bulgarian Communists 131, 137, 150
  attitude to federation 34–5
  Bulgarian letter of good will to 63
  discussing Bulgarian recognition 114, 142
  interpretation of Potsdam by 95
  sanctioning elimination of Bulgarian opposition 143
  talks with Eden (October 1944) 84–5, 88–9, 195
Molotov–Ribbentrop Non-Aggression Pact 42
Momchilov, Nikola 4, 55

monarchy, Bulgarian 31, 148
Montreux convention 80, 92
Morgan, J. S. 41
Moscow 5, 10–11, 23, 28–9, 31, 35, 65, 71, 86–7, 101, 105, 108–10, 115–16, 129–33, 139
  approach to armistice talks with Bulgaria 63
  attitude of Bulgarian opposition to 126
  British approaches to 142, 147, 182, 197
  British criticism of 174
  cooperation with West 67
  declaration of war on Bulgaria 65–6
  Dimitrov in and returning from 83, 115
  directing Bulgarian Communists 43, 48, 112–13, 120, 138,
  disapproval of Bulgarian–Yugoslav agreement 185–6
  Etheridge trip to 116–18
  Fatherland Front government seeking support from 97
  knowledge of British and US special operations 46–7, 57
  links with Bulgarian non-Communists during war 62
  orders to Tito from 94
  'percentages agreement' in: *see* 'percentages agreement'
  pressure on Bulgaria 23, 61, 64
  signature of Bulgarian armistice in: *see* armistice treaty
  support for foreign Communists 161, 181
  talks in (October 1944) 88, 91, 95
  US diplomatic action in 100
  see also 'percentages agreement'; Council of Foreign Ministers, Moscow; Moscow Conference; Moscow decision
Moscow communiqué:
  see Moscow decision
Moscow Conference (October 1943) 30–31, 53, 57, 77, 86, 183
Moscow decision 128–41, 143, 145–6, 149, 155, 197, 200
  clashing interpretations of 132
  British position on 129, 132–6, 138–42
  Bulgarian Communists' view of 129

opposition's view of 130, 136
Soviet attitude to 128, 131
Soviet responsibility for failure of 131, 137
US views of 129, 132–6, 141
see also Vyshinski, Andrei
Moshanov, Stoicho 59–60, 63, 65–6, 68, 87
Moyne, Lord 46, 60, 65, 68
Muraviev, Konstantin 60, 64, 68, 81
Mushanov, Nikola 61, 112
mutiny, Greek forces' 76

National Archive, British 11
National Assembly, Bulgarian 59, 127, 129,
  elections for 100, 112, 126
  proposals for dissolution of 134, 142
  see also Grand National Assembly; Parliament: Bulgarian
Nazi–Soviet breach 74
Near East 121
Neikov, Dimiter 82
NKVD 47–8
Northern Department of Foreign Office 11, 25–8, 161, 163, 171
North Africa 49, 51

Obbov, Alexander 102
occupation, Soviet:
  of Bulgaria 10, 87
  in Europe 73, 80, 92, 98, 179
occupied territories (by Bulgaria) 32
  issue of retention of 57, 63
  withdrawal from 16, 52, 59, 63, 67, 81, 84, 89, 95, 97, 101, 194
Office of Strategic Services (OSS) 46–7
oil fields: *see* bombing: Romania; Ploesti
opposition:
  Bulgarian:
    wartime 17, 38, 44, 48, 57, 61, 194
    non-Communist 99, 129, 155, 166
    appeal to Allies 143, 145
    attitude to, Soviet 112, 118, 130, 137, 143
    attitude to, US 105, 135, 142, 147, 173
    boycott of elections by 114, 119–20
    concessions to, Communist 129–30, 136
    dealing with, British 4, 105, 117, 133,

141–3, 147
  demands of 104,108, 111, 115, 136–7, 141–2, 197
  Etheridge views on 115–17
  interference with, Communist 130
  Moscow decision regarding 130–38
  negotiations with government 135, 140–41, 143, 147
  participation in elections of 148–9, 151
  persecution of 103–4, 115, 120, 122, 143–4, 152–3, 165
  position on referendum of 148
  protests on behalf of, US 172–3
  support for, British 105–6, 108, 110–11, 113, 126, 133, 144–5, 153, 197
  Romanian 9, 138, 145
Ottoman empire 1–2, 15, 17, 182
Overlord 50–51, 55
  see also military landings, Allied
Oxley, General W. H. 109, 113, 136

Paris 140, 141, 144, 147, 149–50, 191
Parliament:
  British 75
    see also House of Commons; House of Lords
  Bulgarian 61, 111, 114, 130, 136, 151, 153, 165
    see also National Assembly
Partisans 25
  Bulgarian 43, 48
    attitude to bombing 67
    British support for 43–4, 46, 53
    contacts with Bagryanov 8
    Soviet help for 48–9, 67
    suspicions towards Britain 45
  Greek 26, 52, 82–3,
    Bulgarian support for 10, 161, 181, 183, 188–9
  Yugoslav 26, 52, 92
pastors' trial 166, 168, 191
Pastuhov, Krustyu 130, 144–5, 196
Pavlov, Todor 111
Peace Conference, Paris 133, 152
peace treaty:
  with Bulgaria 4, 9, 89, 139–40, 153, 164, 181, 185, 192, 197–8
    Article 2 (human rights) 172, 174
    Article 12 (military clauses) 188
    Article 35 (Allied advice) 173
    Article 36 (disputes) 186–8
    attitude to, Communist 166
    inability to uphold, British 175, 177, 191
    interpretation of 173
    involvement regarding, US 172
    links to recognition 142, 148, 150, 152, 155
    negotiations for 136, 141, 147, 149, 160–61
    possible repudiation of 170
    protests regarding violations of, British 174, 188–90
    ratification of 146, 154, 164, 170, 185–6
    signature of 149, 152–3
    violations of 172
  with Italy 109
Pearl Harbor 37
Peloponnese 134
people's courts 99
'people's democracy' 165, 183
'percentages agreement' 6, 10, 96, 195–6, 199
  acceptance by British officials in 79–80
  archival evidence 74
  bearing on Yalta and Potsdam 90–95
  and British concerns for Greece 82–4
  context of 77–81
  Eden's views of 78–9
  final version of 84
  Hungary in 74, 76, 84
  importance for Bulgaria 91, 95–6
  interpretation of 76–8, 80
  relating to Bulgarian armistice 84–6
  Romania in 74, 76, 78–9
  signing of 75–6
  trial period for 79
  Yugoslavia in 74, 76
  see also spheres of influence
persona non grata 168
Petkov, Nikola 104, 112–13, 126, 130, 172, 180
  arrest and accusations of 154, 165

attacks on, Communist 103, 144–5, 150, 191
attitude to, Communist 132
boycotting elections 104, 114–15
British involvement with 104, 114, 136, 196
compromise with 136
execution of 154, 165, 172, 175
meeting Etheridge 115
removal from cabinet 103
Stalin's views of 103, 128, 131, 155
Pinsent, R. P. 146
Pirin 183, 185
  see also Macedonia, Bulgarian interest in
planning, British 2, 4, 7, 12, 15
  long-term military 77, 160–61
  postwar political 25, 27, 67, 69, 193, 195, 199
  wartime 17–18, 44, 50, 82, 198
  see also Post-Hostilities Planning Committee
Ploesti 52
Plovdiv 52
Poland 6, 9, 91, 153
  Communization of 3
  Soviet influence in 25
  strategic importance of 6, 117, 199
Politburo 103, 129, 144, 167
  see also Bulgarian Communist Party
political amnesty 112, 142
political representative in Bulgaria:
  British: *see* Houstoun-Boswall, William; Sterndale-Bennett, John
  Soviet: *see* Kirsanov, Stepan
  US: *see* Barnes, Maynard; Heath, Donald
Political Warfare Executive (PWE) 11, 31, 40
politicians, independent 99, 104
'Popular Front Governments' 24
Post-Hostilities Planning Committee 27, 77
postponement of elections: *see* elections, Bulgarian
Potsdam Conference 8, 90–91, 94–5, 98, 104, 200
Prague 185
Pravda 186
Prazmowska, Anita 9

propaganda 185
  anti-Western 162, 165
  Communist 102, 155, 161
  of democracy 101, 151, 164, 175–9
  wartime:
    Allied 20, 31–2, 37–9, 41, 45, 51, 56, 67, 104
    Soviet 23, 62, 68
    US 46
protest notes: *see* diplomatic notes
Protoguerovists 38–9
public opinion:
  anti-Hitler, Bulgarian 38
  regarding Bulgaria:
    British 171, 175
    international 176
    US 115, 127
    Western 154
publicity 175–7, 186
Public Record Office 11
purges, Communist 172

Quebec Conference 50
Queen Mother, Bulgarian 31

Radio Moscow 64
Realpolitik 5, 162
Red Army 48, 58, 67, 85, 179
  approaching and entering Bulgaria 22, 40, 42, 60, 63–6, 81, 83–4, 87–8, 195, 199
  advance in Balkans 62, 68, 76, 82–4
  advance in Europe 26, 90
  helping Partisans 49
  presence in Bulgaria 97, 111
  withdrawal from Bulgaria 117, 140, 142, 146–7, 149, 152–4, 160, 165, 197
referendum for republic 148
Regency Council: *see* regents, Bulgarian
regents, Bulgarian 103–5, 108, 111, 115, 118
Rendel, Sir George 21–2, 29–32, 38
resistance:
  anti-Axis wartime 9, 17, 37–8, 42–3, 46, 48, 194

anti-Communist 166, 174
Communist: *see* Partisans
rights and freedoms, political:
   see democracy
Roberts, Frank 117, 139, 161–3
Roberts, Geoffrey 6
Robertson, General W. M. 150
Romania 3, 20, 89, 153, 168
  application to UN 190
    see also UN
  Allied tensions over 145
  bombing of: *see* bombing: Romania; Ploesti
  British interest in 8, 28, 91–4, 101, 117
  case against in UN 192
  coup in 59, 63
  Etheridge mission in 127
    see also Etheridge mission
  Moscow decision on 128, 138
  in 'percentages agreement' 74, 76, 78–9
    see also 'percentages agreement'
  prospects for democracy in 6
  SOE mission to 76
  Soviet military advance in: *see* Red Army: advance in Balkans
  Soviet interest in 22, 27, 90
  US policy to 9, 95, 100, 105
  Western demands in 114
Romanos 21
Roosevelt, Franklin Delano 7, 10, 94
  differences with Churchill 50, 57
  opposed to 'spheres of influence' 75, 78
Rothwell, Victor 7
'Russophiles' 2
Russophilia 170
'Russophobes' 2

Sakar 21
Salonika 22, 54, 82, 117
Sargant, Sir Orme 21, 30, 41, 149
  advising firmness to Bulgaria 32
  attitude to SOE 41, 68
  and measures against Soviet advances 92–4, 126, 134, 162
  and 'percentages agreement' 75, 79
  and postponement of elections 108
  sceptical of prospects of democracy in Bulgaria 102
  and strategy memorandum of May 1945 94
  views on Soviet Union of 29, 61, 94
Second front 7
  see also Balkans: Allied offensive on
Second World War 3, 7, 9–10, 16, 18, 194, 198
Serbia 59, 62, 184
spheres of influence 6, 34–5, 75, 78, 94, 96, 114
  see also 'percentages agreement'
Sicily 41, 49, 51
Social Democrats, Bulgarian 82, 104, 111, 180
  British attitude to 166, 176, 196
  members of Fatherland Front government 99, 137
  splinter groups in 103
  in opposition to Fatherland Front 112
  possible inclusion in reorganised government 115, 130
  Communist persecution of 144–5, 166, 176
SOE 11, 194
  arrangements with OSS 47
  attitude to Bulgarian Communists 42–5, 53
  missions to Bulgaria 68
    see also British Liaison Officers; British Military Missions
  mission to Romania 76
  officers in Bulgaria after 9 September 1944 83–4, 89, 98
  proposing cooperation with Soviets 48–9
  recruiting contacts in Bulgaria 38–9
  searching for channels of communication with Bulgaria 40–41, 55
  working with G. M. Dimitrov 39
Sofia 10, 21, 31–2, 37, 43, 54, 86, 103, 107, 116, 120
  arrival of Communist leaders in 112
  as military target 51
  bombing of 51–3, 61
  British minister plenipotentiary in 153–4, 165, 168–74
  British pressure on 110

British representative in 100, 108,
  117–18, 125, 133, 135–7, 141–2,
  145, 150, 152, 166, 175–6
 entry of Soviet army in 65, 84
 Etheridge mission in 116
 exasperating conditions in 140
 expulsions from 168
 return of Moshanov to 59, 63
 SOE missions to 83–4
 Soviet diplomatic presence in 47, 58,
  61, 63
 Tito in 185
 US representative in 136,
 usefulness of legation in 169
 Vyshinski in 131–2
South Slav (con)federation: *see* Balkan
  (con)federation
Southern Department of Foreign Office
  11, 21, 29–30, 101
 advising Soviet pressure on Bulgaria 23
 attitude to possible Bolshevization 22
 avoiding confrontation with Soviets 139
 awareness of Soviet interest by
  146, 180
 considering military deployment to
  Bulgaria 17, 51
 criticism of Bulgarian government by
  119, 153
 difficulty in devising policy to Bulgaria
  by 114, 121, 140, 171, 175
 discussing Bulgarian recognition 146
 exploring pressure on Soviets 182
 interest in Bulgaria of 117
 involvement with opposition 145
 possible break off of relations with
  Bulgaria 169
 promoting democracy 106, 140
 reversal on 177
 reviewing Soviet aims in Bulgaria 26,
  56, 67
 searching for contacts into Bulgaria
  40–41
 support for Balkan front by 49
 view of Moscow decision 138
sovereignty, Bulgarian: *see* independence,
  Bulgarian
Sovietization 8, 198
 see also Communization

Split 22
Stainov, Petko 61, 107–9, 126,
  131, 135
 role in postponement of elections 107
Stalin, Joseph 34, 47, 82, 90, 95, 146, 199
 clash with West 12, 57, 132
 cooperation with Allies 28–9, 53–4, 56,
  92, 94
 criticism of Bulgarian Communists by
  137, 186
 directing Bulgarian Communists 48, 85,
  103, 112–13, 131–2, 137, 144–5,
  151, 155
 interest in Bulgaria 56, 58, 62–6, 87,
  90, 101
 involvement with Greece 90, 104
  see also Greece: Communist Partisans:
   Soviet attitude to
 limits to ambitions of 164
 in Moscow decision: *see* Moscow
  decision: Soviet attitude to
 and origin of Cold War 5–6
 plans for expansion of influence 22–6
  see also Straits, Mediterranean: Soviet
   pressure on
 in 'percentages agreement' 74–8,
  199–200
 policy in Balkans of 58
 security demands of 91, 160
 split with Tito 187–8
 views on Balkan federation: *see* Balkan
  (con)federation: Stalin and
 views on Second front 50
Stamboliiski, Assen 144
Steel, Kit 45
Stephan, Exarch 105
Sterndale-Bennett, John 154, 181–2
 advising firmness against Bulgarian
  government 170–73, 189
 reporting Communist hostility to
  Britain 165–7
 views on publicity of Bulgarian
  infringement of democracy 175–6
Stoyanov, Petko 104
Straits, Mediterranean 16, 81,
  92, 180
 British interest in 15, 28
 Bulgarian proximity to 1–2, 15

Soviet pressure on 34, 73, 78, 80, 85, 180, 200
Turkey's position on 25, 73
see also Mediterranean Sea: Eastern; Dardanelles
Strang, Sir William 86–7, 137, 171
surrender, unconditional 31, 55, 89
Svoboden Narod 144
Switzerland 40, 54

Teheran Conference 50, 55, 57
Temkov, Boris 168
Terpeshev, Dobri 82–3
Theatre, Bulgarian National 130
Third Reich 19, 47
see also Germany
Third Ukrainian Front 84, 89, 144
Thompson, Frank 45
Tito, Josip Broz 48, 86, 94, 101, 185, 188
tobacco 179
Todorov, Bogomil 168
Todorov, Kosta 39
Tolbukhin, Marshal Fyodor 84, 144
Tollinton, Boyd 153
Tolstoy meeting: see 'percentages agreement'
Trachtenberg, Marc 6
trade 170
  British–Bulgarian 15, 19, 153, 163, 169, 178–9
  international 125
trials, political 170
Trieste 94, 101
Tripartite Pact 16, 18–19, 37, 194
Truman Doctrine 165, 181
Truman, Harry 94–5, 105, 129, 154
Tsar Krum Secret Military Organisation 144
Turkey 6, 18, 34, 39, 49, 58, 64, 67, 73, 117
  breaking off with Germany 59
  British focus on 2, 8, 16, 27–8, 192, 199
  Bulgarian peace feeler to 54–5, 63
  in discussions between Churchill and Stalin 76, 79
  fearing Soviet Union 68
  negotiations with Britain 51
  possible territorial acquisition by 21

Soviet pressure on 85, 126, 139, 143, 160–61, 180–82, 184, 196, 200

United Nations (UN) 134, 182, 189
  Bulgarian application to 190
  see also Hungary; Romania; Italy: application to UN
'United Opposition': see opposition, Bulgarian
Universal Declaration of Human Rights 174
UNSCOB 189

Vansittart, Lord 170
Vardar 183
  see also Macedonia
Varna 22
Varsori, Antonio 8
Velchev, Damian 116, 144, 150
Versailles system 19
Vinogradov, Sergey 64
violence, political Communist:
  immediately after 9 September 1944 99
  against non-Communist opposition: see opposition: persecution of
Voroshilov, Kliment 24
Vyshinski, Andrei 135, 142, 144, 150
  intervention in Romania by 100
  meeting with Etheridge 116
  mission to Bulgaria of 130–32
  see also Moscow decision

Wallinger, Geoffrey 171, 175
War Cabinet, British 18, 26–7, 29–30, 78, 93
Warner, Christopher 26, 139, 161
Warner, Geoffrey 145,
Washington 10, 60–61, 109–110, 117, 138, 148
Washington Conference 50
Western missions: see Western representatives
Western representatives / diplomats 137, 170, 199
  attacks against 167–9
  armistice talks with 60, 62, 66
  elections in Bulgaria 100, 108

hostility to 90, 125
and links with Bulgarian opposition 112
obstructions against 90–91, 98
postponement of elections 197
see also Barnes, Maynard; Heath, Donald; Houstoun-Boswall, William; Sterndale-Bennet, John
Western troops: in Balkans 20, 51, 54, 56,
Whitehall 32, 69, 73, 77, 83, 106, 133, 162, 173, 176, 190
Williams, M. S. 138
Wilson, E. M. 28–9
Wilson, General Sir Henry Maitland 18

Yalta agreements: *see* Yalta Conference
Yalta Conference 6, 90–95, 129, 183, 200
   overshadowed by 'percentages agreement' 91–2, 101
   Soviet attitude to 93–4
Yalta Declaration 91, 100
   Bulgarian developments contrary to 125, 149, 154–5
   Soviet implementation of 101

Truman's insistence on adherence to 95
Yugoslavia 8, 22, 31, 40, 47–8, 94, 153, 183–4, 186–8
   autonomy of Macedonia within 32, 183
   British support for 20–21, 27, 37, 42
   Bulgarian troops in / evacuation from 52, 65, 84
   federation / union with Bulgaria 35, 148, 185
      see also Balkan (con)federation
   helping Greek Communists 161, 181, 183
   in 'percentages agreement' 74, 76
   Soviet interest in 25
   Yalta discussions of 92
Yugov, Anton 131, 144

Zachariades, Nichos: meeting with Stalin 181
Zaimov, General Vladimir 48
Zubok, Vladislav 6
Zveno 61, 99, 111, 144
   split within 126, 145

CPSIA information can be obtained at www.ICGtesting.com
Printed in the USA
LVOW10s2135030315

429186LV00001B/197/P

9 781783 084302